THE NEOLIBERAL DELUGE

The Neoliberal Deluge

. . . . .

Hurricane Katrina, Late Capitalism,
and the Remaking of New Orleans

Cedric Johnson, Editor

University of Minnesota Press
Minneapolis
London

Portions of the Introduction were previously published as Cedric Johnson, "The Urban Precariat, Neoliberalization, and the Soft Power of Humanitarian Design," *Journal of Developing Societies* 27, no. 3 and 4 (September 2011): 445–76.

Published by the University of Minnesota Press
111 Third Avenue South, Suite 290
Minneapolis, MN 55401-2520
http://www.upress.umn.edu

Library of Congress Cataloging-in-Publication Data
The neoliberal deluge : Hurricane Katrina, late capitalism,
and the remaking of New Orleans / Cedric Johnson, editor.
    p. cm.
    Includes bibliographical references and index.
    ISBN 978-0-8166-7324-7 (hc : alk. paper) — ISBN 978-0-8166-7325-4
    (pbk. : alk. paper)
    1. Emergency management—Louisiana—New Orleans. 2. Hurricane Katrina, 2005.
3. Disasters—Louisiana—New Orleans. 4. Race discrimination—Louisiana—New Orleans.
5. Neoliberalism. I. Johnson, Cedric, 1971-
  HV551.4.N48N46 2011
  976.3'35064—dc23
                                  2011028098

Printed in the United States of America on acid-free paper

The University of Minnesota is an equal-opportunity educator and employer.

18 17 16 15 14 13 12 11   10 9 8 7 6 5 4 3 2 1

Contents

Part III. Planning

Part IV. Inequality

"Obama's Katrina"

Cedric Johnson

THIS IS A BOOK ABOUT DISASTER. In the most immediate sense, the essays gathered here explore the unique causes and impacts of the 2005 Hurricane Katrina disaster. The massive category 3 storm precipitated catastrophic levee failures, flooding, and social misery in New Orleans and transformed the demographic character of the city, leaving it whiter, wealthier, and less populous than it was before. At the level of theory, this is a book about neoliberalism, the prevailing economic philosophy of our times, and its disastrous ecological and political consequences. The essays in this volume are written against the professed virtues of neoliberalism—the promise of unlimited prosperity and individual freedom through fundamentalist market reforms—and, instead, each illuminates to varying degrees the sociological realities of neoliberalization.

Before my collaborators and I could put the finishing touches on this project, disaster struck the U.S. Gulf Coast once again. In April 2010, an industrial explosion aboard British Petroleum's Deepwater Horizon rig killed eleven workers. After burning uncontrollably for thirty-six hours, the rig capsized, snapping the marine riser a mile beneath the surface and billowing oil into the warm waters of the Gulf. Surpassing the 1989 *Exxon Valdez* disaster, the BP oil spill was the worst environmental disaster in U.S. history and wreaked havoc on marine life for three months as BP made numerous botched attempts to seal the damaged riser. By the time BP finally plugged the spill on July 19, 2010, some 190 million gallons of oil filled the northern Gulf of Mexico. At the peak of the crisis, the surface coverage of the spill was large enough to blanket the state of Maryland.

Most of the workers who lost their lives were white, Republican, family men and so were the many fishermen, bait shop owners, tour guides, hoteliers, and restaurateurs whose livelihoods were threatened by the disaster. Unlike the throngs of urban, mostly black poor who sought refuge in the Superdome and Morial Convention Center and others who waded through floodwaters foraging for food and medicine during the Katrina disaster, these latest victims were the kind of "deserving" middle-class citizens that both parties court during election season. Republican talking heads and politicians seized the political opportunity created by the crisis and quickly termed the BP spill "Obama's Katrina." Although the president's early public statements gave the impression that he would hold BP accountable for the cleanup by working within the established letter of the 1990 Oil Pollution Act, which was passed in the wake of the *Exxon Valdez* spill, such reassurances rang hollow with many Americans who could not comprehend why neither the White House nor BP executives seemed capable of resolving this summer-long crisis. To make matters worse, reports from Obama's own national commission on the BP disaster charged that during the critical early weeks, his administration mislead the public about the full scale of the spill. Moreover, Obama's commitment to the 1990 act was itself deeply problematic because the law afforded considerable autonomy to BP and reflected the spirit of industry self-regulation central to the neoliberal model. Although they were right for the wrong reasons, those who described the BP disaster as "Obama's Katrina" captured a core truth—these two disasters are related not merely by common geography and the populations impacted, but, more fundamentally, both disasters share common roots in neoliberal restructuring. While the catastrophic inundation and death in New Orleans were consequences of state divestment in social services and physical infrastructure, the BP oil disaster stemmed from a deregulatory environment that was crafted by congressional Democrats and Republicans alike.

Prior to the 2010 BP disaster, Transocean, the company that owned the Deepwater Horizon rig, had accumulated one of the worst safety records in the industry. In the period between 2008 and February 2010, Transocean owned only 42 percent of active rigs in the Gulf but was responsible for 73 percent of those with reported safety incidents. Although its root causes ran deeper, the failure of the Obama administration to reform the Minerals Management Service, the chief federal body charged with regulating environmental and labor safety in the oil and gas industries, and to reverse the culture of cronyism and industry self-policing that defined the Bush years made this disaster the Obama administration's own. Many Americans missed these underlying policy continuities stretching between presidential administrations and across the congressional aisles because so much news coverage was defined by a focus on partisan gamesmanship, scrutiny of BP officials rather than the wider industry practices, and the generic preference for human interest stories, such as disappointed beachgoers, the plight of family businesses, etc., rather than sustained analysis of the dangers resulting from lax enforcement of occupational safety and environmental protection standards. More important, Obamanistas were caught unaware because too many failed to separate the symbolic import of his historic campaign from his expressed political views. As well, too many seemed either reluctant or unable to approach his presidency with a mature understanding of the American political process and the relationship between genuine social struggle and substantive political change.

By emboldening left-wing critique of the Bush administration and forcing questions of durable racial inequality back on to the public agenda, the 2005 Katrina disaster created favorable preconditions that made Barack Obama's run for the White House possible. George W. Bush was an already unpopular president when Katrina made landfall, but his administration's callous and ineffective handling of the emergency that unfolded galvanized his opponents and unnerved some of the GOP base. The Katrina effect is only part of the historical equation that delivered victory to the Obama camp. The candidate's biracial background, newcomer status, Ivy League pedigree, rhetorical gifts, unflappable demeanor, and pioneering use of cybermedia campaign strategies also gave him an advantage over others in the field, in particular the GOP nominee, John McCain, who had difficulty energizing the social conservative base, shedding his image as a Beltway insider, and distinguishing himself from the Bush-Cheney camp on economic matters. The unique dynamics of the 2008 presidential election and the media-driven character of U.S. national elections helped to obscure the basic contours of Obama's politics. That is, he is socially liberal in terms of public relations but essentially conservative with respect to productive relations.

With the onset of the 2008 economic crisis and the election of Barack Obama, many announced neoliberalism's demise, and even market stalwarts such as Alan Greenspan were left scratching their heads and reconsidering decades-long monetary practice. Such proclamations of neoliberalism's end were at best premature and at worst amounted to wish-fulfillment. Some have rejected the view that Obama is neoliberal because in public discussion this ideology is too often conflated with classic laissez-faire economics and "smaller government." Neoliberalization does not entail a comprehensive reduction of state spending or capacities; instead, this process crafts a regulatory regime that most enhances the conditions of capital accumulation. The often repeated argument in some corners of the left that this economic crisis would automatically deliver a postcapitalist hereafter was quickly discredited as Obama proceeded to announce the names of his inner circle—a familiar coterie of Washington insiders and Clintonite warhorses. Rather than ushering in the kind of "socialist society" so feared at anti-Obama rallies and on conservative talk radio, the first two years of the Obama presidency have been marked by an effort to preserve investor class power and save capitalism from its own contradictions.

Cass Sustein aptly described Obama as a "University of Chicago Democrat" because of his willingness to pursue aspects of the Democrats' social agenda through market solutions. Surely some radical market libertarians would scoff at this characterization, but Obama's politics share as much core ethical commitment to markets and private sector development as many to his right. The differences between them are differences of degree rather than substance. The key distinguishing factor of Obama's ascendancy is his rhetorical and symbolic repackaging of well-worn, conservative ideas. Recall his frequent campaign trail recitations of underclass mythology, where he asserted that the alleged cultural dysfunction of the black poor was the chief cause of their plight. The incessant references to Franklin D. Roosevelt's New Deal often heard during the 2008 election cycle were generally sloppy and ahistorical, but such comparisons contained a shard of truth—namely, that Roosevelt's administration was equally concerned with developing a viable market society, one that might avoid the problems of overproduction and unregulated stock market activity that led to the 1929 crash and the Great Depression. Obama's light revision of regulatory mechanisms, economic stimulus package, massive federal bailout of Detroit's failing automotive manufacturers, universal health insurance legislation *sans a public option*, and the extension of the Bush-era tax cuts were guided by the same pro-market, "trickle-down" logic that has characterized Republican and New Democratic policies for the past three decades. If Obama's approach to state-market relations should be characterized as socialism, it is the socialization of capitalism's risks rather than the shared collective benefit of society's surplus.

For those who saw Obama as the second coming of Roosevelt, his approach to the economic crisis lacked one of the centerpieces of

New Deal liberalism—old school public works. The Obama administration has advanced its own notion of public works suited to neoliberal times, an approach to national infrastructure improvement and maintenance that is publically financed but executed by private contractors. The Gulf Coast Civic Works Act would have offered a more progressive approach to rebuilding the communities damaged by Hurricanes Katrina and Rita. The brainchild of San Jose State University sociologist Scott Myers-Lipton and supported by numerous student and grassroots organizations nationally, the bill promised to mitigate sheer market dynamics through the immediate employment of displaced citizens and the raising of wage floors, but this policy proposal also accommodates the prevailing practice of funneling public funds toward nongovernmental and religious organizations already assembled and working along the Gulf Coast. More important, the bill has languished in committee and garnered opposition from the Louisiana delegation members, who are undoubtedly committed to the state's firmly established recovery-growth coalition. Despite these limitations and challenges, however, such legislation might have created an opening for a more democratic reconstruction of the Gulf South.

A state-funded and state-managed public works project along the lines of the Depression-era Works Progress Administration might have temporarily provided thousands of jobs to displaced residents and helped the city to retain its population and recover at a much faster rate. Instead of the mass public sector layoffs enacted by New Orleans Mayor C. Ray Nagin, teachers and city employees might have been trained and deployed alongside day laborers and dockworkers in debris removal and cleanup. Like the throngs of students and church volunteers who have descended upon the region, these same residents might have been trained in basic techniques of gutting, drywall installation, mold remediation, and carpentry and employed in the reconstruction of homes, schools, and community institutions. In addition to construction work, displaced residents might have been enlisted to undertake the massive projects of levee repair and wetlands restoration. Such efforts to reverse industrial damage to the natural storm buffers of South Louisiana might have mimicked the long forgotten work of the Civilian Conservation Corps, which employed thousands of young men during the Depression to revitalize parks, trails, roads, and bridges across the nation. The replanting of indigenous marsh grasses throughout coastal Louisiana from Bayou Sauvage on westward to Iberia Bay, the redistribution of alluvial silts from the Mississippi River bed to areas that have suffered acreage loss, and other restorative activities would have provided protection against tropical storms and an even more powerful long-term impact on the citizens who have suffered through this disaster. These temporary work camps might have fostered new friendships and bonds of solidarity, kindled a sense of closeness to the land, offered on-the-ground education in the ecological issues facing the region, and provided disheartened residents with the faith that full recovery was possible—a powerful antidote to the despair that has haunted too many coastal residents in the disaster's aftermath and driven some to depression and suicide. Such a response to the lingering problems of the Gulf Coast region would have required substantial political will and public pressure from below and a political leadership rooted in true vision and radical courage rather than a mere rhetoric of change.

How will we respond to future financial crises, pandemics, and meteorological, industrial, or other man-made disasters? The near destruction of New Orleans and the tortuous process of its rebirth provide an important set of political choices. For some, the horrors of Katrina have engendered deep political cynicism and a new subculture of survivalism where disaster-preparedness is viewed as an individual responsibility. Y2K anxieties, post–September 11 fears of terrorism, premonitions of peak-oil apocalypse, the threat of loose nukes, the 2008 economic crisis, and general angst about impending societal collapse have sent many Americans literally packing—stockpiling canned goods, potable water, global positioning units, power generators, guns, and ammunition. This retreat from society and the creation of individual zones of safety and security for those who can afford to purchase them constitute the logic of neoliberalism gone haywire. Might we surmount our various ecological and social challenges through collective action and democratic planning? In what follows, we address these vital matters of life, death, and civilization that were made so terribly visible in New Orleans and sketch another set of historical possibilities.

There were many people who made this book possible. First and foremost, I must extend my deepest, heartfelt thanks to the contributors. Many of them signed on to this project when it was little more than a notion and they stood by me through various false starts, delays, and rounds of revision. Thank you all for your camaraderie, time, energy, and, most of all, your perceptive insights into so many facets of the Katrina disaster and American politics. There are many people who supported and encouraged me on my journey as an editor and contributor to this project. I am thankful to have had Averill Bauder as a fellow traveler and inspiration in the years following the Katrina disaster. In his former role as director of service learning and civic engagement at Hobart and William Smith Colleges, Ave organized ten trips to the Gulf Coast—most of them to New Orleans—to assist in the rebuilding of homes and lives. His love for the city, capacity for altruism, and stamina on a work site are unrivaled. Teresa Amott, the colleges' provost, and President Mark Gearan were both crucial supporters of my teaching and scholarly interest in the Katrina disaster. Each provided financial and collegial support for my Politics of Disaster course that enabled me to travel with students to New Orleans and provided an invaluable platform for developing my ideas. Thanks to all of my students at Hobart and William Smith Colleges as well who endured those courses, my territorialism about my home state, and my burning passion for this subject matter. Sincerest thanks to Linda Robertson for co-organizing the "Voice Wake Us and We Drown" symposium at the colleges during spring 2009. This event gave faculty and students a chance to refocus our intellectual energies on the Katrina disaster and reconstruction in the Gulf South and share our research with anyone who would listen.

I am forever grateful to so many friends, colleagues, and fellow travelers for their comments and discussions about this subject matter. My homeboy and fellow Rochester transplant, Marcus Watts, was an endless source of information and encouragement. Our discussions took me back home and shaped my thinking about New Orleans and Louisiana politics in immeasurable ways. Roderick Sias has been my comrade, mentor, and inspiration for many years. As this project progressed, he was always a supportive, critical voice and offered a wealth of insight on the many political and social developments in our home state that we both followed on a daily (and sometimes hourly) basis. Although he was not a direct contributor to this volume, his expertise as an architect, historian, and activist and his deep commitment to social justice are imprinted on these pages. Special thanks as well to Roxana Walker-Canton, Tina Morton, David Canton, John Arena, Adolphus Belk Jr., Kevin Dunn, Anna Creadick, Kanate Dahouda, Brian Cooper, Chris Gunn, Donna Albro, Millery Polyné, Bradley Darjean, Eric Chatman, Phil Davis, William A. Johnson Jr., Jonathan Garlock, Vincent Seravallo, Linda

Donahue, Paul Passavant, Nicholas Robertson, Stephen Ward, Nikol Alexander-Floyd, Adolph Reed Jr., Lester K. Spence, Kwasi Densu, Michael Leo Owens, Marcelo Vieta, Elise Thorburn, and Graciela Monteagudo. I am also truly thankful for those colleagues and comrades who created opportunities for me to lecture on this subject. I am especially indebted to Sean Smith and the members of Canadian-Cuban Friendship Association in Toronto for having me as a guest lecturer. Thanks as well to Matthew Birkhold and Ravi Palat, who invited me to deliver a lecture at Binghamton University. Both of these events and many other panel presentations and community events helped me to sharpen my arguments and propel this project to completion.

Many thanks to Pieter Martin for seeing the value of this project early on and for providing me with constant support, helpful criticism, and gentle reminders. I am truly fortunate to have such a gifted editor and colleague. Sincerest thanks to Kristian Tvedten for all his hard work on this project. I am also indebted to the anonymous reviewers who offered critical feedback and support at various stages. And on behalf of all the contributors, I would also like to express deepest thanks to Grace Onderlinde for her copyediting labors and to Sallie Steele for crafting this book's index.

As always, my mother, Ethel D. Johnson, was a source of encouragement and information, providing me with weekly, on-the-ground reports of how Katrina and Rita were transforming my homeland. Thank you as well for being my co-pilot on that rain-drenched sojourn to Simmesport, Louisiana, to survey the Magnaville subdivision. Special thanks to my sister, Cherida Gary, and her family, LaShawn, Nigel, Niyah, and Kenny, for their love and support. My wife and best friend, Sekile Nzinga-Johnson, was crucial to the completion of this work. More than anyone, she weathered some of the earliest statements of these arguments. She also shared in the making of this project through numerous trips to New Orleans and the Gulf Coast. Her questions, wisdom, and critical energy shaped this project from start to finish. My children, Kimathi, Cabral, and Zora, were also vital to this project. Thank you for surrendering the computer when I needed it and for always helping me to see the big picture.

This book is dedicated to the memory of my father, Wadsworth M. Johnson, who died in 2009 amid the fourth anniversary commemorations of the Katrina disaster. A year prior, his cancer treatments were interrupted by an ordeal of evacuation during Hurricane Gustav. His experiences brought me face-to-face with our society's lingering problems of disaster planning and health care and fueled my determination to bring this project to fruition. As I struggled through the trials of graduate school, fatherhood, and life in the tenure tunnel, he was always a patient listener, counselor, and cheerleader. I miss the sound of your laughter, your encyclopedic memory of rhythm and blues history, and your insatiable South Louisiana appetite, but your passion for music, love of life, and unshakable faith in people will always live in my heart. Your penchant for straight talk and ability to detect bullshit in contemporary political life were unparalleled, so I hope this book would have made you proud.

Cedric Johnson
Rochester, New York
December 16, 2010

The Neoliberal Deluge

Cedric Johnson

No one should assume these levees are back to where they need to be . . . they'll protect property, but not protect life.

—Louisiana Governor Bobby Jindal, August 31, 2008

Hurricane Gustav in 2008 was the first major emergency trial for the city of New Orleans since the 2005 Hurricane Katrina disaster. And there was reason to worry. Gustav had reached category 4 strength as it swept across the westernmost end of Cuba days earlier. First-term Republican governor Bobby Jindal's stern warnings to New Orleanians and coastal residents conveyed the lack of progress that had been made in shoring up the city's flood protection system. At a much deeper level, however, his words reflected a rare honesty about the reigning philosophy of governance in the state and nation writ large. The valuation of private property over life, liberty, and the common good had been a guiding principle of American ruling elites long before Hurricane Katrina made landfall. For many Americans, the floodwaters momentarily washed away the roseate democratic veneer of their republic, revealing vulnerability, corruption, indifference, and an unresponsive government. In the immediate aftermath of the storm, leftist political forces were able to popularize critiques of administrative failures and social injustices, but these criticisms have not congealed into a powerful, sustained progressive movement for rebuilding New Orleans and the Gulf Coast. Quite the contrary, the social, economic, and environmental crises that were rendered visible through the disaster have been used to further advance neoliberalization.

The son of Indian immigrants, Jindal's political fortunes crested with Katrina's storm surge. As citizens throughout the state marked the second anniversary of this disaster, Jindal won the governorship in a landslide, becoming the first nonwhite governor of the state of Louisiana since 1872 when P.B.S. Pinchbank, the colored lieutenant governor, temporarily assumed the state's top executive post after the impeachment and conviction of Henry Clay Warmouth. On a more substantive level, Jindal's victory reflected a demographic and political sea change following Hurricanes Katrina and Rita, which devastated coastal Mississippi and Louisiana during the fall of 2005. Although he was initially defeated by Democratic politician and former schoolteacher Kathleen Babineaux Blanco in his first bid for the governorship, her leadership failures during the fall of 2005 disasters created the conditions for his successful run.

As the world watched New Orleanians clinging to rooftops and crowding into the Superdome and Morial Convention Center, Blanco appeared indecisive and she was readily criticized by many pundits and made a scapegoat by Federal Emergency Management Agency (FEMA) officials. In 2007, when Blanco failed to attract a $3.7 billion ThyssenKrupp Steel plant to St. James Parish despite offering a $1.97 billion incentive package, some sensed that it was time for new leadership capable of enhancing and accelerating rebuilding efforts.[1] Although his campaign trail gestures toward insurance industry regulation momentarily rattled some of the state's business leaders, Jindal led the charge in remaking the state into a more attractive site for investors. Within months of taking office, he pushed an omnibus ethics bill through the legislature and pledged to attract more robust investment by cleaning up the state's legendary reputation as a haven of chicanery and backroom deals.

The failure of the New Orleans levee system to hold back Katrina's surge led to catastrophic physical damage, social trauma, and death. At least 1836 people were confirmed dead—1464 in Louisiana and 238 in neighboring Mississippi.[2] The majority of those who perished were over sixty years of age. Another 705 persons were categorized as missing in Louisiana. Some three million residents lost electricity. The city sustained about $22.6 billion in insured and uninsured property losses. Over a million people were displaced from the Gulf Coast region. The large-scale devastation that followed Hurricane Katrina momentarily forced matters of inequality squarely onto the U.S. public agenda like no other event since the 1992 Los Angeles riot. The stunning images of flattened homes, people stranded on rooftops, elderly patients dying in makeshift hospitals, and dead citizens strewn along curbsides and face-down in flood waters all graphically exposed the moral and political contradictions of neoliberal governance and the retreat from public responsibility for the general welfare and safety of the American citizenry.

In mass media, everyday conversations, and academic settings, Hurricane Katrina is still conveniently mislabeled the "worst natural disaster in American history." Katrina was the costliest disaster on record, but other disasters were more destructive in terms of human casualties and the scale of physical devastation. By most metrics, Hurricane Katrina *was not* the worst natural disaster in American history. In the 1900 Galveston hurricane, 8000 people perished. The Great Okeechobee hurricane in 1928 killed over 2500 Floridians, and the 1889 Johnstown Pennsylvania flood left over 2200 dead in its wake. Hurricane Katrina was not even the deadliest disaster in Louisiana's history. The 1893 Cheniere Caminada hurricane's death toll rose above 2000.[3] This "worst natural disaster" characterization stems partially from the historical amnesia that pervades American publics but it persists because of the political cachet this myth carries for the current ruling class.

There were many dimensions of this disaster that were not meterologic at all but rather a consequence of human agency and ideological prerogatives. Surely, the category 3 hurricane that made landfall at Buras, Louisiana, on August 29, 2005, caused massive destruction. The storm surge was responsible for extensive property damage in the Mississippi resort towns of Bay St. Louis, Pass Christian, Gulf Port, Biloxi, Ocean Springs, and Pascagoula. The fifty levee breaches that occurred throughout the New Orleans metropolitan area, however, were symptomatic of a deeper crisis in our national politics. Disaster planning and evacuation failures at the local, state, and national levels reflected a consensus around neoliberal governance. This political reality was lost amid corporate news coverage that portrayed these events as either a string of chaotic, unfortunate missteps, the outcome of partisan gridlock, or simply the result of bureaucratic ineptitude. Much of the death, destruction, and misery that followed Hurricane Katrina might have been minimized through more effective planning and an approach to governance that valued all life and not just that of the investor class.

The contingent social and political disasters that are commonly attributed to Hurricane Katrina were rooted in the project of neoliberalization that has been transforming American life and culture over the past three decades. This volume contributes to ongoing discussions of the

Hurricane Katrina disaster by reframing its underlying social and political contradictions. The Bush administration's wanton disregard for human life, state sovereignty, democratic institutions, and civil liberties represents the most grotesque manifestations of neoliberal governance, but these essays are not solely focused on the well-known transgressions of an unpopular president. Bush, Michael Brown, and FEMA were rightfully the objects of scorn in news media and dinner table discussions in the immediate aftermath of this disaster, but this popular outrage quickly dissipated as the manic news cycle shifted to other matters. More important, this temporary focus on administrative performance failed to ponder questions about the very nature of our society and wider public culpability in this state of affairs. Hurricane Katrina unfolded in the aftermath of the Fordist-Keynesian social compact and the essays in this volume situate this disaster and the reconstruction of New Orleans within a broader context of neoliberal culture and political-economy. The contributors are a diverse group drawn from the disciplines of sociology, political science, education, public policy, and media theory, but we share the basic view that human agency and public choices were more to blame for the death, destruction, and suffering experienced along the Gulf Coast. Forces of nature were instrumental, but policy choices made by local and national publics were more decisive. In that sense, these essays build on other writings that emphasize the "unnatural" aspects of the 2005 Katrina disaster.[4] This volume's emphasis on the role of neoliberalization, however, brings moral and interpretative focus to our prevailing political and economic system in ways that are only partially captured in those analyses that center on institutional racism, the "growth machine," the hubris or incompetence of the Bush White House, or "failed states" arguments.[5] The perspectives gathered here reflect different intellectual traditions, disciplinary roots, and methods but share a critique of that ideological project that elevates market freedoms over all others. The fate of New Orleans is our immediate subject, but these essays speak to the deeper civilizational questions that this story of disaster raises. The social and environmental crises facing New Orleans portend the challenges and states of vulnerability confronting millions in the United States and beyond.

Neoliberal Disasters

Neoliberalism is essentially the ideological rejection of the planner state (both the Soviet state socialist model and the Keynesian welfare state alternative) and the activist promotion of a new order of market rule. David Harvey describes neoliberalism as "a theory of political economic practices that proposes that human well-being can best be advanced by liberating individual entrepreneurial freedoms and skills within an institutional framework characterized by strong private property rights, free markets and free trade."[6] Neoliberalism is a form of world-making predicated on the abatement of labor rights, social provision, public amenities, environmental regulation, and other artifacts of social democracy deemed impediments to capital accumulation. As Jason Hackworth cautions, neoliberalism entails a selective return to the ideals of classical liberalism.[7] Neoliberals do not really embrace classic laissez-faire ideas in a strict sense, but instead favor opportunistic use of the state to colonize all spheres of human activity under market logic. Rather than a regime of unregulated capital, neoliberalism is in fact, as Michael Hardt and Antonio Negri point out, "a form of state regulation that best facilitates the global movement and profit of capital."[8]

Neoliberalism has its genesis in the Cold War. American economist Milton Friedman was this ideology's chief architect and booster. The postwar economic boom provided little traction for Friedman's parlor wars with Keynesian economics. His doctrines and those of his Chicago School peers, like Friedrich von Hayek and Arnold Harberger, gained notoriety among the ruling classes as they attempted to restore their authority and prosperity against global democratic rebellions, falling rates of profit and rising real wages during the late 1960s. Neoliberal reforms were initiated first through the counterrevolutions waged against progressive regimes in the developing world before making their way back to the advance industrial nations of the West. The socialist experiments undertaken throughout the formerly colonized world sought to lessen dependency on the West and meet citizen needs by bolstering national infrastructure, health care, education, and industry. Friedman's brand of economic reforms were implemented through the establishment of local intellectual outposts that trained homegrown "Chicago boys" but more decisively through coup d'état and dictatorship in Latin America's Southern Cone. Trade unionists, teachers, socialists, and others who resisted privatization and social divestment were jailed and murdered en masse under the brutal reign of Augusto Pinochet in Chile and in Argentina's "Dirty War" waged by Jorge Rafael Videla's military government. Elsewhere in the Third World, neoliberal policies were achieved through the structural adjustment measures of the

International Monetary Fund, which required massive cuts in social spending as conditions for loans. During the late 1960s and early 1970s, students, women, minorities, and workers in the advanced industrial nations challenged technocratic power and demanded more expansive democracy in production, education, health care, and politics. The election of Ronald Reagan in 1980, however, marked an effective end to Keynesian approaches in U.S. politics. His avuncular style allowed Reagan to succeed where Barry Goldwater and others had failed. Reagan's administration pursued an agenda of deregulation, tax cuts for the wealthy, an open assault on the social safety net, and other measures designed to liberate market forces. The New Democratic administration of Bill Clinton during the 1990s signaled the defeat of Keynesian liberalism within the Democratic party and the consolidation of American elites around a neoliberal agenda.

Although it is common within American right-wing discourse to conflate the expansion of market regimes with "smaller government," the state does not recede in importance under neoliberal advances. Rather, its role is recast as the market's hand-maiden. The state remains critical to creating and maintaining the institutional underlayment that supports proper functioning of the free market system—the production and regulation of currency, domestic policing, the military, and the courts system. Under neoliberal regimes, state expenditures are re-routed from social goods, such as child care subsidies, housing, education, health care, unemployment insurance, pensions, and the like toward security measures and the subsidization of private sector growth. As the redistributive functions of the state are diminished, social inequalities are increasingly managed through more extensive policing and increasingly invasive forms of surveillance and social control.[9]

Neoliberalism takes root in diverse cultural, social, and government contexts. Not unique to a particular state-form, neoliberal privatization inhabits various politicoeconomic hosts from late Communist China, the urban centers of North America, rural towns and massive slums of Africa and Latin America, the Muslim world, and the traditionally social democratic states of Europe. This latest form of capitalism may not batter down all walls of cultural distinctiveness and national sovereignty as Marx and Engels concluded, but it cuts new doorways for capital mobility and crafts modes of privatization adaptable to local tastes and political arrangements. Indeed, within the neoliberal worldview, the economic choices of free citizens form the central dynamics of markets and prescribe the limits of government authority. This tendency to see such historical arrangements as a natural order circumvents considerations of social power and hierarchy and the differential impact of some citizens' choices over others. Aiwha Ong notes that neoliberalism might be seen as "a new relationship between government and knowledge through which governing activities are recast as nonpolitical and nonideological problems that need technical solutions."[10] For Ong, "neoliberal governmentality results from the infiltration of market-driven truths and calculations into the domain of politics."[11] Neoliberal efforts to marketize politics and privatize information, life, and space threaten the possibility of social equality and meaningful democracy. In a relatively brief period, neoliberal reforms have spawned a global nouveau riche and created wider availability of consumer goods and more expansive playgrounds for tourists and urban elites, but these massive transfers of public wealth into private hands have simultaneously created unprecedented inequality, mass immiseration, and vulnerability for the multitude around the world.[12] Against the ideology of neoliberalism that promises universal benefits through self-regulating market activity, the actual practice of neoliberalization is socially disruptive, inherently crisis-laden, and predicated on pervasive socioeconomic underdevelopment.[13] In response, diverse protest movements—too often crowded under the banner of "antiglobalization"—have challenged the dire social and environmental consequences of neoliberal world-making and the notion that market values should take precedence over human needs, political equality, commons, and environmental integrity.

Our interpretative focus on neoliberalism helps to remedy problems associated with the term "neoconservative," which resonates in American public debate but often conflates opposing tendencies within the Republican Party. For decades, neoconservative appeals to God, country, and capital worked well in securing Republican electoral victories, but this designation concealed cleavages between those whose market fundamentalism ran deeper than their religious devotion, nationalism, or nostalgia for patriarchal family values. We can see evidence of these ideological rifts within the neoconservative bloc in the old pornography/obscenity debates; the latter-day conflicts between the American Pharmacists Association and free-market–oriented conservatives over the legalization of the emergency contraceptive pill Mifepristone; and the simmering tensions between vigilante border patrols in the American Southwest and agribusiness, restaurants, and hospitality industries regarding the use of immigrant labor. A conventional focus on neoconservatism also obscures the extent of bipartisan consensus around market doctrines. Since the Reagan era, Democrats and Republicans, black, brown, and white elites, and state and federal officials have increasingly converged around the view that private institutions and individuals—not government—should bear primary responsibility for social welfare, education, and disaster preparedness, relief, and reconstruction. A focus on neoliberalism also encourages less provincial analyses that link post–Cold War American political and economic development to planetary struggles over privatization.

Although the contributors here are conversant with broader critiques of neoliberal ideology, their respective chapters emphasize "actually existing neoliberalism" through analysis of how neoliberal restructuring projects have been implemented within specific historical-spatial contexts, in particular, though not exclusively, the city of New Orleans. Jaime Peck, Nik Theodore, and Neil Brenner argue that "cities have become strategically important arenas in which neoliberalizing forms of creative destruction have been unfolding."[14] Cities have become chief targets of neoliberal rollback strategies given their historical centrality within the wider Fordist-Keynesian economic system. And as Peck, Theodore, and Brenner contend, "the strategic significance of cities as loci for innovation and growth, and as zones of devolved governance and local institutional experimentation, likewise positions them at the institutional and geographical forefront of neoliberal rollout programs" that introduce new forms of institutional regulation and statecraft.[15] Over the past few decades, the relatively intimate and reciprocal relationships between the federal government, business elites, and locally owned banks that guided urban growth and development under Fordism have been supplanted by a new configuration dominated by transnational banks and the growing influence of bond-rating agencies.[16] Under these new conditions of financialization and global capital mobility, cities are compelled to act entrepreneurially, minimize public expenditures, and incentivize private investment. Neoliberalization not only produces uneven development within cities, but the pressures of competition between locales to attract investment has created a highly variegated order within the international economy where alpha cities like New York, Hong Kong, and London serve as the capitals of finance and political power and cities like New Orleans occupy a diminished, peripheral, and precarious place under these emergent arrangements.[17]

No Longer Inevitable: The Shifting Geopolitics of the Crescent City

In the aftermath of Katrina, Illinois Republican and Speaker of the House J. Dennis Hastert questioned whether New Orleans should be rebuilt given that many residential neighborhoods were susceptible to future flooding.[18] In a similar vein, it was not uncommon to hear pundits and ordinary citizens wonder out loud as to why New Orleanians would build below sea level in the first place. Neither of these comments reflects the reality of how all cities interact with their natural surroundings and challenges—soil composition, water resources, wildlife, climate, elevation, etc. Like most cities, New Orleans developed in ways that were commercially profitable and technologically possible. Montreal's *la ville souterraine* and Tokyo's gleaming, earthquake-resistant skyline are other examples of how cities have adapted technologically to natural challenges. New Orleans was not a backwater exception to good planning and level-headedness as these comments imply. The city featured a mix of both exemplary urban planning and the same wrong-headed land-use practices and radial development that has defined U.S. cities for the past half-century. The spatial development of metropolitan New Orleans, especially the creation of residential subdivisions and strip malls in the former wetlands of New Orleans East and St. Bernard Parish during the 1970s, was driven by market rationality, the short-term self-interests of individual homeowners, developers, contractors, and politicians pursued with little regard to the longer-term consequences for the natural and social environment. Hastert's concerns were those of a diehard fiscal conservative who wished to cut the tap on potential rebuilding funds flowing from the federal government without acknowledging the role of unrestrained market activity in producing vulnerability and disaster. Such comments reflect the deep antiurbanism harbored by many Americans and this particular city's declining stature in our national politicoeconomic constellation. They echo a rationale for New Orleans's abandonment that congealed long before Katrina's storm surge and fiscal neglect cracked open its floodwalls.

New Orleans was created and maintained for its military and commercial advantages and ultimately abandoned as those advantages have diminished amid the ethereal circuits and hyperconnectivity of global capitalism. From its founding in 1718 by colonizer Jean-Baptiste LeMoyne de Bienville, New Orleans occupied strategic military and economic ground near the mouth of North America's largest river.

The original settlement was built on a natural levee—an elevated ridge along the Mississippi's northern banks created through silt deposited by seasonal flooding. Almost completely surrounded by water, the city's tropical climate presented various challenges for drainage, construction, and public health. Throughout the nineteenth century, city residents were plagued by mosquito-borne illnesses such as malaria and yellow fever.[19] The exceptional hydrological challenges and local culture of New Orleans stem from its geographic character as a delta city. Rob Shields notes that such cities are uniquely unstable due to a naturally shifting, adjacent river and an encroaching sea. This instability is further exacerbated by geographic isolation from nearby hinterland and considerable flood hazards due to proximate wetlands.[20] This unwieldy combination of exceptional natural hazards and incredible commercial advantages compelled geographer Pierce F. Lewis to describe New Orleans as "an impossible but inevitable city."[21]

New Orleans developed into the foremost slave-trading center in antebellum America, and by 1840 it was the wealthiest and third most populated city in the country. Like the Panama Canal Zone, Annapolis, Norfolk, and other nodes within the U.S. maritime economy, for much of its history New Orleans provided U.S. statesmen, generals, and captains of industry with ready access to colonial resources. As the twentieth century began, Baldwin Wood's state-of-the-art pump system helped to drain marshlands between the natural levee and the brackish waters of Lake Pontchartrain, enabling the expansion of residential settlement northward. Before the New Deal era, levee protection and disaster preparedness were largely localized matters. At the start of the twentieth century, the New Orleans levee system was a patchwork of privately funded structures.[22] Although the Army Corps of Engineers has its roots in the American Revolutionary period, the Corps did not emerge as a principal force in the development and maintenance of civilian flood protection until the New Deal era.[23] In signing the 1936 Flood Control Act, President Roosevelt elevated flood protection to a matter of federal responsibility. Although contemporary U.S. leftist commentators often emphasize the social munificence of the New Deal as an antidote to the malevolent politics of the New Right, such selective remembrance expunges other ideological motives and material interests animating the Roosevelt administration. The New Deal was undertaken to save the market system and resolve problems of overproduction and speculative crisis by creating a consumer republic.[24]

As New South cities, such as Houston, Richmond, and Atlanta lurched toward modernization in the first few decades of the twentieth century, New Orleans remained a stubborn outpost of the Old South. And even as many companies relocated factories to the Sunbelt during the post–World War II years to tap the region's low-skilled, nonunion workforce, New Orleans never developed a manufacturing base comparable to its Southern neighbors.[25] NASA's acquisition of the Michoud Industrial facility and the federal investment that followed between 1962 and 1966 constituted one ray of Sunbelt development, but overall the picture was increasingly grim. In the aftermath of World War II, civic boosters and politicians shifted their focus toward the development of the local tourist industry. Located at a watery crossroads, the city had always teemed with all sorts of visitors—farmers from nearby parishes, artisans, writers, salesmen, sailors, and assorted adventurers. In 1897, the city created a formal red-light district, Storyville, where early jazz flourished alongside legal sex tourism until it was shut down by federal officials during World War I. Lagging behind their New South competitors, New Orleans's preservationists, entrepreneurs, and civic leaders embellished and marketed the city's Old South charm and Old World streetscape to middle America. Against the prevailing repressive bourgeois norms of post–World War II America, the "Big Easy" was depicted as a haven of social permissiveness, carnality, and preindustrial joys.[26]

Prior to Hurricane Katrina, the city of New Orleans hosted some ten million visitors each year. In addition to being a popular choice for conferences and professional meetings, the city is the annual site of the Jazz and Heritage Fest, the Essence Music Festival, the Bayou Classic and Sugar Bowl collegiate football games, Southern Decadence, and, of course, its storied Mardi Gras celebrations. The hotels that lined Poydras, Canal Street, and the side streets of the French Quarter boasted more than 34,000 rooms. The tourism industry generated more than $5 billion in sales annually with one-fifth of that generated during carnival season alone. Before Katrina, one of every seven city residents worked in the tourist industry. The expansion of the low-wage tourist economy, however, has not provided an adequate alternative to the loss of manufacturing. Unemployment increased in the city for virtually every year from 1966 through 1980. The New Orleans area suffered a net loss of 13,500 manufacturing jobs between 1970 and 2000.[27] During this same period, the service and retail sector expanded dramatically from

38 percent of the total employment in the metropolitan area in 1970 to 52 percent in 2000.[28] Of those sectors that remained in the city amid large-scale deindustrialization, most paid their workers less than the national median wage.[29] Petrochemical drilling and refining as well as shipping continued to define the city's economy, but in the last few decades of the twentieth century, technological and market changes diminished the prominent role these industries once played in the region.

The stretch of the Mississippi River between New Orleans and Baton Rouge is often called the "American Ruhr" because of its dense concentration of industrial facilities. B.F. Goodrich, DuPont, Union Carbide, Dow Chemical, Freemont Chemical, Allied Chemical, Rubicon Chemicals, Vulcan Materials, American Petrofina, Shell Oil, Exxon, Monsanto, and other firms have relied on the Mississippi for water resources, shipping, and waste disposal. As the OPEC crisis waned during the late 1970s and oil prices plummeted, U.S.-based oil and gas companies consolidated their managerial structures, making Houston the oil capital of the country. New Orleans was a casualty of this restructuring with Shell Oil and other companies moving major operations and office staff westward, taking a sizable portion of the city's middle class with them. The city's shipping industry has also experienced declining fortunes.

The South Louisiana port system remains vital, but its centrality to the economy has been challenged by competition from high-tech port terminals in nearby Mobile, Gulfport, Baytown, and Houston. The lower Mississippi River is home to the Port of Baton Rouge, the Port of New Orleans, and the Port of South Louisiana, which is the largest in the Western Hemisphere in terms of raw tonnage volume. Together these three facilities serve as a major point of departure for U.S. agricultural exports. The efforts to keep pace with technological changes, like containerization, have produced greater efficiency and competitiveness, as well as a smaller workforce.[30] And New Orleans has been slower than its competitors in adopting new port technologies. The growing industrial might of China following the procapital reforms under Deng Xiaoping and the corresponding ascendancy of the West Coast ports has also undermined the relative influence of the South Louisiana port complex within the larger domestic economy. Oakland, Seattle, and Long Beach serve as the major gateways for consumer goods produced in the Dickensian factories of Ho Chi Minh City, Manila, Dhaka, and China's Pearl River delta. Although New Orleans was a preeminent entrepôt of mid-nineteenth century American maritime industry and a vital hub of cultural production during the twentieth century, it has been increasingly marginalized in the Information Age's global financial and trade networks. Unlike global cities, which serve as critical centers of communication, finance, and technological development, New Orleans occupies a diminished economic niche of leisure and waterborne commerce more akin to its Caribbean and Yucatan neighbors. The integrity of the city's flood protection system has tracked the same arc as its falling economic prosperity during the forty-year period between Lyndon B. Johnson's 1965 address in the wake of Hurricane Betsy, when he pledged to rebuild a first-class levee system, to George W. Bush's post-Katrina speech in Jackson Square.

Cold War era flood protection policy implemented by the Army Corps, like the Eisenhower highway system, produced universal public benefits, but its chief impetus was to facilitate and enhance commercial activity and national security. A period film produced by the Corps suggested nothing less. The narrator asserted, "This nation has a large and powerful adversary. Our opponent could cause the United States to lose nearly all her seaborne commerce, to lose her standing as first among trading nations.... We are fighting Mother Nature.... It's a battle we have to fight day by day, year by year; the health of our economy depends on victory."[31] Since the 1950s, the Army Corps flood management activities in South Louisiana have sought to maintain the city's commercial and military place against the river's naturally wandering course. In 1963, the Army Corps dammed Old River about 300 miles upstream from New Orleans and developed a structure to control the distribution flows and sediment levels in the Mississippi River and to prevent it from shifting course to the neighboring Atchafalaya basin. The Corps' general approach to maintaining the Mississippi shipping corridor has proven successful, but its efforts toensure protection of residential areas of metropolitan New Orleans have been compromised by design flaws, improper management, and fiscal constraints.

Attempts to subordinate nature to commercial needs often created new hazards. A key case in point where a Corps project created new flood risks is the Mississippi River Gulf Outlet. Known locally as "Mr. Go," this shipping corridor was completed in 1965 as a shortcut to the Gulf of Mexico.[32] Over the years, this little used channel has expanded due to erosion, and it provided a direct path for Katrina's storm surge into suburbs and hamlets of St. Bernard Parish. In November 2009, a federal district court found the Army Corps liable for Katrina damages caused by Mr. Go and awarded $720,000 to the four plaintiffs in the suit.[33] In addition to the Army Corps's role, the city's levee system was compromised by mismanagement. A balkanized system of levee boards was developed and functioned as a form of petty patronage for successive administrations in the city and neighboring parishes. In many cases, these boards failed to enforce basic laws (e.g., regulations forbidding gardening and tree planting near earthen levees) that were crucial to maintaining the integrity of the system. Additionally, the Army Corps was guilty of basic design errors such as the use of I-shaped sheet pilings to reinforce levees rather than inverted T-shaped design more suitable to the region's instable soils.[34] Although the Corps bears responsibility for these and other mistakes, the wider political context should not be ignored. The integrity of the city's levee system was compromised by various factors including technological path-dependency and local malfeasance, but the fiscal constraints imposed by the Bush administration were calamitous.

Upon taking office, Bush embarked on a radical, upward redistribution of wealth that bore dire consequences for public safety. The administration pursued massive tax cuts for the wealthiest Americans and deep cuts in infrastructure improvement and social spending. The Corps withstood various criticisms from environmentalist and others who viewed specific projects as boondoggles. White House officials often evoked these criticisms as a pretext for funding cuts. In February 2001, Bush proposed a $641 million cut to the Army Corps and an additional $390 million the following year. Additionally, half of the funding for the Southeastern Louisiana Flood Control Project and $389 million in disaster relief funding were axed.[35] Although many congressional Democrats would express outrage at the administration's mishandling of the Katrina disaster, they supported these spending cuts. The Bush administration pursued this fiscal assault on the Corps and flood protection despite dissent within the administration and the larger scientific community. Mike Parker, a Mississippi congressmen appointed by Bush to oversee the Corps, warned that extensive cuts to the Southeastern Louisiana Flood Control project would compromise public safety and he was subsequently dismissed from his post. The administration also ignored the 2004 Hurricane Pam simulation conducted by Ivor Van Heerden, then deputy director of Louisiana State University's Hurricane Center. Commissioned by FEMA and the Louisiana Office of Homeland Security, this simulation explored the likely scenario of a slow-moving category 3 hurricane striking southeastern Louisiana. Experts concluded that "Hurricane Pam" would cause catastrophic damage, displace as many as 1 million residents, and destroy over a half million structures.[36] Of course, the administration's prioritization of investor class interests over broader concerns of public safety were clearly reflected in how poorly it reacted when the worst-case scenario materialized.

Damage Control: Neoliberal Disaster Management

The 2005 Katrina disaster and other latter-day catastrophes illuminate the expanding influence and scope of humanitarian-corporate complexes that coordinate, finance, and execute economic development, aid, and post-disaster relief and reconstruction projects worldwide.[37] These complexes are composed of nongovernmental organizations (NGOs), transnational corporations, philanthropic foundations, and private donors; the emergency management agencies, military and coast guards of some nation-states; and international governing bodies. As neoliberal restructuring has hollowed out the welfare safety-net in one nation after another and as fiscal and ideological pressures have diminished the scale and role of centralized state planning, these complexes have evolved as the preeminent means for addressing human need and emergency. Although some more developed nation-states retain a vital role in postdisaster rescue efforts, when disaster strikes, the work of relief, clean-up, and reconstruction is largely undertaken by NGOs and for-profit firms in the United States and beyond. A brief prepared by the United States Institute of Peace following the 2010 Haiti earthquake disaster described that nation as a "republic of NGOs."[38] Prior to the earthquake, the estimated number of NGOs operating in Haiti ranged from 3000 to as many as 10,000. Over 1000 NGOs took up the work of rebuilding Sri Lanka after the 2004 Boxing Day tsunami, with many others operating throughout the flood-damaged coastal regions of Indian Ocean rim. Albeit on a different scale, the same dynamics could be found in post-Katrina New Orleans. Amid widespread criticism of FEMA's failures and public cries for relief, the Bush administration literally capitalized on this disaster and continued its aggressive agenda of corporate privatization by awarding no-bid contracts to political insiders and favored firms (i.e., Bechtel, Halliburton, the Shaw

Group, and others). The administration also created the context for the hyperexploitation of immigrant workers by waiving the Davis-Bacon Act's proof of citizenship and prevailing wage requirements for federal government contractors—a measure that was subsequently reversed under public pressure.[39] Naomi Klein refers to this phenomenon as "disaster capitalism" and argues that neoliberals have seized moments of disaster, social trauma, and political instability as fast tracks for advancing market reforms.[40] Disaster profiteering may be the most visible and reprehensible aspect of the work undertaken by humanitarian–corporate complexes. However, inasmuch as she focuses primarily on the corporate skullduggery and White House patronage streams of the Bush era, Klein's arguments neglect the more pervasive and equally consequential phenomenon of *do-good capitalism* where altruism, good will, and even social antagonisms are harnessed to the profit motive.[41] In New Orleans, short-run clean-up was dominated by disaster capitalism, but the longer-term recovery effort has been characterized by privatization carried out through more benevolent actors—grassroots organizations, neighborhood associations, and charitable groups like Phoenix of New Orleans, Catholic Charities, Contemplatives in Action, Habitat for Humanity, and many others. These emergent disaster management arrangements are a corporate vamping of the peacenik slogan "Food Not Bombs" where economic motives are achieved and new markets are created through humanitarian service.

These maneuvers might be described as *grassroots privatization* because they advance neoliberalization through empowerment and civic mobilization. These efforts did not garner the same outrage as the dispensing of contracts to White House–friendly corporations, but they follow the same logic of government outsourcing and the creation of markets in formerly public sectors—education, housing, security, health care, sanitation, and debris removal. Such measures further the reach of neoliberal privatization by cultivating consensus in unlikely corners of the populace. Education reformers, disgruntled residents, urban planners, liberal academics, students, neighborhood activists, and clergy have embraced the participatory allure of these strategies, but these measures lack the basic fairness, oversight, and potential economic benefits of a truly public works approach to postdisaster reconstruction.

Grassroots privatization depoliticizes the process of reconstruction in a few ways. First, volunteerism typically provides participants with an opportunity to express compassion, without the political risks that accompany working for social justice. Volunteerism may lead to activism in some cases, but this is less likely within organizational contexts where problems that might be addressed through public activity are routinely defined as personal or moral issues with technical and/or religious solutions.[42] Rather than challenging existing patterns of social hierarchy and exclusion, volunteer-led rebuilding efforts coexist alongside local norms and practices. Second, the use of private and religious institutions to facilitate rebuilding also carries little guarantee of constitutional equal protection and often reproduces social inequalities. Reconstruction undertaken by private, charitable groups has typically benefited those sectors of the population who are more educated, articulate, or socially integrated and thus best prepared to negotiate the bureaucracy and subculture of relevant service delivery organizations. Third, the devolution of rebuilding to private institutions encourages participation without substantive power. In other words, these institutions enlist legions of church and student volunteers to carry out rebuilding designs that have already been vetted and sanctioned by celebrity benefactors, nonprofit boards, developers, politicians, and starchitects. Volunteers are vital to the brick, mortar, and drywall phases of rebuilding, but they are largely excluded from and, in many cases, oblivious to the power dynamics that are shaping the larger context and key decisions about resource allocation and priorities. Worse still, residents and displaced evacuees are typically the most marginalized and disempowered in this privatized rebuilding schema. As individuals, Katrina survivors are habitually recruited for design charettes, focus groups, and SWOT analyses, but they often lack the kinds of sustained, effective advocacy organizations that might advance their collective interests.

This Book

This book is organized into four thematic sections—Governance, Urbanity, Planning, and Inequality—with each section dedicated to exploring how these particular aspects of social life in the city and the nation have been influenced, degraded, or transformed by the process of neoliberalization. Part I of this book, "Governance," explores the nature of neoliberal governmentality and how particular discourses and strategies were deployed during the crisis of the Katrina disaster to restore system legitimacy. Contemporary disaster management reflects wider postindustrial changes in economy and culture and the prevailing approach to crisis is fundamentally concerned with controlling the flows and character of information. In chapter 1, Chris Russill and Chad Lavin note that under the current terms of neoliberal governance, states do not pursue legitimacy through public works, but through public relations. These authors consider how discourses of crisis coming from the state and mass media often obscure the political roots of "natural disasters." In particular, they interrogate the use of the "tipping point" as metaphor and theory of epidemiology from its genesis in the popular musings of New Yorker journalist Malcolm Gladwell to its prominence in the congressional testimony of embattled FEMA director Michael Brown. Russill and Lavin conclude that this notion discourages any definitive identification of agency, power, and accountability. Like other authors in this volume, Russill and Lavin urge an approach to crisis that focuses on the political-economy of vulnerability—how public policy, productive relations, and social factors converge to concentrate risks among some sections of the population. In chapters 2 and 3, respectively, Eric Ishiwata and Geoffrey Whitehall and I examine the nexus of racial politics and neoliberal governance.

In the aftermath of Katrina, the racial justice frame quickly emerged as the default interpretation of this disaster in academic, journalistic, and activist circles and its centrality to public discourse shaped the kinds of responses that were crafted by progressive and liberal organizations.[43] The most familiar statement of this sensibility was rap star Kanye West's unscripted "Bush doesn't care about black people" quip during the Red Cross Concert for Hurricane Relief.[44] This basic claim that racism either at the level of executive power or in the deep structures of society was the principal cause of this disaster was developed and advanced in dozens of articles, books, and conference presentations. The fact of racial discrimination seemed apparent enough given the throngs of disheveled and desperate black New Orleanians interviewed and broadcast around the clock in the week after Katrina made landfall. African Americans were also the victims of well-publicized police and vigilante violence in the weeks after the storm.[45] Three days after Katrina struck, as they were walking through the majority-white enclave of Algiers Point, Donnell Hetherington, Marcel Alexander, and Chris Collins were wounded by the shotgun blasts of a racist vigilante, Roland Bourgeois.[46] One of the most heinous acts of post-Katrina violence occurred on Sunday, September 4, 2005, when a group of residents were gunned down by local police on the Danziger Bridge, ending in the death of a forty-year-old, mentally disabled man, Ronald Madison, and seventeen-year-old James Brisette. A coroner's report revealed that Madison sustained seven gunshots into his back. As he lay wounded, Madison was also punched and kicked by one of the officers at the scene. Ronald Madison's brother Lance and several members of the Bartholomew family were also wounded in the attack. Another highly publicized act of aggression against city residents occurred two days after Katrina struck, when a group of about two hundred flood victims sought refuge on the Westbank and were turned away at gunpoint by Gretna police as they attempted to cross the Crescent City Connection bridge on foot.[47] In December 2005, the vicious beating of Robert Davis, a sixty-four-year old re-tired elementary school teacher, by three white New Orleans Police Depart-ment officers was captured on videotape and broadcast nationwide. Such acts of racist violence supported the popular view among social liberals that long-standing, institutional racism was the central motive force animating the injustices of the Katrina disaster and its aftermath.

In chapter 2, Eric Ishiwata examines the Bush administration's dis-avowals of race as a factor in his administration's response to mass suffer-ing in New Orleans. Ishiwata's analysis roots this denial in the colorblind neoliberal politics that have flourished in American life since the rise of Reaganism. In stark contrast to the egalitarian, antiracist posture of the modern civil rights movement, right-wing colorblindness entails a refusal to acknowledge documented patterns of discrimination in labor markets, mortgage lending, college admissions, and other areas of life and a reluc-tance to mobilize state power to remedy inequality. Ishiwata's discussion blends analysis of anti–affirmative action policy, conservative education reform, popular film, and political rhetoric to delineate the core features and limitations of neoliberal colorblindness. He concludes by proposing an alternative approach to contemporary inequality that emphasizes re-lationality and acts of empathy over atomistic individualism, and evades the traps of narrow identity politics. While embracing its ethicopolitical commitments, Ishiwata and other contributors in this volume critique and refine the familiar racial justice argument.

This tendency to cast the 2005 Hurricane Katrina disaster primarily in racial terms remains mired in the grim conclusions of the Kerner Com-mission's report on the 1967 Newark riots, which held that America was becoming two nations—one black, one white, separate and unequal.[48]

Although the media spectacle might suggest that racism was the primary factor shaping the disaster, the actual social landscape of New Orleans was more complex and so were the dynamics shaping life and death during the Hurricane Katrina disaster. For much of its history, race relations in New Orleans were more fluid and complicated—often resembling Caribbean racial hierarchies more than that of other parts of the U.S. South. Through the first half of the twentieth century, the city was defined by higher levels of residential integration than many U.S. cities, such as Detroit and Chicago. Rather than a discrete legacy of slavery and Jim-Crow segregation as some have argued, the hypersegregation of the black poor in New Orleans, which was illuminated during the Katrina crisis, was the consequence of more recent public policy and social processes.[49] Among the more than 1500 residents who perished in Louisiana, class and age were more common denominators than race. The racial justice argument is dull-edged. It still possesses a powerful symbolic resonance, capable of striking a forceful blow against durable inequality in American life, but it is unable to pierce the cultural armament of late capitalism. The racial frame only partially captures the political forces at play in New Orleans. Likewise, with its traditional focus on anti-black racism, the racial justice argument leaves little room for criticism of the culpability of black political leadership in shaping this disaster and the uneven character of post-Katrina reconstruction.

Although his vocal condemnation of Bush during a WWL radio interview suggested someone with a very different political outlook, Nagin's approach to disaster planning and evacuation of the city mirrored the Bush administration's view that individual citizens and private institutions were essentially responsible for the general welfare and not government. The city's contra-flow evacuation scheme was tailored to the needs of automobile owners and biased toward middle-class residents who possessed the resources that might facilitate impromptu travel and an overnight stay (or longer) in another city. Bowing to pressures from international hotel chains amid the tail-end of the summer tourist season, Nagin waited until Sunday morning to call for a mandatory evacuation. The hellish conditions that defined the Superdome as thousands of the city's poorest sought refuge there were an outcome of the local regime's disregard for effective planning. There were no MREs (Meals Ready to Eat), water purification devices, chemical toilets, or designated medical staff at this "shelter of last resort." In his testimony before Congress, Nagin asserted that he had mobilized faith-based institutions in the days before the storm as part of his evacuation plan. As the storm approached, entire fleets of public transit and school buses lay idle—a fact that was quickly exploited by the Right wing commentariat. Nagin skillfully mobilized the racial justice frame in ways that deflected criticism of his mishandling of the evacuation and his alliance with business elites in the city's rebuilding efforts. His public pledge that New Orleans would remain a "Chocolate City" was one such instance where he calmed fears of gentrification and secured enough support from the city's black voters to win reelection. In chapter 3, Geoffrey Whitehall and I examine the limited interpretive and political utility of the racial justice frame by revisiting the "refugees debate" that erupted in the weeks after the disaster.

After Katrina, liberal black leaders and survivors condemned those who described dispossessed residents as "refugees." This term was deemed offensive because of its allusions to Third World poverty and the implicit denial of the storm victims' U.S. citizenship. This line of argument was understandable since these activists hoped to inspire greater federal and local government accountability. The debates over the "refugee" designation, however, revealed the inadequacy of civil rights discourse and obscured the ways that Katrina survivors were in fact acclimated to modes of self-governance in a manner comparable to that experienced by international refugees. Chapter 3 explores the unique terms of neoliberal sovereignty where private institutions and market rationality increasingly create the conditions for meaningful citizenship, mobility, material comfort, and security for some while excluding others. We examine the "Magnaville" settlement created by Canadian industrialist Frank Stronach as an effort to promote neoliberal self-governance in the post-Katrina context. Although this charitable project addressed the immediate needs of some evacuees, its most enduring accomplishment was to advance a privatized approach to relief and reconstruction and legitimate the view that philanthropic work and individual agency can resolve the deep inequalities produced by global capital.

The essays in Part II, "Urbanity," consider the fate of New Orleans's urbanism in the aftermath of Katrina. Pierre Bourdieu aptly described neoliberalism as nothing less than a "programme of the methodical destruction of collectives," and the chapters in this section provide fine-grained portraits of how neoliberalization has transformed the urban social fabric, built environment, public institutions, and traditions of social welfare in the city.[50] In many respects, the essays by Paul Passavant, Adrienne Dixson, and John Arena challenge the familiar notion of Crescent City exceptionalism that lies at the heart of preservationist claims. Such focus on cultural exceptionalism detracts attention from how New Orleans conforms to broader patterns in American urban development. Although its unique history and culture serve as its most precious form of capital, New Orleans is not exceptional. In fact, the problems faced by its residents and civic leaders before and after Katrina are those that confront most American cities albeit in more dramatic form. All the tell-tale markers of North American urban decay—intensification of interlocality competition, population loss, joblessness, poverty, dead commercial corridors, an eroding municipal tax base, the prioritization of downtown tourist and investor interests over neighborhoods, failing schools, and the specter of real and imagined crime were present before the 2005 disaster and continue to form the major axes of struggle in contemporary New Orleans.

In chapter 4, Paul Passavant explores the repressive dimensions of the tourist city. In this historically grounded and nuanced treatment, he examines how New Orleans's cityscape has been reconfigured through neoliberalization to mimic the differentiated niches of marketing mentalities. The post-Fordist city, Passavant argues, produces space in a manner that promotes its brand image to potential tourists and other consumers while at the same time inciting more extensive efforts of surveillance and control. He concludes that the segregative logic and capacities for control were made particularly evident in the wake of Hurricane Katrina when those who were repressed and displaced, literally by post-Fordism's built landscape, returned to those spaces of enclosure and consumption (the Superdome, the Morial Convention Center) in search of refuge and security.

Adrienne Dixson's chapter offers a poignant analysis of the celebrated public school reforms that have been undertaken in Katrina's wake and their implications for African American students, parents, and teachers. Although many residents retained a sense of pride in the athletic teams, marching bands, and communities anchored in the city's schools, prior to Hurricane Katrina, the New Orleans public school system was marked by reputation of a low performance, high dropout rates, violence, and decline. In the aftermath of the Katrina disaster, the city embarked on an aggressive makeover of the public school district that entailed school closures and the proliferation of the charter school model that combines public funding and private management. In chapter 5, Dixson draws on critical race theory to make sense of the privatization of the city's school system and to weigh its effects on educational quality and access. A former Orleans Parish school teacher and now education scholar, she draws on extensive testimony from parents and teachers and creates a portrait that cast considerable doubt on the triumphalist narratives on the virtues of "school choice" that have gained momentum nationwide.

Chapter 6 by John Arena chronicles the struggle to halt demolition of public housing units throughout the city after Katrina. Like the efforts to privatize the city school district, attempts to rid the city of public housing stock were well under way before Katrina, but the conditions of mass exodus and weakened grassroots organizations created an opportunity for opponents of public social provision to advance their agenda. New Orleans was the first U.S. city to build large-scale public housing. Once viewed as a necessary feature of its urban landscape, public housing was the object of scorn in many corners of the city before Katrina, with some viewing the removal of this housing stock as the remedy to the city's crime rates and general economic development woes. In an essay that combines both a broad historical appreciation of contemporary U.S. politics and social policy and an intimate knowledge of local organizations and actors gleaned from his years as a participant in these struggles, Arena explores the rise and fall of local efforts to secure public housing as a basic right. He chronicles the efforts of organizations like Community Concern Compassion (C3)/Hands Off Iberville to defend the right of displaced residents to return to their apartments after Katrina. Arena offers a compelling case for why public housing should not only be defended *but* expanded and improved. He concludes by detailing how various actors, decisions, and ideological postures undermined this local progressive movement. As Arena keenly observes, the local elites, liberal academics touting the virtues of "deconcentrating poverty," and some black activists all ultimately converged around a vision of post-Katrina New Orleans that favored privatized, mixed-income development over the long-standing tradition of social liberalism in the city's public housing practices.

The essays in Part III, "Planning," are united by their focus on rebuilding dynamics and their assertion that models of postdisaster urban redevelopment be guided by an approach that merges ecological sustainability and an emphasis on the social and economic needs of residents.

My chapter 7 and Barbara Allen's chapter 8 both explore the dynamics of rebuilding in one of the most devastated neighborhoods in New Orleans, the Lower Ninth Ward, and how this area has become a laboratory for architectural experimentation. In chapter 7, I examine Brad Pitt's Make It Right Foundation, a private sector effort to rebuild homes and lives in that neighborhood. Pitt's much publicized project evolved as a powerful voice of neighborhood preservation and racial justice at a moment when it appeared that the Lower Ninth Ward would remain vacant due to the lack of investment and support from the city's elite. Although I laud the efforts of MIR supporters to defend black residents' "right of return" and to encourage the use of green building technologies, I argue that this project and the individual homes it has constructed are charming manifestations of the new landscape of neoliberal urbanism where the right to affordable housing and flood protection is determined by market forces and individual access to technological/architectural remedies. Equally important, I hold that the house-by-house strategy undertaken by Pitt and MIR is predicated on bad urbanism—the tendency to prioritize the aesthetics of community over democratic, metropolitan planning.

Whereas chapter 7 focuses on the area to the north of St. Claude Avenue, Allen's contribution looks at the Holy Cross neighborhood, which lies to the south of that thoroughfare. In chapter 8, she uses insights gleaned from science and technology studies and, in particular, the work of Bruno Latour to examine the area's green transformation since Katrina. Allen calls for "just sustainability" that combines traditional sustainability and environmental justice goals—in particular, "the need for distributed environmental goods and harms to all regardless of race or class." In one of the more comparative chapters of this volume, Kanchana Ruwanpura interrogates the geographies of resettlement and reconstruction in Sri Lankan communities following the 2004 Indian Ocean tsunami. In chapter 9, she argues that community concerns and anxieties regarding the politicoeconomic realities of displacement and resettlement were articulated against prevailing fault-lines of war and inequality. With an eye toward the lessons that might be shared with the U.S. Gulf Coast, Ruwanpura concludes that keen attention to local conditions and structural inequalities is vital for rebuilding disaster-torn communities. As an antidote to uneven recovery, all three chapters in this section encourage democratic planning that represents the needs and

interests of women, minorities, workers, and the poor, the very groups
who have been disempowered and dispossessed by neoliberalization.

The final section of this book, Part IV, "Inequality," explores how risks,
vulnerability, and misery have been concentrated among particular segments of the population under neoliberal restructuring. The essays in this
section also examine how prevailing conservative views of poverty and citizenship shaped post-Katrina public policy responses in terms of short-run
relief efforts and long-term public investments. In general, these concluding
essays explore the various deployments of underclass mythology during and
after the disaster. As most of New Orleans stood underwater, wild urban legends swarmed radiowaves, television, and cyberspace. The acts of violence
against black New Orleanians noted above were fueled by an hegemonic
antipathy toward the black urban poor, which cast them as a species apart
from the American mainstream lacking the work ethic, sense of delayed grat-
ification, reverence for family, monogamy and marriage, and other values
allegedly held among the middle classes.[51] Mainstream news media helped
to promote and legitimate these notions of black social pathology as television news anchors and reporters slowly shifted away from renegade critiques
of government malfeasance and back toward more conventional tropes of
disaster coverage including focus on the specter of urban looting. Not surprisingly, as they arrived in places like Lafayette, Memphis, and Houston,
black evacuees were met with a mix of momentary compassion, suspicion,
and, ultimately, demonization. St. Tammany Parish Sheriff Jack Strain openly
worried about receiving "thugs and trash" from New Orleans housing
projects.[52] Black middle-class leaders also participated in the demonization
of black, poor New Orleanians. As his city's population doubled in size to
absorb evacuees, Baton Rouge Mayor Kip Holden expressed concerns
about lawlessness and imposed a curfew on one of the largest hurricane
shelters. When he was later confronted with reports that police were aggressive and discriminatory toward black evacuees, Holden justified his actions
after the disaster, saying he was not going to allow his city to be "overrun
by some people from New Orleans who were hell-bent on committing
crimes."[53] Even as he chastised the Bush administration's failures, anti-
apartheid stalwart and reparations advocate Randall Robinson gave credence to rumors about blacks resorting to cannibalism in New Orleans—
a statement he later retracted.[54] Such tales of murder, gang rape, and mayhem were largely unfounded but stemmed from dominant notions of black
criminality in contemporary American culture.

In chapter 10, Linda Robertson notes that the popular imagery of the black urban poor as lazy, lawless, and ungovernable was readily rehearsed in mass media to frame the social crisis and chaos that enveloped New Orleans. In contrast, another set of semantic narratives were used to describe the experiences of white working-class residents affected during the massive 2008 Midwest floods that devastated Illinois, Indiana, Iowa, Michigan, Minnesota, Missouri, and Wisconsin. Right wing pundits portrayed victims of seasonal flooding as latter-day yeoman—hard-working, virtuous, and independent. For Robertson, such rhetorical maneuvers are dangerous and undermine honest discussions of inequality in American life and the possibility of developing a sense of shared fate among Americans of different regional, ethnic, and class backgrounds.

In chapter 11, Avis Jones-Deweever analyzes the gendered experience of disaster and recovery. Grounding her conclusions in field research and interviews with women in south Louisiana and Mississippi, she contends that women often experience decreased economic capacity, heightened exposure to violence, and sexual assault in the aftermath of disaster and decreased mobility due to caregiving responsibilities. Women disaster survivors must also confront policy practices that privilege patriarchal family structures and the economic reintegration of men in reconstruction efforts. And in the concluding chapter of this volume, Nicole Trujillo-Pagán examines the plight of Mexican, male workers in New Orleans. Although the use of migrant labor drew heavy criticism and scapegoating from some politicians and residents, the overarching narratives of the disaster and their emphasis on anti-black discrimination rendered Latinos invisible—both longtime Latino residents, namely the region's large Honduran population, who were displaced by the hurricane, and the phalanx of migrant laborers who took up much of the immediate postdisaster clean-up and rebuilding work. Drawing on a wealth of fieldwork in the New Orleans metropolitan area, Trujillo-Pagán crafts a rich, fine-grained empirical portrait of labor conditions, particularly in the construction industry. She offers a perceptive treatment of discrimination that illuminates how standing notions of Latinos as hard-working and dutiful facilitated workplace discrimination and the assignment of hazardous, risky work to them. Like the other chapters in this concluding section, Trujillo-Pagán examines the particular impacts of neoliberal political practice on the most dispossessed and marginalized and, as such, provides a unique vantage point from which to contemplate the possibility of more egalitarian modes of economy, urban living, and democratic society.

Notes

1. Louisiana lost the bidding war for this plant to Mobile County, Alabama. The state of Alabama edged out Louisiana with a more substantial incentive package and their proposed site's proximity to Mobile's deepwater port and nearby automotive plants in Huntsville, Tuscaloosa, Montgomery, and Lincoln.

2. Such figures may be underestimated because many citizens died in the weeks and months after the evacuation and once they had reached host states. For example, famed restaurateur Austin Leslie and legendary Louisiana bluesman Clarence "Gatemouth" Brown both died shortly after evacuating to other states. Although the health of these and many other persons was compromised by traumatic experiences, stress, suspended medication, and/or inadequate medical care, such deaths were not classified as "Katrina-related."

3. The 1893 hurricane made landfall at Caminadaville, or Cheniere Caminada, on October 3. Of the village's 1500 residents, 779 were killed. At the time, this fishing village was becoming an increasingly popular resort. A favored destination of novelist Kate Chopin, Cheniere Caminada provided the setting for her 1899 novel, *The Awakening*. See Barry D. Keim and Robert Muller, *Hurricanes of the Gulf of Mexico* (Baton Rouge: Louisiana State University Press, 2009).

4. See Betsy Reed, ed. *Unnatural Disaster: The Nation and Hurricane Katrina* (New York: Nation Books, 2006); Gregory Squires and Chester Hartman, eds. *There Is No Such Thing as a Natural Disaster: Race, Class, and Hurricane Katrina* (New York: Routlege, 2006).

5. William R. Freudenburg, Robert Gramling, Shirley Laska, and Kai T. Erikson's latest book, *Catastrophe in the Making: The Engineering of Katrina and the Disasters of Tomorrow* (Washington, D.C.: Island Press/Shearwater Books, 2009), offers an historically informed examination that emphasizes how design flaws, economic imperatives, and political conflict shaped the Katrina disaster. In this regard, their work comes closest to the interpretative sensibility that unites the essays in *The Neoliberal Deluge*. Nonetheless, while Freudenburg et al. locate some of the contemporary infrastructural problems and inequities in the "growth machine," their analysis does not evoke neoliberalization as such and fails to develop the kind of critiques of politicoeconomic and social processes that define this volume. Noam Chomsky, *Failed States: The Abuse of Power and the Assault on Democracy* (New York: Metropolitan Books, 2006), and Marvin Olasky, *The Politics of Disaster: Katrina, Big Government, and New Strategy*

for Future Crisis (Nashville, Tenn.: Thomas Nelson, 2006), both offer failed states arguments albeit from two opposing ideological poles with Olasky, a former communist and one-time campaign consultant to George W. Bush, using government failure during the Katrina crisis as justification for the further adoption of the neoliberal model.

6. David Harvey, *A Brief History of Neoliberalism* (Oxford, UK: Oxford University, 2005), 4; see also Jason Hackworth, *The Neoliberal City: Governance, Ideology, and Development in American Urbanism* (Ithaca, N.Y.: Cornell University, 2007); Alfredo Saad-Filho and Deborah Johnston, eds. *Neoliberalism: A Critical Reader* (London: Pluto, 2005); and Judith Stein, *Pivotal Decade: How the United States Traded Factories for Finance in the Seventies* (New Haven, Conn.: Yale University Press, 2010).

7. Hackworth, *The Neoliberal City*, 9.

8. Michael Hardt and Antonio Negri, *Multitude: War and Democracy in the Age of Empire* (Cambridge, Mass.: Harvard University, 2004), 280.

9. See Jaime Peck, *Workfare States* (New York: Guilford, 2001); Loïc Wacquant, *Punishing the Poor: The Neoliberal Government of Social Insecurity* (Durham, N.C.: Duke University, 2009); Loïc Wacquant, "Class, Race, and Hyperincarceration in Revanchist America," *Dædalus* (Summer 2010): 74–90; Paul Passavant, "The Strong Neo-liberal State: Crime, Consumption, Governance," *Theory and Event* 8 (2005); Neil Smith, "Revanchist Planet: Regeneration and the Axis of Co-Evilism," *The Urban Inventors* no. 3 (2009), http://www.urbanreinventors.net/3/smith1/smith1-urbanreinventors.pdf (accessed July 26, 2010); Christian Parenti, *Lockdown America: Police and Prisons in the Age of Crisis* (London: Verso, 2008).

10. Aihwa Ong, *Neoliberalism as Exception: Mutations in Citizenship and Sovereignty* (Durham, N.C.: Duke University Press, 2006), 4.

11. Ong, *Neoliberalism as Exception*, 4.

12. Harvey, *A Brief History*, 152–82.

13. Jaime Peck, Nik Theodore, and Neil Brenner, "Neoliberal Urbanism: Models, Moments, Mutations," *SAIS Review* 29 (Winter–Spring 2009): 49–66.

14. Peck et al., "Neoliberal Urbanism," 57; see also Jamie Peck and Adam Tickell, "Neoliberalizing Space," *Antipode* 34 (2002): 380–404; Neil Brenner and Nik Theodore, eds. *Spaces of Neoliberalism: Urban Restructuring in North America and Western Europe* (Malden, Mass.: Blackwell Publishing, 2002).

15. Peck et al., "Neoliberal Urbanism," 57.

16. See Hackworth, *The Neoliberal City*, 17–39.

17. On uneven spatial-economic development within cities and the broader global political economy, see David Harvey, *Spaces of Hope* (Berkeley and Los Angeles: University of California, 2000), 73–96, 133–56; David Harvey, *Spaces of Global Capitalism: Towards a Theory of Uneven Geographical Development* (London: Verso, 2006); Neil Smith, *Uneven Development: Nature, Capital, and*

the Production of Space (Athens: University of Georgia Press, 2008 [org. 1984]); Stephen Graham, *Cities Under Siege: The New Military Urbanism* (London: Verso, 2010); Saskia Sassen, *The Global City* (Princeton, N.J.: Princeton University, 1991); Mike Davis and Daniel Bertrand Monk, eds. *Evil Paradises: Dreamworlds of Neoliberalism* (New York: New Press, 2007).

18. Charles Babington, "Hastert Tries Damage Control after Remarks Hit a Nerve," *Washington Post*, September 3, 2005, A17.

19. See Craig Colten, *An Unnatural Metropolis: Wresting New Orleans from Nature* (Baton Rouge: Louisiana State University Press, 2005).

20. Rob Shields, "Delta City," Phil Steinberg and Rob Shields, eds. *What Is a City? Rethinking the Urban after Hurricane Katrina* (Athens: University of Georgia, 2008).

21. Pierce Lewis, *New Orleans: The Making of an Urban Landscape* (Sante Fe, N.M.: Center for American Places, 2003), 19–20.

22. Craig Colten, *Unnatural Metropolis*.

23. Joseph L. Arnold, *The Evolution of the 1936 Flood Control Act* (Fort Belvoir, Va.: Office of History, United States Army Corp of Engineers, 1988).

24. Lizabeth Cohen, *A Consumer's Republic: The Politics of Mass Consumption in Postwar America* (New York: Vintage, 2003).

25. Arnold R. Hirsh, "New Orleans: Sunbelt in the Swamp," in Richard M. Bernard and Bradley R. Rice, eds. *Sunbelt Cities: Politics and Growth Since World War II* (Austin: University of Texas, 1983), 110.

26. See Mark Souther, *New Orleans on Parade: Tourism and the Transformation of the Crescent City* (Baton Rouge: Louisiana State University, 2006); Kevin Fox Gotham, *Authentic New Orleans: Tourism, Culture, and Race in the Big Easy* (New York: New York University, 2007); Anthony Stanonis, *Making the Big Easy: New Orleans and the Emergence of Modern Tourism, 1918-1945* (Athens: University of Georgia, 2006).

27. Brookings Institution, "New Orleans after the Storm: Lessons from the Past, Plans for the Future" (Washington, D.C.: Brookings Institution, October 2005), 11.

28. Ibid., 11–12.

29. Ibid., 11.

30. Pierce, *New Orleans*, 71–76.

31. Quoted in John McPhee, *The Control of Nature* (New York: Farrar, Straus and Giroux, 1989), 7.

32. Freudenburg et al., *Catastrophe in the Making*, 111–34.

33. Mark Schleifstein, "Corps's Operation of MR-GO Doomed Homes in St. Bernard, Lower 9th Ward, Judge Rules," *Times-Picayune*, November 19, 2009.

34. For an insightful discussion of these and other design flaws made by the Corps, see Jed Horne, *Breach of Faith: Hurricane Katrina and the Near Death of a Great American City* (New York: Random House, 2006), 145–67.

35. See David Sirota, "Hurricanes Rain on Bush Tax Cuts Parade," *In These Times*, September 27, 2005, 16–21, 36–37.

36. Madhu Beriwal, "Hurricanes Pam and Katrina: A Lesson in Disaster Planning," *Natural Hazards Observer*, November 5, 2005; see also Ivor Van Heerden and Mike Bryan, *The Storm: What Went Wrong during Hurricane Katrina and Why–The Inside Story from One Louisiana Scientist* (New York: Penguin, 2007).

37. Aiwa Ong briefly discusses the "growing power of the humanitarian-corporate complexes" in her introductory outline of neoliberal governmentality. See Ong, *Neoliberalism as Exception*, 24; As the sovereign nation-state recedes in historical importance, Ong contends that "increasingly, a diversity of multilateral systems— multinational companies, religious organizations, UN agencies and other NGOs— intervene to deal with specific, situated, and practical problems of abused, naked, and flawed bodies. . . . In short, bare life does not dwell in a zone of indistinction, but it becomes, through the interventions of local communities, NGOs, and even corporations, shifted and reorganized as various categories of morally deserving humanity. Such technoethical situations are an index of the growing power of humanitarian-corporate complexes to grade humanity in relation to particular needs, prioritized interests, and potential affiliations with powers-that-be." Cyberpunk novelist Bruce Sterling describes the same phenomenon as the "emergency rescue complex," but his designation only captures part of the wider phenomenon of disaster management that includes disaster planning, relief, education, and economic development initiatives. See Sterling, "Do-Bad Architecture," *Architectural Record* (October 2008): 86–89.

38. M. Kristoff and L. Panarelli, "Haiti: A Republic of NGOs," United States Institute of Peace Brief 23: 1–3.

39. Mike Davis, "Who Is Killing New Orleans?" *Nation*, April 2006, 10; Mike Davis, "The Predators of New Orleans," *Le Monde Diplomatique*, October 2005; Rita J. King, *Big, Easy Money: Disaster Profiteering on the American Gulf Coast* (Oakland: Corpwatch, 2006); Naomi Klein, *The Shock Doctrine: The Rise of Disaster Capitalism* (New York: Picador, 2007).

40. Klein, *The Shock Doctrine*, 14–15, 20.

41. For more on do-good capitalism or what Žižek terms "cultural capitalism," see Slavoj Žižek, *First as Tragedy, Then as Farce* (London: Verso, 2009), 52–56; Thomas Frank, *The Conquest of Cool: Business Culture, Counterculture, and the Rise of Hip Consumerism* (Chicago: University of Chicago, 1997); Jim McGuigan, *Cool Capitalism* (London: Pluto, 2009); Ong, *Neoliberalism as Exception*.

42. For an especially perceptive account of the interrelated dynamics of volunteerism and the culture of political reticence in the United States, see Nina Eliasoph, *Avoiding Politics: How Americans Produce Apathy in Everyday Life* (Cambridge, UK: Cambridge University 1998), 23–63. Eliasoph is troubled by the "shrinking circle of concern" she encountered while conducting ethnographic work in an

unnamed, fairly typical late twentieth century suburban community. Whether in activist, volunteer, or recreational/leisure settings, the subjects of her study habitually retreat from public-spirited conversation albeit through the use of different strategies of disengagement (non-sequiturs, public-momism, crass humor, cynicism, etc.). Although democratic theorists have often asserted that local issues are "potential schools of wider political concern," Eliasoph concludes that "volunteers shared in this faith in civic participation, but in practice, paradoxically, maintaining this hope and faith meant curtailing political discussion: members sounded less publicly minded and less politically creative in groups than they sounded individually." In their group meetings, "volunteers never drew connections between their everyday acts of charity and public issues. . . . In almost any meeting, the discussion could have widened out to broader questions . . . possibly encouraging citizens to begin permitting themselves to imagine broader solutions. But volunteers assumed that there was no sense sacrificing precious, scarce time complaining and feeling bad about something that could not be fixed; and here was a small, upbeat, hands-on solution that could work right away if enough people would help."

43. In response to Adolph Reed Jr.'s articles in the *Progressive* and *Nation* magazines, which illuminated the class dimensions of the 2005 Katrina disaster, Kristin Lavelle and Joe Feagin reasserted the centrality of the racial justice frame in ways that diminished the implications of the three decades of black municipal rule that predated the Katrina disaster. They opt for a liberal approach to race/class analysis that emphasizes institutional racism: "We argue that race and class have always been used as tools by the white elite and have usually been supported by the white citizenry, first and foremost, to maintain white supremacy and white privilege. We view race and class as inextricably intertwined categories because of this country's centuries of racial oppression. The reason the Katrina disaster seemed like a race issue was because it was. The reason it seemed like a class issue was because it was. In reality, race and class are deeply intertwined in New Orleans primarily because of a long history of well-institutionalized racism." Longtime activist Eric Mann offers an even more assertive statement of the racial justice argument. Although well-meaning and correct in its political allegiances, Mann's arguments for a "Third Reconstruction" draws uncritically on the anachronistic language, interpretations, and political aims of defeated, bygone social movements, such as his references to "oppressed nationalities," "the right to self-determination, including an independent land base in the Black Belt South," etc. Mann writes: "The present period, shaped by the ongoing disintegration of urban centers, as reflected in government attacks on the Black community in New Orleans, intensifies the challenges to build an explicitly pro-Black, pro–people of color, pro–Third World ideology and movement that combats the white supremacy and great

nation chauvinism of this country (too often reflected in the U.S. Left) and challenges the system itself." Adolph Reed Jr., "The Real Divide" *The Progressive*, November 2005, 27–32; Adolph Reed Jr., "Class-ifying the Hurricane," *The Nation*, October 3, 2005; Kristen Lavelle and Joe Feagin, "Hurricane Katrina: The Race and Class Debate," *Monthly Review*, July–August 2006, 52–66; Eric Mann, *Katrina's Legacy: White Racism and Black Reconstruction in New Orleans and the Gulf Coast* (Los Angeles: Frontlines Press, 2006), 11; see also David Roediger, "The Retreat from Race and Class," *Monthly Review* (July–August 2006): 40–51.

44. Some of the writings that advance a racial justice perspective of the Katrina disaster include the following: Michael Eric Dyson, *Come Hell or High Water: Hurricane Katrina and the Color of Disaster* (New York: Basic Civitas, 2006); South End Press Collective, ed. *What Lies Beneath: Katrina, Race, and the State of the Nation* (Cambridge, Mass.: South End, 2007); Manning Marable and Kristen Clarke, eds. *Seeking Higher Ground: The Hurricane Katrina Crisis, Race and Public Policy Reader* (New York: Palgrave-MacMillan, 2008); Hillary Potter, ed. *Racing the Storm: Racial Implications and Lessons Learned from Hurricane Katrina* (Lanham, Md.: Lexington Books, 2007).

45. A.C. Thompson, "Katrina's Hidden Race War," *In These Times*, January 5, 2009, 11–18; A.C. Thompson, "Body of Evidence: Did New Orleans Police Play a Role in the Grisly Death of Henry Glover?" *In These Times*, January 5, 2009, 19–21; Laura Maggi, "Hurdle Lifted in Danziger Bridge Trial," *Times-Picayune*, May 8, 2008.

46. A.C. Thompson, "Katrina's Hidden Race War," *Nation*, January 2009, 11–18; Jarvis DeBerry, "In Algiers Point, a Tale of Vigilante Injustice" *Times-Picayune* online, July 18, 2010. http://ww.nola.com/opinions/index.ssf/2010/07/in_ algiers_ point_a_tale_of_vig.html (accessed on 7/26/10).

47. All of these acts of aggression garnered publicity and criticism from many corners of the African American population and the American Left. Despite a momentary burst of outrage, however, none of these incidents served as a viable flashpoint for organizing civil rights advocates and other activists beyond the city in a sustained and powerful manner. Oddly enough, in September 2007, thousands descended on Jena, a small town in central Louisiana, to protest the convictions of six black teenagers for the assault of a white teen after a series of racial incidents at the local high school. The 2005 Katrina disaster and its aftermath encompassed a complex of issues (poverty, bureaucratic malfeasance, disaster planning, insurance industry self-regulation, social isolation and neglect of the aged, homeless, persons with mental-illness, etc.) that could not be effectively summarized in the "Bush does not care about black people" frame. The Jena 6 case, however, was a perfect storm for the liberal black political elite. The work of activists was made so much easier by the lynching imagery evoked in the white

teens's aggressions, the racist statements of the presiding judge, and the familiar storyline of unequal treatment of black students in a small, southern locale. If the story was shot in black-and-white film and narrated by Julian Bond, it might have passed as a closing episode of the *Eyes on the Prize* documentary series. The court case format also provided familiar terrain for civil rights veterans and millenials looking to reenact movement history. Courtroom dramas provide their own villains, victims, and heroes who are much more alluring and camera-ready than matters of evacuation planning, zoning, or housing policy. The Jena 6 case fit easily within a longer tradition of court cases that became cause célèbre within the African American community and among civil liberties advocates and left social forces—e.g., the Scottsboro Boys, the trial of Emmett Till's murderers, *Brown v. the Board of Education-Topeka, Kansas*; legal defense campaigns for Huey Newton, Angela Y. Davis, the Wilmington 10, Sudiata Acoli, Mumia Abu Jamal, and the Charleston 5. Unlike the segregation era court cases or the imprisonment of Black Power activists, which bore tangible implications for African Americans writ large, contemporary court spectacles from the infamous O.J. Simpson debacle, NFL quarterback Michael Vick's highly publicized trial and conviction on dog-fighting charges and, to a lesser extent, the Jena 6 case carry more symbolic value for the African American population. Although thousands of students and other activists rallied in support, the Jena 6 protest has had little substantive impact on fostering public debate or popular action around the problems of racial profiling, police brutality, mandatory minimum sentencing, incarceration rates, prisoner rights, recidivism and felon disenfranchisement that black youth and adults confront nationally.

48. *Report of the National Advisory Commission on Civil Disorders* (New York: Bantam Books, 1968), 1.

49. Brookings, "New Orleans after the Storm," 5; Lewis, *New Orleans*; Douglas S. Massey and Nancy A. Denton, *American Apartheid: Segregation and the Making of the Underclass* (Cambridge, Mass.: Harvard University, 1993); Daphne Spain, "Race Relations and Residential Segregation in New Orleans: Two Centuries of Paradox," *Annals of the American Academy of Political and Social Science* 441: 81–96; Martha Mahoney, "Law and Racial Geography: Public Housing and the Economy of New Orleans," *Stanford Law Review* 42 (1990): 1251–290;

50. See Pierre Bourdieu, "The Essence of Neoliberalism," *Le Monde Diplomatique* December 1998, http://mondediplo.com/1998/12/08bourdieu (accessed March 30, 2009).

51. Adolph Reed Jr., "The 'Underclass' as Myth and Symbol," in *Stirrings in the Jug: Black Politics in the Post-Segregation Era* (Minneapolis: University of Minnesota Press, 1999); Michael B. Katz, *The Undeserving Poor: From the War on Poverty to the War on Welfare* (New York: Random House, 1989).

52. Quoted in Bill Quigley, "The Right of Return to New Orleans," *Counterpunch*, February 26, 2007, http://www.counterpunch.org/quigley02262007.html (accessed July 26, 2007).

53. Kimberly Vetter, "Post-Katrina Reports Detail Alleged Police Misconduct," *Baton Rouge Advocate* online, March 14, 2010 http://www.2theadvocate.com/news/87599912.html?showAll=y&c=y (accessed July 28, 2010).

54. Randall Robinson, "New Orleans," *Huffington Post* blog, September 2005, http://www.huffingtonpost.com/randall-robinson/new-orleans_b_6643.html (accessed October 5, 2008).

· I ·

Governance

CHAPTER 1

From Tipping Point to Meta-Crisis

Management, Media, and Hurricane Katrina

Chris Russill and Chad Lavin

And in my opinion, it's the responsibility of faith-based organizations, of churches and charities and others to help those people.

—Michael Brown, September 27, 2005

In the Wake of Katrina, America Is at a Tipping Point.

—MoveOn.org press release title, September 21, 2005

Political discourse teems with crisis. Often, this is hyperbolic and opportunistic rhetoric mobilized in the service of a particular agenda or a media strategy to increase ratings. Sometimes, as during the first days of September 2005, when much of New Orleans lay beneath water, and when thousands of the most vulnerable residents were stranded without food, medical supplies, and toilets, narratives of crisis are unavoidable. It is true that not everyone witnessed the same crisis. While some saw an ecological crisis after a massive storm and levee failure destroyed so many homes and lives, others saw a humanitarian crisis as various organizations and institutions seemed incapable of coordinating an effective response. Some saw a political crisis, noting the race and class of the victims, while others witnessed a crisis of civil society, focusing on the quick devolution to Hobbesian brutality within the city. Most cynically, Jon Stewart quipped on *The Daily Show* that the actions of federal officials in coordinating photo ops and press conferences suggested that the true crisis was the president's plummeting approval ratings.

The proliferating visions of the crisis marked the clear failure of the Bush administration's attempt to manage the crisis. Typically, narratives of crisis result from a ritualistic process dominated by government officials and media professionals, and these rituals distribute assumptions regarding how crises emerge, how a society responds, and how reoccurrence is prevented. In 2005, these rituals broke down, as media elites and citizens largely rejected the official narratives of events coming from government officials. Why did this happen? We argue that an insufficient notion of crisis organized the managerial strategies of key Bush officials, namely, Director of the Federal Emergency Management Agency (FEMA) Michael Brown and Secretary of Defense Donald Rumsfeld. Brown and Rumsfeld both used a "tipping point" perspective to manage crisis in accord with the radical assumptions of the Bush administration. Both failed in spectacular fashion.

Here, we focus on the failure of tipping point explanations of crisis in the flooding of New Orleans. First, we revisit Michael Brown's congressional testimony and examine his account of what went wrong. We develop in greater detail the tipping point metaphor animating Brown's remarks and show how it encourages particular ideas of political agency and responsibility. Second, we propose a fuller conception of crisis through Eric Klinenberg's "political economy of disaster vulnerability." Third, we discuss how theories of crisis organize understandings of political agency and responsibility through narrative and media practice. Fourth, we examine how media coverage helped generate reflection on crisis, provoking what we call a "meta-crisis" in which established narratives of crisis were themselves thrown into crisis. We also discuss how the reflective potential of the "meta-crisis" in New Orleans has been appropriated.

The Tipping Point

On September 27, 2005, Michael Brown appeared before the House of Representatives Select Bipartisan Committee to Investigate the Preparation for and Response to Hurricane Katrina. Testifying in response to criticism that FEMA and the Bush administration had failed in their response to this disaster, the recently removed FEMA director's account was much anticipated. Few surprises had emerged from the earlier testimony of the National Hurricane Center and National Weather Service directors, which amounted to a clear message: *We told them the storm was coming.* Brown would have to answer the question of what went wrong. As Representative Thomas M. Davis III noted in opening congressional questioning of the witness, "Like it or not, fair or not, FEMA in general and Mr. Brown in particular have become the symbol of what went wrong with the government's response to Katrina."[1]

In a long day of testimony, Brown maintained two key talking points. First, he argued that the system of response in place at FEMA was adequate such that this was a failure of execution rather than planning; as he put it more than once, "We were prepared but overwhelmed." Second, Brown claimed that incompetent and defamatory media coverage contributed to the inadequacy of the response in general and his personal ineffectiveness in particular:

> While FEMA was trying to respond to probably the largest natural disaster in the history of this country . . . [our] press office became bombarded with requests to respond immediately to false statements about my resume and my background.

Brown supported these talking points by characterizing key moments of decision as "tipping points." In the most prominent and widely quoted of these statements, Brown blamed state and local officials for failing to manage the evacuation, claiming that, "The failure to evacuate was the tipping point for all the other things that either went wrong or were exacerbated." Later, discussing his public blunder in admitting that he was unaware of the thousands of survivors still stranded at the Morial Convention Center, Brown stated, "That was one of my personal tipping points, too, because I was just tired and misspoke." If the failure to evacuate was a failure of state operations, this second failure is slightly different—a failure of state–media interactions. Earlier, Representative Davis similarly identified the decisive nature of this particular failure:

> When Michael Brown admitted to reporters that he didn't know thousands of survivors were stranded at the New Orleans convention center without food or water, even though T.V. journalists had been reporting that fact for hours, his appearance before us today became inevitable.

A third and more illuminating use of the term comes in a significantly less assured moment in Brown's testimony, when he is explaining the inability to move the necessary supplies to the affected region:

> Not enough people in place and not enough—again, couple that with the logistics problem of getting stuff in, so if you don't have enough to begin with . . . the flood and then the logistical problem itself, it all just—it reaches its own tipping point.

Here, Brown's frustration is palpable. His inability to control the situation in New Orleans is matched by his inability to meet the demand that he explain it. The term "tipping point" signals the limit of the explanation; Brown can explain important elements leading up to the crisis, but eventually his words fail just as thoroughly as the disaster response. The narrative, like the affair itself, eventually reaches a point at which established concepts and institutions do not work; the "tipping point" is the point at which rational description of the situation becomes cumbersome or visibly breaks down—where apparent order becomes obvious disorder. For anybody interested in crisis or disaster response, this is exactly the point at which the story gets most interesting.

Unfortunately, as Brown tells it, this is where the story ends. Even more unfortunately, nobody in the hearing asked Brown what he meant by the term "tipping point." One might chalk this up to the term's familiarity in popular discourse. Or perhaps given the ubiquity of "sound bite" media coverage and political grandstanding, it is not terribly surprising that nobody bothered to interrogate Brown's explanatory device. But for a six-hour interrogation into the most visible failure of a federal agency in U.S. history—an interrogation that often turned to quite technical aspects of the agency's mandate, organization, and operational strategies—it is noteworthy that the use of "tipping points" as a mechanism for explaining how disaster occurred was never questioned or elaborated. Indeed, although there was plenty of scrutiny regarding how FEMA responds to crisis, there was no discussion at all of how FEMA (or its director) *conceptualizes* crisis.[2]

So what exactly is a tipping point, and how did a government official come to explain the devastation of a major American city in these terms? The notion circulates rather freely in mass media and popular discourse, surely reaching its cultural apex through Malcolm Gladwell, a *New Yorker* staff writer who claimed in a 1996 essay that the idea "should change the way we think about whether and why social programs work."[3] Gladwell parlayed that idea into a reported $1.5 million advance for the pop cultural phenomenon *The Tipping Point: How Little Things Can Make a Big Difference*, and nearly a decade later, this book remained on the *New York Times* bestsellers list.[4]

Gladwell spent the months before Katrina in a media blitz. His second book, *Blink*, hit bookstores in early 2005, and with *The Tipping Point* displayed prominently in airport bookstores around the world, it was the year of the tipping point. With profiles in such magazines as *Fast Company* (January 2005) and *Brand Strategy* (April 2005), christened one of the world's most influential people by *Time* (April 2005), and commanding speaking fees in the neighborhood of $40,000, Gladwell had achieved a rare hybrid status as literary celebrity, political analyst, and business guru.[5]

Gladwell had blown up into a full-fledged managerial fad a year or so earlier, with the *Harvard Business Review* promoting "tipping point leadership," a program that weds familiar do-more-with-less efficiency mantras to Gladwell's own focus on "social epidemics."[6] In rather derivative fashion, W. Chan Kim and Renee Mauborgne extend the very example Gladwell used in popularizing the term (the idea that violent crime in New York spreads like a virus) and emerge with a theory of the successful attributes of management leadership.

> Contrary to conventional wisdom, meeting a massive challenge is not about putting forth an equally massive response. Rather it is about conserving resources and cutting time by focusing on identifying and then leveraging the factors of disproportionate influence in an organization.[7]

The appeal of this approach to managerial crises is not surprising, since it marries the desire to legitimate corporate downsizing to arguments for unleashing entrepreneurial creativity in an "information economy." It is more surprising that such theories would inform managers of war and crisis. Yet, tipping points were the theoretical touchstone of both Rumsfeld and Brown. For Rumsfeld, military success in Iraq was always one tipping point away. In 2003, he sold President Bush on the Iraq Interim Authority concept by suggesting its value as a tipping point for democracy.[8] In 2004, he argued that a military victory in Fallujah would constitute a tipping point in the war, and elaborated:

> When I use this phrase "tipping," people don't go from here over to there, they move this way, just a slight bit, and pretty soon the overwhelming majority are over in this area, recognizing that that's the future.[9]

By 2005, the tipping point in Iraq would be the elections: "That has to cause a tipping of support for the government, whoever is elected, because of the confidence that all of those people have to feel as a result of seeing so many others of the same view."[10]

A number of influential pundits were enrolled into this way of viewing crisis, not least of which were Malcolm Gladwell and newly inspired tipping point proponent, Thomas Friedman, the New York Times foreign policy columnist. On February 22, 2005, Gladwell appeared with Friedman on ABC's Nightline to explain the potential of tipping points for managing war in Iraq.[11] Straightforwardly, Ted Koppel asked Gladwell which factors were important for determining whether the 2005 Iraqi election was a tipping point. Gladwell's answer emphasized the malleability of human perception and recommended attention to the way people reframe an issue. Koppel, in seeking a concrete example, pointed to the toppling of the Saddam statue and Bush's "Mission Accomplished" speech as two examples that fit Gladwell's requirements. These examples draw attention to the stage-managed and manipulative media events encouraged by this way of thinking, and although Gladwell wisely refrained from committing himself to these examples, he did not object or correct Koppel's suggestion either.

After a commercial break, Koppel again asked Gladwell to apply the tipping point perspective to events in Iraq. Gladwell emphasized three key aspects from his book: the role of socially influential people in advancing an idea, the multiple elements implicated in social change, and the rapid, contagious nature of such change. Gladwell tried to avoid prognosticating on tipping points in Iraq, always referring instead to historical events, such as the spread of rock and roll or the fall of the Berlin Wall; yet, when Thomas Friedman showed no such restraint, Gladwell agreed Friedman's discussion of the Iraqi election was a good example. In brief, Friedman and Gladwell argued that the tipping point perspective is necessary to a proper understanding and strategy for social change in Iraq. Change can catch on fast; it can result from leveraging only some of the multiple elements of a situation; opinion-leaders can drive change by reframing how people see a situation. Only two days later, Friedman expanded the scope of his perspective, identifying three tipping points that spanned "the Middle East playground."[12]

Brown was clearly convinced by the efficacy of this point of view; he continued to use the term—and to recommend Gladwell's book—after his removal from FEMA and "tipping points" have remained part of his evolving explanations for failure.[13] It is important to recognize, however, that Gladwell's book contains only a partial account of tipping points. In his 1996 essay on tipping points, Gladwell traced the concept back to the "foundational work" by Nobel Prize–winning economist Thomas Schelling.[14] In Gladwell's subsequent book, however, Schelling is downgraded to an endnote, and his work is categorized as one among "several classic works of sociology" that describe the tipping point model.[15] In fact, Schelling, an economist and applied game theorist, had adopted the term from political scientist Morton Grodzins.[16] Grodzins and Schelling had sought to explain the same phenomenon: white neighborhoods seeing increased numbers of black residents eventually reach a "tip point" that triggers what is commonly referred to as white flight. White families do not leave individually as black families move in; rather, they leave en masse when the neighborhood reaches a critical threshold of nonwhite households.

Grodzins saw this situation as the most pressing social problem of the immediate future; quite correctly, he expected a political struggle over the direction of American cities, even forecasting "a new round of repression aimed at Negroes," and characterizing metropolitan space as a "racial problem."[17] Grodzins noted that the idea of "tipping" a neighborhood belonged to the common parlance of real estate professionals and community planners, and that it generally entailed a focus on controlling African American mobility. Grodzins's broader lesson was that avoiding the unjust outcomes that resulted, like racial and economic ghettoization, required a federal commitment to public infrastructure and urban planning; otherwise, the overcrowding of impoverished residents and disinvestment in major American urban centers would result, and this would "accentuate the evolution of central cities into lower class ethnic islands."[18]

Schelling's lesson was rather different. Working with Rand Corporation, a think-tank criticized for the ideological production of knowledge to contest investment in social infrastructure, Schelling argued an abstract point: one cannot infer individual intentions or preferences from patterns of social interaction.[19] Schelling used this argument, and a raft of examples designed to support it, to recast political problems as ubiquitous and largely banal situations amenable to abstract mathematical modeling. In Schelling's work, the influence of illegal racist activities and poverty is circumscribed, and he amplifies the importance of other variables in modeling neighborhood segregation patterns. It turns out urban segregation is not a "racial problem" at all; in fact, it is not even segregation, but rather aggregation, a byproduct of very general features of social interaction.[20] It is difficult not to see the uptake of Schelling's arguments as consistent with the general strategy of benign neglect used to combat proponents of economic and racial justice, like Grodzins.[21]

Gladwell reflects on this phenomenon to insist on a different point, which is the priority of sudden change.[22] Social policy is gradualist and assumes steady progression, but social phenomena are "non-linear"; crime waves, for example, do not wax or wane in direct proportion to the obstacles or incentives put in their way. Instead, they move in fits and starts. A favorite example for Gladwell is William Bratton, the transit authority policeman Rudy Giuliani appointed to head the NYPD, who lowered crime rates not by marshalling a larger police force but rather by managing public perceptions of urban disorder by replacing broken windows and cleaning graffiti. Bratton's approach, drawing on the "broken windows theory" of crime introduced by James Q. Wilson and George L. Kelling, was predicated on the idea that the problem of crime in New York City could best be met not through a massive mobilization of police repression but through superficial "quality of life" reforms that would be inordinately influential on community dynamics.[23]

Gladwell's point is that "liberal" social planners from the 1960s failed to account for this pattern and so pursued ineffective, inefficient, and overpriced strategies to fix social ills. Once the nature of threshold-based sudden change is recognized, you learn the value of concentrating resources on tightly focused interventions, or "Band-Aid solutions."

> The Band-Aid solution is actually the best kind of solution because it involves solving a problem with the minimum amount of effort and time and cost. We, of course, have an instinctive

disdain for this kind of solution because there is something in
all of us that feels that the true answers to problems have to be
comprehensive. . . . The problem, of course, is that indiscriminate
application of effort is something that is not always possible.
There are times when we need a shortcut, a way to make a lot
out of a little, and that is what Tipping Points, in the end, are all
about. The theory of Tipping Points requires, however, that we
reframe the way we think about the world.[24]

In a culture suspicious of social engineering and enamored of market
models, the metaphor entails a drastically reduced vision for collective
human agency, and it justifies the restriction of state intervention. It is
clear from the earliest concerns with economic and racial segregation
up through Gladwell's work and Michael Brown's testimony that tipping
points are implicated in concerns regarding federalism, public policy, and
urban planning. In this light, Michael Brown's insistence that FEMA was
"prepared" for a massive hurricane in New Orleans depends entirely on
his belief that FEMA's responsibilities for dealing with such a crisis were
quite limited. Indeed, Brown explicitly claimed in his testimony that it was
not FEMA's job to help evacuate the city: "in my opinion, it's the responsibility of faith-based organizations, of churches and charities and others
to help those people."[25] Brown identified the failure of such local organizations to assist threatened populations as the first tipping point for the
disaster, and his invocation of "tipping points" divorces the affair from
FEMA's merging into the Department of Homeland Security, the reduced
funding for maintaining levees, the concentration of poverty in specific
neighborhoods, the ongoing erosion of the Louisiana wetlands that protect against storm surges, the housing of hazardous material next to urban
populations, or the increased willingness to leave individuals personally
responsible for their own safety. For Brown, intent on identifying tipping
points in the hours after the storm hit, these conditions are not relevant to
determining whether FEMA was prepared to do its job.

Charles Perrow, the sociologist famous for explaining how massive
failures in complicated organizations are, in fact, "normal accidents,"[26]
identifies how a tipping point explanation works in this respect:

This explanation does not assume deterioration on the part of the
agency's ability to deal with natural disasters. It assumes a tipping

point, and when disasters are involved, the tipping point may bring about a sudden, rather than gradual, decline. Once it is challenged beyond its capabilities, the failures can be sudden and widespread even if the organization is not weak.[27]

The trouble in applying a tipping point explanation to FEMA is that FEMA exists to prepare for and organize response to crises that overwhelm local and state agencies. When pressed on his claim that FEMA was prepared but simply overwhelmed, Brown eventually defaulted to a restricted understanding of federalism and states' responsibility, claiming that a larger policy debate was needed if FEMA was to be prepared for events like Katrina: "Because what you're doing is driving toward a policy debate about what the role of the federal government is." In Brown's view, the crisis outstripped the capacity of the agency to respond; in our view, Brown's tipping point perspective carries an understanding of agency that encourages the very crises it purports to explain. Indeed, the most remarkable feature of both Rumsfeld's and Brown's leadership was an inability to recognize failure, and to claim success in obviously worsening conditions. In each case, the failed strategy would necessitate a massive "surge" in military deployment.

The Political Economy of Disaster Vulnerability

An alternative to the tipping point explanation is found in Eric Klinenberg's sociology of disaster. In his "social autopsy" of the 1995 Chicago heat wave blamed for the deaths of 739 citizens, Klinenberg focuses not on particular moments of nonlinear change but instead on what he calls "the political economy of disaster vulnerability."[28] Klinenberg asks why most of the people who died were old, alone, and poor, as well as disproportionately African American, and he asks why these disparate mortality rates did not figure prominently in popular or official accounts of the disaster. Indeed, the disaster is largely forgotten (despite a death toll that dwarfs that of many more well-known disasters such as the 1989 San Francisco earthquake), and its rootedness in features of urban social organization is unacknowledged. A select list of factors that Klinenberg identifies as heightening the vulnerability of both specific and general populations in Chicago would be: the social ecology of the city that isolates its residents, the aging urban infrastructure that limits the mobility and relations of the poor and the elderly, the differential access to cold water and air conditioning, and the defunding of public services that reduces the competence and efficiency of emergency response when it is needed. Klinenberg uses this neighborhood-level analysis to supplement the individual-level focus of public health agencies, including an official report from the Centers for Disease Control and Prevention. The result is a clear pattern of mortality, where residents of specific neighborhoods were significantly more likely to perish in a heat wave than were residents of other neighborhoods.

> A key reason that African Americans had the highest death rates in the Chicago heat wave is that they are the only group in the city segregated and ghettoized in community areas with high levels of abandoned housing stock, empty lots, depleted commercial infrastructure, population decline, degraded sidewalks, parks, and streets, and impoverished institutions.[29]

Focusing less on the punctuating moment of the heat reaching 106 degrees Fahrenheit and more on the production and unequal distribution of vulnerability across the city, Klinenberg sees in the Chicago case not a "natural disaster" but, in the words of one interviewee, "murder by public policy."[30] The crisis in Chicago, like that in New Orleans ten years later, was not meteorological in origin but was produced by a neoliberal style of governance and exacerbated by unequal access to reliable transportation, communication, and healthcare networks. Government agencies and administrations are organized for ineffective response because they are committed to market based operating principles regarding the role of individuals, public sector, and the state. There are direct implications to these commitments for disaster management. In Chicago, the commissioner of human services viewed the dead as individuals who had neglected themselves, and the mayor blamed families for failing to care for their relatives.[31] These views lead emergency planners to beseech individuals and families to ameliorate the crisis.

Only this is wrong. The organization of the social environment, not individuals and their families, explains why the pattern of crisis occurred. The evidence Klinenberg brings to bear on his analysis is exhaustive—he explores the demographic, political, economic, and architectural history of the city to explain why certain types of people were more likely to die in a heat wave.[32] The result is not a recommendation that the health commissioner or mayor be blamed for the heat wave. As he puts it, "It is pointless to organize an inquiry into the heat wave as a search for a guilty party, as only the crudest forms of analysis could reduce such a complex event to a single actor, causal agent, or social force."[33] The conclusion is that neglecting the political economy of disaster vulnerability in organizing crisis response is dangerous and deadly.

Klinenberg's "social autopsy" is designed to denaturalize disaster, to illuminate the role of the state in producing disaster vulnerability, and to show how public officials and media "render invisible both the political economy of vulnerability and the role of the state."[34] He shows how government and media professionals alike had internalized the crisis as a "natural disaster," and he explores the effect this had on news narratives of crisis: "The natural framing of the disaster, it seemed, had structured the editors' own perception of the crisis."[35] For example, Klinenberg shows how newspaper headlines maintained that those perishing in the heat wave were "just like most of us," even as the details in those stories indicated that the victims were primarily elderly, disproportionately black, and largely concentrated in specific neighborhoods—that is to say, *not* like most of us.[36] Klinenberg challenges this framing to root the Chicago death toll not in unpredictable and unavoidable climatological shifts but in the actions and decisions that concentrate populations and neglect services in a manner that unequally, although systematically, distributes vulnerability across the population.

Klinenberg's story is the converse of Brown's tipping point testimony. Brown's narrative is organized around the principled ascription of responsibility and the steadfast refusal of federal liability for the failed emergency response, whereas Klinenberg, in failing to hold anybody directly responsible, ultimately distributes responsibility across society such that only a systemic, collective agent could wage an appropriate response. For Klinenberg, the crisis is not locatable at the peak of the heat wave but rather in the decade leading up to the heat wave as city services and public infrastructure declined to the great neglect of so many residents. His account does not fit crisis to the existing capabilities of institutions, or fashionable theories of abrupt change, but requires that the social production of vulnerability inform debate on disaster management.

One lesson of Klinenberg's model is that it is remarkably difficult to sustain public discourse on the political nature of disaster vulnerability. For this reason, it is unfortunate that no one queried Brown's tipping point meta-phor and its underlying presumptions of management and agency. Instead, attention focused on Brown's unabashed allocation of responsibility to Louisiana state officials for the failed evacuation, typically reproduced via his summary judgment that "Louisiana is dysfunctional." It is tempting to see shoddy journalism or political expediency behind the "blame game" or "scapegoat" character of the ensuing public discourse, although strategies of responsibility displacement are probably as old as disaster itself. Respon-sibility displacement is encouraged, however, by the constricted vision of crisis and political agency informing such claims making. Without a politi-cal economy of disaster vulnerability, the complex set of relations between citizens, media, and state that render populations disproportionately vul-nerable to meteorological or political violence are only partially evident. The tipping point vision is damaging in this respect. Its faith in the priority of small-scale and even counterintuitive Band-Aid solutions to social problems, its emphasis on changing perception rather than reorganizing material conditions, and its predisposition for explaining social change as the result of moments of abrupt change, all work against a broader analysis.

In summary, Klinenberg does not shift responsibility for the heat wave from nature to the government, and he does not merely change the frame from "natural disaster" to "man-made disaster"; he directs attention to a fundamentally different theory of crisis, one that is rooted in a different set of commitments about the responsibilities and capacities of the state. The "social autopsy" does not simply identify an underreported crisis; it opens the question of what a crisis *is*.

What Is a Crisis?

As Colin Hay explains it, "crisis" comes from the Greek *kríno*. *Krísis* means "to decide"; a crisis is "*a moment of decisive intervention . . . a moment of objective contradiction yet subjective intervention*."[37] When people are suffering heat stroke or are being flooded out of their homes and when hospitals are overflowing and cities lack facilities to treat ill or endangered citizens, decisions have to be made on how to intervene. However, in most cases, the decisions are shaped not by objective and unmediated conditions but rather by the narrative explanation of the situation. Crisis, in other words, is not *incidentally* but *fundamentally* about agency; crises do not merely arise but are produced when political actors characterize the world in a manner that emphasizes the possibility of responding to a particular situation. The identification of a crisis always projects a possible response, and requires narratives of these responses to resonate culturally.

Hay's work engages a tradition of crisis theory covered in Jürgen Habermas's *Legitimation Crisis,* in which the state aims primarily to recast endemic and irresolvable economic antagonisms as episodic and manageable political disagreements.[38] The state, in this analysis, is an essentially conservative institution, offering its specific policies up for sacrifice in times of turmoil so as to protect its underlying institutional logic; in times of economic difficulty, "a potentially profound crisis of capitalism deriving from its inherent economic conditions . . . becomes, through displacement, merely a crisis of a *particular regime* of the capitalist state."[39] Just as Habermas characterizes the narrative construction of a political crisis to shield capitalism from critique, Klinenberg chronicles the narrative construction of a "natural disaster" to distract from the production and distribution of vulnerability by urban decay and market-based governance.

The displacement of crisis for Habermas is not conspiracy, or dupery, but mandated by the internal structure of the state itself: in order to maintain legitimacy, it needs to present itself as capable of solving crises, so it needs to cast each crisis as one that it can solve or recast unaddressed crises as tragedy and fate (which is to say, not crises at all). In Hay's discussion of Thatcherism, however, there is a new twist to the story, as the extension of state power to ameliorate the inevitable crises produced by the contradictions of capitalism becomes its own crisis, exploited by opponents of "big government." The latest turn, and the most radical version of this story, is found in Naomi Klein's idea of "disaster capitalism," where crises like that in New Orleans are exploited by neoliberal reformers descending on vulnerable populations during moments of shock.[40] (Hence the popular refrain in the media that Wal-Mart was more successful than the government in providing aid.)

Hay's observation is an important one. It is not merely the imperatives of particular organizations but the different narratives of crisis and responsibility that condition the types of responses that are possible. Klinenberg makes a similar point. Situating the heat wave in an era of privatized services and a declining sense that government bears responsibility to care for the well-being of its citizens, Klinenberg suggests that the ability to recognize a crisis depends on established ideas about appropriate responses. When the political economy of Chicago and its unequal distribution of air conditioning, water, or medical care are not considered in discussions of the heat wave, the conditions of deprivation that lead to fatalities (conditions produced economically through housing and labor markets and politically through municipal budget and zoning decisions) are, precisely, naturalized—written out of the story and placed beyond the scope of legitimate political control. The story suggests a very limited set of possible responses to situations of public danger—evacuate the stranded, feed the hungry, rebuild the levees. But because Klinenberg sees the situation in Chicago as a situation of persistent vulnerability rather than unpredictable meteorological chance, he encourages reflection on a much wider set of possible responses— rebuild public infrastructure, invest in public health, deliver public services, and ensure equal protection.

Klinenberg's model is especially valuable for its sensitivity to the way media "render invisible both the political economy of vulnerability and the role of the state in the reconstructions of the disaster they produce, reconstructions that not only dominate public representations of the event but help organize the terms of scientific studies as well."[41] He details how the Chicago mayor's office was not only "spinning out of the crisis" but how successfully it had strategized to have the public record support its account of disaster, one involving a "sophisticated politics of denial to diffuse responsibility."[42] Klinenberg dedicates an entire chapter, "Governing by Public Relations," to media practices, and he observes first-hand how public relations professionals have become "a fundamental part of the emergency political response" to disasters.[43] This is not a conspiracy, but the messy interface of journalistic routine, the changing organization of the news industry, and a professionalized public relations perspective on managing emergencies that had staged the crisis to promote regional integration and consensus with "just like most of us" stories.

The organization of news production is generally synchronized with the practices of state and public officials, and the results are familiar narratives of disaster in times of crisis. Pierre Bourdieu argues that "the journalistic field" governing the production of news tends to produce narratives that "cut [events] off from their antecedents and consequences," leaving viewers with "a series of apparently absurd stories" that are "stripped of any political necessity" that "can at best arouse a vague humanitarian interest."[44]

It's almost a journalistic ritual, and certainly a tradition, to focus on simple events that are simple to cover. As for the victims, they're not presented in any more political light than those of a train derailment or any other accident. We see nothing that might stimulate any sort of truly political cohesion or revolt.[45]

Klinenberg, in adapting Bourdieu's work for his model, emphasizes four features of the field of news production that impoverish disaster coverage. First, the commercial nature of the media industry encourages spectacular rather than social treatments of disaster, as stories must reflect common sense rather than analysis, and complex material must be rendered in a simple and attention-getting way. Second, the personal and professional relationship between journalists and politicians cannot be risked through excessive criticism, and this relationship provides public officials with extraordinary opportunity to define and explain an event. Third, journalists are not sociologists; they are trained to write for a market and do not have the specialized understanding required to articulate the political economy of disaster vulnerability. Elite media professionals, in particular, are largely unfamiliar with the daily struggles or social environments of urban poverty. Finally, media production schedules preclude in-depth investigation.[46]

In Chicago, journalists and political officials rendered invisible the political economy of disaster vulnerability and the role of market-based governance in producing it. The result was not produced by conspiracy or cynical adherence to organization demands, and official disaster myths did not circulate in order to avoid throwing the political system into turmoil; rather, largely unstated assumptions about government responsibility naturalized economic and racial segregation and in large part exonerated the state from its responsibility for public safety. In Chicago, this understanding of crisis continued to organize state–media relationships, such that the "natural disaster" frame largely carried the day, Mayor Daley emerged from this affair with his reputation relatively unmarred, and the American public today is generally unaware that hundreds of people died as a result of reduced municipal services. During the disaster in New Orleans in 2005, however, these ideas of crisis failed, the state–media relationship was reconfigured, and the result was an unexpected meta-crisis, when established narratives for recognizing crisis were themselves throw into crisis.

The Meta-Crisis

Media coverage of crisis in New Orleans took a remarkable turn, as journalists and public officials diverged in their narratives of the situation. Initial coverage of Hurricane Katrina conformed well to what might be called the "Weather Channel" template, with a de-politicized focus on the visual and affective dimensions of crisis prevailing in stories of property damage, human suffering, and individual heroics. The use of media to produce "consensual or integrative forms of ritual news coverage," or even a "sphere of consensus," is now a formal and institutionalized aspect of crisis response—a tool of governments to protect their legitimacy when their constituents are suffering.[47] And although scholars differ on how these "ritual" processes work, they are a frequent touchstone for descriptions of media practice and only rarely discussed positively. Simon Cottle, for instance, observes that while these stories "proclaim international solidarity and collective compassion," they also tend to "encode relations of national hierarchy and power" and they lack the political perspective needed to encourage contention or challenge to that power.[48]

By all accounts, this crisis template failed in the aftermath of the storm. Journalists lost interest in property damage, missing pets, and acts of individual bravery or suffering, and the usual rituals for producing news of crisis were abandoned. In an important insight, Frank Durham concludes that it was not simply the news content or production rituals that changed but that there was a "changed relationship of the media to the state in this crisis moment"[49]—media, that is, largely abandoned their reliance on official government sources and risked their collegial working relationship in rejecting the state's version of events as self-serving and inadequate. Durham's explanation for this change is a good one. He emphasizes how the desire to resonate culturally with the broader audience's experience of the crisis introduced a populist dimension to media coverage, and he observes how the techniques and norms of tabloid journalism played a stronger role as a result. Given our concerns, however, we cannot help but emphasize how the prevailing idea of crisis, which had previously organized state-media-citizen relationships, could no longer do so.

At first glance, it is remarkable that government officials failed to recognize and adjust to shifts in media practice. Brown had presumed that media institutions could be managed to produce narratives of crisis organized around national hierarchy and humanitarian compassion. The timing and content of his statements were organized to facilitate that end. From Brown's perspective, emergency management requires the use of media to build support and legitimacy for the official government response; his role was to offer a steady stream of assuring statements through press conferences to secure political order. Holding regular press conferences, for example, is a standard technique for encouraging the press to consistently report the statements of public officials, as these officials establish a coherent storyline, as they establish the authority to maintain that storyline, and as they discourage the search for "man-on-the-street" counternarratives. In short, Brown's strategy of managing media coverage is designed to avoid the political organization of social unrest that can result from disaster and crisis.

When journalists became critical and challenged the government's narrative of the crisis, the fact that the bulk of government activities were organized around media management became a salient story in itself. Mayor Ray Nagin pleaded for a moratorium on press conferences; Anderson Cooper challenged Louisiana Senator Mary Landrieu out of irritation with politicians thanking and congratulating each other on camera; and three separate news anchors publicly challenged Brown's inability to aid people in the Morial Convention Center. Brown's adherence to the media rituals that usually attend disaster was now recognized as a manipulative effort to manage public perception irrespective of material conditions in New Orleans.

The extent of Brown's commitment to this view of media management in crisis situations is remarkable.[50] He explicitly identified the failure to manage the relationship to media as one of FEMA's two primary failures (the other was failing to realize how incompetent state and local authorities would be), and he described the changed relationship as his "personal tipping point." He seems to imply that things could have been very different had he managed media practices differently, or had journalists acted more responsibly. It is a tempting conclusion, even for progressives, since it leads to the suggestion that journalists had recovered their public role once again, and served as a populist watchdog of government practice on behalf of the people.

In rejecting Brown's story, however, journalists did not have a broader notion of crisis through which to organize their reporting, and what we call a "meta-crisis" ensued. The result was confusion, and even today media scholars do not agree on the precise nature of the resulting coverage or its implications. Some scholars identified a "meta-narrative" of government failure, one underpinning a populist turn in media coverage and carrying more progressive possibilities.[51] Dixon, for example, identified in the shift to criticism of governmental institutions an overtly sympathetic perspective among journalists toward victims.[52] Grusky and Ryo summarized a familiar sentiment in noting the attention given to race and class in America:

> The coverage of Katrina is fascinating precisely because it converted a conventional story about a natural disaster into an unconventional and high-profile story about the socially constructed disasters of poverty, inequality and racism.[53]

International coverage was also fascinated by this conversion, and Cottle observes how global media used the opportunity to criticize the Bush administration.

> By such means, Hurricane Katrina also exposed the normally invisible inequalities of race and poverty in American society and became an opportunity for political appropriation by different projects and discourses worldwide.[54]

Others, however, emphasized a shift in narrative to stories of civil unrest and urban insurgency, which were organized in terms of a "war-zone" metaphor.[55] This narrative began with the media focus on the supposed dominance of armed gangs wandering the city, but culminated in the celebrations of General Russel Honoré, "The Category 5 General," to quote *The Washington Post*, or, in the words of Mayor Nagin, "a John Wayne dude . . . that can get some stuff done."[56] Tierney et al. conclude, "The overall effect of media coverage was to further bolster arguments that only the military is capable of effective action during disasters."[57] (Again quoting Nagin: "They ought to give that guy [Honoré] . . . full authority to get the job done, and we can save some people.") Indeed, it was the military and private paramilitary contractors that intervened decisively in New Orleans, and in this respect, the moment of meta-crisis is not without its dangers. Durham points out that the movement toward populism in Katrina coverage did not come from a shared set of experiences of the audience and the victims but rather "from the immediate shock of this overwhelming moment."[58] For Klein, these moments of shock and collective trauma are the very situations exploited by ideologues to extend neoliberal reforms.[59] But one does not have to subscribe to Klein's thesis to recognize the dangers inherent in recommending that the military be more involved in solving domestic problems.

These alternative narratives were established when journalists engaged in an adversarial relationship with government officials.[60] However, it is important to view the meta-narrative of government failure as the result of a failed notion of crisis and of the neoliberal style of governance organizing this notion of crisis; otherwise, there will be a continuing failure to recognize the political economy of disaster vulnerability. In the opinion of Grusky and Ryo, the shift in media coverage from natural disaster to stories of poverty and racism did not produce a discernible change in public attitudes toward these features of social organization. It is not enough, then, to simply shift frames and to displace natural disaster stories with narratives of poverty and racism; the connection between these accounts must be established and narrated in terms of a political economy of disaster vulnerability. Otherwise, stories of government failure serve only to displace responsibility for crisis or recommend increased military control. Indeed, it is worth noting that while the media celebrated Honoré for his critical military intervention in New Orleans, few noticed his later commentary that the current disparity in access to healthcare constitutes a major obstacle to effective disaster response.[61]

Despite these dangers, two specific aspects of the "meta-crisis" deserve attention. First, there is the obvious conclusion drawn by many experiencing the disaster and its continuing effects: do not trust and do not depend on the government. The lesson is found in the streetwise lyrics of rap artist Juvenile, who tells folks to stop feeling sorry for themselves and to "get ya hustle on," since "the government wasn't going to do nothing for you anyway"; it is also arguably encouraged by Naomi Klein's admiration of "direct-action reconstruction," in which local residents proceeded to rebuild New Orleans without dependence on government aid.[62] It is difficult not to sympathize with those drawing this conclusion. However, if the emphasis on bureaucratic failure implies still greater dependence on non–government-organized responses to crisis, then the result is to reinscribe arguments for privatization that continue to create social vulnerability.

Second, there is the ubiquitous refrain of non-news media flows, which have continued to organize state–media relationships through a narrow vision of crisis. For example, the priority of a neoliberal understanding between citizens and government is the main lesson found on the Weather Channel, where individual preparedness for weather-related disaster infuses almost all aspects of their programming and marketing.[63] Although Weather Channel partners with federal emergency relief agencies, it organizes its disaster coverage and marketing appeals around reliance on nongovernment responses to weather-related disaster. Their good example has not gone unnoticed. As Ouellette and Hay report, Secretary of Homeland Security Tom Ridge pointed to such coverage in his remarks to a public preparedness symposium:

> If you've ever watched the Weather Channel when they talk about some of the individual stories in the midst of some of these horrific natural events and how the people actually saved themselves because they knew what to do before the event occurred and they just did it; it was a reflex. They had it prepared. They had thought about it and did it.[64]

If Weather Channel affirms the importance individual preparedness for crisis, media personalities like Dr. Phil McGraw privatize the disaster twice over. When Dr. Phil showed up at the Houston Astrodome to treat Katrina victims, he focused on reconnecting families and offered access to an array of nongovernmental resources to displaced people (his foundation continues to direct people only to nongovernmental aid sources).[65] At the same time, Dr. Phil addresses the civil unrest and anger toward FEMA in psychological terms and demonstrates how therapeutic techniques and personal life management philosophies can be drawn upon for help. His recurring "Take Care of Yourself" message is not merely motivational but also effectively neoliberal.[66]

These are not unique examples. As Ouellette and Hay observe, television extends the reach of government by privileging a neoliberal relationship between the state and its citizens, as both become "more reliant upon privatized, commercial resources."[67] Government roles are outsourced, in a manner of speaking, to television, not unlike the way disaster management and policing were contracted to Blackwater USA and DynCorp in New Orleans. The relationship established between government and citizens via commercial media presents formidable obstacles to the reorganization of crisis response in terms of a political economy of disaster vulnerability.

It is in this situation that the resonance between tipping point leadership and neoliberal governance is firmly established. It simply is *not* within the legitimate scope of governmental authority to maintain infrastructure and ensure the basic safety of millions of residents against disaster, although the appropriate response to catastrophic loss of life is to leverage media representations of the affair so that individuals and nongovernmental organizations can proceed "unhindered" to take care of themselves. Brown's view of crisis response corresponds to a worldview in which the government has privatized the delivery of services and state legitimacy is secured through media coverage and public opinion. It is only within this context that recommendations to take care of yourself during a flood of biblical proportions could make sense.

In this respect, the reflective potential found in "meta-crisis" is severely circumscribed by contemporary media practices that are extensions of neoliberal governance, and disasters like Katrina may result not in the questioning of the theoretical assumptions informing social organization but rather in the extension of paramilitary control in times and spaces of crisis.

Conclusion

Years after Hurricane Katrina, public opinion still ranks the federal, state, and local responses to the flooding of New Orleans as one of the greatest failures—and, indeed, shames—of U.S. history. This seems unlikely to change anytime soon. But the reasons for this failure remain, as yet, relatively ill-defined. Despite some thoughtful attempts to situate this disaster in a crisis of neoliberal governance, a declining commitment to public welfare, and the enduring significance of race even in an Obama era, little has been done on the metaphorical construction of crisis in management literatures such as *The Tipping Point* or their resonance in popular media. Although academics often scoff at such literature, these works have tremendous impact on the production of public consciousness and public policy. With their implicit assumptions about the value of human life and the responsibility and ability of institutions to remedy situations, these vocabularies not only provide management professionals and public officials with strategies for dealing with public problems; they also provide the public with narratives for evaluating responsibility of public institutions.

In this essay, we have tried to reveal how some dubious assumptions of familiar vocabularies contribute to the very catastrophes they claim to address, and also how these assumptions proved so visibly inadequate in the days after Hurricane Katrina.[68] Perhaps more than anything else, the flooding of New Orleans brought to the surface all of the displaced costs of a neoliberal approach to governance and public safety, as the water rendered it impossible to ignore the impoverished populations, slashed budgets, and environmental racism that kept the Crescent City afloat. The ensuing meta-crisis provoked long-overdue (if perhaps fleeting) attention to the racial and economic segregation predicted by Grodzins, the unequal distribution of vulnerability in our society, and the real consequences of environmental collapse.

This particular meta-crisis was facilitated by five specific characteristics of the situation. First, the high visibility of FEMA, both as the federal agency ostensibly charged with coordinating response to such situations and as the symbolic face of the Bush plan for national security after 9/11; the media could not help but notice the Department of Homeland Security stumbling upon entering its own coming-out party.[69] Second, the visceral and visual seduction of floods as a media event provided inordinately more coverage than other "natural" disasters and provoked politically resonant comparisons to impoverished countries and warzones. Third, an unmistakable and shocking racial component to the suffering was demonstrated in a country that generally prefers to see racism—particularly in the South—as part of its regrettable past. Fourth, an inability to manage the media and public relations was exemplified by Brown's public admission that he did not know about the convention center, and that he had lied. Fifth, the specific place that New Orleans occupies in the American consciousness compelled nationwide dissonance organized around a realization of how the city's famous hospitality is predicated on the brutal poverty endemic to a postindustrial service economy in the South.

However, although media coverage unmistakably called attention to the failed policies of the Bush administration, and probably created greater willingness to criticize the administration's similarly disastrous handling of the war in Iraq, it seems naïve to suggest that the meta-crisis has resulted in a challenge to neoliberal strategies of management and governance writ large. Instead, as in Iraq, criticism targeted feckless bureaucrats and inept officials, while the values and commitments that informed the overseas invasion and the neglect of American cities have emerged intact. In this sense, while meta-crises mark an opportunity for rethinking the assumptions about agency and responsibility that define a culture's approach to governance and public safety, the dominance of neoliberal refrains in both official and unofficial sources always threatens to overpower alternative narratives of the flooding of New Orleans. When this happens, representations of even this most devastating example of disaster vulnerability tend to revert to the neoliberal mantras of personal responsibility, corporate organization, and state security.

Notes

1. All quotes from Michael Brown and his interlocutors, unless otherwise indicated, are drawn from his testimony before the House of Representatives Select Bipartisan Committee to Investigate the Preparation for and Response to Hurricane Katrina, September 27, 2005.

2. Brown continued to use the phrase in later interviews, identifying the moment President Bush declared that he was doing a "heckuva job," the moment Michael Chertoff arrived in New Orleans and challenged his authority, and an August 31 reprimand from Chertoff as "tipping points." See Douglas Brinkley, *The Great Deluge: Hurricane Katrina, New Orleans, and the Mississippi Gulf Coast* (New York: William Morrow, 2006), 550, and House Select Katrina Response Investigation Committee, "A Failure of Initiative," 109th Congress, 2d Session, Report 109-396, 13. When we asked Brown what he meant, he promised a quick answer but then failed to follow through and did not answer follow-up queries.

3. Malcolm Gladwell, "The Tipping Point," *New Yorker,* June 3, 1996.

4. Malcolm Gladwell, *The Tipping Point: How Little Things Can Make a Big Difference* (New York: Little, Brown, 2000); and Gavin McNett, "Idea Epidemics," *Salon,* March 17, 2000.

5. Rachel Donadio, "The Gladwell Effect," *New York Times,* February 5, 2006.

6. W. Chan Kim and Renee Mauborgne, "Tipping Point Leadership," *Harvard Business Review* 81 (April 2003): 60–69; and "Tipped for the Top: Tipping-Point Leadership," *INSEAD Quarterly* 3 (2004): 3–7.

7. Kim and Mauborgne, "Tipped for the Top," 3.

8. Donald Rumsfeld, *Memorandum for the President,* April 1, 2003.

9. Donald Rumsfeld, *Department of Defense News Briefing,* November 8, 2004.

10. Donald Rumsfeld, *Department of Defense News Briefing,* February 3, 2005.

11. ABC News, *Nightline,* February 22, 2005.

12. Thomas Friedman, "The Tipping Points," *New York Times,* February 27, 2005.

13. Brown: "You read the book *The Tipping Point.* It's a short book—you would probably like it, it's called *The Tipping Point.* Probably less than a hundred pages and it's all about how different factors can accumulate and there's a tipping point where you know, suddenly everyone in the country has a certain kind of sneaker" (Brown's interview with Douglas Brinkley, February 5, 2006; transcript provided by Brinkley). See also Brinkley, *The Great Deluge,* 550, and Ed O'Keefe, "FEMA's Michael Brown, Five Years Later," *Washington Post,* http://voices.washingtonpost.com/federal-eye/2010/08/michael_brown_five_years_later.html (accessed April 25, 2011).

14. Gladwell, "The Tipping Point."

15. Gladwell, *Tipping Point,* 261, 282.

16. Thomas Schelling, *Models of Segregation* (Santa Monica, Calif.: The Rand Corporation, 1969); Schelling, "Dynamic Models of Segregation," *Journal of Mathematical Sociology* 1 (1971): 143–86; Schelling, *Micromotives and Macrobehavior* (New York: Norton, 1978), 91–102; Morton Grodzins, "Metropolitan Segregation," *Scientific American* 197 (October 1957): 33–41; and Grodzins, *The Metropolitan Area as a Racial Problem* (Pittsburgh, Pa.: University of Pittsburgh Press, 1958).

17. Grodzins, "Metropolitan Segregation"; Grodzins, *Metropolitan Area.*

18. Grodzins, "Metropolitan Segregation."

19. For criticism of Rand Corporation, see Deborah Wallace and Rodrick Wallace, *A Plague on Your Houses: How New York Was Burned Down and National Public Health Crumbled* (New York: Verso, 1998), and Mike Davis, *Planet of Slums* (New York: Verso, 2008).

20. Schelling, *Micromotives,* 153–55.

21. Similarly, although the term "tipping point" does not appear in Schelling's *Arms and Influence* (New Haven, Conn.: Yale University Press, 1966), the book recommends small military engagements as a means to avoiding larger ones—for securing international peace by finding, and then leveraging, the factors of disproportionate influence in geopolitics. Fred Kaplan traces a relatively straightforward link between this approach to international conflict and the escalated bombing in North Vietnam (Kaplan, *The Wizards of Armageddon* [New York: Simon and Schuster, 1983]).

22. Gladwell, *Tipping Point,* 12.

23. Wilson and Kelling's article and its bearing on the decrease in urban crime in the 1990s have become a flashpoint for discussion among popular commentators seeking to advance pet theories of counterintuitive and disproportionate influence, including most famously the dust up between Malcolm Gladwell and Steven Levitt (the coauthor of *Freakonomics,* who credited abortion laws with the decrease in crime). The relationship of such apparently apolitical discussion to the conservative politics implied by Wilson and Kelling's support for the

informal order-maintenance function of policing deserves closer attention. See James Q. Wilson and George L. Kelling, "Broken Windows: The Police and Neighborhood Safety," *Atlantic Monthly* (March 1982).

24. Gladwell, *Tipping Point*, 256–57.

25. James Loy, deputy secretary to DHS, echoed this sentiment on PBS's *Frontline*, going so far as to say that claims that FEMA should have been more involved in the evacuation lead to "a logic path that takes you to pretty Orwellian nature." See *Frontline*, "The Storm," http://www.pbs.org/wgbh/pages/frontline/storm/etc/script.html (accessed April 21, 2011).

26. Perrow suggests that the accident at Three Mile Island, for example, did not begin when the reactor started to melt, but when the decision was made to construct a complicated nuclear power plant that would eventually, inevitably, have problems. His warning is that such accidents are "normal," whereas approaches that emphasize tipping points suggest they are abnormal. See Charles Perrow, *Normal Accidents: Living with High Risk Technologies* (Princeton, N.J.: Princeton University Press, 1999).

27. Perrow admits the argument can be persuasive but rejects it in this instance. See Charles Perrow, "Using Organizations: The Case of FEMA," *Understanding FEMA: Perspectives from the Social Sciences* (June 11, 2006), para. 16, http://understandingkatrina.ssrc.org/Perrow/ (accessed April 21, 2011).

28. Eric Klinenberg, *Heat Wave: A Social Autopsy of Disaster in Chicago* (Chicago: University of Chicago Press, 2002); and Klinenberg, "Denaturalizing Disaster: A Social Autopsy of the 1995 Chicago Heat Wave," *Theory & Society* 28 (1999): 239–95.

29. Klinenberg, *Heat Wave*, 127.

30. Ibid., 136, 268.

31. Ibid., 172–76.

32. Klinenberg applied this approach to Hurricane Katrina in a short essay co-authored with Thomas Frank, arguing that the devastation resulted largely from a series of decisions to privatize risk and dismantle government protections. The essay concludes with a warning that this same story will be told again after the flu pandemic that is on the inevitable horizon. See Eric Klinenberg and Thomas Frank, "Looting Homeland Security," *Rolling Stone* (December 15, 2005). Frank later made this same argument in more general terms about neoliberals since the 1980s in *The Wrecking Crew: How Conservatives Ruined Government, Enriched Themselves, and Beggared the Nation* (New York: Metropolitan Books, 2008).

33. Klinenberg, *Heat Wave*, 32.

34. Klinenberg, "Denaturalizing Disaster," 242.

35. Klinenberg, *Heat Wave*, 207.

36. Ibid., 18–20.

37. Colin Hay, "Rethinking Crisis: Narratives of the New Right and Constructions of Crisis," *Rethinking Marxism* 8 (1995): 63.

38. Jürgen Habermas, *Legitimation Crisis*, trans. T. McCarthy (Boston: Beacon Press, 1975).

39. Colin Hay, *Re-Stating Social and Political Change* (Buckingham, UK: Open University Press, 1996), 91.

40. Naomi Klein, *The Shock Doctrine: The Rise of Disaster Capitalism* (New York: Metropolitan Books, 2007).

41. Klinenberg, "Denaturalizing Disaster," 242.

42. Klinenberg, *Heat Wave*, 180.

43. Ibid., 35.

44. Pierre Bourdieu, *On Television*, trans. Priscilla Parkhurst Ferguson (New York: The New Press, 1996), 6–7.

45. Ibid., 8.

46. Klinenberg, "Denaturalizing Disaster," 278–79.

47. Simon Cottle, "Global Crises in the News: Staging New Wars, Disaster, and Climate Change," *International Journal of Communication* 3 (2009): 504; and Frank Durham, "Media Ritual in Catastrophic Time: The Populist Turn in Television Coverage of Hurricane Katrina," *Journalism* 9 (2008): 95.

48. Cottle, "Global Crises in the News," 503.

49. Durham, "Media Ritual in Catastrophic Time," 111.

50. When asked about the inconsistency in his statements regarding the preparedness of Louisiana and New Orleans for Hurricane Katrina, Brown was unapologetic: "Because I'm not going to go on television and publicly say that I think that the mayor and the governor are not doing their job, and they don't have the sense of urgency. I'm not going to say that publicly. I don't think that's the proper thing to do. So yes, when I go on a news show, I'm going to talk about the state's doing the best job they can and I'm pleased with the way they're working. And then I'm going to get off that news show, and I'm going to pick up the telephone, and I'm going to keep urging them to get busy and do what needs to be done." *Frontline* interview, October 14, 2005, http://www.pbs.org/wgbh/pages/frontline/storm/interviews/brown.html (accessed April 21, 2011).

51. Durham, "Media Ritual in Catastrophic Time," 96.

52. T. L. Dixon, "Understanding News Coverage of Hurricane Katrina: The Use of News Frames and Racial Stereotypes by Network Television News" (paper presented at the annual meeting of the NCA 94th Annual Convention, San Diego, California, November 20, 2008).

53. David Grusky and Emily Ryo, "Did Katrina Recalibrate Attitudes Toward Poverty and Inequality? A Test of the 'Dirty Little Secret' Hypothesis," *De Bois Review* 3 (2006): 74.

54. Cottle, "Global Crises in the News," 504–5.

55. Kathleen Tierney, Christine Bevc, and Erica Kuligowski, "Metaphors Matter: Disaster Myths, Media Frames, and Their Consequences in Hurricane Katrina," *Annals of the American Academy of Political and Social Science* 604 (2006): 57–81; cf. Cottle.

56. Lynne Duke, "The Category 5 General," *Washington Post,* September 12, 2005; Nagin interview with WWL-AM (September 2, 2005). In many ways, Honoré was the perfect folk hero for the "warzone" narrative—a Louisiana native (Pointe Coupee), a graduate of Southern University–Baton Rouge, and the embodiment of a no-nonsense militaristic approach to evacuation. His depiction in corporate media coverage illuminates the dangerously simplistic view of military intervention that dominated such narratives, as Honoré's own views on New Orleans emphasize the impact of health disparities, poverty, and other elements important to a political economy of vulnerability. See Russel Honoré, "Health Disparities: Barriers to a Culture of Preparedness," *Journal of Public Health Management and Practice* 14 (2008): 5–7. We thank Cedric Johnson for drawing this point to our attention.

57. Tierney et al., "Metaphors Matter," 61.

58. Durham, "Media Ritual in Catastrophic Time," 105. Durham points out that regular media routines are established rather quickly and that the process of "redress" in the case of Hurricane Katrina needs greater attention.

59. Klein, *The Shock Doctrine.*

60. Of course, the coverage should not be idealized. The scholarship on media depictions of race during Hurricane Katrina has been troubling. Miller and Roberts argue that despite the inclusion of race and poverty in media coverage of Hurricane Katrina, white victims and white officials predominated in national news coverage. In this respect, African Americans were seen and not heard: "The authorities who spoke were white, the victims who spoke were white, and African Americans were seen only in the rest of the video and most often in a negative manner." Andrea Miller and Shearon Roberts, "Race in National vs. Local Television News Coverage of Hurricane Katrina: A Study of Sources, Victims, and Negative Video" (paper presented at the annual meeting of the Association for Education in Journalism and Mass Communication, Brabham, D.C., August 6, 2008, 19). Similarly, Dixon (2008) and Summers et al. (2006) suggest African Americans were associated with the majority of the lawbreaking in media coverage. See Samuel R. Summers et al., "Race and Media Coverage of Hurricane Katrina: Analysis, Implications, and Future Research Questions," *Analyses of Social Issues and Public Policy* 6 (2006): 1.

61. Honoré, "Health Disparities: Barriers to a Culture of Preparedness."

62. Shaheem Read, "Juvenile Tears into Cash Money, Lil Wayne—And FEMA," *MTV*, March 9, 2006, http://www.mtv.com/news/articles/1525684/20060308/juvenile.jhtml (accessed April 21, 2011); Klein, *The Shock Doctrine*, 464.

63. Laurie Ouellette and James Hay, *Better Living through Reality TV* (Oxford, UK: Blackwell, 2008), 156–58.

64. Ibid., 168.

65. Ibid., 63.

66. Ibid., 77–79.

67. Ibid., 218–19.

68. In another essay, we consider characterizations of the Mississippi River and the levees in New Orleans as a battleground in a "war on nature," similarly arguing that the resonance of this phrasing indicates a broader problem in American politics. See Chad Lavin and Chris Russill, "The Buoyancy of Failure: Fighting Nature in New Orleans," *Space and Culture* 9 (2006): 48–51.

69. Hurricane Katrina was not the new FEMA's first disaster; various scholars have talked about the 2004 hurricane season as the agency's trial by fire. But in a special issue of the political science journal *The Forum* printed soon after Hurricane Katrina, one article claimed that FEMA's performance in 2004 "was viewed as a complete mismanagement," while another asserted that it was "well-regarded." Clearly, the jury was still out on the new FEMA until Katrina. See Amanda Lee Hollis, "A Tale of Two Federal Emergency Management Agencies," and Patrick Roberts, "What Katrina Means for Emergency Management," both in *Forum* 3, no. 3 (2005).

CHAPTER 2

"We Are Seeing People We Didn't Know Exist"

Katrina and the Neoliberal Erasure of Race

Eric Ishiwata

O N September 1, 2005, four days after Hurricane Katrina struck the Gulf Coast, Jim Lehrer interviewed Michael Brown (then-director of FEMA) on PBS's *NewsHour*. Five minutes into the interview, after becoming exasperated by Brown's stilted refrain—"we're moving as fast as we can"—Lehrer read a list of FEMA's failings and asked: "So what does 'as soon as we can' mean at this stage of the game, Mr. Brown?"[1] Only slightly unnerved, Brown began his two-part answer by lauding FEMA's accomplishments, noting that the evacuees at the Convention Center and Superdome had been supplied with "meals every day they've been there."[2] While such praise was suspect, particularly when set against the ubiquitous images of suffering and despair, it was in fact the remainder of Brown's response that stood out as most striking:

> The second part of my answer, Jim, which, I think, again, the American people understand how fascinating and unusual this is—is that *we're seeing people that we didn't know exist* that suddenly are showing up on bridges or parts of the interstate that aren't inundated.[3] [emphasis added]

Remarkable for its insensitivity, Brown's response was equally significant for the ways it signaled a rupture in the prevailing discourse on race in the United States. To be sure, this disruption was triggered less by Brown's comments on *NewsHour* than the disaster itself. Nevertheless, Brown's remarks remain instructive in the sense that they stand as one of the earliest indications of a shift in the popular framings of race in a post-Katrina America.

To set Brown's comments along such a trajectory is to treat his "we're seeing people that we didn't know exist" as a moment of national import, one that transcends the bounds of the televised interview. A reading such as this is facilitated in part by the duplicity of Brown's subject *we*. Interpolating not only FEMA's agents-on-the-ground but also the entirety of the viewing public as well, Brown's *we* foregrounds the fact that it was, after all, "We the People" who were doing the *seeing*; that the extensive media coverage had extrapolated Katrina's local effects to the level of national spectacle. And it is here, within this trope of visibility (i.e., Brown's *seeing*), where the sharpest indication of a racial transformation lies. Not since the 1992 Los Angeles riots or, more properly, the civil rights movement, had the United States en masse been compelled to *see* what *Newsweek* would later term "the Other America."[4] And, in the wake of Katrina, these American Others—racial minorities in particular, the socioeconomically disenfranchised in general—were doing more than simply "showing up on bridges." They commanded the center stage of national attention.

The "suddenness" of their visibility warrants critical attention as it marks both a rupturing of America's racial discourse and the deleterious effects of the nation's pre-Katrina racial order. Put differently, the abrupt emergence of the "Other America" evinces the degree to which a large segment of Katrina's victims had, to the point of the disaster, been cast as *personae non grata*—citizen-subjects rendered invisible by the reigning neoliberal ideology of a "colorblind America." The stark images disseminated by Katrina's media coverage brought into sharp focus the lived experiences of racially coded socioeconomic disparities and, as a result presented a conspicuous challenge to the allegedly "race neutral" policies of the neoliberal state. Responding to this dissonance, politicians, pundits, and journalists alike devoted an unprecedented amount of energy to either quell the transformatory potential of Katrina and recuperate the neoliberal order or leverage public outrage in hopes of garnering widespread support for a race-based identity politics.

This chapter draws attention to a series of public statements to explore how America's racial discourse was disrupted, reinflected, and (however slight) transformed. To this end, my engagement with Katrina sets out on a path dissimilar to the literature that immediately followed the disaster.[5] Unlike the prevailing mode of inquiry that sought to corroborate whether racism exacerbated the storm's devastation, my approach contends that the "facts" of Katrina are inextricable from prevailing values, that words are something more than the innocent mirrors of objects and events, and that analyses are always already inflected by the "realities" they seek to represent.[6] Thus, while efforts to document *what* exactly transpired are inarguably important, I argue there is at least an equal need for treatments that examine *how* the "realities of Katrina" were framed, read, and communicated through the conceptualization of the event.[7] Responding to this need, here I work to demonstrate the disparate ways that race circulated through the "event" of Katrina. I am primarily concerned with how race was spoken about, in disclosing who was doing the speaking, in identifying the positions and viewpoints from which they spoke, and in determining the institutions that both prompted people to speak and distributed the things that were said.[8] In short, while I remain mindful of the loss and grief attached to the disaster itself, my focus here is to explore the *event of Katrina* as a broader symptom of America's political present—as a backdrop for an examination of the current state of race and racism in the United States.[9] In this regard, my investigation will work to (1) locate the "event" of Katrina within the broader context of American neoliberalism; (2) trace the key positions that fought to either recuperate or reinflect the nation's racial order after the storm; and (3) affirm that which I find to be a more creative and democratic engagement with Katrina, one commensurate with bell hooks's notion of a "beloved community."[10]

Decentering Katrina

I want to begin by framing Katrina as less an (un)natural disaster than a disruptive event, one exemplary of Jacques Rancière's *topos* of encounter. Defined as an "opening of the space and time in which those who do not count are counted,"[11] Rancière suggests that it is from such a *topos* where democracy—conceptualized here as a mode of subjectification rather than an ideology or structure[12]—takes place. To be clear, this is a departure from the more familiar sense of consensus democracy whereby negotiations take place between known actors, "parties [that] are presupposed as already given."[13] Instead, Rancière's democracy is predicated upon disruptive moments that extend political qualification to those who previously had "no part on the reckoning of society's parties."[14] Such a conception resonates closely with the *event of Katrina* as both evoke an "evanescent moment when [the] tensions arising from human being-in-common produce instances of disruption, generating sources of political action."[15]

In the case of Katrina, the event enabled America's Others to emerge as politically actors in both the national consciousness and mainstream political debates. Yet, within the contested narratives surrounding Katrina, these actors circulated as largely unmarked bodies that did not wholly "coincide with parties of the state of society."[16] While the suddenness of their visibility may have forced the nation to confront its complicity with racism, poverty, and an uneven distribution of rights and protections throughout its citizenry, the actual social positions of these subjects remained largely unsettled. Identified alternately and conflictingly as "victims," "refugees," "evacuees," "minorities," the "underclass," the "culturally bankrupt," and the "socially irresponsible," this chapter argues that exactly *how* these subjects were counted speaks much to the present-day politics of race and inequality.

Calling into question the very terms of the event works to decenter Katrina, treating it as something other than an "exceptional, metaphysical or nihilistic act that stands outside of history and politics,"[17] I am therefore interested in engaging with Katrina as an event that unsettled, if not transformed, contemporary American racial politics. My disposition draws largely from Wendy Brown, who has suggested there is "a world of difference between reading events and theorizing the conditions and possibilities of political life in a particular time."[18] To merely read or respond to events, therefore, "runs the risk of limiting [political theory's] capacity as a domain of inquiry capable of disrupting the tyranny of givenness of the present, and expanding the range of possible futures."[19] A decentering of Katrina, in this regard, requires a critical attentiveness to emergence (*enstehung*) over origins (*herkunft*).[20] Once framed in this manner, Katrina can be read as less the casual outcome of the march of history (i.e., cultural bankruptcy, federal neglect, or institutional racism) than as an event produced by a "hazardous play of dominations."[21] In the same manner that Foucault declared the body as "an inscribed surface of events,"[22] the sudden visibility of America's Others can be read as the effect of power—namely, the "colorblind" policies of the neoliberal state.

It needs to be stated, however, that references to the "sudden emergence" of the Other America should in no way suggest that the United States, prior to Katrina, was free of racially coded inequalities. On the contrary, racism was inextricably bound with the working of the state.[23] Yet, America's Others had been rendered invisible by the ideological force of "colorblind racism," a neoliberal fantasy that has effectively recoded the incongruent effects of systemic racism in stringently individual and nonracial terms (i.e., a "lack of effort, loose family organization, and inappropriate values").[24] What reigned, then, was an artfully pliable form of governmentality that structured political life in terms of race, gender, sexuality, and class while simultaneously disavowing the very significance of these categories in a post–Civil Rights era America.[25]

The Pre-Katrina Neoliberal Order

The contours of America's neoliberal order can be laid bare in three moments that typify the racial context that immediately preceded Katrina's landfall: (1) President George W. Bush's 2003 condemnation of the University of Michigan's affirmative action policies; (2) the implementation of the Department of Education's 2001 No Child Left Behind Act; and (3) Paul Haggis's 2004 Academy Award–winning film, *Crash*. While far from all-encompassing, when taken together these three moments disclose how state power, public policy, and popular culture worked simultaneously to empty the concepts of race and institutional racism of their Civil Rights era meanings.

In a January 15, 2003, presidential address decrying the University of Michigan's affirmative action policies, George W. Bush opened by insisting he was an adamant supporter of "diversity of all kinds, including racial diversity in higher education."[26] The promise of this egalitarian gesture, however, was quickly tempered by a caveat that warned "as we work to address the wrong of prejudice, we must not use means that create another wrong, and thus perpetuate our divisions."[27] As an example of such a "wrong," Bush referred to the University of Michigan's practice of allotting minority applicants "20 points out of a maximum 150," emphasizing that these points were granted "not because of any academic achievement or life experience, but solely because they are African American, Hispanic or Native American."[28] Bush continued by attacking Michigan's Law School, noting that "some minority students are admitted to meet percentage targets while other applicants with higher grades and better scores are passed over."[29] This, in Bush's estimation, demonstrated that applicants were "being selected or rejected based primarily on the color of their skin"—the unambiguous mark of a racial discriminatory policy.[30] It is here, in his unconditional and decontextualized declaration that "discrimination is wrong,"[31] where Bush's neoliberal position turns the once-progressive commitments of fairness and equality on their head. His privileging of "race-neutral" or "merit-based" policies function as a seemingly benign means of undermining the very corrective structures established to mitigate the historic and continued prejudice experienced by America's native and minority populations. Once decontextualized from the specificities of enduring institutional racism, Bush's attack against minority entitlements is primed to masquerade as "egalitarian," "fair," and "just."

This privileging of "merit" over racial justice is equally present in the Department of Education's 2001 No Child Left Behind Act (NCLB). As Eric Freeman has noted, NCLB situates public schools as discrete domains disassociated from broader socioeconomic inequities.[32] As such, Freeman continues, "NCLB suggests that the best way to view the problem of inequitable schooling is as a set of self-contained conditions that experts can manipulate adequately and independently of the external environment within which schooling is contained."[33] The racial and socioeconomic differences among schools and students are thus couched within the antiracial flatness of "normative incrementalism."[34] Echoing Freeman, Rebecca Goldstein and Andrew Beutel note that within the framework of NCLB, "it is no longer acceptable to consider who students are and where they are from; rather, what is most important is to maintain one's high standards and expectations, regardless of reality."[35] In other words, by concentrating on individualized academic performance, NCLB established a "putatively rational baseline that appears to be neutral in terms of race, class, and gender."[36] The end effect of this "idiosyncratic enterprise," Freeman argues, is a "policy mechanism carefully constructed to ensure that racial progress in education remains under the control of colorblind politicians and school officials, unfolding in a broadly acceptable and gradual manner."[37] To state it flatly, this form of governmentality is problematic because it disassociates education reform from broader socioeconomic contexts. The NCLB solution, therefore, is "tantamount to confronting the historical permanence of racial injustice with one eye shut,"[38] rendering invisible entire segments of America's Others.

Last, Paul Haggis's film *Crash* offers an equally revealing glimpse of the nation's pre-Katrina racial order.[39] Released theatrically on May 6, 2005, and praised widely for its gritty, neorealist treatment of race, *Crash* can be read as a mechanism that fortified the neoliberal discourse of colorblindness, albeit in conspicuous ways. While much has been made about its calculatingly diverse yet emotionally impoverished characters,[40] it is the film's central metaphor that most readily "reinforces conservative thinking about race and fails to challenge racist narratives that are deep-seated in the American imagination."[41] Established in the opening mono-logue, Don Cheadle's Detective Graham Waters outlines the premise for *Crash*'s humanist framing of race:

> It's the sense of touch. In any real city, you walk, you know? You brush past people, people bump into you. In L.A., nobody touches you. We're always behind this metal and glass. I think we miss that touch so much, that we crash into each other, just so we can feel something.[42]

Sylvia Chan rightly notes that "the whole idea that you don't have to think about race until you 'crash' into it is not what most people have the luxury of doing."[43] This nostalgia for contact, Chan continues, is exactly "what white privilege is . . . not having to think about race."[44] To this end, *Crash* works to erase not race per se but rather the continued salience of institutional racism. While the film does contain several references to structural inequalities (i.e., "I know all the sociological reasons why—per capita—eight times more black men are incarcer-ated than white men . . . schools are a disgrace, lack of opportunity, bias in judicial system, all that stuff"), it is staged in such a cursory manner that, in the words of Derek Smith, it "insinuates that America's systemic racism is old news, hardly worth mentioning."[45] The "crash" metaphor, in this regard, casts America's racial tensions as less the outcome of histori-cal and systemic racism than the product of individual prejudices that are distributed uniformly across a society that is "out of touch."[46] In lieu of engaging with the "complicated 'sociological' reasons that black men too often end up on the wrong side of the law," Smith observes, *Crash* injects "a more tangible and easily dramatized explanatory symbol . . . we deduce that Peter may have turned to crime because he is the child of a drug-addicted, black single mother."[47] Thus, by reducing racism to an individual and moral phenomenon, the film compels viewers to confront personal prejudices, but only in a manner that allows those in privileged positions to evade collective responsibility for social inequalities.[48]

When taken together, these three moments trace the contours of the nation's racial discourse at the interstice of pre- and post-Katrina

America. In their concealments of the continued effects of systemic racism, Bush's critique of affirmative action, NCLB, and *Crash* combined to support an environment that denounced all provisions that failed to correspond to the logic of the neoliberal market; where the privileging of merit and the atomization of equality reconfigured the public domain into a wellspring of entrepreneurialism. It is though these means that America's Others were rendered invisible: the pre-Katrina America was coded as an undifferentiated space of citizenship whereby the logic of colorblindness laundered the state's relationship to racism and relieved the public from its commitments to racial and socioeconomic justice.[49] In short, the United States *had* become a "colorblind society," but not in the sense that race no longer mattered. Instead, concerns regarding historical and racial inequity were made unintelligible by the presumably "race neutral" logic of neoliberalism, and the nation *writ large* had collectively turned a blind eye to discrimination, injustice, and ethnoracial violence.

All of this faced a formidable challenge in the wake of Katrina. And, it is within this period of disruption that society's regulatory forces fought unabashedly to recuperate America's neoliberal order. To extend my inquiry, then, is to examine these modalities of value and meaning—to locate the "'mechanisms of coercion' that hover around the contemporary coding of events as experience."[50]

"Order Words" and the Event of Katrina

While the "event proper" of Katrina was produced by the storm itself, the intelligibility of Katrina-as-event was expressed though texts—both visual and linguistic. It is here where a turn to Gilles Deleuze and Felix Guattari proves particularly useful as their work can be used to examine the "role of language and other forms of representation in the actualization or effectuation of everyday events."[51] Within the context of Katrina, such a move allows for a departure from the positivistic accounts by approaching the act of understanding as less the recognition of "facts," than a constitutive event.[52] The intelligibility of events, in this regard, "emerge[s] as a result of an imposition"—impositions that are performed through what Deleuze and Guattari deem "order words,"[53] which hold normative function and operate within the pragmatics and politics of language.[54] When understood in these terms, Paul Patton adds, the primary function of language is less the communication of information than a matter of *acting in or upon* the world.[55] For this very reason, Patton suggests, "politics frequently takes the form of struggle over the appropriate description of events."[56]

Katrina-as-event, insofar as it figured in the social imaginary, was a complex phenomenon that included its own forms of representation in media reports, official statements, political speeches, and popular culture. Katrina is in this sense exemplary in that it offers specific examples of how the "representation of events, in television and print media, has become part of the unfolding of events themselves."[57] While it would be too much to claim that events are reducible to their representations, it should be "equally implausible to claim that events and their representations are entirely distinct from one another."[58] To this end, rhetorical and textual representations of Katrina give expression to the "incorporate dimension" of the actual event. Thus, the remainder of this chapter proceeds by using textual analyses to map the key positions—or perhaps *impositions*—that sought to recuperate or reinflect America's racial order in the wake of Katrina.

Conservative Recuperations of America's Racial Order

In the days that followed Katrina's landfall, the disturbing images and harsher realities of flooded streets, distraught evacuees, and abandoned bodies left the typically vociferous conservative pundits as ill-equipped as their official counterparts. Before their preferred narrative of Katrina congealed into the present-day critique of Governor Kathleen Blano's and Mayor Ray Nagin's competence (gendered and racialized respectfully), conservative critics mustered little more than an attack of Kanye West's patriotism in light of his "George Bush doesn't care about black people" ad lib.[59] Significant for the purposes of this chapter, however, is that prior to settling on this safer, presumably "anti-racial" terrain of competence, conservative pundits actually engaged with the concepts of race and racism, if only to disavow their significance in the disaster. While a more robust study could readily trace the trajectory of conservatives' commentaries—from dumbfoundedness to their denial that racial factors to accusations of incompetence—for the purposes of the present study I will lean on two articles that stand out as emblematic of their treatment of race: John McWhorter's "'Racism!' They Charged: When

Don't They?" and James Q. Wilson's "American Dilemma: Problems of Race Still Cry to be Solved."

McWhorter's September 26, 2005, article, "'Racism!' They Charged: When Don't They?" is significant because it was one of the first conservative responses to substitute the post-Katrina racial discourse with one of neoliberal entrepreneurialism. While McWhorter's article recognizes "that in New Orleans, as in so many other places, to be poor is often to be black," he was either unprepared or unwilling to attribute the "tragic realities of racial disparity" to the legacies of racism.[60] Instead, McWhorter capitalized on the gravity of Katrina's destruction to evade such considerations. Given "the prospect of finding many thousands of dead as the waters recede," he asserted, "historical debates of this kind can and should wait."[61] However, McWhorter's reverence grew decidedly less pronounced as he launched into the crux of his argument:

> To claim that racism is the reason that the rescue effort was so slow is not a matter of debate at all: It's nothing more than a handy way to get media attention, or to help sell a new CD. It's self-affirming, too, if playing the victim is the only way you know to make yourself feel like you matter. It is also absurd.[62]

Through the progression of his argument, it becomes clear that McWhorter's charge of absurdity was directed toward those "black nationalists" who, in his assessment, have confused FEMA's colorblind failures with institutional racism. His charge of absurdity is more than dismissive. It strives to foreclose national discussions regarding racism (i.e., it is "not a matter of debate at all") while simultaneously trivializing identity-based politics, which McWhorter characterized as being little more than the posturing of victimhood.

Within these attacks, McWhorter aimed to reconstitute the event of Katrina as markedly antiracial. He assumed a liberal conception of citizenship—one founded upon the same ideals that animated Bush's anti-affirmative action position as well as the policies of NCLB—and intimates that because all are equal before the law, none should receive preferential treatment (in this case, federal assistance), even in the event of a calamitous disaster. Writing against a widespread demand for increased federal assistance and an outpouring of private donations, McWhorter's argument strove to reestablish atomized entrepreneurialism as the central feature of social exchange such that notions of public responsibility are converted into opportunities for private gain.[63]

The political effects of this position were laid bare in McWhorter's conclusion. Instead of recognizing Katrina as a national issue and the rebuilding effort as a federal responsibility, McWhorter recoded the destruction of the Gulf Coast as an event that bestowed "poor blacks" with "an opportunity to create a coherent all-black enclave."[64] Arguing that Katrina is the closest semblance to a "Second Civil Rights Revolution" that the United States will likely encounter, McWhorter supposedly "eagerly anticipated" the emergence of a "thriving black working class in New Orleans."[65] This ostensibly benign vision turned problematic once, without the least bit of irony, McWhorter described the benefits of black self-sufficiency: "Older blacks fondly recall the struggling but coherent black communities that integration dissolved—sometimes a little 'segregation' can be a good thing."[66] This romantic harkening to the "good old days" of Jim Crow, a time when the federal mitigation of racial disparities was at its minimum, demonstrates the "benevolent" violence enabled by the decontextualizing effect of American neoliberalism. McWhorter's bootstrap fantasy of an ahistorical and antiracial America was taken to even more severe ends in James Wilson's "American Dilemma: Problems of Race Still Cry to Be Solved."[67]

Similar to McWhorter, Wilson used Katrina as an opportunity to recode the emergent issues of institutional racism and socioeconomic inequality. Yet, whereas McWhorter argued for the empowerment of "poor blacks" (if only to justify the removal of federal assistance), Wilson found in Katrina an opportunity to chastise the African American community for what he deemed to be a lack of social capital. Published three months after the storm's landfall, Wilson's commentary reflects an emboldened conservative position that argued the federal government has already provided more than its share and it is now time for "poor blacks" to help themselves.

Wilson begins his piece by applauding the gains of the civil rights movement. "In the space of just a few decades," Wilson writes, "the legalized suppression of a racial minority was ended, the public with trivial exceptions embraced an anti-racism ideology, and a large middle class emerged."[68] However, after presenting anecdotal evidence of black mobility (i.e., "about one-third of all blacks now hold middle-class," "the percentage of blacks living below the poverty line has declined," "the median income of black women is now about 90 percent that of white women"), Wilson deploys his central critique:

> At the same time the percentage of single-parent black families has grown hugely, the advances that black women have made are not equaled by those of black men, and the rate of serious crime among blacks is much higher than it is for non-Hispanic whites and vastly greater than it is for Asian Americans.[69]

With the connection between Katrina and Wilson's single-parent black families growing faint, he asserts that "everyone knows these facts but hardly anyone discusses them publicly."[70] "Instead," he continues,

> the veil of political correctness has descended on this topic, a veil much in evidence during the media's coverage of the effect of Hurricane Katrina on New Orleans. We have been repeatedly told that most of New Orleans residents are "poor" and that it is the fault of the rest of us that they are poor.[71]

It is here where Wilson resonates with McWhorter's call for a minimization of state involvement. He argues that those who try to implicate the lives of "good Americans" with the plights of the "incompetent blacks" stranded by Katrina fail to recognize the "extraordinary efforts that the government and private enterprise have made to help the poor: welfare payments, Medicaid, food stamps, public housing, affirmative action, and the compulsive search by firms and universities for any competent black who can be hired or educated."[72] Thus, in a manner less subtle than McWhorter, Wilson's piece advocated for a restriction of state involvement in the rebuilding of New Orleans because doing so, in his estimation, would infringe upon the African American community's prerogative to "make it on their own."[73]

Like McWhorter, Wilson went to great lengths to disavow the significance of racism, albeit in curious ways. For example, challenging a speech by President Bush claiming that the poverty exposed by Katrina was the result of racial discrimination and lack of opportunity, Wilson appealed to statistics from the 2000 U.S. Census, noting that "35 percent of blacks in New Orleans were poor, even though only 25 percent of the blacks nationally are poor."[74] From this discrepancy, it would appear that

Wilson hoped his readers to infer that (1) the poverty in New Orleans was not an effect of racism and (2) there is a factor other than historical racial and ongoing inequalities that better explains why New Orleans' African American poverty race is 10 percent higher than the national average. His answer, in an uncanny mirroring of *Crash*'s parable, suggested that

> discrimination did not produce what we see in New Orleans, where almost half the black families with children under 18 are headed by single women. They outnumber married black families with children by over 18,000. We do not know who the looters were, but among black thieves, I imagine that most came from single-parent families.[75]

What Wilson may have lacked in deductive reasoning was made up for by his consistency. "As the nation's observance of civil rights has grown," he continued, "the proportion of children living with unmarried mothers has also grown."[76] The consequences of this phenomenon, according to Wilson, include "high rates of crime and imprisonment, heavy rates of drug use, poor school performance, and a willingness to loot unguarded stores."[77] He therefore concludes by declaring that these "scarred (fatherless) youngsters" are the source of America's gravest social problems. In searching for solutions, Wilson predictably argues against any form of state intervention. He derides liberal public policy commentators for being "determined to talk about giving everybody more money so that they can minimize work and indulge their fantasies."[78] Further, he suggests: "To assume that these problems can be fixed by simply spending more money or creating more jobs reflects a mindless rejection of the evidence of the last half-century: We spent more and created more jobs and problems got worse."[79]

The real damage of Wilson's argument, however, stems from the way in which he problematized "the black family." Identifying black family structures as the "key to the persistence of a large and criminal lower class," he proposed that the "main domestic concern of policy-engaged intellectuals, liberal and conservative, ought to be to think hard about how to change these social weaknesses."[80] Wilson's problematization of "the black family" is neither novel nor unique. In 1965, Daniel Patrick Moynihan's report on "the Negro family" famously faulted the economic disparities between blacks and whites on the absence of fathers and the resulting matriarchal structure of black families.[81] Hortense Spillers, in a poignant critique, questioned the ways in which the Moynihan Report was framed:

> "Ethnicity" itself identifies a total objectification of human and cultural motives—the "white" family, by implication, and the "Negro Family," by outright assertion, in a constant opposition of binary meanings. Apparently spontaneous, these "actants" are wholly generated, with neither past nor future, as tribal currents moving out of time. Moynihan's "families" are pure present and always tense.[82]

Commensurate with the Moynihan Report, McWhorter and Wilson's reactions to Katrina presented "good Americans" and "poor blacks" in a mutually exclusive relationship that was thoroughly gutted of politics and history. The authors' investments in minimizing federal and state involvement therefore compelled both to pathologize racial difference in ways that recuperated neoliberalism's *modus operandi*: survival-of-the-fittest qua individual responsibility.

Identity Politics and the Reinflection of America's Racial Order

If the initial disruptive force of Katrina caught conservative pundits off guard, America's identity-based politicians quickly coded the disaster in terms of race. Prominent political, religious, and cultural figures issued nearly univocal statements underscoring how the disaster was differentially experienced by the black community. Notable among these, Representative Charlie Rangel, for example, addressed the Congressional Black Caucus by linking President Bush to Theophilus "Bull" Conner, stating Katrina proved that "if you're black in this country, and you're poor in this country, it's not an inconvenience—it's a death sentence. . . . If there's one thing that George Bush has done that we should never forget, it's that for us and for our children, he has shattered the myth of white supremacy once and for all."[83] In a similar vein, Reverend Jesse Jackson released a string of public statements pronouncing that "many black people feel that their race, their property conditions and their voting patterns have been a factor in the response"[84]; that the insufficiencies of the federal emergency response were consistent with a "historical indifference to the pain of poor people and black people"[85]; and that the constitution of the federal response team was unconscionable: "How can blacks be locked out of the leadership, and trapped in the suffering?"[86] And, while Kanye West's "George Bush doesn't care about black people" may have been the most prominent celebrity sound bite, Spike Lee—commenting on the conspiracy theory that New Orleans' Ninth Ward had been deliberately flooded by authorities—stated, "I don't put anything past the United States government. I don't find it too far-fetched that they tried to displace all the black people out of New Orleans."[87] Of course, not all Katrina-related statements issued by African Americans appealed to identity-based politics. Nevertheless, this sampling suggests identity politics was a significant—if not the prevailing—mode of engagement.

To be clear, my examination of identity-based politics is not designed to challenge or refute the merit of the aforementioned statements. Given the well-documented unfolding of events, Rangel, Jackson, West, and Lee's assessments have proven difficult to contest. Moreover, I am not particularly interested in rehashing the well-tread critiques of identity politics (i.e., that it is essentialist, reductive, and exclusive), however relevant they may continue to be. Instead, I want to fold these identity-based responses into my larger critique of neoliberalism by (1) exposing how their political efficacy was met with diminishing returns due to their inability to escape conservative appropriations of once-progressive rhetoric and (2) gesturing toward a potentially transformatory tension that emerged between community and democracy, specifically within Mayor Ralph Nagin's renowned "Chocolate City" address.

The enduring merits of identity-based politics are tough to refute. Group identities—whether race, gender, sexuality, or religion—continue to provide the most readily available platforms for building political solidarity and the event-of-Katrina proved no different. While the previously mentioned drawbacks raise undeniable concerns (although it should be noted that political theorists such as Tommie Shelby and Francis Kornegay have taken significant strides toward recuperating these deficiencies within the context of black leadership[88]), I would argue that identity-based politics are currently plagued by a more debilitating inadequacy; namely, its inability to fend off the conservative appropriations of the Civil Rights era notions of "fairness," "justice," and "equality."

As a testament to the cultural impact of the civil rights movement, overt declarations of sexism and racism are no longer deemed acceptable in the public domain (not that naked acts of sexism and racism no longer permeate American society). Yet, when overt antagonisms do arise, particularly when expressed by public figures, they are roundly condemned by liberals and conservatives alike and are frequently framed as potentially career-ending "gaffs." In this respect, the American public has grown intolerant to unconcealed intolerance. What has remained, then, is a climate of "benign racism," whereby seemingly innocent small-scale interactions rehearse the cruder patterns of large-scale racism, albeit "in a muted way that is difficult to notice until the effects of many small-scale discriminations have been totaled up."[89]

With respect to the conservative reactions to Katrina's identity-based politics, those working to preserve white patriarchy have been forced to repackage their projects in ways that obscure the prejudices that animate their politics. These reactions to identity politics disclose how the forced exclusions previously enacted through legislation (i.e., Jim Crow) currently appear as "benign" enforcements of a colorblind meritocracy. Taking as fact that the post–Civil Rights era *de jure* equality is commensurate with de facto equality, conservative politicians, pundits, journalists, and activist organizations such as the Institute for Justice, the Center for Individual Rights, the Center for Equal Opportunity, and the American Center for Law & Justice[90] justify their efforts by clinging to the neoliberal fantasy that American society already operates on a "level playing field." In an attempt to substantiate this fantasy, conservatives foreground anecdotal confirmations of barrier-free social mobility. While these accounts typically assume the form of individual success stories (i.e., evocations of Oprah Winfrey, Colin Powell, Condoleezza Rice, and, most recently, Barack Obama), they are increasingly framed in terms of group advancement (i.e., Asian Americans as the "model minority," the growth of the black middle class, and financial gains from Indian gaming). The purpose of these success stories is to impart the notions that artificial impediments to socioeconomic advancement have been removed and individual success is solely a matter of talent and effort. While perhaps more palatable than prior regimes of overt domination, inclusive forms of racism remain injurious because their privileging of "equality" over justice locates the blame and burden of America's problems on those historically marginalized groups unwilling to "move beyond" the injuries incurred by conquest, slavery, and discrimination. In this regard, the conservative "push back" to post-Katrina identity politics can be read as an effort to supplant historically asymmetric relations of power with an unsituated antiracial flatness.

In reaction to Rangel's Bush–Bull Conner comparison, for example, Tracey Schmitt, spokeswoman for the Republican National Committee, argued that "by making such an outrageous comparison, Rangel is simply emulating the hateful divisiveness of the past," adding that President Bush "remains more committed than ever to expanding access to the American dream, and Democrat leaders should repudiate such hateful attacks."[91] Furthermore, in light of the Democratic National Committee chairman's refusal to rebuke Rangel's remarks, Schmitt added that Democrats "might be disappointed to learn that their party leader [Howard Dean] considers hate speech an acceptable alternative to an agenda."[92] Similarly, responding to Reverend Jackson's statements regarding Katrina, Former House Speaker Newt Gingrich declared on *The O'Reilly Factor* that "there are some people in America who have made a career out of being despicable racists on their own side" and "Jesse Jackson in that sense behaves essentially as a racist."[93] Gingrich continued by arguing the "fact is [Jackson] wants to see a color-defined America . . . that is a purely racist position."[94] Modeling a presumably more progressive, postracial disposition, Gingrich suggested that

the rest of us ought to take this kind of vicious attitude head on and just point out that there were an awful lot of New Orleans police-men of all backgrounds ethnically, trying to protect that city. . . . There were an awful lot of people out there of all backgrounds, firemen and volunteer workers, trying to help those people. And having Jesse Jackson's viciousness undermines that entire process.[95]

And, on the cultural front, First Lady Laura Bush condemned Kanye West's ad lib by stating, "I think all of those remarks were disgusting because, of course, President Bush cares about everyone in our country."[96] Last, Nicholas Kulish's otherwise positive *New York Times* review of Spike Lee's Katrina documentary argued, "Mr. Lee undermines the latter goal [of drawing attention to the continued misery of the victims and encour-aging a new rush of aid and assistance for those struggling to rebuild] whenever his film reduces Katrina to a black problem."[97] The end effect of all these conservative reactions, then, is that all forms of minority/identity-based politics can be reduced to "reverse racism," "race monger-ing," "victimology," or "playing the race card." This of course is only made sensible through the antiracial, ahistorical lens of neoliberalism.

Spilling over to the domain of public discourse, their efforts have contributed to an atomization of the American citizenry that not only launders the State's relationship to racism but individuates social responsibility in a manner that has relieved the public from its commitments to minority—racial or otherwise—concerns. As such, prior social assurances (even in their most emaciated forms) to empower historically marginal segments of society have been rendered unintelligible, if not unconstitutional, by the "colorblind" neutrality and universality of the law. Herein lays the critical disjunction between the conservative rhetoric of "equality" and the similar-sounding appeals initiated in the civil rights movement. The politics of the civil rights movement strove, albeit in diverse and uneven ways, to dismantle the gender, racial, and sexual divisions that sustained the upward consolidation of power, wealth, and privilege. These struggles, propelled by the emergence of identity-based politics (i.e., women's movement, black nationalism, the American Indian movement, Chicanismo, and the gay rights movement), forced the United States to not only acknowledge but also address past and continued forms of oppression. What followed, at least until the Reagan administration, was the establishment of federal policies and programs that encouraged a broader distribution of resources and opportunity.[98] To this end, the civil rights movement's politicization of racial identities facilitated the establishment of a limited welfare state, a questioning of unrestrained capitalism, and an imperilment of America's white patriarchy.[99]

The present conservative push back against identity-based politics, though presumably founded on similar ideals of egalitarianism, is qualitatively different. These latest evocations of "equality" are part of a countermovement that has, since the 1970s, fought to systematically dismantle the gains made by the civil rights movement, albeit in ostensibly innocent ways.[100] With the aim of resecuring America's racial hierarchies, the conservative countermovement has increasingly used the discourse of rights to seize the primary institutions of the state, thereby rerouting federal funds away from "social issues" (welfare programs, affirmative action, etc.) and toward private interests.[101] The consequence, in short, has been a popular denouncement of all provisions that fail to correspond to the Darwinistic laws of the market. As neoliberal ideologues implore citizens to surrender their understandings of the public domain as a terrain of empowerment, mantras of "individual responsibility," "privacy," and "personal initiative" have been used to justify a "cutting of losses" and the curbing of state involvement. Notable here is House Speaker Dennis Hastert's initial reaction to Katrina: when asked if he supported dedicating billions of dollars toward rebuilding New Orleans, he responded, "I don't know. That doesn't make sense to me" and "It looks like a lot of that place could be bulldozed."[102] It is from within such a logic that the ideological force of neoliberalism has replaced the ethos of social obligation with a privileging of "individualism" and "meritocracy."

"Chocolate City," a Beloved Community, and Democracy

The pressing question becomes: Are there forms of American race politics that can operate outside of neoliberalism's seemingly benign atomistic, market-based dominations? Is it possible to contest conservatives' disavowal of white patriarchy while simultaneously evading their "post-racial" condemnations of identity-based politics? The need, in this regard, is for a "way forward" that (1) transposes neoliberalism's individualism with relationality, (2) confounds the survival-of-the-fittest mentality with acts of empathy, and (3) evades both the real and alleged exclusivities of identity politics. This is obviously a tall order, and while I do not know exactly what such a politics would look like, there were a couple of post-Katrina moments that offered hope. Although perhaps counterintuitive at first glance, Mayor Nagin's "Chocolate City" speech provides a productive point of departure.

On January 16, 2006, at the commencement of New Orleans' first post-Katrina Martin Luther King Jr. parade, Mayor Ralph Nagin let loose with a now-infamous invocation:

> We, as black people, it's time. It's time for us to come together. It's time for us to rebuild a New Orleans—the one that should be a *chocolate* New Orleans. And I don't care what people are saying uptown or wherever they are, this city will be *chocolate* at the end of the day. This city will be a majority African American city. It's the way God wants it to be.

In the controversy that ensued, Nagin was cast in a number of shades—none of which were gray. To some, he was a champion of the black community, a straight-shooter who rightly addressed the fear that New Orleans would be rebuilt richer and whiter. To others, he was an opportunistic politician, one whose sudden commitment to "chocolate" flew in the face of his administration's near-total assault on public services. And to others still, he was a racist who declared in no uncertain terms that white would not be welcomed in the *new* New Orleans. In this respect, the controversy generated by Nagin's speech foreground the present-day complexities of American race politics.

Nagin's controversy, however, is equally significant for the ways it staged a broader political concern; namely, the tension that exists between identity-based politics and the egalitarian commitments of a liberal democracy. This tension, while implicit in the quote above, was made all the more evident in Nagin's subsequent exchanges with reporters. When asked to reconcile the seemingly divisive nature of his Chocolate City imagery with the more inclusive spirit of the parade's namesake (off-camera reporter: "Do you think that is a bit divisive though, on MLK Day?"[103]), Nagin defensively replied:

> Do you know anything about chocolate? How to you make chocolate? You take dark chocolate, you mix it with white milk, and it becomes a delicious drink. *That's* the chocolate I'm talking about. New Orleans was a chocolate city before Katrina. It's going to be a chocolate city after. How is that divisive? It's white and black working together—coming together and making something special.

While this was, in all likelihood, a case of political backpedaling if there ever was one, Nagin's response provides a provocative first move toward a "way forward." Whereas the reporter's question presumes that Nagin's efforts to "keep it real" with New Orleans' African American community compromised his role as a public official, the mayor's equivocation is far from a retraction. Instead, his delicious drink analogy, though ungainly, can be viewed as an evasion of the traditional limits of identity politics: the mutual-exclusive choices between "dark chocolate" and "white milk," between Nagin's "people" and his constituents, and, last, between community and democracy.

My reading here, while perhaps overly generous, is not dissimilar to Francis Kornegay's conclusions in his "Post-Katrina New Orleans: The Crisis of Black Leadership Revisited." Drawing inspiration from Harold Cruse's 1967 *Crisis of the Negro Intellectual*, Kornegay outlines the dangers of racial separatism and highlights the heterogeneity of the "African American community." His conclusion: African Americans —nationalists and nonnationalists alike—will have to muster a level of multicultural sensitivity that has not been amply evident from past political encounters between black political actors and constituencies and other nonwhite ethnic groups."[104] What follows is not a dilution of (African American) identity-based commitments, but instead a nuanced coalitional formation analogous to Chantal Mouffe's "radical democratic politics"; that is,

> the articulation of the democratic demands found in a variety of movements: women, workers, blacks, gays, ecological, as well as other "new social movements." The aim is to construct a "we" as radical democratic citizens, a collective political identity articulated through the principle of democratic *equivalence*.[105]

The key here—the element that makes Mouffe's concept different from classic liberal formulations that empty gender, racial, sexual, and historical distinctions for the sake of the "greater good"—is that "such a relation of *equivalence* does not eliminate *difference*."[106] Instead, Mouffe's radical democratic politics emphasizes the "numerous social relations in which situations of domination exists that must be challenged" and affirms the "common recognition by the different groups struggling for an extension and radicalization of democracy that they have a common concern."[107]

    In terms of Kornegay's formulation, this requires the interplay of two efforts. The first would be the creation of an independent all-black political party, one that supported progressive Republicans and Democrats alike, which focused almost exclusively on a "limited objective strategy of mobilizing an urban black political, economic, and social reconstruction agenda" for New Orleans.[108] This all-black independent political party strategy, Kornegay insists, "would, of necessity, need to be coupled and calibrated with interracial coalition-building to give voice and momentum to a broad urban progressive reform 'social movement' of renewal."[109] Referencing the Coalition of Black Trade Unions (CBTU) as a possible spearhead, Kornegay suggests the "formation of an all-black or black-led independent political party [...] with the CBTU as its nucleus, could motivate the consolidation or a range of disparate progressive initiatives" that, echoing Mouffe's racial democratic politics, could "shape a broader, interracial and multicultural Urban Progressive Alliance that would engage interactively, in tandem, with an independent black political base."[110]

While a Kornegay-Mouffe strategy begins to flesh-out Nagin's delicious drink of "white and black working together—coming together and making something special" and holds the potential to evade the exclusivities of conventional identity politics, it does not in and of itself address the contestation of neoliberalism's individuality and survival-of-the-fittest ideology. It is here that a final turn to bell hooks's extrapolation of Martin Luther King Jr.'s notion of a "beloved community" proves instructive.

"Most folks in this society have become so cynical about ending racism," hooks writes, "so convinced that solidarity across racial differences can never be a reality, that they make no effort to build community."[111] Adding to these difficulties are the suspicions produced by the notion that people "must give up allegiances to specific cultural legacies in order to have harmony."[112] While hooks concedes that such suspicion is healthy, she warns that as long as "black Americans are succumbing to and internalizing the racist assumption that there can be no meaningful bonds of intimacy between blacks and whites," no resistance to white supremacy can take place.[113] Arguing that "we must not allow the actions of white folks who blindly endorse racism to determine the direction of our resistance," hooks (re)introduces "love" as the only antithesis to the will to dominate and subjugate.[114] This love, for hooks, is not sentimental or naïve love; it does not obscure the fact that racism is deeply systemic. Rather, the small circles of interracial love "we have managed to form in our individual lives represent a concrete realistic reminder that *beloved community* is not a dream, that it already exists for those of us who have done the work of educating ourselves for critical consciousness in ways that enabled a letting go of white supremacist assumptions and values."[115] To create and sustain a *beloved community*, therefore, necessitates a collective renewal of "our commitment to a democratic vision of racial justice and equality."[116] Thus, intertwined with the strategic formulations of Kornegay-Mouffe, hooks's appeal to *beloved* interracial relations holds the potential to establish what Wynton Marsalis deemed "not only a new tone for New Orleans, but believe it or not, a new tone for our nation."[117]

Notes

1. Michael Brown, interview by Jim Lehrer, *The NewsHour with Jim Lehrer*, PBS, September 1, 2005.

2. Ibid.

3. Ibid.

4. Jonathan Alter, "The Other America," *Newsweek*, September 19, 2005, 42. While Alter does not credit Michael Harrington's 1962 work of the same name, for my purposes it is worth noting that Harrington's *Other America* was a politically influential work that foregrounded the intersection between poverty and race/immigration.

5. Michael Eric Dyson, *Come Hell or High Water: Hurricane Katrina and the Color of Disaster* (New York: Basic Civitas, 2007); Douglas Brinkley, *The Great Deluge: Hurricane Katrina, New Orleans, and the Mississippi Gulf Coast* (New York: Harper Perennial, 2007); Jed Horne, *Breach of Faith: Hurricane Katrina and the Near Death of a Great American City* (New York: Random House Trade Paperbacks, 2008); Christopher Cooper, *Disaster: Hurricane Katrina and the Failure of Homeland Security* (New York: Holt Paperbacks, 2007); Ivor van Heerden, *The Storm: What Went Wrong and Why during Hurricane Katrina—the Inside Story from One Louisiana Scientist* (New York: Penguin, 2007); Gregory Squires, *There is No Such Thing as a Natural Disaster: Race, Class, and Katrina* (New York: Routledge, 2006); and Walter Brasch, *'Unacceptable': The Federal Government's Response to Hurricane Katrina* (Charleston, S.C.: BookSurge, 2005).

6. James der Derian, "Global Events, National Security, and Virtual Theory," *Millennium: Journal of International Studies* 30, no. 3 (2001): 669–90, 672. Although der Derian's article predates Katrina, his treatment of "global accidents" is appropriate.

7. Ibid., 685.

8. Michel Foucault, *History of Sexuality: Volume I* (New York: Pantheon, 1978), 11. Foucault's "sex" has been transposed with "race."

9. Wendy Brown, "The Time of the Political," *Theory & Event* 1, no. 1 (1997): 1–8, 4. Brown does not specifically engage with race yet her concepts and phrasing proved helpful in the formulation of this move.

10. bell hooks, *killing rage: Ending Racism* (New York: Henry Holt and Co., 1995). Thanks to Michelle Holling, who referred this work.

11. Jacques Rancière, 97, quoted in Michael Dillon's "A Passion for the (Im)possible: Jacques Rancière, Equality, Pedagogy, and the Messianic," *European Journal of Political Theory* 4 (October 2005): 445.

12. Jacques Rancière, *Disagreement: Politics and Philosophy* (Minneapolis: University of Minnesota Press, 1999), 99.

13. Ibid., 102.

14. Ibid., 99.

15. Aamir Mufti, "Reading Jacques Ranciere's 'Ten Theses on Politics': After September 11th," *Theory & Event* 6, no. 4 (2003): 1–10, 1.

16. Rancière, *Disagreement*, 99–100. Rancière actually uses the term "floating subjects" to refer to the unmarked. However, given the unfortunate literal confluence with the gruesome realities of the disaster, I elected to omit it from the main text.

17. der Derian, "Global Events," 689. Changed from plural to singular and transposed "acts" with "stands."

18. Brown, "The Time of the Political," 4.

19. Ibid., 5.

20. Michel Foucault, *Discipline and Punish: The Birth of the Prison* (London: Penguin, 1977), 148.

21. Ibid.

22. Ibid.

23. Michel Foucault, *"Society Must Be Defended"* (New York: Piscador, 2003), 258; and Lisa Duggan, *The Twilight of Equality: Neoliberalism, Cultural Politics, and the Attack on Democracy* (Boston: Beacon, 2003), 14.

24. Eduardo Bonilla-Silva, *Racism without Racists: Color-Blind Racism and the Persistence of Racial Inequality in the United States* (Lanham, Md.: Rowman & Littlefield, 2003), 40.

25. Duggan, *The Twilight of Equality*, 2003.

26. "Briefing Room: The White House," www.whitehouse.gov/news/releases/2003/01/20030115-7.html.

27. Ibid.

28. Ibid.

29. Ibid.

30. Ibid.

31. Ibid.

32. Eric Freeman, "No Child Left Behind and the Denigration of Race," *Equity & Excellence in Education* 38, no. 3 (August 2005): 190–99, 194.

33. Ibid.

34. Ibid.

35. Rebecca A. Goldstein and Andrew R. Beutel, "The Best Democracy Money Can Buy: NCLB in Bush's Neo-liberal Marketplace (a.k.a., Revisioning History: The Discourse of Equality, Justice, and Democracy Surrounding NCLB)," *Journal of Education Controversy* 3, no. 1 (Winter 2008).

36. Freeman, "No Child Left Behind and the Denigration of Race," 196.

37. Ibid., 198.

38. Ibid., 194.

39. The film was originally released in 2004 but was not widely distributed until 2005 so it could qualify for Oscar consideration. www.imdb.com/title/tt0375679/triva.

40. Derik Smith, "Investigating the *Crash* Scene," www.blackcommentator. com/175/175_crash_scene_smith_guest.html; Earl Ofari Hutchinson, "A Crash Course on Stereotypes," www.alternet.org/story/22064/a_crash_course_on_ stereotypes/ (accessed April 26, 2006); Jeff Chang and Sylvia Chan, "Can White Hollywood Get Race Right?" www.alternet.org/movies/23597/ (accessed April 26, 2006); and Robert Jensen and Robert Wosnitzer, "'Crash' and the Self-Indulgence of White America," www.blackcommentator.com/176/176_ think_crash_jensen_wosnitzer.html (accessed April 26, 2006).

41. Smith, "Investigating the *Crash* Scene."

42. *Crash*, DVD, directed by Paul Haggis, 2004. (Los Angeles, CA: Lions Gate Films Home Entertainment, 2005).

43. Chang and Chan, "Can White Hollywood Get Race Right?"

44. Ibid.

45. Smith, "Investigating the *Crash* Scene."

46. Chang and Chan, "Can White Hollywood Get Race Right?"

47. Smith, "Investigating the *Crash* Scene."

48. Jensen and Wosnitzer, "'Crash' and the Self-Indulgence of White America."

49. Reference to "undifferentiated space of citizenship" is derived from Michael J. Shapiro, "Genres of Nationhood: The 'Musico-Literary' Aesthetics of Attachment and Resistance," *Strategies: Journal of Theory, Culture & Politics* 13, no. 2 (November 2000): 141–61. The concept of "laundering" is drawn from Wahneema Lubiano, "Black Ladies, Welfare Queens, and State Minstrels: Ideological War by Narrative Means," in *Race-ing Justice, Engendering Power: Essays on Anita Hill, Clarence Thomas, and the Construction of Social Reality,* ed. Toni Morrison (New York: Pantheon, 1992), 353.

50. Michael J. Shapiro, *Cinematic Political Thought: Narrating Race, Nation, and Gender* (New York: NYU Press, 1999), 16–17.

51. Ibid., 20.

52. Ibid., 21.

53. Ibid., 21.

54. Ibid., 22.

55. Paul Patton, *Deleuze and the Political* (New York: Routledge, 2000), 27.

56. Ibid., 28.

57. Ibid., 9.

58. Ibid., 9.

59. Sean Alfano, "Rapper Blasts Bush Over Katrina," September 3, 2005, www. cbsnews.com/stories/2005/09/03/katrina/main814636.shtml.

60. John McWhorter, "'Racism!' They Charged: When Don't They?" *National Review,* September 26, 2005.

61. Ibid.

62. Ibid.

63. Ibid.

64. Ibid.

65. Ibid.

66. Ibid.

67. James Wilson, "American Dilemma: Problems of Race Still Cry to Be Solved," *National Review,* December 11, 2005.

68. Ibid.

69. Ibid.

70. Ibid.

71. Ibid.

72. Ibid.

73. Ibid.

74. Ibid.

75. Ibid.

76. Ibid.

77. Ibid.

78. Ibid.

79. Ibid.

80. Reference drawn from Michael J. Shapiro, "Literary Geography and Sovereign Violence: Resisting Tocqueville's Family Romance," *Alternatives* 25, no. 1 (January 2000): 27–50.

81. Ibid.

82. Ibid.

83. Meghan Clyne, "President Bush is 'Our Bull Conner,' Harlem's Rep. Charles Rangel Claims," *New York Sun,* September 23, 2005, www.nysun.com/national/president-bush-is-our-bull-connor-harlems-rep/20495/.

84. David Gonzalez, "From Margins of Society to Center of the Tragedy," *New York Times,* September 2, 2005, www.nytimes.com/2005/09/02/national/nationalspecial/02discrim.html?_r=1.

85. Doug Simpson, "Jackson Blasts Bush Over Katrina Aid," *Associated Press,* September 2, 2005, www.breitbart.com/article.php?id=D8CCAOI81&show_article=1.

86. Ibid.

87. "Lee to Take Spiky Look at Katrina," *Guardian UK,* October 13, 2005, www.guardian.co.uk/film/2005/oct/13/news.spikelee.

88. Tommie Shelby, *We Who Are Dark: The Philosophical Foundations of Black Solidarity* (Cambridge, Mass.: Belknap Press, 2007); and Francis A. Kornegay, "Post-Katrina New Orleans: The Crisis of Black Leadership Revisited," *The Black Commentator,* November 3, 2005, 157, www.blackcommentator.com/157/157_kornegay_post_katrina_no.html.

89. Robert Ackerman, *Heterogeneities: Race, Gender, Class, Nation, and State* (Amherst, Mass.: Massachusetts, 1996), 42.

90. While the Institute for Justice and Center for Individual Rights are currently the most prominent legal organizations, others include but are not limited to: the Washington Legal Foundation, the Pacific Legal Foundation, the Landmark Legal Foundation, the Independent Women's Forum, the American Civil Rights Institute, the Federation for American Immigration Reform, and the Alliance Defense Fund.

91. Meghan Clyne, "Rangel's Jibe at President Draws Support from Democrats," *New York Sun,* September 27, 2005, www.nysun.com/national/rangels-jibe-at-president-draws-support-from/20580/.

92. Meghan Clyne, "DNC Stands By Rangel after 'Hate Speech'," *New York Sun,* September 28, 2005, www.nysun.com/new-york/dnc-stands-by-rangel-after-hate-speech/20654/.

93. "Interview: Former House Speaker Newt Gingrich on Katrina Aftermath," *The O'Reilly Factor,* September 6, 2005, www.foxnews.com/story/0,2933,168567,00.html.

94. Ibid.

95. Ibid.

96. Juan Williams, "Examining Race, Class, and Katrina," *NPR News,* September 16, 2005, www.npr.org/templates/story/story.php?storyId=4850509.

97. Nicholas Kulish, "Spike Lee Films the New Orleans Disaster His Way," *New York Times,* August 21, 2006, www.nytimes.com/2006/08/21/opinion/21mon4.html.

98. Duggan, *Twilight of Equality,* 9.

99. Ibid., xi.

100. Ibid., ix.

101. Ibid., xi.

102. Charles Babington, "Hastret Tries Damage Control after Remarks Hit a Nerve," *Washington Post,* September 3, 2005, www.washingtonpost.com/wp-dyn/content/article/2005/09/02/AR2005090202156.html.

103. "Nagin Apologizes for 'Chocolate' City Comments" *CNN,* January 18, 2006, www.cnn.com/2006/US/01/17/nagin.city/index.html.

104. Kornegay, "Post-Katrina New Orleans, 157.

105. Chantal Mouffe, "Feminism, Citizenship, and Radical Democratic Politics," in *Everyday Theory* (New York: Pearson Longman, 2005), 413–414.

106. Ibid., 414.

107. Ibid., 413.

108. Kornegay, "Post-Katrina New Orleans," 8.

109. Ibid.

110. Ibid.

111. hooks, *killing rage,* 264.

112. Ibid., 256.

113. Ibid., 269.

114. Ibid., 265.

115. Ibid., 264.

116. Ibid., 271.

117. "Wynton Marsalis: Renewal Series Address," January 16, 2006, http://www2.tulane.edu/marsalis011606.cfm.

CHAPTER 3

Making Citizens in Magnaville

Katrina Refugees and Neoliberal Self-Governance

Geoffrey Whitehall and Cedric Johnson

I am not a "refugee." I wasn't shipped here. . . . We are not refugees. You hold your head up. We are United States Citizens, and you be proud of that. A lot of us are taxpaying, honest, hardworking people. I'm like, when did I come from another country? That's what they used to call people that was in the boats, and that was sneaking over here. I am a survivor.

—Sharon White, New Orleans resident in Baton Rouge shelter, quoted on National Public Radio's *All Things Considered,* September 7, 2005

The people we're talking about are not refugees. . . . They are Americans and they need the help and love and compassion of our fellow citizens.

—President George W. Bush, quoted during visit to shelter in Baker, Louisiana, September 2005

THE 2008 FILM *TROUBLE THE WATER* was heralded as the best Katrina film in many corners for its first-person account of Kim Rivers Roberts's struggle to survive and rebuild her life after the waters consumed her Upper Ninth Ward neighborhood. The film stands out because filmmakers Tia Lessin and Carl Deal drive the narrative through Kim's priceless hand-held footage of the slow and catastrophic inundation of her neighborhood and the efforts of residents to save themselves. The film provides a more intimate account of government failure than that circulated widely in corporate news coverage of the disaster. *Trouble the Water* reveals the vulnerability and disunity experienced by citizens in the United States, and it invites further reflection about the practices of citizenship and politics in the redemption of contemporary neoliberal sovereignty.

The film documents how, for the span of a week, thousands of the most vulnerable residents in New Orleans and the Gulf Coast were refugees. Kim and her fellow New Orleanians existed without the minimum protections one expects as a citizen in an advanced industrial society. On the contrary, Scott Roberts (Kim's husband) recounts a chilling episode in which he and dozens of other residents were turned *away* from a local naval support station at gunpoint when they sought refuge there. In another segment, Kim and Scott's fellow traveler, Brian Noble, is denied relief assistance in Memphis because he lived in a halfway house prior to the hurricane and could not produce an address for proof of residency. In one of the most powerful moments in the film, a relative of Kim puts words to the broader social predicament when she laments that the poor and the marginalized in America are in fact living without a government.

Kim, Scott, and Brian are honest and terribly likable personalities. Their Katrina stories are told in a direct and unvarnished fashion. Each seems buoyed by the endurance that has developed from hard-scrabble lives (evidenced by the physical scars that adorn them and the deeper wounds reflected in their tales of love, violence, and loss) that predated the events of 2005, a deep faith in Christ, and the possibility of deliverance from earthly travails. *Trouble the Water* is uplifting because it overturns depictions of black New Orleanians as savages who resorted to murder, rape, and destruction during a time of crisis. Through each personal testimony of survivors, we glimpse the spirit of altruism and community that permeated many neighborhoods as the streets filled with water and 911 emergency calls went unanswered.

This film was a huge hit among art house patrons and activists, but it follows a plot arch of trouble, tragedy, and redemption that most American movie-going audiences have come to expect. The film's theme of redemption resonates with the Christian Right, Obamanistas, and antiwelfare conservatives alike. What is crucial to our argument in this chapter is that Kim and Scott must undergo a makeover as the film progresses. In a sense they are remade in the likeness of Middle America or at least an image that is more tolerable to the professed values of middle-class America. For much of the film, they appear haggard and unkempt, but for the closing shots we find them made over, donning crisp attire, pearly white sneakers, carefully manicured dreadlocks, a salon-quality perm, and the like. This cosmetic makeover suggests a more fundamental ideological one: that ne'er-do-wells can assimilate to bourgeois culture if they are only given a chance. By the end of the film, Scott has secured a job working in construction, and Kim is working to promote her music career. And by extension, a society that failed so miserably to protect the lives of its most vulnerable citizens can in fact be redeemed through individualism and kind deeds. The film's Christian undertones and the closing sequences move the narrative back toward the familiar ground of early twenty-first century American politics.

Given their commitments to labor politics, both Lessin and Deal obviously wish to portray New Orleans' black working class with dignity. Lessin and Deal opt for cinéma vérité, which juxtaposes the Bush administration's press maneuvers with on-the-ground (and underwater) experiences of survivors in order to underscore the gross negligence and hypocrisy of ruling elites. However, because the film operates primarily at the level of survivor testimony—a smarter version of the familiar human interest story common to corporate news media, this aesthetic choice leaves the lineaments of power shaping this disaster and the process of recovery largely unexplored. The film closes with a rousing brass-band performance amid a protest, but little information is revealed about the political content or intentions of this action, which was in fact a demonstration against the proposed demolition of public housing units in the city. The film's plot arch might refract a different message: that the black urban poor can be made respectable. Therefore, although the film portrays flood victims with dignity, it forecloses the possibility of alternative lives for New Orleans' laboring class, lives that transcend the crime, despair, and deprivation of urban poverty but also the insecurity, consumerism, and pretentiousness that accompany middle-class life.

This tension between vulnerability and redemption speaks to two broad themes we wish to address more fully in this chapter. First, the raw home-video footage and survivor stories testify how Americans have been made increasingly vulnerable by neoliberal governance—a refugee-like status was revealed and debated during the Katrina disaster. This status problematizes the fiction that the state is our protectorate and invites speculation into the contours of contemporary progressive politics and neoliberal sovereignty. Second, the film illustrates a contemporary sociopolitical desire to make citizens and citizenship work. The vulnerability created by neoliberalism is, ironically, to be solved by the very same forms of citizenship it champions. Instead of citizenship taking the form of collective well-being, neoliberal citizenship is rooted in individualizing responsibility. And even individual well-being is left to the persistent sense that if one does not comply they will become a refugee. In sum, *Trouble the Water* is a gateway into a broad sociopolitical process of assimilating and mobilizing disaster stories in the process of redeeming American neoliberalism.

This chapter begins by revisiting media debates over usage of the term "refugee" to describe disaster victims. We contend that such debates revealed the inadequacy of civil rights discourse for addressing new states of vulnerability and exclusion under neoliberalism. Arguments over semantics obscured the ways that Katrina survivors were in fact acclimated to modes of self-governance in a manner comparable to that experienced by international refugees fleeing state terror, civil war, and natural disaster. In the remaining sections of this chapter, we explore the unique terms of neoliberal sovereignty, in which private institutions and market rationality increasingly create expressions of meaningful citizenship in terms of mobility, material comfort, and security for some, while excluding others. We note how states of emergency—war, pandemic, disaster, gang warfare, and the like—increasingly provide the ruling classes with opportunities to advance their interests and attain popular legitimacy through active promotion of neoliberal modes of self-governance. The closing portion of this chapter examines one such project—Magnaville, a transitional residential settlement created by Canadian industrialist Frank Stronach—as an experiment in neoliberal citizen-making.

The "Refugees" Debate Revisited: Civil Rights Liberalism Meets Neoliberalism

As images of the mostly black, destitute, and desperate survivors were circulated internationally after the Katrina disaster, many newscasters and journalists referred to them as *refugees*. Some survivors were angered by the use of the term. Tyrone McKnight, a New Orleans resident who found shelter in Baton Rouge after the flood, rejected the implications of the term stating: "The image I have in my mind is people in a Third World country, the babies in Africa that have all the flies and are starving to death. . . . That's not me. I'm a law-abiding citizen who's working every day and paying taxes."[1] When asked about the use of the term *refugees,* Sharon White, who also evacuated to Baton Rouge, quipped, "A lot of us are taxpaying, honest, hardworking people. I'm like, when did I come from another country? That's what they use to call people that was in boats and that was sneaking over here. I am a survivor."[2] Many Katrina evacuees responded in this manner, first disassociating themselves from the Third World connotations of the term and then making a claim to relief by reasserting themselves as liberal democratic citizens—hard-working, law-abiding, tax-paying. Black politicians like California Congresswoman Diane Watson and Maryland Congressman Elijah Cummings rejected the use of the term on similar grounds. And veteran civil rights leaders like Al Sharpton and Jesse Jackson appeared on numerous television programs to denounce the designation. Jackson charged that it was "racist to call American citizens refugees." However, the refusal to accept the term *refugee* on the basis of one's legal status as an American ignores actual practice.

The Katrina disaster set in motion the largest mass displacement in U.S. history, surpassing the Dust Bowl migrations of the 1930s in scale.[3] Over the span of two weeks, more than one million evacuees were relocated to every state in the Union. For an outside observer who witnessed hours of footage of residents dying from heat exhaustion, dehydration, and the lack of adequate emergency services; others struggling to find basic necessities; and many other scenes of mass misery, the adamancy with which some rejected the term refugee might seem puzzling. Were Gulf coastal residents *not* experiencing the same realities of displacement, sheer need, and desperation seen elsewhere? New Orleans was, after all, a manifestation of the "Third World" in the "First," and the disaster was a violent reminder for many middle-class citizens in the United States that large-scale misery is a fact of real life and not merely the stuff of *Grand Theft Auto, The Wire,* and other slumdog fantasies.

The visceral reaction against the use of the term can only be understood within the context of late twentieth-century African American political development and the unchallenged centrality of civil rights liberalism within black public discourses from the 1970s onward. The rejection of Third World references among African American working people and elites reflects the triumph of liberal integrationist ideology over other visions of race advancement since the 1960s. The knee-jerk rejection of affiliation with the Third World gives the impression that the Black Power movement never happened. It forgets how, as Jim Crow segregation buckled under the pressure of local activist campaigns and congressional civil rights acts, many black activists embraced the notion of the Third World as an alternative frame of reference. Moreover, the Third World was a utopian project seeing the national liberation movements unfolding throughout the colonized world as the embodiment of new modes of being that promised to overturn imperialist power and Western cultural hegemony.[4] Black Power militancy sought to create a revolutionary politics on domestic soil, with many arguing that blacks in the United States were, in fact, an internal colony. Liberal civil rights leaders generally scoffed at these more militant, internationalist aspirations, choosing instead to confine their political activism to the enforcement of constitutional equal protection in the hope of pushing Cold War liberal contradictions toward greater racial justice reforms.[5]

Black activists used similar conventional civil rights arguments after Katrina in an attempt to compel greater accountability from the current administration. Bush parried such criticisms by asserting that Hurricane Katrina was an "equal opportunity destroyer," thus minimizing his administration's culpability and the stark social dimensions of the disaster. In many respects, the claims of liberal civil rights discourse have been rendered anachronistic by the decades-long gutting of the Keynesian New Deal social compact and transformations in the global political economy. Multinational corporations and supranational financial institutions are increasingly responsible for shaping real wages, population flows, labor, and civil rights and are beyond the reach of traditional levers of democratic citizenship.

Ironically, the mainstream press, in defending its use of the term *refugee*, was prescient in grasping the reality of political vulnerability revealed by the Katrina disaster. Kathleen Carroll, executive editor of the Associated Press, asserted "the AP is using the term 'refugee' where appropriate to capture the sweep and scope of effects of this historic natural disaster on a vast number of citizens."[6] In a similar vein, *New York Times* Communications Chief Catherine Mathis defined the use of the term, noting its appropriateness for describing the social realities experienced by survivors: "We have used ['refugee'] along with 'evacuee,' 'survivor,' 'displaced' and various other terms that fit what our reporters are seeing on the ground. *Webster's* [dictionary] defines a refugee as a person fleeing 'home and country' in search of refuge and it certainly does justice to the legions driven from their homes by Katrina."[7] However, there is something more than semantics at stake in this term *refugee*.

Humanitarian Crises and Neoliberal Self-Governance

In times of emergency, the state is traditionally swept up in a wave of redemption. The emergency not only provides the opportunity to expand the governmental reach of the state but, equally important, also provides the necessary justification to normalize a geographically and historically contingent (and generally outdated) way of organizing political community and social life. In times of emergency, subjects are likely to lower their resistances to the injustices that the state enforces and become patriotic citizens willing, in some cases, to pay the ultimate sacrifice for the very instrument they previously challenged. Contrary to popular belief, therefore, those who support statecraft organize themselves around the next impending emergency, threat, or risk. Emergencies, threats, and risks (like crime, illness, and ignorance) do not complicate statecraft; they offer its core justification. The state form constitutes a complicated tension between taming and creating moments of its antipathy—a formless emergency. Following Giorgio Agamben, we call this *the state of emergency*. The state of emergency is simultaneously a suspension of state law and the moment in which the state reaches its greatest fulfillment. In this sense, there is a growing concern in contemporary political circles that the state of emergency is becoming the norm and not the exception. In this way, the character of our contemporary vulnerability is a normalized refugee.

In the wake of the Katrina emergency, given the U.S. government's failure to respond to the threat of a Class 5 hurricane and the subsequent debacle of its response, we might ask, what is the status of the statecraft? Did the champions of statecraft *fail* to react? Did they react in a *new* way that does not fit with our conception of the way that government *should* work? In other words, is it possible that the U.S. government did not fail to respond to the emergency but instead is operating within a new logic, and that this is the real emergency? A new force was swept up in the tide of redemptions, thereby further complicating the logic of statecraft with the logic of the market. Jason Barker suggests that "unlike the recent past, the State is no longer under any pressure to respond to genuine antagonisms in order to justify the consolidation of empires. It simply does whatever it wants under the benign pretext of providing security for human beings in a world of infinite uncertainty."[8] In order to understand the *failure* to respond to Katrina in this light, it is important to understand this new force.

Michael Dillon has argued that we are in the midst of a profound shift, a shift as weighty as that marked by Michel Foucault at the end of his seminal work *The Order of Things,* in which he predicts that as swiftly as it emerged, the image of man might be washed away like a face in the sand. The war on terror, the avian flu, the HIV and SARS epidemics, the Asian financial crisis and the Mexico debt crisis, and the response to the Katrina hurricane and the Asian tsunami are all symptoms of this profound shift in the organizing principles of *modern political life.* Dillon identifies the shift between the principle of security (organized around the maintenance of a populations and territory) and a global regime that is organized around a new image of life that exceeds the modern image of state citizenship and the rights of man. Building on Foucault and Agamben's arguments that politics is organized around managing life and what life can mean, Dillon argues that the traditional emphasis on emergencies, threat, and risk have been amplified within a generalized contingency. This new image of life, and therefore life's new definition, is contingency—a mixture of circulations and connectivity. In other words, life is no longer guaranteed because it exists; it exists because it is in the midst of circulating connections. Governance, therefore, is no longer organized around maintaining the health of the nation (whatever that means); instead, we are witnessing the governance of contingency. Contingency, he argues, now rivals society and economy. A great transformation is under way, in which the competing organizing narratives have met their match. He states, "Liberal governance, articulated biopolitically, grounds its freedom in an ontological contingency of species being newly understood and newly experienced socially, politically and scientifically as radically contingent because it is ontologically emergent."[9] The end is not yet in sight, but its transformation is under development.

Setting aside how this new life will be experienced scientifically (i.e., gene therapy, biocomputing, preemptive triage), the social and political transformation that Dillon identifies can be witnessed in the conflict over whether Katrina victims were refugees or émigrés. Political correctness got in the way of political acumen when the progressive forces in the United States fought to label Katrina refugees as émigrés. Agamben has argued that the refugee betrays the fiction of the state. The state is not your protectorate. The desire to name those displaced by the floodwaters émigrés betrays the insight that at various historical moments blacks have not had a state to protect their interests, bodies, and futures. It would also be productive to read the history of blacks in America through the lens of the perpetual refugee/prisoner of war produced by the conquest of an entire continent and then of an entire population. In this light, Agamben's pronouncement is chilling: "The camp is the space that is opened when the state of exception begins to become the rule." America is a refugee camp that has become normalized for/by some and governed for/by others. Nevertheless, the contemporary desire to relabel Katrina refugees as émigrés is more dangerously committed to maintaining a fiction of national citizenship. A refugee, Agamben argues,

> must be considered for what he [sic] is: nothing less than a limit concept that radically calls into question the fundamental categories of the nation state, from the birth nation to the man-citizen link, and thereby makes it possible to clear the way in which bare life is no long-overdue renewal of categories in service of a politics in which bare life is no longer separated and excepted, either in the state order or in the figure of human rights.[10]

In other words, "by breaking the continuity between man and citizen, nativity and nationality, . . . [the refugee puts] the originary fiction of modern sovereignty in crisis."[11]

As such, the Katrina emergency and the disappointment that most had with the U.S. government's response (it should be noted that the international community, as it was with the Asian tsunami, was quick to offer aid in this *humanitarian* crisis) is indicative of a larger set of questions concerning the possibility of engaging in contemporary progressive politics. The proliferation of contingency and the parallel emergence of a circulatory and connective global assemblage constitute the contemporary terrain of political action.

In this sense, we can also say that the emergency provides an opportunity. Agamben's pessimism that "when life and politics—originally divided, and linked together by means of the no-man's land of the state of exception that is inhabited by bare life—begin to become one, all life becomes sacred (capable of being killed without it being murder) and all politics becomes the exception"[12] is profound. However, it is precisely in such instances that traditional philosophical definitions of the political (i.e., deliberation, communication, and consensus) are replaced with a creative practice of politics.[13] As Dillon argues, "If you wish to contest biopolitics, you cannot do so simply by taking issue with distributive economy, geopolitical alliances, imperializing practices or murderous promotion of reproductively developmental life planet-wide: (as Rumsfeld stated) 'they will either succeed in changing our way of life or we will succeed in changing theirs.'"[14] In the midst of an emergency, a new politics must emerge. Setting the stakes clearly, Alain Badiou states, "The essence of politics is not the plurality of opinion. It is the prescription of a possibility in rupture with what exists."[15] Such a politics must be immanent to the practices that it contests, and as such, it is important to understand those practices, or what we are exploring as neoliberal sovereignty.

Setting aside the broader epistemic similarities between state sovereignty and neoliberal sovereignty, we find an attention to neoliberal sovereignty useful to understanding the long-term reaction to Hurricane Katrina. When the practices that constitute, condition, and cajole citizenship are no longer the sole purview of the state and instead occur within the express logic of the market, we can speak about the emergence of neoliberal sovereignty. In this sense, it is the logic of the market that decides the exception or, in other words, decides what counts and what does not. Similarly, the market sets the conditions under which the training of the good life of American citizenship is supposed to occur. Neoliberal sovereignty is becoming the norm in state practice.

In the American context, for example, it is rarely the state nowadays that decides whether a life is worth living; instead, it is a health management organization (HMO) that decides whether an individual should receive treatment and which treatment should be given. The argument that individuals of a society have the right to good health has been superseded by a new opportunity to consume an active lifestyle, part of which includes making choices about purchasing HMO coverage. Cultivating this decision-making process, however, occurs in the early depths of a disciplinary apparatus. For example, we increasingly find corporate values and case studies (i.e., figuring out the profit margins of Pepsi Co. in math class) infiltrating the curricula of the public and private school system. School, we are told, needs to be made relevant to the realities of a market-oriented society-world. Similarly, students are as likely to be encouraged to participate in charitable service because of the value it gives to their society-world as they are to be encouraged because of the value it gives to their resume or college applications. Gaining valuable experience, as such, occurs within a different register. The decision about whether you count or not, therefore, is increasingly narrated through individual consumer purchases (good insurance, quality education, nice neighborhood, and reliable friends) that often require short-term sacrifice for long-term gain.

Within this milieu, we can imagine the tension that would emerge if something beyond an individual's consumer choice, like a hurricane, sets the horizon of potential individual action and responsibility. Old arguments that are tailored toward structural conditions of classism, racism, and sexism are heightened in an event that appears to arrive from a geographic or historic elsewhere. The clash between the neoliberal individual and secured state subject, seen in the tension between naming victims refugees or émigrés explored previously, results in an important political moment. Ranciére usefully explains that a political moment occurs when the normal distribution of appearances is disrupted by a voice/vision that could not be heard/seen before. The Katrina emergency, therefore, had the effect of renewing the vigor of these arguments by revealing the disjuncture between what has been promised and what has been actualized in the American experiment. In this political space, the hurricane became a social phenomenon (federal cutbacks left the levees weak, capitalist planning left the most disadvantaged in the most flood-prone zones of New Orleans). In the space of this disjuncture, neoliberalism needed to renew its credibility beyond hypocritically pointing out that the state (after cutbacks), once again, proved itself to be ineffective. If sovereignty is to have any purchase, then it must retain its standard as the most convincing mechanism for solving problems or disagreements between universal and particular needs and demands. Therefore, if something like neoliberal sovereignty is emerging, as such, its practices will be an attempt to bridge the breach.

"A Hand Up . . . Not a Hand Out": Neoliberal Self-Governance in Magnaville

In December 2005, when much of New Orleans still lay in fetid ruins, Frank Stronach literally pitched a revival tent to launch his new settlement for Katrina survivors. An Austrian native, Stronach was the colorful founder and chairman of Magna International, Inc., an auto-parts manufacturer worth over $20 billion as well as the now bankrupt Magna Entertainment

Corporation (MEC), a racetrack and gaming company.[16] As New Orleans flooded, he and his right-hand man, former Liberal Party Canadian MP Dennis Mills, leapt into action. First, they airlifted 260 New Orleanians to one of Stronach's MEC horse training facilities in Palm Springs, Florida, and later Stronach marshaled his wealth and social connections to create a semipermanent settlement near Simmesport, Louisiana. Like other philanthropic projects undertaken in the wake of Katrina, Magnaville might be described as *benevolent neoliberalism.* Such projects obviously entail an ethical commitment to those in need but simultaneously promote market-centric approaches to disaster relief and seek to manage inequality through the inculcation of neoliberal technologies. Magnaville belongs to the same constellation of neoliberal approaches as Roland Fryer's economic incentivization experiments on elementary students through Harvard University's Education Innovation Laboratory, South Bronx native Geoffrey Canada's celebrated Harlem Children's Zone, and Father Greg Boyle's Homeboy Industries in Los Angeles, which trains and employs gang members in small-scale enterprises like tattoo removal parlors.[17] These roll-out projects take up the former social functions of the welfare state and simultaneously advance market-logics among the marginal, the excluded, and middle-class citizens alike. Such projects are the logical outgrowth of government outsourcing of social services undertaken by New Democratic and New Right politicians since Reagan. George H. W. Bush's "Thousand Points of Light" appeal to voluntarism, the Temporary Assistance to Needy Families and Hope VI programs enacted under Bill Clinton that remade social provision and public housing, respectively, and George W. Bush's faith-based and community initiatives all used state power to spur market-based remedies to inequality and social need. Stronach's Magnaville was the beneficiary of this decades-long assault on the public social safety net, and by demonstrating that private institutions could respond quicker than government in moments of crisis, the project served as a powerful ideological justification of neoliberalization. When he launched the Magnaville project in December 2005 amid much fanfare, Stronach was clear about his intentions.

After a warm-up sermon from local black Baptist minister Joshua Dara, Stronach took the microphone and preached his own gospel of hard work and money. Magnaville would "fight poverty" according to Stronach, by providing residents with the means to self-reliance. Stronach was not merely concerned with providing shelter, but over the long haul, he hoped this planned community that would also serve as a means of teaching values of autonomy and self-sufficiency. "You know the old saying," Stronach reminded the audience of new residents and underwriters, "if you give someone a fish, you feed them for a day. Teach them to fish and you feed them for a lifetime."[18] Magnaville—or "Canadaville," as it is known to the locals—was constructed on 920 acres that had formerly been used for sugarcane farming near Simmesport, Louisiana. In a planning decision driven by either pure irony or cruel humor, Magnaville was built about 100 meters from a levee, near the northernmost reaches of the Atchafalaya River flood control system. The subdivision was designed by the Toronto-based architecture firms Giffels Associates and NORR. From December 2005 to January 2011 when it was disbanded, the settlement housed 150 residents in forty-nine prefabricated homes, each containing three bedrooms and two bathrooms. To execute their vision, Stronach and Mills drew on over fifty project partners, including Habitat for Humanity, Air Canada, Indigo Books, IBM, and Sharp Electronics.

Why did Stronach choose Simmesport, a small, isolated, and economically depressed town, to create his answer to the Katrina disaster? Why did he hire a reputable architectural firm like Giffels, with its dense portfolio of signature buildings and big-ticket projects, to design something so mundane? He could have purchased the same prefab "double-wides" at any dealer in south Louisiana. With the exception of the central square with its lush grove of live oak trees, the development is unremarkable. Why would he relocate these urban dwellers to an area without any of the amenities, cultural offerings, social contacts, etc., that many had known their entire lives?

Stronach biographer Wayne Lilley contends that Magnaville provided its creator with a much-needed wave of good publicity at a moment when Stronach's lobbying efforts for legalization of slot machines in Florida and California were being met with controversy and intense political opposition.[19] Stronach's motivations, however, ran deeper than a short-run publicity stunt. Magnaville is the most mature manifestation of his standing ideological commitments to liberal capitalism. So the legend goes, Stronach arrived in Toronto with $200 and began his auto-parts empire as a humble garage operation. Although Magnaville may be his most ambitious effort at social engineering, this project and others (such as his investment in a vocational-technical school for low-income residents in Baltimore) all reflect his desire to help those in need. Given his legendary antiunion and antiregulatory posture, Magnaville might also be viewed as an extension of Stronach's will to manage class contradictions in his factories and in society more generally, through the promotion of liberal individualism and techniques of self-governance that erode traditional urban, industrial modes of solidarity and collective action.

By and large, residents really see Stronach as a godsend and Magnaville as a blessing. They often compare their situation to the more dismal prospects of other survivors. Compared to similar philanthropic projects, Stronach's more conscientious and substantial investment in rebuilding the lives of Katrina's victims may have more long-term consequences for the residents of Magnaville and for the way that philanthropists and nongovernmental organizations approach postdisaster reconstruction in decades to come.

Oprah Winfrey's Angel Lane subdivision outside Houston, Texas, provides an interesting comparison to Stronach's Magnaville. Both are residential projects undertaken by billionaires and both benefactors are equally committed to the promotion of bourgeois subjectivity, but Oprah's project is less sophisticated and conscientious. Oprah responded to the Katrina disaster by providing extensive and emotionally gripping coverage of the victims during the week after the storm made landfall. In her trademark style, she reframed the catastrophe in a manner that pruned away its political and social roots. Instead, she opted for a conventional journalistic style, which reduced the storm victims' collective plight and shared experience of alienation to an emotionally overwhelming procession of disembodied human-interest stories, lost pets, bureaucratic snarls, and tearful reunions, ad nauseam. Surely, this approach riveted millions of viewers to her daily television program and elicited sympathy from onlookers. True to form, however, this framing was typical of the Oprah brand, which approaches most personal and social challenges of postindustrial life as curable through New Age self-help and philanthropic largesse.[20]

In the self-serving fashion that is her hallmark, Oprah unveiled her post-Katrina relief project on national television. She assembled a group of disaster survivors who were under the impression that they were interviewing for a finite set of Habitat for Humanity homes, only to be treated to a "big reveal," where she announced that they would all become neighbors in the Angel Lane subdivision. Lowe's Home Improvement provided toolboxes to the ecstatic and sobbing families. Sixty-five people were chosen to live in the subdivision. Each household was expected to earn $1500 per month. If the homeowners missed three mortgage payments, they would lose their homes. As well, all residents were expected to be active participants in the homeowners' association.

Little has been published about the fate of Angel Lane residents since its establishment. A February 2009 news story in the *Houston Chronicle* reported that Angel Lane was becoming overrun by crime and that some residents felt more vulnerable and fearful than they did in New Orleans. Despite her cultish popularity, Oprah's efforts at social engineering have not been successful as of late. Angel Lane has apparently suffered the same fate as the Leadership Academy for Girls that Oprah established in South Africa, which was plagued by sexual abuse scandals. In comparison to Oprah's poorly planned Angel Lane development, Magnaville featured much more extensive capital investment and a conscientious strategy for creating new lives for its residents.

Stronach's project should be understood within the context of the new capitalist culture radically reshaping work, life, and leisure across the planet. In many respects, his approach to the social trauma and standing poverty of Katrina survivors was a civil society manifestation of his method of handling labor conflicts in his Magna factories. His approach to managing class contradictions in both instances is to displace conflicts through institutions that preempt working class solidarity and, instead, promote modes of consciousness and behavior that are amenable to his immediate interests and those of the investor class more generally. Like "quality circles," worker discussion groups, and other forms of participatory management, the Magna model "empowers" workers in ways that do not threaten the power of management. Wayne Lewchuk and Don Wells have studied the managerial style used by Stronach's Magna International plants, and they concluded that within the Magna model of industrial relations, redistributive conflicts are recast as opportunities for mutual gains through profit sharing.[21] In a similar vein, the Magnaville settlement depoliticizes the drama of disaster and displacement and the progressively redistributive claims that might arise through public-spirited discussion and activism. Stronach scores points as a corporate giant who cares for the least of these. His plan entailed a more extensive effort to mold displaced New Orleanians into citizens whose labors and aspirations were commensurate with market logics.

Stronach's project reflects all the conventional thinking about how to best "ameliorate" poverty. His plan to relocate black urban dwellers to a pastoral setting was guided by assumptions about "deconcentrating poverty" that were forcefully articulated in the aftermath of the disaster. A derivative of underclass discourse, this argument suggests that housing policy efforts targeting the poor should be designed to break up zones of poverty and create mixed-income neighborhoods, with the underlying logic being that class contact would end the social isolation experienced by the poor and provide them with middle-class modeling and guidance in behavioral modification. Even as the on-the-ground reporting of the Katrina disaster was still difficult and patchy, right-wing commentators began to explain the sources of the tragedy in the language of the underclass myth. The University of Maryland's Douglas Besharov and University of California–Berkeley professor and Manhattan Institute Fellow John McWhorter both asserted that those who died or were left stranded on rooftops were not the victims of a natural disaster, institutional racism, or state divestment but rather the victims of a culture of welfare dependency, especially acute in New Orleans, that discouraged their capacity to act independently even in times of extreme duress. [22]

Fueled by the mass-mediated images of destitution and wild urban legends, right-wing arguments about poverty maintained their preflood hegemony and, in some corners, gained new converts. *New York Times* columnist David Brooks pointed out the "silver lining" of this disaster. In a September 8, 2005, opinion piece, Brooks wrote that that hurricane "has given us an amazing chance to do something serious about urban poverty."[23] For Brooks and many others, the dispersion of evacuees across the United States provided an opportunity to "break up zones of concentrated poverty" and to test hypotheses about cultural integration that have been in circulation among social scientist and policy makers for decades. Brooks argues, "The only chance we have to break up the cycle of poverty is to integrate people who lack middle class skills into neighborhoods with people who possess these skills and who insist on certain standards of behavior."[24] Liberals took up this rhetoric as well.

The Urban Sociology Section of the American Sociological Association circulated a petition titled, "Moving to Opportunity in the Wake of Hurricane Katrina." Led by William Julius Wilson and Xavier Briggs, the petitioners echoed Brooks's language as they described the hurricane as an "historic opportunity to lift thousands of the nations' most vulnerable families out of ghetto poverty and the associated physical and social risks . . . so vividly illustrated in recent weeks."[25] The petition goes on to reference a "growing body of scientific research" that demonstrates that "moving to lower poverty, lower risk neighborhoods and school districts can have significant positive effects on the well-being and economic opportunity of low-income children and their families." The petitioners claim that they "do not seek to depopulate the city [of New Orleans] or its historically black communities," but the overall thrust of the petition tends to override this disclaimer. The petition makes no mention of the grassroots efforts that were being waged by public housing tenants and advocates in New Orleans and along the Gulf Coast.

Although the deconcentration argument has been taken up by conservatives and New Democrats as a pretext for the razing of public housing stock, such arguments have their origins in mid-twentieth-century criticisms of the scalar, social, and design problems of U.S. housing for the poor. When large cities like Chicago erected massive tower blocks during the 1950s, left liberals and radicals were quick to scrutinize the underlying regulatory posture, racially segregative logic, and other problems associated with warehousing the urban minority poor in large-scale public housing tracts.[26] Contemporary adoptions of the deconcentration argument, however, are most often alloyed with revanchist motives. In a searing critique of the petition circulated by Briggs and Wilson, Adolph Reed Jr. and Stephen Steinberg argue that the deconcentration rhetoric advances an ulterior agenda that benefits local developers more than the poor. They note that the "Moving to Opportunity" strategy "is not part of a comprehensive policy to attack poverty and racism: to rid the United States of impoverished ghettos that pockmark the national landscape. Rather the policy is enacted in places where poor blacks occupy valuable real estate."[27] The "Moving to Opportunity" discourse, like most discussions of poverty since the Great Society era, tends to portray the ghetto as an aberration within liberal democratic society, rather than a constituent element of capitalist social organization. The ghetto is not represented as a community that can be rebuilt, transformed, or renewed but rather as a zone that must be razed, escaped, avoided, or policed. In effect, this discourse reproduces the commonsensical notion that the black urban poor are the objects of elite overtures and benevolence rather than independent agents possessing political will. Never do the poor themselves enter into these narratives as subjects in history.

What is especially insidious about this broader rhetoric of creating opportunity through dispersion, especially when applied to Magnaville, is that many of its residents were not poor before the flood. Carl Tipton, a retired school teacher and former professional football player, and his wife, Gwen, were among the first residents. In much post-Katrina public discourse, the terms "poor," "black," "flood victim," "evacuee," and "refugee" are used interchangeably and strung together in ways that discourage more accurate, nuanced analysis of the political-economy of this particular disaster and sideline any effective way of discerning comparative harm and claims to redress.

Unlike Brad Pitt's Make It Right Foundation, which aims to rebuild 150 sustainable homes for residents of the lower Ninth Ward, projects like Magnaville, Oprah's Angel Lane, and the "adoption" of Katrina victims by local churches all construe the relocation of New Orleanians from the city to suburban and rural locations as unqualified progress. Obviously, some Magnaville residents appreciated the calm, quiet nights of rural South Louisiana. One promotional video featured footage of kids at play and suggests that, unlike their past lives in crime-ridden New Orleans, families can allow their children to play unattended. No gunshots, no drama, no worries. Some residents welcome the clean air and open space of the pastoral setting, but others express nostalgia for New Orleans, and after a stint in Magnaville, some returned to the city, citing the difficulty transitioning to the slower-paced lifestyle, finding employment, and adjusting without the kinship networks and rich social bonds that made New Orleans home. Their exodus reveals the patent limitations of the Magnaville settlement.

Beyond its closeness to nature and "peace and quiet," Magnaville, as a housing development, was deeply antiurban and not guided by the kinds of best practices that might create a rich social life for its residents. Magnaville was designed to transform them from urban dwellers into modern-day yeomen. Gone were the grid street network, sidewalks, public transit, and other amenities Magnaville's residents were accustomed to in New Orleans. These streets were not made for walking, and furthermore, there was nowhere to walk to. Magnaville was isolated from Simmesport's existing residential neighborhoods, designed to be a relatively self-contained community like other suburban developments and small-town trailer parks, with a playground, basketball courts, and a baseball diamond. The underlying message here is that cities, the loci of social innovation, creativity, and civilization for millennia, are no longer necessary or desirable. This latter-day North American disdain for all things urban takes physical form in Magnaville.

The subdivision eschews the most common global, urban form of cohabitation, the apartment building, in favor of the single-family, detached home. Even Brad Pitt's Make It Right project incorporates some more flexible dwellings that accommodate a granny flat or small apartment at the rear, which can offer some autonomy to an adult member of a blended family or serve as a source of income for the principal tenant. Architecturally, Magnaville falls somewhere between the middle-twentieth-century Levittowns constructed in Long Island and Pennsylvania and a FEMA trailer park. It fuses the suburban biases and industrial monotony of the former with the transitory aesthetics and conservative politics of the latter. The site selection, land use practices, and exclusive use of single-family homes reassert postwar suburban housing as normative. The choice of "double-wides" over newly constructed homes or renovated ones also embodies the same the neoliberal logic that guided the creation of workfare and the continued use of FEMA trailers when more durable dwellings, like Katrina Cottages, could be produced for less cost. The underlying message here, written in vinyl siding and pressure-treated lumber, is that too much charity, especially when guaranteed by the state, will undermine the self-reliance and motivation of the poor. The sensory landscape of Magnaville communicates that its residents should be grateful, but they should not be contented with their new surroundings. They should aspire to something more.

Stronach's vision was to create a community of self-sustaining individuals. Residents were provided rent for the first five years, and during that time period, each would be expected to contribute to the community through various forms of unpaid service. Stronach and his collaborators hoped to create an organic farm manned by residents that would supply fresh produce to Whole Foods supermarket. They enlisted Calvin Walker, a professor of animal science at Southern University–Baton Rouge, and Sustainable Innovations, Inc. in the hopes of creating Louisiana's first organic poultry and pork operation and developing future plans for meat processing and beef production.

Some critics took issue with the idea of work requirements for residents, charging that over the benevolent aspects of Stronach's largesse this proposed wedding of industrial farming and black labor was eerily similar to the system of debt peonage whose ghosts still haunt the memories of blacks throughout the lower Mississippi Delta. Walker rebuffed these claims that Magnaville's work requirements were a Jim Crow throwback, saying, "Anyone who makes jokes about slavery is just ignorant."[28] It is not surprising that he would defend Magnaville in this way, given his own immediate interests in the project's success as a researcher and beneficiary of consulting contracts. As a matter of historical interpretation, however, Walker is correct. Magnaville is neither the Parchman Farm nor the former sugar plantation that once stood there. Long gone are the most brutal forms of vigilante violence and legal apartheid that subordinated black peasants to the interests of the Southern planter class for a century from the fall of Reconstruction to the civil rights reforms of the Johnson administration. As a rhetorical strategy, reference to sharecropping can be powerful, but as historical analysis, it is not. The analogy calls attention to the implicit power dynamics in the project but fails to clarify the nature of these arrangements.

In a video-recorded statement for Magnaville's first anniversary, former Governor Kathleen Babineaux Blanco lauded Stronach and Magnaville for giving evacuees a hand up rather than a hand out. The strategy here is one of rehabilitation. How might lower-income city dwellers reach their fullest market potential? The Magnaville project's work prescriptions, pastoral setting, and attempts to create a profitable organic farm were intended to cultivate an entrepreneurial spirit — a new way of life that may offer some measure of economic independence and self-sufficiency to the residents.

Conclusion

The Magnaville project officially ended on Friday, January 7, 2011, as the last residents were nudged off the property. Technically, they were given the option of remaining in their homes at the cost of $500 per month (plus, a $500 deposit), but such a rental rate was hardly feasible given that so many had failed to find consistent work in the Simmesport area. One month before Magnaville ended its rent-free phase, the Chicago Housing Authority closed the last remaining building in the notorious Cabrini-Green public housing complex in the city's gentrified Near North Side. The discontinuation of both public housing and Stronach's exercise in disaster relief is predicated on the same neoliberal model of social engineering. Stronach's five-year experiment, like the public housing reforms and workfare policies that began during the Clinton years, was predicated on the view that social provision should not be open-ended if it is to spur independence among the poor. The literal success of the Magnaville project—whether Stronach and Mills actually created new yeomen citizens out of New Orleans expatriates—may be less significant than the ideological work that this project has already accomplished. The Magnaville launch provided Stronach with good publicity, but more substantially, the fulsome praise of the project by government officials, flood victims, and reporters legitimated the neoliberal claim that private institutions and philanthropy are better suited to undertake social redress than the state.

Projects like Magnaville and Angel Lane are forms of benevolent neoliberalism that attempt to manage inequality and social misery by advancing market logics. These projects are benevolent in their immediate effects, but they bear an ideological dimension that is socially pernicious. Charter schools, like Chicago's Urban Prep Academy for African American boys, are cherished by local communities for producing results—safer learning environments, higher graduation rates, increased numbers of college-bound students, and a renewed sense of possibility among students, teachers, and the wider community.[29] Such schools, which wed public funding and private management, however, are limited in scope and social impact, and yet, they are often deployed as a weapon to further erode universal, public education in favor of increased privatization. As Adrienne Dixson's contribution to this volume illustrates in the case of New Orleans schools after Katrina, charterization often sacrifices access, deliberation and transparency, and the collective-bargaining rights of teachers and staff in the interest of delivering a better "product" and "customer service." Such neoliberal roll-out projects are further legitimated at the level of everyday life, as the livelihoods and economic security of various beneficiaries—the poor, the unemployed, low-wage workers, and disaster victims but also middle-class researchers, students, politicians, grantees, etc.—are hitched to private funding streams and market logics as the state's role in social service delivery fades from view. The philanthropy of entertainers such as Stronach, Céline Dion, Oprah Winfrey, and Sean Penn and that of nongovernmental organizations, such as Habitat for Humanity, Phoenix of New Orleans, and dozens of others, is made all the more valuable in the context of government divestiture in public amenities. The political rhetoric of these organizations ranges from left liberal criticism of Bush administration failure to overt endorsements of privatization. Within the emergent phenomenon of benevolent neoliberalization, stalwart capitalists, disenchanted liberals, and millennial do-gooders converge to advance a project of empowerment through individual self-help.

Herein lies a conundrum for the post-Seattle left: How does one organize against forms of privatization engaged in "good works," activities that feel good or right for those who participate? How does one challenge philanthropic projects that provide relief, shelter, and education in lieu of public alternatives? How do we politicize a cherished concept like citizenship if it now functions to reproduce the very problems that it used to solve? More participation, individual action, and self-responsibility are used to dismantle the collective promises that they (with limits) were able to achieve. Much of New Orleans is being remade, therefore, not solely by what Naomi Klein terms *disaster capitalism* (e.g., the clandestine handiwork of Pinochet, the Chicago School, Halliburton, etc.) but by *do-good capitalism* (e.g., the heavily publicized, Facebooked and Twittered labors of celebrity socialites, church groups, and mercurial student volunteers) that is more difficult to politicize and contest. The popular mode of left criticism, however, habitually misses the more subtle but no less consequential aspects of neoliberal governmentality that advances market-logic at the level of everyday life. Such pressure often unwittingly has the effect of furthering neoliberalism's advance. Wal-Mart's cartoonish smiley face and Bush's bewildered one are easy targets, but the new convivial face of capitalism is a more formidable adversary.

Notes

1. Quoted in Robert E. Pierre and Paul Farhi, "'Refugee': A Word of Trouble," *Washington Post*, September 7, 2005, C1.

2. Michelle Norris, "Katrina Survivors Contemplate Whether to Go Home," *All Things Considered*, September 7, 2005, online transcript, http://www.npr.org/templates/story/story.php?storyId=4836564 (accessed March 16, 2010).

3. Peter Grier, "The Great Katrina Migration," *Christian Science Monitor*, September 12, 2005, http://www.csmonitor.com/2005/0912/p01s01-ussc.html (accessed January 25, 2010).

4. Cedric Johnson, *Revolutionaries to Race Leaders: Black Power and the Making of African American Politics* (Minneapolis: University of Minnesota, 2007); Vijay Prashad, *The Darker Nations: A People's History of the Third World* (New York: New Press, 2007); and Michael O. West, William G. Martin, and Fanon Che Wilkins, eds., *From Toussaint to Tupac: The Black International Since the Age of Revolution* (Chapel Hill: University of North Carolina Press, 2007).

5. Derrick Bell, *Silent Covenants: Brown v. Board of Education and the Unfulfilled Hopes for Racial Reform* (Oxford: Oxford University, 2004).

6. "Calling Katrina Survivors 'Refugees' Stirs Debate," *Associated Press*, September 7, 2005, www.msnbc.com (accessed January 25, 2010).

7. "Calling Katrina Survivors"; William Safire, "Katrina Words," *New York Times*, September 18, 2005.

8. Jason Barker, "Translator's Introduction," in Alain Badiou, *Metapolitics*, trans. Jason Barker (New York: Verso, 2005), xvi.

9. Michael Dillon, "Governing Terror: The State of Emergency of Biopolitical Emergence," *International Political Sociology* 1, no. 1 (2007): 15.

10. Giorgio Agamben, *Homo Sacer: Sovereign Power and Bare Life*, trans. Daniel Heller-Roazen (Stanford: Stanford University Press, 1998), 131.

11. Ibid., 131.

12. Ibid., 148.

13. Here we are siding with Alain Badiou's critique of political philosophy; see Alain Badiou, *Metapolitics*, trans. Jason Barker (New York: Verso, 2005).

14. Dillon, "Governing Terror," 20.

15. Badiou, *Metapolitics*, 24.

16. Thomas Watson, a senior writer at *Canadian Business*, reported on the five-year anniversary of the Magnaville settlement. He captured the wide-ranging entrepreneurial and personal pursuits and voracious ambition of Magnaville's benefactor: "As corporate Canada's self-styled philosopher king, Stronach has always been a larger-than-life entrepreneur that some people just can't help kicking around. Even a few Magna loyalists joke that the boss is a 'visionary with an attention-span disorder.' When not focused on expanding his $20-plus-billion autoparts conglomerate or breeding one of the world's largest stables of thoroughbreds, Stronach has tried his hand at a wide range of ventures. Over the years, he has opened a disco, run a restaurant, published an alternative business magazine, launched an energy drink, tried building a massive amusement park in Vienna, proposed an airline for the rich, tried transforming prestigious racetracks into entertainment destinations for the masses, and attempted to beat Magna's car-making customers at their own game. The man's nonbusiness activities range from managing the Austrian soccer league to running for a seat in Ottawa (where he planned to push for radical parliamentary reforms)." See Thomas Watson, "Magnaville's Unfinished Dream," *Canadian Business*,

October 11, 2010, http://www.canadianbusiness.com/managing/strategy/article.
jsp?content=20101011_10023_10023 (accessed October 15, 2010).

17. Paul Tough, *Whatever It Takes: Geoffrey Canada's Quest to Change Harlem and America* (New York: Houghton Mifflin, 2008); Geoffrey Canada, *Fist Stick Gun Knife: A Personal History of Violence in America* (New York: Beacon Press, 1995); and Greg Boyle, *Tattoos on the Heart: The Power of Boundless Compassion* (New York: Free Press, 2010).

18. Thomas Watson, "Stronach's Louisiana Purchase," *Canadian Business,* January 16–29, 2006, 37; and Amber Hildebrandt, "The End of 'Canadaville'" *CBC News,* August 31, 2010, http://www.cbc.ca/world/story/2010/08/30/f-canadaville-magnaville-stronach.html (accessed August 31, 2010).

19. Wayne Lilley, *Magna Cum Laude: How Frank Stronach Became Canada's Best Paid Man* (Toronto: Douglas Gibson Books, 2008).

20. Jane M. Shattuc, *The Talking Cure: TV Talk Shows and Women* (New York: Routledge Press, 1997).

21. Wayne Lewchuk and Don Wells, "When Corporations Substitute for Adversarial Unions: Labour Markets and Human Resource Management at Magna," *Relations Indutrielles/Industrial Relations* 61, no. 4 (2005): 639–65; Luc Boltanski and Eve Chiapello, *The New Spirit of Capitalism* (London and New York: Verso, 2007); and Peter Fleming, *Authenticity and the Cultural Politics of Work: New Forms of Informal Control* (Oxford: Oxford University, 2009).

22. See "Race, Poverty, and Katrina," *Talk of the Nation,* National Public Radio, September 22, 2005. Online transcript, http://www.npr.org/templates/transcript/transcript.php?storyId=4859257 (accessed January 5, 2008).

23. David Brooks, "Katrina's Silver Lining," *New York Times,* September 5, 2005.

24. Ibid.

25. New Vision Institute, "Moving to Opportunity in the Wake of Hurricane Katrina," September 15, 2005, http://www.newvisioninstitute.org/Moving OppotunityScholarsPetition.pdf (accessed January 8, 2008); See also Xavier de Souza Briggs, Susan J. Popkin, and John Goering, *Moving to Opportunity: The Story of an American Experiment to Fight Ghetto Poverty* (Oxford and New York: Oxford University Press, 2010); David Imbroscio, "'United and Actuated by Some Common Impulse of Passion': Challenging the Dispersal Consensus in American Policy Research," *Journal of Urban Affairs* 30, no. 2 (2008): 111–30; Stephen Steinberg, "The Myth of Concentrated Poverty," in Chester Hartman and Gregory D. Squires, eds. *The Integration Debate: Competing Futures for American Cities* (New York: Routledge, 2010), 213–27.

26. Jane Jacobs offers one such critique of the socially isolating character of public housing design in mid-twentieth century America. She writes: "One of the unsuitable ideas behind projects is the very notion that they *are* projects,

abstracted out of the ordinary city and set apart. To think of salvaging or improving projects, *as projects*, is to repeat this root mistake. The aim should be to get that
project, that patch upon the city rewoven back into the fabric—and in the process
of doing so, strengthen the surrounding fabric too" [emphasis original]; Jane
Jacobs, *The Death and Life of Great American Cities* (New York: Random House,
1993), 511; see also Arnold Hirsch, *Making the Second Ghetto: Race and Housing
in Chicago, 1940-1960* (Chicago: University of Chicago, 1998 [1983]); and Sudhir
Venkatesh, *American Project: The Rise and Fall of Modern Ghetto* (Cambridge,
Mass.: Harvard University Press, 2000).

27. Adolph Reed and Stephen Steinberg, "Liberal Bad Faith in the Wake
of Hurricane Katrina," *Black Commentator,* May 4, 2006, http://www.
blackcommentator.com/182/182_cover_liberals_katrina_pf.html (accessed
June 20, 2006).

28. Watson, "Louisiana Purchase," 40.

29. Duaa Eldeib, "Every Urban Prep Senior Is College Bound," *Chicago Tribune,*
March 5, 2010.

· II ·

Urbanity

CHAPTER 4

Mega-Events, the Superdome, and the Return of the Repressed in New Orleans

Paul A. Passavant

HURRICANE KATRINA PUTS BEFORE US once more the question of the state and neoliberalism.[1] The contemporary state is represented in contradictory ways. The neoliberal state is represented as being small and weak due to a preference for market-based solutions to problems and a propensity to privatize its functions. Alternatively, the state is described as so strong that its sovereign decisions create unprivileged, disposable human life contained within a contemporary equivalent to the concentration camp. As a marker of contemporary confusion, some scholars hold both views. In fact, both conceptions of the state have been used to understand Hurricane Katrina's immediate aftermath. Perhaps we can learn something about the distinctive characteristics of the neoliberal state if we examine Hurricane Katrina as a weeklong mega-event that showcased New Orleans as does the Super Bowl. Let's consider how New Orleans handled the mega-event of Hurricane Katrina in light of how it handles mega-events like the Super Bowl.

As New Orleans's prior handling of the Super Bowl demonstrates, the neoliberal state should not be understood as weak simply because it governs through privatization or consumption. Through privatization, the state can extend its reach and intensify its effects for those governed within particular places. Because the state governs through privatization and market-based mentalities, a binary logic of sovereign decisions creating privileged inclusion and disposable exclusion does not capture what is unique to contemporary conditions. Without dismissing tendencies toward exclusion and disposability—indeed, I will dwell on some of these here—the neoliberal state governs through differentiated and hierarchized distributions or zones. Finally, the contemporary state is invested not only in technologies of consumption like consumer databases that it mines for security purposes but also in spaces of consumption.[2] These spaces of consumption include the development of entertainment zones or the creation of mega-events, such as the Democrat or Republican Party conventions, and major sporting events like the Super Bowl, as a way to market a place in the interurban competition for visitor dollars. The development and promotion of entertainment zones and mega-events allow us to pose better questions: rather than asking whether the neoliberal state is weak or strong, it lets us grasp how the neoliberal state acts, and what it cares to do (or not to do).

We might say, then, that the neoliberal state governs, in part, although the mentality of the consumer-criminal double. This consumer-criminal double influences the valid objectives of governance and the institutional infrastructure in which our lives take place. This infrastructure governs through a drive for containment by zoning bodies to spaces or by criminalizing bodies out of place—regardless of whether we are speaking of consumerism or criminalization. Rather than operating as a zero-sum binary, the logic of the consumer-criminal double is one of distributed differences like market niches. Nor are consumerism and criminalization mutually exterior categories. Fear of crime influences the design of spaces dedicated to consumption while security services are thoroughly marketized and commodified.[3]

Hurricane Katrina highlights certain neoliberal aspects of "the state" in New Orleans, Louisiana. First, and contrary to those who contend that the neoliberal state is weak, I indicate how the contemporary neoliberal, post-Fordist landscape was produced, significantly, through state practices. Second, the way that many aspects of the built environment in New Orleans functioned during the storm and its immediate aftermath shows how neoliberal development has created or intensified zoned, segregated spaces that are containable and defensible. I will focus, third, upon the Superdome as dramatically manifesting the tendencies of neoliberal, post-Fordist state practices. The Superdome is an institution of consumer entertainment created by the state where events are staged not only for the viewing pleasure of the audience but also to market New Orleans's capacity both to stage such events and to market New Orleans as a place for potential visitors or tourists. Staging such spectacles, however, is premised upon an ability to control the environment so that their production will have occurred without disturbance.[4] In other words, being an institution of control is simply the flip side of being an institution for consumer entertainment. This is illustrated vividly by how easily the Superdome "flipped" from an institution of consumer entertainment where mega-events such as the Bayou Classic, the Sugar Bowl, and the Super Bowl have been hosted to becoming the functional equivalent of a prison for those who sought refuge in it during the weeklong mega-event constituting Katrina's first chapter. Hurricane Katrina's immediate aftermath, then, does not show that the neoliberal state is incapable of governing. Rather, it manifests *how* we are governed under contemporary conditions.

The Neoliberal State

Two associated developments during the last quarter of the twentieth century have deeply influenced the context and conduct of urban governance—the decline of Fordism and the rise of post-Fordism, on the one hand, and the rise of neoliberalism, on the other. Fordism refers to mass production, mass consumption, a social welfare state, and a steadily improving aggregate national political economy valorizing production. Post-Fordism refers to the loss of manufacturing in North American cities, economies demanding flexible labor and just-in-time production for segmented market niches, and the valorization of consumption. Neoliberalism is closely associated with post-Fordism. Neoliberalism privileges privatization, market-based logics, and is antagonistic toward the appearance of "state intervention" in markets or state responsibility in the areas of social welfare and public health. Such logics justify slashing the welfare state, which, in turn, forces labor to accept a more "flexible" position.[5]

For many, the neoliberal state should be understood as weak and small due to privatization, in contrast to the social welfare state of the mid-twentieth century. According to Nikolas Rose, the securitization of identity and extensive surveillance accompanying the "mobilization of the consumer" are "not best understood in terms of a relentless augmentation of the powers of a centralizing, controlling, and regulating state."[6] Or, as Michael Hardt and Antonio Negri declare: "the state has been defeated and corporations now rule the earth!"[7] Likewise, a number of studies focusing on urban public space find such public space to be disappearing due to privatization and an increased private control over such "zones of privilege," through, for instance, the use of "a private police force."[8] In other words, privatization is opposed to state power as its limit or antagonist.

The weak state approach informs both journalistic and more scholarly efforts to grasp the disaster of Hurricane Katrina in New Orleans. Writing for the online journal *Alternet*, Joshua Holland concludes that the disaster in New Orleans illustrates the problem not of "too much government, but too little, too late."[9] Peter Feng, writing in another online journal, *Counterpunch*, sounds similar themes when he describes a tradeoff between corporate governance and state governance, invoking the aspirations of "corporatists" like Grover Norquist who want to shrink government to the point where it can be drowned in a bathtub.[10] In a more scholarly vein, Henry Giroux argues that Katrina displayed the flaws of hollowing out the state through "privatization schemes," rendering the neoliberal state an "incompetent, impotent bystander."[11] The neoliberal state is a weak state, and Hurricane Katrina demonstrates its lack of capacity.

For others, the state is better understood in accordance with the work of philosopher Giorgio Agamben. Agamben conceptualizes the state in the image of an all-powerful, unitary sovereign. This sovereign acts by declaring ever more frequent states of exception or states of emergency. Such states of emergency abandon humans to the lawless will of those who will arbitrarily decide their fate, much like those condemned to the Nazi death camps.[12] Despite his use of the weak, neoliberal state paradigm to describe the disaster of Hurricane Katrina, even Giroux cannot resist the appeal of Agamben as an alternative, if contradictory, explanation of Katrina's aftermath. The camp, according to Giroux, has become the "key institution and social model of the new millennium," serving as a dumping ground for lives not useful for consumer capitalism, hence rendered "disposable." Therefore, "Agamben's theory of biopolitics rightly alerts us to the dangers of a government in which the state of emergency becomes the fundamental structure of control over populations."[13] Although Giroux believes that we must attend to the specifics whereby some lives are made more valuable (or more disposable) than others, he otherwise finds Agamben's model of sovereignty and states of exception or emergency to be a useful prism through which to understand the human costs of Hurricane Katrina.

Neither the pole of a neoliberal state in "retreat" and "impotent" nor that of an all-powerful sovereign declaring ever more frequent states of emergency captures *how* the neoliberal state governs. More nuanced approaches, though, have resulted from studies of "actually existing neoliberalism."[14] Certain works in the fields of international relations, comparative politics, geography, urban studies, and criminology find neoliberalism to be more complex than a simple weakening of the state. Urban geographers Jamie Peck and Adam Tickell argue that neoliberalism is a "regulatory 'project' or 'regime'" that is not simply anti-statist. More specifically, neoliberalism is better understood as the "*destruction* and *discreditation* of Keynesian-welfarist and social-collectivist institutions," and a process of "*construct*[ing] and *consolidat*[ing] . . . neoliberalized state forms, modes of governance, and regulatory relations." It is a project of "active state-building."[15]

How does the neoliberal state govern? To begin, we should note that privatization does not indicate a retreat or impotence of the state. Rather, as the criminologist David Garland contends, "state agencies activate action by non-state organizations and actors." The state seeks to "enlist[ ] the 'governmental' powers of private actors, shaping them to the ends of crime control."[16] In the way that historian Michel Foucault discusses "governmentality" as the strategy of structuring the field of action of others, we can say that the neoliberal state uses privatization to "govern at a distance."[17] By governing through privatization, the neoliberal state seeks to mobilize private actors to state purposes, re-presenting state power over space and time.[18] Neoliberalism is not a weakening of state power; it is a distinctive manner of exercising state power.[19]

Urban Fiscal Crisis, the State, and Neoliberalism's Landscape

In the United States, cities began to suffer from deindustrialization and depopulation shortly after World War II. Rather than being caused by an abstract market logic, state actions during the middle of the twentieth century helped to produce a landscape of economic inequality and racial segregation that crystallized as the "urban fiscal crisis."[20] As World War II came to a close, most white collar jobs, in addition to manufacturing jobs, were located in cities. The federal policy to build an extensive interstate highway system, however, hurt urban economies. Although some may have thought that highways would help cities by funneling people to downtowns, highways meant that white collar workers could keep jobs located in the city but move to the suburbs, diminishing the property tax base of cities used for infrastructural upkeep. Additionally, urban routes were located in "blighted areas," leading to the removal of black homes and communities.[21]

Quickly, cities became poorer and blacker, while "suburbia" grew in the United States, becoming in the process wealthier and whiter than urban areas. As historian Lizabeth Cohen writes, between "1947 and 1953, the sub-urban population increased by 43 percent." Although it represented 19 percent of the U.S. population, suburban residents "spent 29 percent of its income."[22] Department stores responded by opening suburban branches that would soon outsell the downtown flagship and account for "nearly 78 percent of all department store business."[23] "Limited access highways," according to urban planner Robert Beauregard, "created high value intersections throughout the suburban periphery, and these locations became ideal sites for regional shopping malls."[24] The growth in the U.S. retail economy, then, was signifi-cant job growth that occurred in suburbs. Not only did the location of shop-ping malls provide shoppers and business owners an insulating distance from blacks and urban poverty, but by being built on private property mainly accessible by automobile, these shopping malls could become environments tightly controlled for the promotion of consumption and increasingly free from disruption by labor unions, which could picket department stores when they were located in a city's central business district.[25]

Not only was suburbia increasingly segregated economically speak-ing after World War II, it was racially differentiated as well. This outcome was due to the use of race in restrictive covenants between the seller of a property and the buyer, and the institutionalization of racial consider-ations in numerous federal programs to assist home buying or to rate the risk of a neighborhood for lending. When private lenders utilized federal government residential security maps, the effects of the latter's use of race was multiplied. These institutions pervasively influenced the construc-tion of American suburbia.[26]

State policies such as the 1956 Highway Act, the Supreme Court's 1976 about-face refusal to enforce its public forum doctrine in the case of shopping malls hurting political protestors and union organizers, and the institutionalized use of racially restrictive covenants, then, have deeply influenced the U.S. landscape. They facilitated the economic demise of American cities, enabled the creation of highly controlled and policed suburban "public spaces," and promoted the exclusion of the poor and nonwhites from suburbia. As retail anthropologist Paco Underhill puts it, the suburban shopping mall is a "monument to the moment when Americans turned their back on the city."[27]

After 1978, the federal government turned its back on cities as well. During the Reagan and Bush years of 1981 to 1992, "federal funding of urban programs dropped 68 percent," and direct aid to localities was replaced by block grants administered through state governments.[28] Nor did aid from state budgets substitute for the loss of federal money—indeed, the 1978 passage of Proposition 13 in California and the 1982 passage of Proposition 2½ in Massachusetts signaled that state governments would also turn their backs on cities.[29] For those remaining in cities, poverty increased and became more concentrated. As socioeconomic inequalities grew, cities became increasingly polarized. Or, in the words of one author referring to New York City, it "became a different place."[30]

The value of the suburban shopping mall was in its very difference from "the city," as a place of cleanliness, control free from disruption, and, most important, free from crime.[31] The suburban shopping mall represented the negation of the city. Yet from the very moment of the suburban shopping mall's emergence that would come to doom the city, it was already being proposed as the city's salvation. Salvation through negation. As early as 1955, the father of the shopping mall in the United States, Victor Gruen, proposed that the shopping mall could be the "salvation of downtown."[32] By 1962, Gruen had established the first downtown enclosed urban shopping mall—Midtown in Rochester, New York.[33] Gruen was a pioneer, but even the most adventuresome or successful developers were reticent to follow his lead. In 1973, the largest shopping center developer in the United States, Edward DeBartolo, stated that he would not want to invest "a penny" in a shopping center located downtown because people stay away from the downtown due to "danger." Without "amazing subsidies," his advice was to stay in the suburbs.[34]

By the end of the 1970s and into the 1980s, however, mall developers turned to cities and cities turned to mall developers. On the one hand, in the 1970s, after an incredible ninety malls were built between 1971 and 1976 by the most significant shopping mall developers in the United States, malls began to saturate suburbia and their growth rate there slowed.[35] On the other hand, cities were forced to become more "entrepreneurial" to address the loss of the middle class, deindustrialization, and severe reductions in federal aid.[36] To respond, cities began thinking about ways to raise revenue from those who did not live in the city but who might be persuaded to visit the city—to shop or as a tourist, for example.

To this end, urban redevelopment projects oriented city services to "visitors," as cities entered an increasingly global interurban competition for tourist dollars. This has entailed constructing what urban scholar John Hannigan describes as urban entertainment destinations—themed venues, themed restaurants, themed places, museums, aquariums, IMAX theatres, arenas, sports stadia, and, of course, shopping.[37] James Rouse's redesign of Boston's Faneuil Marketplace, which reopened August 26, 1976, was an early exemplar of the emerging trend for downtown redevelopment. Beginning in the 1970s and quickening in the 1980s, cities became the locus for new shopping malls—cities were co-investors in three of every four shopping mall projects between 1970 and 1985. These projects included Baltimore's Harbor Place and New York City's South St. Seaport, both of which are Rouse-developed "festival marketplaces."[38]

In the process of constructing and aggressively marketing this "fantasy city," through hosting and promoting mega-events, for example, cities also constructed "tourist enclaves" or a "tourist bubble"—a zone sanitized of urban disorder, with security, and, more important, signs of security or an aesthetics of security, to make visitors feel safe.[39] Not only did crime need to be prevented in order to lure the middle class back to the city as tourists or shoppers, but the *perception* of danger or disorder needed to be controlled.[40] The symptoms of the urban crisis needed to be rendered invisible within the "analogous" or "fantasy" city produced for visitors.[41] Therefore, the emerging police practices coinciding with post-Fordist urban redevelopment strategies were "zero-tolerance" or "quality of life" (QOL) policies that targeted not only actual crime but also any signs of disorder or poverty to signal to shoppers and tourists that they were secure and in a controlled setting.

The city, which had achieved a reputation as "dangerous," needed to become rebranded as "fun." QOL policing was integral to this process.[42] In other words, authoritarian modes of policing are the flip-side to the celebrated fun city of consumption, from the use of militarized policing to clear the poor or homeless from a space being readied for redevelopment, to a "zero-tolerance" attitude toward visible signs of minor disorder by cities implementing the QOL policing paradigm.[43] Today, it can be said that we are governed through a consumer-criminal double as the numbers of incarcerated in the United States have increased by a stunning 500 percent since the early 1970s—even when crime rates were declining.[44]

Neoliberalism's Landscape and the State in New Orleans

Over the course of the twentieth century, the experience of New Orleans paralleled that of other major cities in the United States as it flipped from being a city that was 69.7 percent white and 30.1 percent black in 1940 to a city that had become 26.6 percent white and 66.6 percent black by 2000.[45] As the region experienced slow population growth, the city (Orleans Parish) lost population, with the consequence that 54 percent of the metropolitan population lived in the city in 1970 but only 36 percent did in 2000. Additionally, while the city lost 18 percent of its population between 1970 and 2000, the African American population grew by 27 percent. Those leaving New Orleans were racially distributed as well. That is, most of those able to move to the suburbs were white, although blacks were able to move to Jefferson Parish to the west and into New Orleans East. Finally, during the same period, New Orleans lost manufacturing jobs, which tended to pay better than the service jobs that replaced them.[46] Although the oil industry is an important segment of the Louisiana economy, many of these better-paying jobs are found in the suburban parishes.[47] In sum, New Orleans has lost population while its suburban neighbors have gained population, and New Orleans has also become a predominantly black city. Not only is New Orleans less racially mixed within the city and more racially segregated in the second half of the twentieth century than in the first half, with the loss of manufacturing, it has also become a center of poverty—the "poverty rate for the city of New Orleans is roughly double that of the surrounding suburban area," according to urban sociologist Kevin Fox Gotham, and it is the sixth poorest metropolitan region in the country with an 18 percent poverty rate.[48]

These trends of segregation were not produced by market forces freed from state restraint. In important ways, state actions during the middle of the twentieth century helped to produce this landscape of inequality. As much as federal loans and the federal highway program helped to subsidize the growth of the suburbs at the expense of cities throughout the United States, the highway program also decimated black neighborhoods within New Orleans and forced the creation of neighborhoods that were less mixed and had increased concentrations of blacks. Highways help bring tourists to special events in New Orleans. Their actual *locations*, however, have had a segregating effect. As New Orleans historian Peirce Lewis writes regarding highway construction in New Orleans, "there is no direct evidence that highways were deliberately located in black neighborhoods, [however] a comparison of racial maps with highway maps makes that conclusion inevitable."[49] Referring to I-10 (Interstate 10), for example, Lewis notes that the city built it along North Claiborne Avenue, the main street of New Orleans's largest African American neighborhood. What had once been a "broad, landscaped boulevard" was converted into a "dingy, concrete cavern."[50] Of course New Orleans is not unique among U.S. cities with its tendency to locate freeways such that they disproportionately displaced black communities through a mixture of intention and the lack of political clout these communities had in comparison with others—opponents of a Robert Moses–inspired plan for a Riverfront Expressway, for instance, were able to resist a similarly likely blighting of the French Quarter.[51] Nevertheless, the consequences of these decisions have been to damage the social fabric of those targeted black communities and to cause population displacements that further intensify residential racial segregation. Highways allowed the white middle class to move to the suburbs, spurred the growth of retail in suburban shopping centers outside of the city, and allowed white collar professionals to move to another location yet keep jobs in the city (or to take what new jobs that

Figure 4.1. Old North Claiborne Avenue lined with oak trees, undated photo; courtesy of the New Orleans Public Library, Louisiana Division, City Archives.

Figure 4.2. Peoples Hurricane Relief Fund rallies on North Claiborne Avenue underneath I-10 in January 2007. Photograph by John Arena.

were created in urban areas), while damaging middle class black communities with their placement.

In addition to Jim Crow, other state practices that increased segregation in New Orleans include the federal housing programs that built public housing, in conjunction with state and local input. These housing programs enhanced both racial segregation, as they were officially segregated (St. Thomas was the only mixed project) and, in some cases, geographic isolation (the huge Desire project was cut off from the rest of New Orleans by two canals and two sets of railroad tracks). Public housing—enclaves of poverty—in New Orleans became virtually 100 percent black due to those demographic changes that were structured, in part, by the state as subsidized private housing, for instance, was systematically closed off to blacks.[52] A landscape of racial and economic segmentation in the New Orleans metropolitan region, then, was shaped in important ways by federal, state, and local policies.

These housing and highway policies of the Fordist era created the context for post-Fordist and neoliberal New Orleans. Other state policies regarding revenue raising also created the conditions within which New Orleans would need to rely on consumption as a major component of its urban economy and, more specifically, the consumption of non–New Orleanians—tourists. As Gotham describes, in 1974,

> the Louisiana State legislature passed several statutes that significantly reduced the ability of local governments in the state to raise revenue. These fiscal constraints included: a reduction in the ability of local governments to collect income taxes, thereby increasing their reliance on sales tax; a statute that two-thirds of both houses of the state legislature had to approve any increase in any existing local tax; and an expanded exemption on home-owners' property taxes.[53]

With an increasingly impoverished and shrinking urban population, and with fiscal constraints produced through a significant reduction in federal money as a proportion of its city budget, New Orleans needed a source of revenue and was constrained—by a poor local population and by state legislation—regarding possible sources of funds. This conjuncture of events, influenced significantly by the state, made the reorientation of New Orleans infrastructure away from its residents and toward tourists an attractive option.[54] Like other cities in the United States, New Orleans had to become more "entrepreneurial" and become more of a producer of entertainment for visitors.

This effort to make cities into producers of entertainment means that cities are aggressively marketed and promoted through a logic of branding in the interurban market for tourism. It also means, ironically, that cities become more like each other even as they are driven to become "distinctive" from each other for their branding strategy. As a result of these developments, there is increasing crossover between entertainment corporations like Disney and urban planning—a process that many refer to as the "Disneyfication of urban space."[55]

We can see how New Orleans's post-Fordist entrepreneurialism strikes these chords familiar to other cities—the mall, corporate entertainment, and themed enclaves—with coinciding segregating effects. Malls moved to downtown locations across the United States in the 1980s due to the convergence of suburban saturation and post-Fordist urban recruitment. In parallel with other cities, New Orleans developed the Canal Place

Figure 4.3. The Riverwalk Marketplace shopping mall designed by James Rouse, July, 2008. Photograph by the author.

shopping center in 1983 and the James Rouse–designed Riverwalk along the Mississippi in 1986.

With the decline in manufacturing, New Orleans followed in the footsteps of other cities, and the production of entertainment became a more significant aspect of its urban economy.[56] New Orleans took part in a major trend in urban planning—one strongly supported by the Urban Land Institute, from which New Orleans solicited urban planning advice in the aftermath of Hurricane Katrina—and created urban entertainment destinations: themed and branded districts or enclaves distinct from adjacent neighborhoods and constructed around spectacle to design "experiences" for a risk-adverse middle class.[57] New Orleans was already famous for architecture, culture, and ethnic neighborhoods in light of its history as a European colony and for its importance in the history of jazz. From this foundation, it developed a "museum" or "arts" district out of hosting the 1984 World's Fair. In addition to its domed stadium and urban festival marketplace designed by Rouse, New Orleans participated in the "theming of America," with a convention center and theme parks like Jazzland

Figure 4.4. Harrah's Casino, New Orleans, July 2008. Photograph by the author.

(renamed Six Flags but destroyed by Hurricane Katrina), other museums that are both fun and educational like Aquarium of the Americas, an IMAX theatre (located in Aquarium of the Americas), themed eateries and bars like the Hard Rock Café and Coyote Ugly, and a casino (Harrah's Casino).

Of course, New Orleans is famously branded and "place-marketed" around its French Quarter (Vieux Carré) entertainment zone and Mardi Gras as an annual tourist destination that has become central to New Orleans–linked commodity production year-round. The steep increase in revenues that the city of New Orleans receives from Mardi Gras speaks to the significance of tourism to the local economy. While in 1986, the city received $4.3 million in annual revenues from Mardi Gras parades, by 2000, this had increased to $21.6 million—over a 500 percent increase from this revenue stream.[58]

These processes are dramatically expressed in the changes to the French Quarter as New Orleans has become more aggressive about competing in the interurban global tourist market. As the French Quarter has become more gentrified and more of an entertainment complex, it has also become more socially homogeneous. While the percentage of the white population in the rest of New Orleans was in decline, Gotham finds that the Vieux Carré changed from being 79 percent white in 1940 to a district that was 91.9 percent white in 2000.[59] Meanwhile, during the 1990s, rents increased substantially, often between 50 and 100 percent. The quarter became wealthier and whiter as its commercial base became reoriented away from residents and toward tourists. So, instead of grocery stores or hardware stores (the numbers of which declined from 44 to 4 and 31 to 1, respectively, between 1940 and 2000), the French Quarter is now the location of souvenir and T-shirt shops (26 to 110), music clubs (7 to 27), hotels (21 to 40), and tourism information centers (a 32 percent increase since 1950). Since the early 1990s, corporate entertainment chains have also been introduced to the French Quarter or its vicinity, like Larry Flynt's Hustler Club, House of Blues, Coyote Ugly Bar, Planet Hollywood, Harrah's Casino, and the Aquarium for the Americas. The process of turning New Orleans into a tourist city has been a process

Figure 4.5. The Aquarium of the Americas, with IMAX theater, located along the Mississippi close to the Riverwalk Marketplace shopping mall and a short walk from the French Quarter, July 2008. Photograph by the author.

of turning the city's landscape into one of segments that are increasingly internally socially homogeneous and increasingly socially different from other segments, as creating one socially unitary space entails influencing the social constitution of others.[60]

We should not neglect the role of the state in constructing the entertainment city, in either its more overt and forceful or its more subtle actions. In terms of more forceful applications of state power, New Orleans shares with other cities an effort to implement zero tolerance, QOL policing. New Orleans's private, nonprofit New Orleans Police Foundation (a business group that promotes crime reduction) hired Jack Maple in 1996 as a consultant (along with John Linder) to overhaul the New Orleans Police Department (NOPD) along the lines of QOL policing that Maple had helped to pioneer when he worked under New York City Police Commissioner William Bratton. NOPD Superintendent Richard Pennington, upon announcing the program and the fact that he would be implementing Maple's suggestions, made clear the tourism-oriented purposes of the policy: "I'm very concerned about the tourist season. . . . I'm concerned about the major events that we have coming up. I want to make sure that when we have tourists come to this city, we have enough capability in the areas they frequent."[61] The results in New Orleans of zero tolerance and QOL policing were similar to those of other cities: "declining crime rates" and skyrocketing numbers of "police brutality" complaints.[62] The preparation and maintenance of places dedicated to consumerism through zero tolerance, QOL policing strategies illustrate how we are governed through a consumer-criminal double.

In Hurricane Katrina's wake, as the New Orleans City Council voted to proceed with demolishing its "Big Four" public housing developments to convert them into mixed developments with severely reduced space reserved for public housing—although rents have increased in New Orleans by 40 percent post-Katrina—public housing residents gathered to protest the demolition of their homes. Referred to by one member of council as "terrorists and demagogues," many were kept from entering the meeting by barricade, foot police, mounted police, pepper spray, and the use of newly acquired Taser guns Mayor Nagin would so proudly tout as an achievement in a "state of the city" speech late in his second administration.[63] Fifteen were arrested.

With higher rents in post-Katrina New Orleans, reduced public housing options, and high levels of unemployment as the U.S. economy lurched toward disaster, tent-cities of homeless sprung up throughout New Orleans, including Duncan Plaza across from City Hall. When Duncan Plaza was cleared of the homeless, fenced, and declared a construction site, many of the homeless moved to a more chaotic site under I-10 at the Claiborne exit, from where they were also removed (Duncan Plaza was self-governed by "Homeless Pride," which tried to enforce nighttime quiet and prevent drug sales, while the Claiborne site became a virtual crack market).[64] These sites were cleared when Mayor Nagin threatened to enforce the city's public habitation "laws," and the homeless advocacy group UNITY struck a deal with the city whereby this social services group would remove the homeless in order to prevent the kind of violent confrontation between the police and the poor that had ensued when the city council voted to demolish the Big Four public housing developments.[65]

At the time of this writing, there are an estimated 6,000 squatters living in abandoned buildings throughout New Orleans.[66] When this real estate becomes valuable enough to redevelop, the state—or a social service organization acting one step ahead of the police—will remove, by force if necessary, those inhabiting the properties targeted for redevelopment. Even in the case of real estate–led economic development, the state is deeply involved, often quite forcefully, in these neoliberal processes of producing consumer-friendly space by effectively criminalizing those who must be removed from the space for it to become invested with credible value.

Let's take the Louisiana Superdome, to which I will return later, as a useful example of the more subtle forms of neoliberal state action to produce post-Fordist space. The Superdome is where many special events are hosted, from the Essence Music Festival or the Super Bowl to the Southern Baptist Convention and the Republican National Convention. The Superdome project was a response to the decline of manufacturing and an interest in enhancing tourism in New Orleans. It was built on land either cleared or made valuable through the use of eminent domain powers. It was funded through a state-guaranteed bond. Debt payments and a fund for renovations and maintenance come from a local tax on hotel and motel room usage. The Superdome is governed by a legislatively created entity called the Louisiana Stadium and Exposition District, the entity that levies the occupancy taxes. The state pays the New Orleans Saints "compensation" to keep the football team in New Orleans since its stadium deal is not as lucrative as others that some National Football League (NFL) teams have been able to negotiate elsewhere, and New Orleans

Figure 4.6. A squatter's residence near the Superdome, New Orleans Centre Mall, and the Hyatt, adjacent to the central business district, July 2008. Photograph by the author.

could not host the Super Bowl if it was not home to an NFL team. After Hurricane Katrina damaged the Superdome, the governor of the state, Kathleen Blanco, "fast-tracked" repairs on the Superdome, as opposed to, say, New Orleans's neighborhoods, Charity hospital (see Figure 4.7), or the public school system. These repairs—and upgrades so that the Superdome could remain a competitive, state-of-the-art facility for the Super Bowl—were funded by the state: 90 percent of these repairs and improvements were financed by the Federal Emergency Management Agency (FEMA), at a time when homeowners in New Orleans were not able to get aid to rebuild their homes, and ten percent was funded by the state of Louisiana.[67] From construction to post-Katrina renovation, the Superdome is a product of state action. The neoliberal, post-Fordist landscape is deeply structured by the state.

The neoliberal landscape is also a segregated one—it is a series of segments. It is a set of mutually constitutive containerized spaces or enclaves and distinctive zones, influenced by market-based logics and marketing on the one hand and by fear of crime and an interest in containing dangerous

Figure 4.7. Charity Hospital in New Orleans (July 2008), which was closed after the storm and remains closed as of this writing. Photograph by the author.

populations on the other. Building the Superdome entailed less direct displacement than it might otherwise have because of its location by railway yards and the earlier construction of the New Orleans civic center—the new city hall and other government buildings—from the 1940s through the early 1950s by then-Mayor DeLesseps "Chep" Morrison.[68] Nevertheless, the removal of black New Orleanians from the site for the civic center in the 1940s helped to create the conditions that enabled the construction of the Superdome nearby twenty years later. The bulldozing for the civic center was viewed favorably by those who secured financial backing for the Superdome because it provided vital "protection" for the central business district and the Superdome project.[69] Unfortunately, it also caused, as New Orleans historian Edward Haas describes, greater residential segregation in New Orleans since it forced blacks to crowd into "predominantly Negro sections of the city" due to a failure by the city to provide other housing options for those displaced by the project.[70] Thus, the Superdome is part of a process where creating one type of enclave in one part of the city has reciprocal effects—like squeezing air out of a balloon at one end and watching it bulge at another—on other city zones. Indeed, it is a deep irony that progressive-minded New Orleanians attacked Jim Crow, in part, to become more attractive to tourists and yet, as a tourist city, it is more deeply segregated than it was during the years of official segregation.[71]

Container Spaces

Initial use of the term "state of emergency" to understand the mega-event of Hurricane Katrina obscures how Katrina brings into focus long-term processes that structured the creation of a city with distinctive zones and containable enclaves.[72] Furthermore, New Orleans shares a broader post-Fordist experience with other U.S. cities, as I have demonstrated by referring to recent scholarship in the field of urban studies. In the remainder of this essay, I describe a spectrum of city spaces in the immediate aftermath of the hurricane.

The variety of urban spaces allows us to understand how New Orleans as an exemplar of post-Fordist urbanity is a city constituted by a series of zones or enclaves that are spaces of control, although differentiated in how they control or for what purpose. These spaces manifest a spectrum within the consumer-criminal logic of governance. This illustrates how acts of enforcement (and criminalization) constitute spaces dedicated to consumption. It also illustrates how consuming spaces and criminal spaces are containment spaces—so that consumers are buffered from nonconsumers, and those deemed a threat to consumption are also contained. Finally, this spectrum illustrates how control is not only present in a prison but in a variety of "free" spaces—particularly those spaces dedicated to the (post-Fordist) production of consumer experiences, or entertaining mega-events, free from disruption.[73]

Prisons

In the period coinciding with the rise of neoliberalism, the number of inmates incarcerated in the United States, a statistic that has been historically fairly steady in the United States and which declined during the Fordist period of the mid-twentieth century, began to rise dramatically. By 2005, the year Katrina struck, over 7 million people in the United States were under some form of correctional supervision.[74] Louisiana and New Orleans are notorious within the context of governing through crime.[75]

Louisiana led the nation in 2005 (the year Katrina struck) with its incarceration rate of 797 per 100,000 residents, beating out Texas, Mississippi, Oklahoma, and Alabama for this dubious honor.[76] In fact, Louisiana consistently had the highest total incarceration rate in the nation throughout the 1990s.[77] The incarceration rate in New Orleans is even higher, at 1,480 per 100,000, which is the highest incarceration rate of any city in the United States.[78] While Louisiana's population is 32 percent black, its prison population is 72 percent black. New Orleans has a 40 percent illiteracy rate, and over 50 percent of black ninth graders will not graduate from high school in four years. Louisiana is noted for its Angola prison, a former slave plantation, where over 90 percent of inmates sent there will die there, and they will perform manual labor until they do. New Orleans is home to the infamous Orleans Parish Prison (OPP), the eighth largest jail in the nation, located in downtown New Orleans not far from the Superdome and described as a "warehouse" for human beings.[79] Stunningly, Louisiana accounts for almost 25 percent of the *national* jail population, and it is the only state where inmates might serve out their entire sentence in a local jail as opposed to a state prison.[80]

At any given time, though, 60 percent of OPP's population are "individuals being held on attachments, traffic, or municipal charges." In other words, they are either convicted of very minor offenses or they are being held for processing or while awaiting trial (i.e., they are legally presumed innocent). When Katrina hit, there was no operational evacuation plan for these prisoners, and they were abandoned to their cells. Most would have served a jail term that would have been a couple weeks at most but, due to the response to Katrina, wound up spending months in the state prison system.

With the approach of the hurricane, the jail went into lockdown.[81] Eventually, the inmates were taken to state prisons like the Hunt correctional facility. At Hunt, the evacuees were put in the middle of a football field and left there for days on end where many suffered abuse. Their evacuation, however, began as they were herded to central lock-up and then taken by boat to the Broad Street Overpass on I-10.

It was on the overpass where they would wait for hours and even days to be taken to state facilities. On the overpass, the prisoners were placed in rows and ordered to remain seated back-to-back and often assaulted when they tried to stand to urinate. The prisoners were given little or no water or food while being kept by guards on the overpass in the hot sun.[82] The incident is telling because we typically think of highways as arteries and not as spatial containers. But just as interstates displaced black communities, they are also containers occupying (haunted) space whereby the middle class could safely travel from suburbs to city and back again. In some urban areas, for example, rotaries are used so that cars do not have to stop in dangerous neighborhoods.[83] The segregating attribute of interstates as spaces separated from others is indicated by how OPP deputies were able to turn a highway overpass into the functional equivalent of a jail for a period of days in the immediate aftermath of Hurricane Katrina.

Highways

Sociologist Loïc Wacquant has described black hyperincarceration in the United States historically as a process whereby the prison comes to substitute for Jim Crow to segregate blacks from the rest of society and, institutionally, as a substitute for the ghetto to keep blacks in their *place*. For Wacquant, the post–Civil Rights ghetto and the U.S. carceral system have become "linked by a triple relationship of functional equivalency, structural homology, and cultural fusion" that has spawned a "carceral continuum" for, especially, young black males that extends from prisons through ghettos to low-wage jobs.[84] Wacquant's argument regarding a carceral continuum becomes compelling when we consider how, when flushed by Katrina's waters from their normal spatial locations, ghetto and prison met in a new dimension on I-10 in New Orleans.

Thousands were reportedly stranded at the intersection of I-10 and the Lake Pontchartrain Causeway.[85] Many were dropped on highways after they had been rescued from their flooded homes, while others struggled to reach the highways for "vertical evacuation."[86] Regardless of how they got to the highway, once there, the highway itself became an ordeal to survive without food or water, and sitting in the hot sun, often for days. One evacuee went so far as to describe herself as a "detainee" at the Causeway. According to the congressional testimony of Leah Hodges, when she and others were dropped off, they were "fenced in, and penned in, by military vehicles," within the space of the interstate. She described the conditions on the highway as comparable to a "concentration camp."[87]

We can see how governing through a consumer-criminal double involves a policing of bodies to spaces according to a logic of containment by following those who walked along I-90 toward the bridge that crosses the Mississippi, linking New Orleans with Gretna. Gretna is a middle class suburb of 17,500—a population that is mostly white but has a significant black minority of 35 percent. Those evacuees walking toward Gretna were 95 percent black—a mixed group of New Orleanians and tourists who had been forced to leave their hotels, which were closing now that the storm had been weathered.[88] Dehydrated and bedraggled, they staggered over the bridge only to be faced with a line of armed Gretna police who were mostly white. The police chief, Arthur Lawson, had decided to "seal off Gretna," and the officers fired warning shots from their shotguns to make sure that the evacuees understood that they were being contained and could not proceed into Gretna. The chief saw his job as "secur[ing] our city" against terror and mayhem, while Mayor Ronnie Harris supported the chief's decision, saying, "Something had to be done," since "within that crowd was a criminal element." The city council also passed a resolution stating that allowing those individuals to enter the city would have posed "an unacceptable risk to the safety of the citizens of Gretna."[89] Black bodies out of place were immediately read as "criminal" and as an unacceptable risk. We might note that Governor Blanco also ordered the National Guard to various points of exit from New Orleans to keep people from walking out, making many feel as if they were being kept prisoner within the city of New Orleans.[90]

Gated Communities

At first, a gated community for the wealthy might seem to have little in common with a prison that concentrates poverty and illiteracy within its walls. This, however, is to miss how, in the postrehabilitative era where the main function of a prison is to contain its inmates, prisons share a segregating logic of a control space with gated communities. Criminologist Mona Lynch notes how those states where gated communities predominate (the South and Southwest) map onto those states with the highest levels of incarceration and a proclivity for building "supermax" prisons. She urges us to understand the prison as trending toward becoming a self-contained "lifestyle community" for the underclass now that it has given up on rehabilitation. She suggests that these institutions of gated community and prison merge in public housing, an institution that is increasingly becoming gated, with security officers, cameras, electronic pass cards, and strict regulations regarding who may visit. Indeed, having been subjected to criminal background checks and a constant threat of eviction if institutional regulations are violated, some residents start to wonder whether they are in public housing or prison themselves.[91]

New Orleans is seeking to do as other cities like New York City have done or sought to do: pursue "redevelopment" by trying to exchange the residents a city has for residents a city would prefer to have.[92] Those New Orleanians whose homes were in public housing are experiencing the brunt of this policy in Katrina's aftermath. Residents of public housing, already more heavily policed by Nagin's policy of increasing the number of surveillance cameras in public housing, returned to find their homes had been gated and doors and windows secured with armor when the floodwater receded.[93] This space had been recoded in order to exclude its former residents, leases notwithstanding. The exclusion by gating of the former public housing residents is a symptom of New Orleans's idea of redevelopment as four of New Orleans's public housing developments have been demolished in favor of economically mixed residential projects.[94] This is a harsh example of neoliberal urban development seeking to make the post-Fordist city uninhabitable for the poor who are not well contained and, if possible, the poor period. Zoning former residents out of public housing also demonstrates the spatial logic of the post-Fordist city and how it is forcefully secured.[95]

While many of New Orleans's poor and black residents of public housing are now scattered around the country, especially in the Houston, Texas, and Atlanta, Georgia, regions, others of New Orleans's poor were placed in FEMA trailer parks—until they were later closed so the people could "move on."[96] Interestingly, the Renaissance Village trailer park in Baker, Louisiana, was gated, with private security. This trailer park, like public housing, blurs the line between prison and community. FEMA rules made it difficult for reporters to speak to residents. In fact, they were forbidden from speaking freely to residents within the park and even in the resident's home, the trailer. No interview could occur within the installation without a FEMA representative acting as chaperone. Security guards (the private security firm Corporate Security Solutions [CSS] has this FEMA contract) took action to prevent free conversations between park residents and reporters and would call the police if a reporter persisted. The news media were also prohibited from taking pictures of the trailer park or its residents.[97] As the Katrina disaster washed away some of the "path resistance" to neoliberalism in New Orleans and elsewhere, we can better comprehend neoliberalism's geographic logic as one of controlled, segregated spaces.

"Private" Security

One unique aspect of the neoliberal state is the way that it governs through privatization. When St. Bernard Parish hired personnel from the private security corporation DynCorp in the wake of Katrina, it had them live in the same trailers that other employees of the sheriff's department would live, eat the same food, wear the same uniforms, and it deputized them to make legal arrests and to carry weapons.[98] The "private" is not primarily a limit on the state or antagonistic toward the state, as we can see from this example.

The private security industry can be made to function, then, as an extension of state power. Along with other private security firms, Blackwater arrived, armed to the teeth, in New Orleans in the immediate aftermath of Hurricane Katrina and then stayed. It is tempting to view the presence of Blackwater, and other private security firms, as an extrajudicial force beyond law.[99] So, while the rest of New Orleans suffered, the gated community Audubon Place was guarded by the Israeli security firm ISI— the wealthy have a law unto themselves.[100] This view, however, misses how private security functions as an extension to state power. Blackwater helped the National Guard patrol the city's streets and also provided a security detail to FEMA workers, under a $73 million FEMA contract.[101] The security firm Able Security, specialists in disaster security, established the perimeter of George Bush's visit to New Orleans.[102] These examples show how the state governs through privatization and can expand its reach by mobilizing private security forces.

The Tourist Landscape: Hotels

Hurricane Katrina also allows us to see where and for whom infrastructural investments have been made in post-Fordist New Orleans. The NOPD set up their command at Harrah's Casino. When the NOPD lost their communications center in the French Quarter, they moved it to the

Aquarium of the Americas, which wanted police protection from possible looting anyway.[103] The geography of sites of public authority or municipal service to address Katrina's immediate impact tracked the neoliberal landscape built for tourists.

We may profitably contrast the response of Starwood Hotels (owners of the Sheraton) to Katrina with that of the City of New Orleans. Because of the frequency of hurricanes in the southeast United States, the company has learned to require that each hotel general manager has a hurricane checklist.[104] An emergency command is established and daily communications are set up between a team of corporate leaders and the regional recovery team. Guests are updated and given safety instruction. A final list of guests and workers is established. Before the hurricane, Starwood's major hotels in New Orleans made sure to have enough food and water to anticipate difficulties in the days after the storm. When the storm hit, guests were moved to protected ballrooms, with large screens set up so adults could watch the news and children could watch movies. Monday morning, cooks served a hot breakfast. The information technology staff kept telephone and Internet service intact, and the sick and infirm were provided medical care. After the levee collapsed, Starwood found buses (when the city and FEMA apparently could not) and coordinated carpooling in order to evacuate (with security escorts to maintain a continuing and distinguishing buffer between guests and the risks of the unknown). Illustrating the organizational interpenetration of state and private security, the director of security for the Sheraton is also a commissioned deputy sheriff. Thus, Starwood hotels were able to arrange NOPD escorts to get supplies through roadblocks (ultimately, they contracted for additional security from Blackwater). When the city had no pumps working, they had a contract with a company to pump sewage out and thus allow the hotels to pump water in to feed the fire protection system and cooling towers. By Sunday night, they had received septic tanks and the last generators that would allow them to relight exterior signage for all three Starwood hotels in New Orleans. That gave them the ability to take stock of needed repairs. Two weeks to the day after Katrina struck, they took their first paying guests. During the ordeal, the Sheraton provided facilities to the Fifth District station of the NOPD (about 150 officers), an area fire station, and about 400 U.S. Immigration and Customs Enforcement agents.

The Hyatt became Mayor Ray Nagin's command center. Although closed to the public, it continued to house and provide meals to the mayor, as well as fire and police personnel, the National Guard, FEMA, and the Army Corps of Engineers for three months after Katrina.[105] The Hyatt was also one of the first facilities to receive power following the hurricane.[106] The Hyatt is connected to the Louisiana Superdome. Illustrating how the post-Fordist landscape is constituted by container-ized spaces, Nagin was able to shield himself from the refugees in the Superdome by staying in the Hyatt.[107] This changed, however, when the National Guard began to evacuate the Superdome and needed to move people onto buses that would be in front of the Hyatt. In order to maintain the zoned, enclaved logic of these containable spaces now that there was about to be a breach, the National Guard lined the walk-way through the hotel with 150 armed personnel so that the evacuation could proceed smoothly: the evacuees would remain contained and the hotel guests protected. The evacuation went smoothly once it began, although it was interrupted at one point so that about 700 guests and employees from the Hyatt could slide in ahead of them and be evacu-ated themselves. The correlation of security risks and access to service to differentiated consumer profiles indicate we are being governed by the consumer-criminal double.[108]

Superdome

The Superdome was built to boost tourism to New Orleans, and when Katrina struck, no other city had hosted more Super Bowls than New Orleans in the Louisiana Superdome. When the seri-ousness of Hurricane Katrina began to dawn on Mayor Nagin, he directed New Orleanians unable to evacuate to go to the Superdome as a shelter of last resort, which in theory could withstand hurricane-force winds. Quickly, a long line formed around the perimeter of the stadium as the National Guard performed security checks before allowing anyone to enter.[109]

Perhaps no place during Hurricane Katrina and its immediate aftermath are as symptomatic of our post-Fordist spatial organization as the Superdome. The Superdome, a cathedral to the post-Fordist reproduction of sports into corporatized entertainment, flipped and changed into a prison. The apparent ease with which the walls changed their meaning once those normally kept out of the stadium in favor of middle class spectators became the predominant population of the stadium tells us how the institutions of post-Fordism are built upon an infrastructure enabling containable space. It is indicative of the premise of control within the logic of consumer capitalism. The built environment of post-Fordism differentiates spatial segments, sifting those allowed into a given place, and providing for the containment, if not control, of those within its parameters.

The discourse of those who described the scene at the Superdome, and those who weathered the hurricane there, is one that compares the experience to having been in a prison or worse. "Superdome refuge 'worse than a prison,'" reads an *International Herald Tribune* headline.[110] According to an Associated Press (AP) story, "The refugees are being housed in what was, until earlier this week, a minimum-security prison. Ironic, since a favorite synonym for the Superdome seemed to be 'jail.'"[111] We are told by another AP article that even for those police officers who spent the storm at the Dome, it was "their prison, too."[112] A woman who had been at the Superdome said that she would "rather be in jail."[113] One CNN viewer, upset at reports of looting in New Orleans, suggested converting the Superdome into a jail.[114] Actually, the Superdome has a jail on the premises that is used for unruly fans at New Orleans Saints football games. The jail was used during the hurricane for a man accused of molesting children and for a man accused of shooting a National Guardsman (although it turns out the Guardsman was either shot by a fellow officer accidentally or shot himself accidentally).[115] The unimaginably horrible conditions at the Superdome made the refugees there and the Guardsmen tense. At one point, the Guard reportedly went into "lockdown mode," calling in reinforcements, erecting razor-wire fences inside concourses, and ordering the evacuation of all nonessential personnel. To many crowded into the Superdome, the National Guard "was treating them like prisoners."[116]

When the Superdome refugees were evacuated, they were taken in prison buses to "Reliant City," the sports and convention center complex in Houston, Texas.[117] Illustrating how the state builds itself into private spaces, Reliant City was given its own zip code, post office, and a government. Members of a Reliant maintenance crew described it as being like a "Super Bowl everyday." From the arrival of the first evacuees, the goal at Reliant was "order." Arrivals received a security screening and barricades and checkpoints were set up around the complex (although police made "surprisingly few arrests"). For "security reasons," everyone "must be identified" with differently colored wristbands depending on whether they resided at the Astrodome, the convention center, or the downtown convention center. Bodies were policed to spaces. And when lines got out of control, police instituted a lockdown at Reliant City, too.[118] Here, Reliant City was using the same discourse and producing the same institutional effect of control as a prison lockdown.

As described earlier, renovations of the Louisiana Superdome were "fast tracked." Once repaired and renovated one year after the hurricane, the Superdome's restoration was taken to be symbolic of a "rebirth for New Orleans."[119] This rebirth occurred to the musical accompaniment of U2 and the Goo Goo Dolls and was televised on ESPN (owned by the Disney Corporation), but it was a rebirth with fewer poor and black residents.[120] Salvation through negation.[121]

For the 2007–2008 college football season, New Orleans hosted both the Fiesta Bowl and the Sugar Bowl. From an organizational standpoint, this was said to be akin to hosting "two major political conventions at once." According to Mayor Nagin, every day, the City of New Orleans gets stronger in its ability to "handle a major event," by which he means a media or convention event. Nagin hoped that by hosting both Bowl games, New Orleans would "create the synergies . . . to have a world-class event." The post-Fordist city promotes spectacle to create a brand name for itself, seeking to appeal to tourists and conventioneers, rather than worrying about infrastructure for its residents. Giving a dramatic illustration of this in the case of New Orleans, the *New York Times* reports that in the "downtown area where the Superdome, the French Quarter, and a majority of the hotels are located, there is little evidence of Katrina's devastation."[122] In fact, there are "more restaurants open downtown now than before Katrina."[123] These areas are in "stunning contrast to nearby areas that many tourists do not see" (unless they are on a disaster tour). Other neighborhoods still look like "an atomic bomb wiped them off the face of the earth."[124] The differences in New Orleans's urban landscape that existed prior to Katrina have only been exacerbated by the neoliberal approach to its reconstruction.

The choice of words used to describe the organizational effort to pull off two college bowl games as being similar to "conducting two major political conventions at once" is symptomatic as well. Not only does it speak to how the Democratic and Republican National Conventions have become performances of a convention, rather than actually being a convention that does the work of making political decisions, it also speaks to why cities want to play host to such generators of spectacle, by putting them on a par with a college bowl game from the standpoint of place-marketing.

From a security standpoint, the major party conventions are National Special Security Events (NSSEs). This designation comes from a still-classified Presidential Decision Directive number 62 (PDD-62) issued by then-President Clinton. The Secret Service becomes the lead agency for developing an operational security plan, and the FBI takes the lead with respect to intelligence, crisis management, hostage rescue, and counterterrorism. There is no higher security classification of an event. Other NSSEs include a presidential inauguration or funeral and the Super Bowl.[125] Security arrangements for NSSEs include smart cards and biometrics for employees, walk-through metal detectors plus handheld devices, and facial recognition technology to compare faces in the crowd to criminal databases; hard and soft perimeters are established; and the airspace is secured by the North American Aerospace Defense Command (NORAD). Coordination must occur among approximately fifty federal, state, and local agencies, in addition to the private security firm managing security inside the stadium at game time.[126] The first time a Super Bowl ever received a designation as an NSSE was in 2002, when the Super Bowl was played in the Louisiana Superdome.

While "only" thirty-five agencies were involved in the security arrangements in 2002, coordinating even this kind of an organizational effort is no small task.[127] Nevertheless, at the time Katrina hit, no city had pulled off more successful Super Bowls than had New Orleans. With the renovations of the Superdome, the practice of hosting the Sugar Bowl and the Fiesta Bowls during the same week, and with winning bids for the National Collegiate Athletic Association (NCAA) Division I Men's (2012) and Women's (2013) Final Fours, the NCAA collegiate football championship game (2008, 2012), and the National Basketball Association's All-Star game (2008), the stage was set for New Orleans to put in a bid to host its tenth Super Bowl.[128]

On May 19, 2009, the NFL owners voted to award New Orleans the 2013 Super Bowl.[129] Congressman Scalise, whose congressional district includes the Superdome, took the award as a "sign that New Orleans is still a world-class city," recognizing "our ability to host one of the largest events in the world."[130] As the general manager of the Hilton's New Orleans Riverside Hotel stated, the Super Bowl promotes New Orleans and "helps to attract these meetings and conventions that are really our bread and butter."[131] According to the president of the

New Orleans Convention and Visitors' Bureau, with the Super Bowl, New Orleans has been "re-established" as the "pre-eminent special-events city."[132]

Not only does the Super Bowl assist New Orleans in terms of place-marketing, with so many successful bids for major sporting events, New Orleans is now working to "place-brand" itself in terms of sports. As part of these efforts, plans are under way to build a 92,000 square-foot "fan zone" adjacent to the Superdome that will become part of a new "sports entertainment district."[133] It will be located in the complex of commercial space that includes the Hyatt and the mall that attaches to the Superdome, which have largely remained empty, except for squatters, since Katrina struck in 2005 (see Figure 4.6).

If past practice is any guide, New Orleans will govern the complexities of the 2013 Super Bowl with success. This success, and its past successes, as in 2002, however, will stand in stark contrast to the organizational nightmare of Hurricane Katrina. While both weeklong mega-events involve massive organizational coordination between federal, state, local, and private assets and both are governed by the neoliberal state, one functioned smoothly— the Super Bowl of 2002—and one did not—Hurricane Katrina.

Therefore, let us not say that the neoliberal state has been weak-ened by privatization and so cannot govern. Let us give praise where praise is due: the organizational coordination to produce the mega-event of the Super Bowl is impressive. Moreover, the private security helping to produce an environment conducive to the spectacle that both the NFL and the post-Fordist city hope to generate is part of a se-ries of articulated organizations governed by the neoliberal state. The neoliberal state is more effective at producing Super Bowls, in part, because they occur annually. Through repetition, organizational linkages become forged, turning an organization flow chart into institutionalized social practices. The same could happen for hurricanes in the southeast-ern region of the United States—especially as global climate change seems to affect the frequency and intensity of the hurricanes that reach land yearly. It just doesn't.

Conclusion

The response to Hurricane Katrina brings the neoliberal state into sharp relief. Neither an absolute sovereign nor weak and hollowed out, the neoliberal state is not limited by privatization but rather governs through privatization. Within the post-Fordist city, the landscape has become reconfigured to mimic the differentiated niches of marketing mentalities. Indeed, the post-Fordist city needs to produce space in a way that will promote its brand image to potential tourists and other visitors, and its landscape and infrastructure are reshaped to this task. That is, space is segmented into containable units that can be controlled for the specific aesthetic purposes of niche-based consumerism. Those who are not valuable as consumers, then, are either forgotten or repressed.[134]

The segregating logic and capacities for control of the post-Fordist city were made particularly evident in the wake of Hurricane Katrina when those repressed and displaced, literally, by post-Fordism's built environment returned to those locations from which the poor and blacks had been displaced over the course of the twentieth century in New Orleans. This return of the repressed was structurally determined by a lack of gas money and a lack of public transportation. It disturbed the world's conscience by bringing to our collective attention the poverty and racial segregation that neoliberalism produces and which neoliberalism must guard against to secure its privileged spaces. The preoccupations of the neoliberal state are shown by the contrast between the return of the repressed to I-10 and the Superdome, on the one hand, and the moderate success of the contraflow traffic plan for hurricane evacuation designed by Governor Blanco for those with cars, on the other.[135]

The return of the repressed nonconsumer manifests how we are governed by a consumer-criminal double as these black bodies out of place were preemptively criminalized and spatially policed. It also illustrates how technologies of control are embedded within this post-Fordist landscape as institutions for consumption quickly flipped and became equally serviceable as detention centers. New Orleans's design and management of consumer space are influenced by an affliction, fear, or threat: the threat that those repressed and displaced for the construction of post-Fordist spaces might actually return.

The neoliberal state is not a weak state. One of the unfortunate lessons of the response to Katrina, compared to the Super Bowl, is that the neoliberal state does have a capacity to govern. We just should not judge its capacity to govern by the tasks that it does not care to do.

Notes

I would like to thank Jodi Dean, Cedric Johnson, Chad Lavin, and the two anonymous reviewers for very productive comments on an earlier version of this essay. I would also like to acknowledge helpful discussions about these matters with Jay Arena, Mike Howells, Roderick Dean, and Cody Marshall.

1. Adolph Reed, "Undone by Neoliberalism," *Nation*, August 31, 2006, http://www.thenation.com/ (accessed July 9, 2007), aptly situates the event of Hurricane Katrina in the context of neoliberalism.

2. Paul A. Passavant, "The Strong Neo-liberal State: Crime, Consumption, Governance," *Theory and Event* 8 (2005).

3. On the "consumer-criminal double," see Passavant, "The Strong Neo-liberal State"; and Jodi Dean, *Democracy and Other Neoliberal Fantasies* (Durham, N.C.: Duke University Press, 2009), 67–71, 131.

4. Sophie Body-Gendrot, "Cities, Security, and Visitors: Managing Mega-Events in France," in *Cities and Visitors: Regulating People, Markets, and City Space*, ed. Lily Hoffman, Susan Fainstein, and Dennis Judd, 39–52 (Malden, Mass.: Blackwell, 2003).

5. Ash Amin, "Post-Fordism: Models, Fantasies, and Phantoms of Transition," in *Post-Fordism: A Reader*, ed. Ash Amin, 1–39 (Cambridge, UK: Blackwell, 1994); and David Harvey, *A Brief History of Neoliberalism* (New York: Oxford University Press, 2005), 2–3.

6. Nikolas Rose, *Powers of Freedom* (Cambridge, UK: Cambridge University Press, 1999), 18, 243–45.

7. Michael Hardt and Antonio Negri, *Empire* (Cambridge, Mass.: Harvard University Press, 2000), 306 (italics removed). See, generally, Susan Strange, *The Retreat of the State: The Diffusion of Power in the World Economy* (Cambridge, UK: Cambridge University Press, 1996), although she excludes the United States from her claims.

8. Margaret Kohn, *Brave New Neighborhoods: The Privatization of Public Space* (New York: Routledge, 2004), 160–62; and Robyn Turner, "The Politics of Design and Development in the Postmodern Downtown," *Journal of Urban Affairs* 24 (2002): 533–548, 543.

9. Joshua Holland, "Hurricane Reality vs. Right-Wing Ideology," *Alternet*, September 8, 2005, http://www.alternet.org/ (accessed July 8, 2007).

10. Peter Feng, "Neoliberalism, Katrina, and the Asian Tsunami," *Counterpunch*, January 21–22, 2006, http://www.counterpunch.com/ (accessed July 9, 2007).

11. James Carroll, "Katrina's Truths," *The Boston Globe*, September 5, 2005, A17, quoted in Henry Giroux, *Stormy Weather: Katrina and the Politics of Disposability* (Boulder, Colo.: Paradigm Publishers, 2006), 41, 86 (accessed by Giroux online), in part.

12. Giorgio Agamben, *Homo Sacer: Sovereign Power and Bare Life*, trans. Daniel Heller-Roazen (Stanford, Calif.: Stanford University Press, 1998).

13. Ibid., 18–19; for a discussion of Agamben on the state, see Paul A. Passavant, "The Contradictory State of Giorgio Agamben," *Political Theory* 35 (April 2007): 147–74. Giroux is borrowing significantly, as well, from Zygmunt Bauman, *Liquid Love* (London: Polity, 2003).

14. Neil Brenner and Nik Theodore, "Cities and the Geographies of 'Actually Existing Neoliberalism,'" in *Spaces of Neoliberalism: Urban Restructuring in North America and Western Europe*, ed. Neil Brenner and Nik Theodore (Malden, Mass.: Blackwell, 2002), chap. 1. See also Jason Hackworth, *The Neoliberal City: Governance, Ideology, and Development in American Urbanism* (Ithaca, N.Y.: Cornell University Press, 2007).

15. Jamie Peck and Adam Tickell, "Neoliberalizing Space," in *Spaces of Neoliberalism*, ed. Brenner and Theodore, 37, italics in original.

16. David Garland, *The Culture of Control* (Chicago: University of Chicago Press, 2001), 124.

17. Michel Foucault, "The Subject and Power," *Critical Inquiry* 8 (Summer 1982): 777–95.

18. Passavant, "The Strong Neo-liberal State."

19. See also Béatrice Hibou, ed. *Privatizing the State*, trans. Jonathan Derrick (New York: Columbia University Press, 2004), for a similar approach to that taken here in the fields of international relations and comparative politics.

20. In what follows, I build upon Paul A. Passavant, "Policing Protest in the Post-Fordist City," *Amsterdam Law Forum* 2 (2009): 93–116.

21. Robert Beauregard, *When America Became Suburban* (Minneapolis: University of Minnesota Press, 2006), 84–85; and Bernard Frieden and Lynne Sagalyn, *Downtown, Inc: How America Rebuilds Cities* (Cambridge, Mass.: MIT Press, 1989), 20–22, 28–30.

22. Lizabeth Cohen, *A Consumer's Republic: The Politics of Mass Consumption in Postwar America* (New York: Knopf, 2003), 195.

23. Ibid., 273.

24. Beauregard, *When America Became Suburban*, 85.

25. Paul A. Passavant, "The Governmentality of Consumption," *Interventions* 3 (2004): 381–400.

26. Cohen, *A Consumer's Republic*, 204.

27. Paco Underhill, *The Call of the Mall: The Geography of Shopping* (New York: Simon and Schuster, 2004), 32.

28. Ester Fuchs, "The Permanent Urban Crisis," in *Breaking Away: The Future of Cities*, ed. Julia Vitullo-Martin (New York: Twentieth Century Fund Press, 1996), 62–63.

29. Demetrios Caraley, "Washington Abandons the Cities," *Political Science Quarterly* 107 (Spring 1992): 11–12 (states not a substitute for decline in federal aid).

30. J. Phillip Thompson, "Urban Poverty and Race," in Vitullo-Martin, *Breaking Away*, 13–15.

31. The relevant differences of the suburban shopping mall in comparison to a city's downtown are described by Frieden and Sagalyn, *Downtown, Inc.*, 66; see also Passavant, "Governmentality of Consumption," 394 (discussing *New Jersey Coalition against the War in the Middle East v. J.M.B. Realty Corp.* 138 NJ 326 [1994]).

32. "Downtown Needs a Lesson from the Suburbs," *Business Week*, October 22, 1955, 64.

33. Victor Gruen, *The Heart of Our Cities: The Urban Crisis* (New York: Simon and Schuster, 1964), 300ff.

34. Frieden and Sagalyn, *Downtown, Inc.*, 5.

35. Ibid., 70, 81.

36. This is not a phenomenon limited to the United States. See Tim Hall and Phil Hubbard, eds. *The Entrepreneurial City: Geographies of Politics, Regime, and Representation* (New York: John Wiley and Sons, 1998).

37. John Hannigan, *Fantasy City: Pleasure and Profit in the Postmodern Metropolis* (New York: Routledge, 1998).

38. Frieden and Sagalyn, *Downtown, Inc.*, 171–72.

39. Dennis Judd, "Constructing the Tourist Bubble," in *The Tourist City*, eds. Dennis Judd and Susan Fainstein (New Haven: Yale University Press, 1999), 35–53; and Dennis Judd, "Visitors and the Spatial Ecology of the City," in *Cities and Visitors: Regulating People, Markets, and City Space*, ed. Lily Hoffman, Susan Fainstein, and Dennis Judd (Malden, Mass.: Blackwell Publishing, 2003), 23–38.

40. Christian Parenti, *Lockdown America: Police and Prisons in the Age of Crisis* (New York: Verso, 1999), 100–101.

41. In addition to Hannigan, *Fantasy City*, see Trevor Boddy, "Underground and Overhead: Building the Analogous City," in *Variations on a Theme Park: The New American City and the End of Public Space*, ed. Michael Sorkin (New York: Hill and Wang, 1992), 123–53.

42. For a discussion of quality of life policing in the context of New York City, including the observation that QOL policing was pioneered by Mayor Dinkins, although perfected under Mayor Giuliani, see Alex Vitale, *City of Disorder: How the Quality of Life Campaign Transformed New York Politics* (New York: New York University Press, 2008).

43. For a discussion of the battle between the New York City police and the homeless over Tompkins Square Park, see Neil Smith, *The New Urban Frontier: Gentrification and the Revanchist City* (New York: Routledge, 1996), 218ff., and passim Ash Amin, "Collective Culture and Urban Public Space," *City* 12 (April 2008): 5–24, then, celebrates the city of consumption with little regard to how it is inextricably linked to punitive forms of policing.

44. Garland, *Culture of Control*.

45. Kevin Fox Gotham, "Tourism Gentrification: The Case of New Orleans' Vieux Carré (French Quarter)," *Urban Studies* 42 (June 2005), 1099–1121, 1104.

46. The Brookings Institution, "New Orleans after the Storm: Lessons from the Past, a Plan for the Future" (Washington, D.C.: The Brookings Institution, October 2005), 9–11, http://www.brookings.edu/ (accessed May 30, 2007).

47. Michael Peter Smith and Marlene Keller, "'Managed Growth' and the Politics of Uneven Development in New Orleans," in *Restructuring the City: The Political Economy of Urban Redevelopment*, revised edition, ed. Susan Fainstein et al. (New York: Longman, 1986), 128.

48. Kevin Fox Gotham, "Marketing Mardi Gras: Commodification, Spectacle, and the Political Economy of Tourism in New Orleans," *Urban Studies* 39 (2002): 1742; Brookings, "New Orleans after the Storm," 4, 20–23; and see, generally, Gotham, "Tourism Gentrification."

49. Peirce Lewis, *New Orleans: The Making of an Urban Landscape*, second edition (Santa Fe: Center for American Places, 2003), 98.

50. Ibid.

51. Smith and Keller, "'Managed Growth' and the Politics of Uneven Development in New Orleans," 137; see also Tom Lewis, *Divided Highways: Building the Interstate Highways, Transforming American Life* (New York: Viking Penguin, 1997), chap. 8.

52. Martha Mahoney, "Law and Racial Geography: Public Housing and the Economy in New Orleans," *Stanford Law Review* 42 (1990): 1251–90; and Brookings Institution, "New Orleans after the Storm," 21–22.

53. Gotham, "Tourism Gentrification," 1103–4.

54. On the inequities of reorienting services away from city residents and toward tourists and other city visitors, see Peter Eisinger, "The Politics of Bread and Circuses: Building the City for the Visitor Class," *Urban Affairs Review* 35 (2000): 316–33.

55. Michael Sorkin, "See You in Disneyland," in *Variations on a Theme Park: The New American City and the End of Public Space*, ed. Michael Sorkin (New York: Hill and Wang, 1992).

56. Tourism has long figured in some way throughout the history of New Orleans, but its significance has become heightened over the past thirty years. See Kevin Fox Gotham, *Authentic New Orleans: Tourism, Culture, and Race in the Big Easy* (New York: New York University Press, 2007).

57. Hannigan, *Fantasy City*; and Mark Gottdiener, *The Theming of America: Dreams, Visions, and Commercial Spaces* (Boulder, Colo.: Westview Press, 1997).

58. Gotham, "Marketing Mardi Gras," 1746.

59. Gotham, "Tourism Gentrification," 1106.

60. Peter Marcuse, while not disputing the deep and deepening divisions between rich and poor in cities around the world, urges urban studies to recognize

the many enclaves and divisions within contemporary urban space, and the adoption of the "quartered" metaphor to emphasize that actions are taken that produce these divisions and that producing one enclave necessarily has social effects elsewhere in the city; hence, these enclaves are not sociologically separated from each other but are, rather, mutually constitutive. See Peter Marcuse, "'Dual City': A Muddy Metaphor for a Quartered City," *International Journal of Urban and Regional Research* 13 (1989): 697–708; and Peter Marcuse, "Not Chaos, but Walls: Postmodernism and the Partitioned City," in *Postmodern Cities and Spaces*, ed. Sophie Watson and Katherine Gibson (Cambridge, Mass.: Blackwell, 1995), 243–53.

61. Michael Perlstein, "Pennington Promises Safe City, Safe Streets; Focus Shifts to N.O.'s 8 District Stations," *Times-Picayune*, October 15, 1996, A1.

62. Parenti, *Lockdown America*, 84–85.

63. For a thorough accounting of the events of the city council meeting on December 19, 2007, see the real-time postings at www.nola.com: Gwen Filosa, "Live Updates on Demolition Vote from Council Chambers," http://www. nola.com/news (accessed November 2, 2009); see also Cain Burdeau, "Dozens Protest Projects' Razing," *Associated Press*, December 21, 2007, http://truthout. org (accessed November 2, 2009). For a report of how Nagin "heralded" the acquisition of Taser guns as one of his accomplishments, see Michelle Krupa and Frank Donze, "Nagin Reveals Plan for Dwindling Term," *Times-Picayune*, May 21, 2009, 1, national edition.

64. Katy Reckdahl, "Social Workers Clear Camps for Homeless," *Times-Picayune*, July 18, 2008, 1, national edition; John Moreno Gonzales, "After Despair, New Orleans Homeless Camp Cleared, *Associated Press*, July 18, 2008, Lexis-Nexis (accessed November 3, 2009); and Katy Reckdahl, "Homeless Camp Springs Up on Claiborne Avenue; Many Say They Came from Duncan Plaza," *Times-Picayune*, January 1, 2008, 1, metro edition.

65. Katy Reckdahl, "City May Move Homeless from Underpass to Shelter; Plan Targets Those at Claiborne Camp," *Times-Picayune*, February 9, 2008, 1, national edition; Richard Webster, "New Orleans' Homeless Policy on Shaky Legal Ground," *New Orleans City Business*, February 18, 2008, Lexis-Nexis (accessed November 3, 2009); and John Moreno Gonzales, "Group Helps House New Orleans' Homeless," *Associated Press*, December 22, 2007, Lexis-Nexis (accessed November 3, 2009). As Reckdahl's and Webster's articles explain, however, the most likely city ordinance to which Nagin might have been referring, a "public habitation ordinance," was ruled unconstitutional in federal court in 1986. Nevertheless, the New Orleans Police Department made arrests under the invalid ordinance until the city council voted to repeal it in 2001. Confusion continued to surround this "ordinance," however, because of the Municipal Code Corporation's failure to remove it from subsequent publications of the municipal code, meaning that if one looked at the municipal ordinance book, one would still

see the ordinance as if it were a valid legal rule, although it has not been a valid legal rule for over twenty years. Arrests were made under the "ordinance" as recently as 2002 in a "clean up" of the French Quarter.

66. Angela Patterson, "Testimony by Angela Patterson, Director, UNITY Welcome Home," House of Representatives, House Financial Services Subcommittee on Housing and Community Opportunity Hearing, August 21, 2009, Lexis-Nexis (accessed November 2, 2009).

67. William Wallace, "Louisiana Superdome: The 'People Place,'" *New York Times,* November 4, 1971, 61; William Wallace, "Coliseums: The Game Is Profits," *New York Times,* January 16, 1972, F15; Jeff Gerth, "Superdome a Bottomless Pit for Taxpayer Funds," *New York Times,* January 13, 1978, A13; Jimmy Smith, "Dome Alone as Domed Stadiums Elsewhere Become Obsolete, The Superdome Approaches 25 as Vibrant as Ever," *Times-Picayune,* July 11, 1999, C1; Shelly Sigo, "Louisiana Superdome Panel," *Bond Buyer,* July 19, 2001, 39; Tedra DeSue, "The Superdome Deal: Fixing the Roof and Raising Spirits," *Bond Buyer,* December 28, 2006, 24A; U.S. Census Bureau, "Governments: Louisiana," http://www2. census.gov/govs/cog/gc0212la.pdf (accessed July 5, 2007); Betsy Ziobron, "After the Storm," *Communication News,* November 2006, 12; and David Barron and John Lopez, "The Superdome Reopens," *Houston Chronicle,* September 26, 2006, 1.

68. Smith and Keller, "'Managed Growth' and the Politics of Uneven Development in New Orleans," 134–35; Edward Haas, *DeLesseps S. Morrison and the Image of Reform* (Baton Rouge: Louisiana State University Press, 1974), 58, 290–91; and Agnes Meyer, "New Orleans Sheds Its Shackles," *Washington Post,* May 5, 1946, B1.

69. Smith and Keller, "'Managed Growth,'" 134–35.

70. Haas, *DeLesseps S. Morrison,* 290–91.

71. J. Mark Souther, "Into the Big League: Conventions, Football, and the Color Line in New Orleans," *Journal of Urban History* 29 (2003): 694–725.

72. CNN, *Katrina: State of Emergency* (Kansas City: Andrews McMeel, 2005).

73. Use of the "container" metaphor resonates in numerous ways for those who have lived in New Orleans. As a port city, the New Orleans economy relies, in part, upon opening itself up to global trade. New Orleans serves as a nodal point in the commerce of goods that are shipped into and out of the United States in containers (much as its economy also relies, in part, upon opening itself up to outsiders in the form of the tourist). Post–September 11, 2001, however, those with "homeland" security anxieties have focused upon these containers flowing through New Orleans as a risk to be policed in a similarly zero-tolerance manner as New Orleans's container spaces: is there a threat lying, unknown, within a container? Can "we" contain that which threatens "us"?

74. Bureau of Justice Statistics, "The Number of Adults in the Correctional Population Has Been Increasing," U.S. Department of Justice, n.d., http://www. ojp.usdoj.gov/bjs/glance/corr2.htm (accessed May 31, 2007).

75. Jonathan Simon, *Governing through Crime* (Oxford: Oxford University Press, 2007); and Garland, *Culture of Control.*

76. Bureau of Justice Statistics, "Prisoners in 2005," *Bureau of Justice Statistics Bulletin* (Washington, D.C.: U.S. Department of Justice, Office of Justice Programs, November 2006), www.ojp.usdoj.gov/bjs/p05.htm (accessed May 31, 2007). Actually, Louisiana coasted to the national lead in this statistical category as its prison population actually declined in 2005 by 2.3 percent.

77. Allen J. Beck, "Prison and Jail Inmates at Midyear 1999," *Bureau of Justice Statistics Bulletin* (Washington, D.C.: U.S. Department of Justice, Office of Justice Programs, April, 2000), http://www.ojp.usdoj.gov/bjs/pub/ascii/pjim99.txt (accessed May 31, 2007).

78. American Civil Liberties Union, *Abandoned and Abused: Orleans Parish Prisoners in the Wake of Hurricane Katrina* (ACLU National Prison Project, August 10, 2006), 13, www.aclu.org/pdfs/prison/oppreport20060809.pdf (accessed May 31, 2007).

79. Jordan Flaherty, "Imprisoned in New Orleans," *Colorlines*, Spring, 2006, http://www.colorlines.com (accessed May 31, 2007).

80. C. J. Schexnayder, "What Price Incarceration," *Best of New Orleans*, November 19, 2002, http://www.bestofneworleans.com (accessed May 31, 2007).

81. ACLU, *Abandoned and Abused*, 40.

82. Ibid., 65. Sitting in the sun on the hot asphalt, 20 reportedly passed out before deputies even considered bringing water.

83. Mike Davis, *Planet of the Slums* (New York: Verso, 2006).

84. Loïc Wacquant, "Deadly Symbiosis: When Ghetto and Prison Meet and Mesh," in *Mass Imprisonment: Social Causes and Consequences*, ed. David Garland (London: Sage, 2001), 83–84.

85. Douglas Brinkley, *The Great Deluge: Hurricane Katrina, New Orleans, and the Mississippi Gulf Coast* (New York: William Morrow, 2006), 288–89.

86. Ibid., 375, 403, 456, 464, 467, 591.

87. Leah Hodges, "Written Testimony for the Record," Select Bipartisan Committee to Investigate the Preparation for the response to Hurricane Katrina, December 6, 2005, htt://www.katrina.house.gov/hearings/12_06_05/hodges_120605.rft (accessed November 3, 2009).

88. "The Bridge to Gretna," *60 Minutes* (CBS News Transcripts, December 18, 2005); Brinkley, *Great Deluge*, 468–69.

89. "Bridge to Gretna."

90. Brinkley, *Great Deluge*, 472–73.

91. Mona Lynch, "From the Punitive City to the Gated Community: Security and Segregation across the Social and Penal Landscape," *University of Miami Law Review* 56 (2001): 95, 103.

92. The efforts of Mayors Koch and Giuliani, if not of Dinkins as well, to reorient New York City away from the poor and toward the middle class and tourists, if not the rich, have born fruit as recent census figures show that New York City has become more wealthy—leading one essayist to complain in the *New York Times* about the difficulty of living in the city for under $500,000. See Susan Fainstein, *City Builders: Property Development in New York and London, 1980–2000* (Lawrence: University of Kansas Press, 2001); Smith, *The New Urban Frontier*; Sam Roberts, "Census Shows a More Diverse and Prosperous New York," *New York Times*, December 9, 2008, A27; Allen Salkin, "*You* Try to Live on 500K in This Town," *New York Times*, February 8, 2009, 1, Sunday Styles section.

93. Martha Moore, "Cities Opening More Video Surveillance Eyes," *USA Today*, July 17, 2005, www.usatoday.com (accessed June 21, 2007); Bill Sasser, "Locking Out New Orleans' Poor," *Salon.com*, June 12, 2006, http://www.salon.com (accessed June 21, 2007); Craig Morse and Elliot Dale, "New Orleans Battle for Public Housing," *Z Magazine Online*, February, 2007, http://www.zcommunications.org/zmag (accessed June 22, 2007).

94. Susan Saulny, "5,000 Public Housing Units in New Orleans Are to Be Razed," *New York Times*, June 15, 2006, http://www.nytimes.com/ (accessed June 21, 2007); Anita Sinha, "Prepared Statement of Anita Sinha, Senior Attorney, Advancement Project," House Committee on Financial Services, Subcommittee on Housing and Community Opportunity, Field Hearing on the Status of the "Big Four" Four Years After Hurricane Katrina (August 21, 2009), http://www.house.gov/apps/hearing/financialsvcs_dem/sinha.pdf (accessed August 25, 2009).

95. Housing activist and then-sociology graduate student (he is currently an Assistant Professor) Jay Arena followed the neoliberalization of New Orleans and its biopolitical logic in depth. See Jay Arena, "We're Back! Reopen Our Homes Now!" *Z Magazine Online*, February 26, 2006, http://www.zcommunications.org/zmag (accessed June 11, 2007); Jay Arena, "The Contradictions of Black Comprador Rule," *Z Magazine Online*, January 26, 2006, http://www.zcommunications.org/zmag (accessed June 21, 2007); Jay Arena, "The War at Home," *Z Magazine Online*, November 12, 2005, http://www.zcommunications.org/zmag (accessed June 21, 2007). See also Bill Quigley "Urban Removal," *Black Commentator*, June 28, 2007, http://tompaine.com/ (accessed June 28, 2007).

96. Michael Kunzelman, "FEMA Closing Trailer Parks on Eve of Hurricane Season," Associated Press, May 28, 2008, Lexis-Nexis (accessed November 7, 2009).

97. "FEMA's Dirty Little Secret: A Rare Look Inside the Renaissance Village Trailer Park, Home to Over 2,000 Hurricane Katrina Evacuees," *Democracy Now*, April 24, 2006 (transcript), http://www.democracynow.org/ (accessed July 2, 2007); Sandy Davis, "Empty FEMA Trailers; Hundreds of Units Stand Unoccupied in Louisiana," *The Advocate*, July 16, 2006, A1.

98. Renae Merle, "Storm-Wracked Parish Considers Hired Guns," *Washington Post*, March 14, 2006, A1, http://www.washingtonpost.com/ (accessed July 8, 2007); "Statement of Robert B. Rosenkranz, President, Government Services Division, DynCorp International before the Subcommittee on Management, Investigation, and Oversight Committee on Homeland Security," House of Representatives, Hearing on "Increasing the Number of U.S. Border Patrol Agents," June 19, 2007, homeland.house.gov/sitedocuments/20070619152426-71242.pdf (accessed July 8, 2007).

99. Jeremy Scahill, *Blackwater* (New York: Nation Books, 2007), 332.

100. Jamie Wilson, "Mercenaries Guard Homes of the Rich in New Orleans," *Guardian*, September 12, 2005, http://www.guardian.co.uk/ (accessed July 8, 2007).

101. Joanne Kimberlin and Bill Sizemore, "Blackwater on American Soil," *Virginia-Pilot*, July 27, 2006.

102. "Disaster Security: Protecting People and Property during Times of Crisis," PR Newswire US, October 27, 2005, Lexis-Nexis (accessed June 22, 2007).

103. Brinkley, *Great Deluge*, 302, 519–520.

104. This and the following information is taken from Kevin Regan, "Statement of Kevin T. Regan, Vice President, Operations, Starwood Hotels and Resorts," Private Sector Response to Katrina, United States Senate, Homeland Security and Governmental Affairs Committee, *Congressional Quarterly Testimony*, November 16, 2005, Lexis-Nexis (accessed June 12, 2007).

105. Kathy Bergen, "Hotel Manager Stood Tall in the Chaos All around Him," *Chicago Tribune*, December 18, 2005, 1.

106. Curtis Herbert, "Statement of Curtis Herbert, Executive Vice President, Entergy Corporation," United States Senate, Testimony before the Energy and Natural Resources Committee, October 6, 2005, Lexis-Nexis (accessed July 19, 2007).

107. Brinkley, *Great Deluge*.

108. Bergen, "Hotel Manager Stood Tall," 1; Mary Foster, "2000 Stranded as Superdome Exodus Halted," *The Sun Herald* (Sydney, Australia), September 4, 2005, 3; on correlating risk assessments to consumer profiles, see Passavant, "Strong Neoliberal State."

109. Brian Thevenot and Gordon Russell, no title, Newhouse News Service, September 25, 2005, Lexis-Nexis (accessed June 22, 2007); Brinkley, *Great Deluge*, 78.

110. Joseph Treaster, "Haven from the Flood Becomes a Purgatory; Superdome Refuge 'Worse Than a Prison,'" *International Herald Tribune* (September 2, 2005), 5.

111. Matt Sedensky, "Final Chapter in Storm Exodus Is Epic Bus Journey," *Associated Press*, September 3, 2005, Lexis-Nexis (accessed June 22, 2007).

112. Tim Dahlberg, "Two Police Officers Return to the Superdome That Was Their Prison, Too," *Associated Press*, September 7, 2005, Lexis-Nexis (accessed June 22, 2007).

113. Mary Foster, "Storm Refugees Snarl Superdome Evacuations," *Associated Press Online*, September 2, 2005, Lexis-Nexis (accessed November 7, 2009).

114. Tom Foreman, et. al., "Thousands Feared Dead in New Orleans," *The Situation Room*, Cable News Network Transcript, August 31, 2005, Lexis-Nexis (accessed June 22, 2007).

115. Lee Jenkins, "Superdome Stars: Everyday People Confronted Chaos," *New York Times*, August 6, 2006, 1, sports section.

116. Jeff Duncan, "Superdome: Refuge of Last Resort," *Times-Picayune*, August 30, 2006, 1, sports section.

117. Tim Harper, "Chaos Katrina: The Scene," *Toronto Star*, September 1, 2005, A1.

118. Lisa Rein, "'Reliant City': For Evacuees, a Home Away from Home; Mini-Town Set Up at Sports Complex," *Washington Post*, September 12, 2005, A8.

119. "Louisiana Superdome Sports Nortel Secure Converged Network for Anywhere, Anytime Game Action," *Canada NewsWire*, November 13, 2006, Lexis-Nexis (accessed June 22, 2007).

120. Stacey Plaisance, "Superdome Reopening Draws Celebrities," *Associated Press Online*, September 26, 2006, Lexis-Nexis (accessed November 8, 2009).

121. Rigorously understood, salvation of anything occurs through a constitutive negation. What we see in post-Katrina New Orleans is what, specifically is deemed worthy of salvation and what, specifically, is the constituting negation.

122. Pete Thamel, "2 Major Bowls Will Test New Orleans's Recovery," *New York Times*, sec. 8, April 29, 2007, 5.

123. Ibid.

124. Ibid.

125. Department of Homeland Security, "National Security Special Events," http://www.dhs.gov/ (accessed July 11, 2005); United States Secret Service, "National Special Security Events," http://www.secretservice.gov/nsse.shtml (accessed July 11, 2005); Larry Copeland, "Big Easy Lets Its Hair Down, but Not Its Guard," *USA Today*, December 11, 2001, A3.

126. Michael Gips, "Faster, Stronger, Safer," *Security Management*, February, 2002, http://www.securitymanagement.com/ (accessed April 30, 2009); David Shepardson, "Super Bowl; Super Security," *Detroit News*, January 25, 2006, http://www.detnews.com/ (accessed November 8, 2009); "Super Bowl XL Security: NORAD and U.S. Coast Guard," American Forces Press Service, February 4, 2006, http://www.michnews.com/ (accessed March 7, 2006).

127. Copeland, "Big Easy Lets Its Hair Down, but Not Its Guard;" R. V. Baugus, "Super Safe," *Facility Manager*, September–October, 2003, http://www.iaam.org/ (accessed July 11, 2005).

128. Mary Foster, "New Orleans Gets Final Four," *Associated Press*, November 19, 2008, Lexis-Nexis (accessed November 8, 2009); Ted Lewis, "New Orleans to Host Women's Final Four," *Times-Picayune*, November 15, 2008; Brett Martel,

"New Orleans Officially Seeking 2013 Super Bowl," Associated Press, March 28, 2009, Lexis-Nexis (accessed November 8, 2009).

129. Tim Reynolds, "Dome Sweet Dome: New Orleans Gets 2013 Super Bowl," Associated Press, May 19, 2009, Lexis-Nexis (accessed November 8, 2009).

130. "Scalise Congratulates NFL for Choosing New Orleans for 2013 Super Bowl," *States News Service*, May 19, 2009, Lexis-Nexis (accessed November 8, 2009).

131. Jaquetta White, "Extra Points; Super Bowl XLVII Will Pay Off for Years, Tourism Officials Say," *Times-Picayune*, May 20, 2009, 1, money section.

132. Brett Martel, "Return of Major Sports Aids New Orleans' Recovery," *Associated Press Online*, May 23, 2009, Lexis-Nexis (accessed November 8, 2009).

133. "Who Dat Rebuilding Poydras?" (editorial) *Times-Picayune*, September 19, 2009, 6, metro edition.

134. Zygmunt Bauman, *Globalization: The Human Consequences* (New York: Columbia University Press, 1998).

135. Brinkley, *Great Deluge*, 54–55.

CHAPTER 5

Whose Choice?

A Critical Race Perspective on Charter Schools

Adrienne Dixson

It took the storm of a lifetime, to create the opportunity of a lifetime. . . . This is a once-in-a-lifetime opportunity. We must not let it pass us by.

—Kathleen Babineaux Blanco

IN FALL 2005, Louisiana Governor Kathleen Babineaux Blanco signed into law Legislative Act 35 (LA 35), which gave the state power to control failing school districts. As a result of LA 35, the state board of education established the Recovery School District (RSD) and took control of 107 of 128 New Orleans Public Schools (NOPS). As part of the rebuilding effort and with the support of federal funds from the U.S. Department of Education, the state developed a plan to reopen schools in New Orleans. Currently, forty of seventy-nine public schools are charter schools. The RSD runs twenty-two of the forty charter schools. The remaining eighteen are either independently run or operated by the Orleans Parish School Board (OPSB). While a number of scholars have examined charter schools, New Orleans provides an interesting case in that the landscape of public schooling has been radically transformed and exists essentially as a city without a traditional single school district.[1] Given the recent history of school reform of this magnitude, specifically the reform efforts in Chicago, Philadelphia, Washington, DC, and Milwaukee, little research exists that examines the complete overhauling of public schooling on the scale found in New Orleans. That is, while large urban school districts have certainly experienced school reform in various iterations, reform of this nature is relatively new and understudied.[1] For example, the loss of human capital, specifically, the firing of black teachers and principals by the Orleans Parish School Board months after Katrina, rivals the loss of employment for black teachers and administrators after the *Brown vs. Board of Education* decision.[2]

The purpose of the larger ongoing study from which this chapter is drawn is to examine the rebuilding of public education in post-Katrina New Orleans from the perspective of stakeholders—parents, teachers, and community members. The aspect of the study that I focus on in this chapter is their responses to and understanding of the hybrid nature of public schools in New Orleans that contain both traditional public schools (i.e., schools that exist and existed as part of the New Orleans Public Schools) and charter schools. Specifically, the following research questions guide the project: What happens when traditional public schooling is replaced by a hybrid, free-market model? And how do these reforms impact communities of color, specifically as it relates to educational and racial equity? Given that the popular rhetoric of charter proponents is that charter schools help to address educational inequity by offering parents, especially low-income parents of color, the opportunity to choose a school for their child as opposed to the normal route of neighborhood school assignment by the school district, this chapter shows some of the challenges that parents encounter as they navigate a system of schools that is emerging as a three-tiered system that may exacerbate racialized educational inequity. Thus, this project ultimately considers what happens to democratic public education when given sway to the notion of "100% choice" and charter schools.

As demonstrated by the displacement of black teachers and the challenges parents face in finding a school for their child, the data from this ongoing study also offer some insight into the racial landscape of public education in New Orleans. I locate my analysis within critical race theory (CRT). In the tradition of CRT, I use counternarrative to describe pre-Katrina public education and embed other tenets of CRT, namely, restrictive versus expansive notions of equality and whiteness as property.

Theoretical Framework

CRT has its origins in the law and emerged in response to the neo-Marxist critical legal studies, or CLS, movement of the 1970s. CLS scholars were critical of U.S. *jurisprudence* and argued that remedies that addressed class disparities would also address all disparities.

Gloria Ladson-Billings and William F. Tate IV introduced CRT to education in 1994. They argued that race was undertheorized in education and that explanations for educational inequity failed to consider the impact of racism on the educational outcomes of students of color.

According to CRT scholar Charles Lawrence,

> Critical Race Theory focuses on the persistence of conditions created by and traditionally associated with racist practice. As opposed to liberal theory, which promotes the equality of individuals through process, Critical Race Theory promotes substantive equality as the result of legislative and judicial action. By reflecting the perspective of the subordinated, Critical Race Theory articulates a theory of equality and human dignity that is grounded in anti-subordination principles.[3]

CRT scholars in education have engaged in scholarship that critiques the liberal ideology of early multicultural education scholarship;[4] examined the school curriculum as a form of property for which access to high-quality and rigorous curricula is afforded primarily based on race;[5] examined the impact of affirmative action and school desegregation policies;[6] analyzed the inequities of school funding;[7] looked at the relationship between the color-blind discourse and teachers' pedagogies in low-income urban schools;[8] and argued for a critical race methodology.[9]

For the purposes of this chapter, and in light of the topic's personal meaning for me, I am drawing on the CRT tradition of using "the word"[10] to describe the preliminary findings. It is important to note that because this is an ongoing study, the findings I offer are preliminary and emerging.[11]

Post-Brown and Pre-Katrina: Race and Education in New Orleans

Norman Rockwell's famous portrait, "The Problem We All Live With," that depicted U.S. Marshals walking a young black girl into a school building poignantly captured the context of race and public education in New Orleans in the 1960s. The girl in Rockwell's portrait was not an image conjured by his imagination but rather was Ruby Bridges, a six-year-old girl who bravely integrated William Franz Elementary School on November 14, 1960.[12] Although Franz School and McDonogh 19[13] were integrated, it was not until the 1969–1970 school year that OPSB was fully desegregated through the twelfth grade.[14] While the district experienced fluctuations in its enrollment among black and white students from the 1970s through the 1980s, by the 2004–2005 school year, the district had a black enrollment of 94 percent. In addition, 77 percent of the student enrollment in OPSB was also eligible for free/reduced lunch.

As the student enrollment in New Orleans integrated racially, so did the teaching force. In 1937, black teachers formed their own union as an affiliate of the American Federation of Teachers (AFT). They established the Local 527. The local chapter of the National Education Association was segregated and only open to whites. Establishing the Local 527 was the only way black teachers could organize and protest the disparity in pay between themselves and their white counterparts.[15] In 1972, the two unions combined and formed the United Teachers of New Orleans (UTNO) and represented nearly 5,000 teachers in the city. By 2005, UTNO represented 7,500 teachers and other school staff. The racial demographics of the OPSB teaching force were 90 percent African American representing nearly 4,000 teachers. After Katrina, those numbers have shifted most dramatically in the RSD schools where Teach For America teachers (see Table 5.1) comprise the majority of teachers in RSD direct-run schools.[16]

TABLE 5.1

New Orleans Teachers by Years of Experience before and after Katrina

	0–1 YEARS	2–3 YEARS	4–10 YEARS	11–14 YEARS	15–19 YEARS	20–24 YEARS	25+ YEARS
2004–2005	9.7%	7.3%	24.7%	9.0%	8.9%	10.9%	29.5%
2007–2008	36.7%	17.2%	19.3%	4.8%	5.5%	4.9%	11.6%
Change (04–05 and 07–08)	27.0%	9.9%	−5.4%	−4.2%	−3.4%	−6.0%	−17.9%

Source: Cowen Institute, 2009.

"The Storm of a Lifetime": Legislative Act 35

Authored by a bipartisan group of sixteen state senators and representatives, Louisiana Legislative Act 35 (LA 35), was signed into law by Governor Kathleen Babineaux Blanco during a special session of the Louisiana Legislature on November 22, 2005. Eleven of the twenty representatives from Orleans Parish voted against the legislation. LA 35 was a revision of Louisiana Legislative Act 9 (LA 9) passed in 2003. Act 9 was authored by six of the same state senators and representatives who authored LA 35. LA 9 allowed for the establishment and governance of the RSD, a state-run school district that would take over a failed school(s). LA 9 identifies four criteria for determining a failed school:

(a) fails to present a plan to reconstitute the failed school to the state board, as required pursuant to such an accountability program, or (b) presents a reconstitution plan that is unacceptable to the state board, or (c) fails at any time to comply with the terms of the reconstitution plan approved by the state board, or (d) the school has been labeled an academically unacceptable school for four consecutive years.

In Louisiana, the primary state accountability program is the Louisiana Educational Assessment Program (LEAP), the standardized testing program designed to measure students' academic achievement.[17] The LEAP was part of the composite that made up the School Performance Score (SPS).[18] LA 9 allowed the RSD to take over "academically unacceptable" (AU) schools with an SPS of 45 for four years. In 2004, the state legislature raised the SPS score to 60. The average SPS for the State of Louisiana was 86.2 in the 2004–2005 school year. By July 2004, the RSD had taken over one school run by the OPSB. As late as May 2005, just three months before Hurricane Katrina and six months before Governor Blanco signed LA 35 into law, the RSD had only taken over four OPSBs.[19]

Among other issues relative to accountability, funding, and oversight of public elementary and secondary schools, LA 9 was also an entrée for charter schools in Louisiana. The specific language in the legislation is thus, "to establish and provide for a Type 5 charter school; to eliminate the termination of the authority for certain chartering authorities to enter into certain types of charters; to provide for an effective date; and to provide for related matters."

With the passage of LA 35, the minimum SPS was raised to "below" the state average of 87.4. Indeed, OPSB schools were above the SPS cutoff of 60 yet still taken over by the RSD. In fact, LA 35 not only allowed the RSD to take over individual schools but also expanded its jurisdiction to entire school districts that had 30 or more schools that were AU. OPSB was one of the fourteen school districts in the state that had at least thirty schools. According to Dr. Barbara Ferguson, founder of the Center of Action Research on New Orleans School Reform, the Board of Elementary and Secondary Education only applied the SPS score cutoff to schools in Orleans Parish.[20] Both Ferguson's 2010 report on what she describes as the "double standard" of the SPS scores (see Table 5.2) and a 2010 report by the Cowen Institute at Tulane University show that no other schools the state that had been taken over by the RSD had SPS scores above 60 (see Table 5.3).

Prior to Hurricane Katrina, OPSB operated 128 schools and was the only district in the state with that many schools. As a result of LA 35, RSD was able to take over 112 of the 128 schools run by OPSB. The law was changed such that schools did not have to be AU for four consecutive years before RSD could take them over. In addition, Blanco signed two executive orders that expanded chartering options. The first executive order removed timelines with respect to when the RSD could take over a school. The second executive order lifted the requirement that parents and teachers approve of the charter. For many stakeholders, especially teachers and UTNO, it appeared that LA 35 was designed to target OPSB and create the conditions that led to the firing of the entire teaching force in OPSB and effectively dismantle the teachers' union.[21] This maneuvering created the "system of systems" currently in place for public education in New Orleans (see Figure 5.1).

According to a 2007 report by UTNO, teachers in New Orleans, whether in an RSD school (charter/noncharter) or an OPSB school (charter/noncharter), unlike their colleagues in neighboring parishes, have no collective bargaining agreement with their employers and their work conditions are often more stringent—longer work days and larger class sizes. They also have no job security because of the absence of a tenure system and working on an "at-will" contract from year to year. In some charter schools, teachers are forbidden from discussing their salaries because they are negotiated on an individual basis. Discussing and/or

TABLE 5.2

Pre-Katrina School Performance Scores (SPS) for Schools in Orleans Parish School Board (OPSB)

SCHOOL NAME	GRADES	BASELINE SPS 04–05
Henry W. Allen Elementary School	Pre-K–7	65.6
Thurgood Marshall Middle School	7–8	77.6
Stuart R. Bradley Elementary School	Pre-K–6	78.5
Parkview Fundamental Magnet	Pre-K–6	85.7
Mary D. Coghill Elementary School	Pre-K–6	76.6
John Dibert Elementary School	Pre-K–6	65.8
Dwight D. Eisenhower Elementary School	Pre-K–6	67.6
William J. Fischer Elementary School	Pre-K–6	73.8
Gentilly Terrace Elementary School	Pre-K–6	65.5
William J. Guste Elementary School	Pre-K–6	66.2
Paul B. Habans Elementary School	K–6	64.2
Thomy Lafon Elementary School	Pre-K–6	61.5
Ronald G. McNair Elementary School	Pre-K–6	70.6
McDonogh 15 Creative Arts Magnet	Pre-K–6	63.5
McDonogh #07 Elementary School	Pre-K–6	64.6
Harriet Tubman Elementary School	Pre-K–6	73.3
Mildred Osborne Elementary School	Pre-K–8	62.6
Rabouin Career Magnet High School	8–12	61.1
H.C. Schaumburg Elementary School	Pre-K–8	72.1
Sherwood Forest Elementary School	Pre-K–6	64.5
New Orleans Free School	K–8	63.6
Dr. MLK Elementary School for Science and Technology	Pre-K–6	81.8
New Orleans Charter Middle School	6–8	70.5
Lake Area Middle School	7–8	63.0
New Orleans Technology High School	9	61.7

Source: Barbara Ferguson, New Orleans Schools Decline Following State's "Double Standard" Takeover, Center for Action Research on New Orleans School Reforms, February 2010.

TABLE 5.3

Schools in Other Louisiana Parishes with SPS Scores below 60

SCHOOL NAME	BASELINE SPS 2008–2009
Linear Middle School	52.9
Linwood Middle School	51.1
Banks Elementary	52.4
Capitol Middle School	54.6
Crestworth Middle	49.5
Dalton Elementary	54.4
Kenilworth Middle School	55
Lanier Elementary	56.6
Parker Elementary	49.4
Take over school average	52.8
Louisiana SPS average	86.2

Source: Cowen Institute, March 2010.

disclosing their salary can be grounds for dismissal.[22] These conditions are in stark contrast to pre-Katrina conditions for teachers in OPSB. Teachers who were not dues-paying members of UTNO were covered by the benefits of the collective bargaining agreements. However, one veteran teacher I interviewed who worked in OPSB pre-Katrina and has returned to an RSD charter believes that working in the charter is in many ways better than under the old system.[23] For this teacher, a twenty-year veteran, native New Orleanian and graduate of a teacher education program at a local historically black college, teaching in a charter school affords her more autonomy and control over the curriculum. Moreover, she appreciated that school administrators were responsive to her requests for curricular and teaching materials. She also appreciated the fact that she did not have to navigate the bureaucracy of a central office to get what she believed she needed to effectively teach her students. It is important to note, however, her school is one of the few schools, within the current schooling context in New Orleans, where most of the teachers in her school, with the exception of two new teachers, are veteran OPSB teachers.[24] Both the principal and assistant principal taught in OPSB. The

GOVERNANCE STRUCTURE
September 2009

**Board of Elementary and Secondary Education (BESE) &
Louisiana Department of Education
State Superintendent: Paul Pastorek**

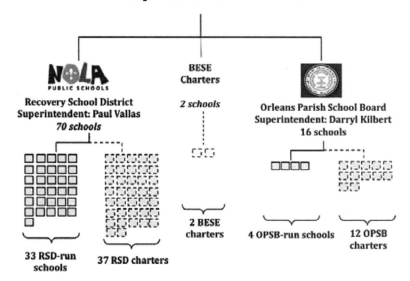

Figure 5.1. Public School Governance in New Orleans. From Cowen Institute, Creating a
Governing Framework for Public Education in New Orleans: School District Political
Leadership *November 2009 and Louisiana Department of Education, September 2009.*

principal led a school for nearly ten years before Hurricane Katrina. Thus,
while this teacher enjoys control, she also enjoys working in a school with
a stable and experienced faculty, which in many ways allows her to focus
on her instruction rather than on climate and discipline issues. This teacher's
preference for her charter school over OPSB supports the finding by the
AFT that teachers value stable and positive working conditions, supportive administrators and feeling comfortable working with particular groups
of students over higher salaries and benefits.[25]

They're Trying to Wash Us Away

For many New Orleanians, especially African Americans, returning to the city is difficult given the shortage of affordable housing options, an unfamiliar school terrain, and uncertain employment opportunities. Several of the participants in the study also described the trials of trying to return to New Orleans and rebuild their lives. One participant, Ken Brock,[26] a father of two sons who have autism and the founder of a nonprofit advocacy agency for parents with children with special needs, described the financial and emotional drain of rebuilding post-Katrina. In addition, he described the challenges for parents of children with special needs trying to navigate a complicated network of schools that do not share information or records and who seem indifferent about serving those children.[27]

> The training of personnel is still the major issue. It was a major issue then [before Katrina] and it's still the major issue as far as I'm concerned. People are not trained to do some of the things they are being asked to do. And, you have to keep saying it. I've had these conversations with Margaret [Director of Special Education for the RSD] just recently about the training stuff. She understands that trying to implement Positive Behavior Support, that people are not trained. And, so, you have this expectation that they are [teachers and school level personnel] going to buy into something, I'm not sure that they know what they're buying into. It's a difficult situation. Because right now, this charterized system is very difficult. It's hard to figure out where to go [for information on special education supports]. I just don't know.[28]

This need for special education is no small matter, especially in post-Katrina New Orleans, where students' needs might have been exacerbated by the trauma of Katrina. Moreover, exact numbers of students with special needs are difficult to ascertain as student records were lost during the storm and schools have been slow to reevaluate students to determine their classifications. However, in the RSD, about 12 percent of their student population have special needs.[29]

Two weeks before Hurricane Katrina made landfall, I had been hosting in my home in Columbus, Ohio, Lashonda, a young woman who was in the first six-grade class I taught at Charles E. Gayarre Elementary[30] in

New Orleans in the early 1990s. Because her biological mother was mostly absent due to persistent drug addiction, I have been an othermother[31] to Lashonda since she was twelve years old. From the time that she was in the sixth grade and until I left New Orleans for graduate school, she would stay in my home for extended periods, often accompanying my children and me on vacations. We maintained contact and she visited me while I was working on my doctorate, attended my graduation, and visited me when I had my first academic job. In May 2005, I returned to New Orleans to be the "mother of the bride" at her wedding. Several months after her wedding, Lashonda came to visit me in Columbus for a few weeks in August 2005. She was scheduled to return to New Orleans on August 28, 2005.

I had been through this before, this "mess" with hurricanes. I was living in New Orleans when meteorologists predicted Hurricane Andrew was going to sink the city. With my two small sons in tow, I drove through the miles of traffic on Airline Highway to Baton Rouge, only to be stuck there for three days because the heavy rains flooded the city. Andrew bypassed New Orleans but devastated Miami.[32] My friends and family teased me for evacuating for Andrew since many had stayed for other hurricanes, with all of them citing Betsy as the worst. Yet, for Katrina, most heeded the calls to evacuate. My cousin's husband worked offshore in Houston, and although she maintained a household in New Orleans, his company made arrangements for her and their youngest son to go to a hotel in the French Quarter. One-by-one I received telephone calls or text messages from people letting me know they were headed out of the city and that they would be in touch when they were home in a few days. While we watched the news, Lashonda and I worked on changing her ticket since she was supposed to return to New Orleans on the day the hurricane was scheduled to make landfall. The airlines were unwilling to reroute her before Sunday in the event that the hurricane did not hit New Orleans. We managed to get her re-routed to Houston on Monday, August 29, where she ended up living with her husband, son, and mother-in-law for the next year and a half. They had lost everything during Katrina, and although they did not own a home, they were able to recoup some of their losses through the FEMA funds and the SBA loan Lashonda qualified for to compensate her for the loss of her cosmetology equipment. She had been gainfully self-employed before Katrina as a hair stylist and was renting a booth at a thriving salon in the Gentilly area of the city. Because she was on vacation when the storm hit, she was not able to make provisions for all of her equipment in anticipation of the storm. In addition, because she was new to Houston, she was not able to build a client base that matched the one she had in New Orleans pre-Katrina. In the hopes of rebuilding her business and being closer to her family, in November 2007, Lashonda, her husband, and now two children returned to New Orleans to rebuild their lives. Like many returnees, her first order of business was to find a school for her son, Andrew, who was in the first grade.[33] For many parents and caregivers who wanted to return to New Orleans, finding affordable housing and a quality school for their children is key to ensuring economic stability for their families.[34] Even after the fifth anniversary of Hurricane Katrina, affordable and viable housing options are still issues that make living in New Orleans economically untenable for most returning families.[35]

Although she was living in New Orleans East in a FEMA trailer attached to her grandmother's home that was being renovated, Lashonda enrolled her son in the New Orleans Free Academy (NOFA)[36] located on Camp Street in Uptown New Orleans about nine miles away. Like most of the charter schools, NOFA offered free busing, something new for native New Orleanians.[37] In February 2009, Lashonda learned that the principal had been told that her contract would not be renewed and the faculty were being terminated; NOFA would be closing at the end of the school year due to poor test scores. She was informed that although NOFA was closing, she could send Andrew to the charter operator's other school located near City Park. At the meeting they also gave the parents a guide that listed all the schools in the city to which she could apply for admission for her son for the next year.[38]

Prior to finding out about NOFA's closing, Lashonda had asked me about schools in the area since she was aware of my research on schooling in the area. She and her family had since moved out of the FEMA trailer and into an apartment farther away from NOFA. She had given birth to her third child, a daughter, in September, one week after evacuating the city for Hurricane Gustav. Her husband was training to be a firefighter and had to stay in the city as a first-responder. As a result of the new baby's birth, her husband's change in work schedule as a firefighter, and their move farther into New Orleans East, Lashonda was looking for a school that was closer to her apartment or her mother-in-law's house in Gentilly so that Andrew could get home from school earlier and in the event that there was an emergency and someone needed to get to the school. In order to get to school on time, Andrew had to get on the bus by 6:30 a.m. and was dropped off at the bus stop near his home at 5:30 p.m.[39] Since I could not give her a personal recommendation for any of the RSD schools or other schools that were closer to her, I recommended the one school I was working with, McDonogh 42 Charter School, since the board president is my former principal and many of the teachers are veteran teachers and my former colleagues from Charles E. Gayarre Elementary School.[40] She decided to wait until the end of the school year to move Andrew. NOFA's announcement about closing provided her with the opportunity to "shop" for another school. She decided to apply to Edward Hynes Charter School, an OPSB charter. Prior to Katrina, Hynes had a good reputation and was one of the better performing schools in OPSB. Hynes' reopening, however, has a contentious history.

Currently, Hynes is housed in the St. James Major building located in Gentilly—a Catholic school that the archdiocese did not reopen after Katrina. The old Hynes building was demolished and not slated for renovation. In the 2006–2007 school year, students were housed on two separate campuses. Like most of the school buildings and other public facilities that suffered damage from Katrina in the city, FEMA cites the Stafford Act to justify repairing buildings only to their pre-Katrina conditions. As a result, a number of buildings that were fifty years old and, in many ways, historical buildings were demolished rather than refurbished, in large part due to funding discrepancies among FEMA, the state, and Orleans Parish.[41] Kimberly Boudreaux, a white woman who is divorced, the mother of three biracial sons (African American and white), and one of the writers of the original charter for Hynes to reopen after Katrina, expressed feeling pressured to write the charter to reopen Hynes because that was the only financial support for reopening schools.[42] She expressed frustration at how the school has been run as a charter and feels that it does not reflect the vision of the group of parents and former Hynes teachers who helped to write the charter. She believed that the charter, in its current iteration, does not reflect the "community priorities, community understanding and knowledge and does not serve the needs of families"[43] and believes the rewritten charter was designed to prevent low-income and presumably low-performing students from attending the school. In fact, Act 35 and the provisions made to facilitate the chartering process by Governor

Blanco's executive orders made it possible for charter operators to open schools that did not reflect the interests or approval of parents and teachers. Thus, as Michael Apple[44] aptly notes,

> The religious status of neoliberalism assumes particular things. Choice, competition, markets—all of these supposedly will lead us to the promised land of efficient and effective schools. The key word here is "supposedly." This is a crucial caveat, since we know that school choice policies, especially those involving marketization and privatization, often involve schools choosing students and parents as much as parents choosing schools.[45]

Apple's insight on the inverse effect of choice describes the experiences many families, most of whom were African American, had trying to enroll their children in school.[46] The Center for Community Change (CCC) reported that in early 2006, as many as 170 students were turned away from schools in New Orleans as they tried to register their children.

Sierra Jones, an African American mother who works as an advocate for parents with children of special needs, has worked with a group of parents to open a traditional public high school in her community. She has been working with RSD to get the school opened because the parents in the community want a neighborhood high school that is not a charter school. While her group has been successful at getting the high school opened in the 2009–2010 school year, she, too, felt the pressure to open it as a charter. She cites the funding that is available from the state as well as from the U.S. Department of Education, the support from foundations and nonprofit agencies in the city to develop school plans, and the support from Paul Vallas of RSD for charters that she believes are not available for traditional public schools.[47] In fact, more funds from the federal government, under both the Bush and Obama administrations, were and are available to open a charter or to convert an existing school to a charter than there are to open a new school under the OPSB or the RSD.[48] These differences in funding the reopening of schools support Apple's insights on what he calls neoliberal school choice policies. These policies and how they are operationalized currently in New Orleans school reform appear to foreclose opportunities for democratic school choice but rather create the forced choice of charter schools.

Wading through the Water of School Enrollment

Despite applying nearly a month before the March 30, 2009, deadline on April 1, 2009, Lashonda received a letter from Hynes stating that Andrew was placed on a waiting list. If the school did not have an opening by October, his name would be removed from the waiting list. The school's process for admissions is open unless they have more applicants than they have spaces available. In the event that they have more applicants than available space, they will hold a lottery to select students. While that appeared to be fair, Lashonda's letter indicated that the lottery was held on March 20, 2009, a full ten days before the application deadline. It is not clear why the school would conduct a lottery before presumably all of the applications have been submitted. Harper Smith, an RSD administrator, expressed frustration with the differential rules for charter school admissions and those for RSD.[49] According to Mr. Smith, charter operators have been able to use the admission caps as justification for turning students away. The RSD, however, cannot turn any student away despite having capacity issues that are manifesting in hiring decisions and the ability to deliver services to students. Despite only living in New Orleans since after Katrina, he did not like the direction that public education in New Orleans was going and believed that families did not, in fact, have a choice in the schools to which they sent their children. "Parents who have social capital can do what they need to do for their kids. The schools are getting further segregated with white schools and black schools. There are more people wedded to 'the experiment.' There will be schools that have the kids that nobody wants."[50] Mr. Smith's observation echoes the findings by UTNO and AFT in their 2006 report on post-Katrina public education.[51]

Conclusion: Who's Choosing Whom?

In this chapter, I have tried to represent the context of education reform in post-Katrina New Orleans through the voices of those stakeholders who, besides the children, are in direct contact with how it is conceptualized and implemented. For the participants in the study that frames this chapter, the current context of public education in New Orleans indeed feels like an experiment on a number of levels: human capital with respect to recruiting and hiring teachers and administrators; school governance with respect to state versus local control; and, school choice/admission with respect to charter versus traditional RSD or OPSB-run schools. Harper Smith's belief that educational reformers in New Orleans are more committed to the experiment than the children could be more than just conjecture and pessimism.

Currently, RSD schools are commonly referred to as the "schools of last resort." Parents do, in fact, shop for schools, yet many are not able to get their first choice, especially if they attempt to enroll their children in the newly chartered schools that were formerly high-performing OPSB schools. The New Orleans Parent Organizing Network emerged to help parents learn how to navigate the "system of schools" that now exists in New Orleans. Yet, understanding how to apply for schools does not ensure that parents are exercising their choice. Instead, parents are forced to choose among a host of schools that have an unproved or unknown record of success as illustrated by Lashonda's experience with the Leona Group's New Orleans Free Academy. Her only guaranteed choice is to register Andrew in the Leona Group's other charter school or to continue to shop for a school that may or may not admit him. While data on the results of the lotteries for the charters are not available, for families like Lashonda's, the process does not suggest it is fair. From a CRT perspective, the lottery system that currently operates in New Orleans is an example of the restrictive versus expansive notion of equality.[52] According to Crenshaw, the restrictive perspective of equality privileges the process that allows access to particular opportunities and institutions. If the process is one that is transparent and presumably fair because *anyone* can participate, the specter of discrimination has been removed. If the process yields access to only a few people of color or others historically marginalized and discriminated, that is just an unfortunate consequence because everyone, theoretically, had an opportunity to apply or attempt to participate. For Crenshaw, this does not address the persistent inequity that a discriminatory history has created and does not ensure that everyone in fact can and does have access to opportunity. She argues that the focus of equality policies has to be on the material outcome of the policies. In other words, if we are to redress historic and persistent inequity, we need to ensure that not only is access fair but also, in fact, that those who have been denied opportunities actually get the opportunity to participate in institutions. In terms of the lottery for charter schools, if the demographics of the schools do not represent the larger public school population such that only a select type of student can enroll, district administrators and other policymakers must reconsider the process such that the school provides opportunities to students who have not had access to it previously.

In light of Lashonda's experience and the challenges for parents of children with special needs as expressed by Ken Brock, the hybrid school system in place in New Orleans is often one that engenders a great deal of frustration and confusion. Moreover, parents and community members who have tried to reopen schools in their neighborhoods report feeling pressured to reopen the schools as charters. This raises the question as to whether charters are the will of the community or the desire of the state. In other words, whose choice is it to have choice in New Orleans?

In the 2009 Emerging Knowledge Forum hosted by the Annenberg Institute and held in New Orleans, Paul Vallas, the current superintendent of the RSD, stated that his goal is to make New Orleans the first school district in the nation that is 100% choice.[53] While Vallas articulates a desire to provide choice for parents, it appears that the only choice will be charters. The schools that the OPSB currently operates or oversees—charter and traditional—are the most selective schools in the city. One of the most selective and highly resourced schools prior to Katrina, Lusher, now has two campuses located uptown in the St. Charles / Tulane University area.[54] Its first priority is to admit who they describe as "in-district" students and will open slots to "community" students "based on a scoring matrix that includes artistic talent, prior classroom grades, standardized test scores and parental involvement."[55] For parents whose children do not show artistic talent, Lusher is not a choice or an option. While racial equity is a part of the public discourse about school reform in New Orleans, the manifestations of the school reform suggest that it is far from racially equitable. As a number of the participants have articulated, 100% choice is a laudable goal if parents actually have the freedom to choose the school they want for their child and if a system is in place to support that choice. The current path of school reform suggests that parents will be forced to choose whatever school is available. This perpetuation of a multi-tiered system of schools seems to suggest that racial inequities will remain intact in New Orleans.

Notes

1. M. Alexander, "Reinventing a Broken Wheel? The Fight to Reclaim Public Education in New Orleans," *Social Policy* (Spring/Summer 2007): 18–23; Katrina E. Bulkley, "Bringing the Private into Public: Changing the Rules of the Game and New Regime Politics in Philadelphia Public Education," *Educational Policy* 21, no. 1 (2007): 155–84; Paul T. Hill and Jane Hannaway, *The Future of Public Education in New Orleans* (Washington, D.C.: The Urban Institute, 2006); Lynne Huntley, *Education after Katrina: Time for a New Federal Response* (Atlanta, Ga.: Southern Education Fund, 2007); Linda A. Renzulli, "Organizational Environments and the Emergence of Charter Schools in the United States," *Sociology of Education*, 78, no. 1 (2005): 1–26; Linda A. Renzulli, and Vincent J. Roscigno, "Charter School Policy, Implementation, and Diffusion across the United States," *Sociology of Education* 78, no. 4 (2005): 344–66; United Teachers of New Orleans (UTNO), Louisiana Federation of Teachers (LFT), and American Federation of Teachers (AFT), *No Experience Necessary: How the New Orleans School Takeover Experiment Devalues Experienced Teachers,* June 2007.

2. Daniella Cook, "Cooperation, Collaboration, and Solidarity: Black Educator Fictive Kinship Networks in Post Katrina New Orleans," *Southern Anthropologist* (in press).

3. C. R. Lawrence, "The Word and the River: Pedagogy as Scholarship, as Struggle," *Stanford Law Review* 65 (1992): 2231–98.

4. G. Ladson-Billings and W. F. Tate IV, "Toward a Critical Race Theory of Education," *Teachers College Record* 97, no. 1 (1995): 47–68.

5. Daniel G. Solorzano, "From Racial Stereotyping to Deficit Discourse toward a Critical Race Theory in Teacher Education," *Multicultural Education* 9, no. 1, (2001): 2–8.

6. Ed Taylor, "Critical Race Theory and Interest Convergence in the Backlash against Affirmative Action: Washington State and Initiative 200," *Teachers College Record* 102, no. 3 (2000): 539–60.

7. Kevin Brady, Timothy Eatman, Laurence Parker, "To Have or Not to Have? A Preliminary Analysis of Higher Education Funding Disparities in the Post-Ayers v. Fordice Era: Evidence from Critical Race Theory," *Journal of Education Finance* 25, no. 3 (Winter 2000): 297–322.

8. A. D. Dixson, "'Taming the Beast': Race, Discourse, and Identity in a Middle School Classroom," in *Literacy as a Civil Right: Reclaiming Social Justice in Literacy Teaching and Learning,* ed. Stuart Greene (New York: Peter Lang Publishers, 2008).

9. T. K. Chapman, "Interrogating Classroom Relationships and Events: Using Portraiture and Critical Race Theory in Education Research," *Educational*

Researcher 36, no. 3 (2007): 156–62; and M. Lynn and L. Parker, "Introductory Overview to the Special Issue. Critical Race Theory and Education: Recent Developments in the Field," *Equity & Excellence in Education* 35, no. 2 (2002): 87–92.

10. Lawrence, "The Word and the River."

11. I am conducting a qualitative study in New Orleans. From August 2008 to January 2009, I was on a ten-week research leave that allowed me to live full-time in the area. I continued to return to New Orleans twice a month from January until June or July 2009 to conduct interviews, attend community meetings, visit schools, and understand the educational landscape of New Orleans. I am still recruiting participants because I would like to have a sample that represents the diversity of the stakeholders. At this point, my sample includes twelve people. I have been able to interview two administrators in the Recovery School District (RSD), one person from the state board of education, one former teacher and two current teachers, three parents, and four people from the educational nonprofit sector. As the study continues, I will interview current teachers in different types of schools, principals, and parents.

12. Ruby Bridges, *Through My Eye* (New York: Scholastic Press, 1999).

13. In the late 1870s, John McDonogh was a wealthy trader and slave owner who left his entire estate to the city to open public schools. There were twenty schools named after John McDonogh and they were numbered. McDonogh 35 opened in 1917 as the only black high school in the city. Until Katrina, McDonogh 35 was one of the premier high schools in the city. Booker T. Washington was opened in 1940 as a career training high school and was also a premier all-black high school in the city. Prior to Katrina, its reputation had declined significantly. Both schools have reopened as charters with McDonogh 35 as an OPSB charter school servicing grades 7 through 12.

14. Cowen Institute, *Recovery School District of Louisiana* (New Orleans, La.: Cowen Institute, Tulane University, 2010).

15. In the 1937–1938 school year, the annual salary for white teachers was $1,193 compared to $504 for black teachers.

16. Cowen Institute, *Recovery School District of Louisiana*.

17. In response to the *No Child Left Behind* legislation (NCLB), Louisiana revised its statewide, high stakes testing program, LEAP is a criterion-referenced, high-stakes examination that schools administer to students in fourth and eighth grades. The LEAP measures students' achievement in English/language arts (ELA), mathematics, science, and the social studies. The LEAP has five achievement ratings: advanced, mastery, basic, approaching basic, and unsatisfactory. Students who do not score "basic" or higher on ELA and mathematics will not be promoted to the next grade level (fifth or ninth grade).

Students in grades 3, 5, 6, 7, and 9 take the Integrated Louisiana Educational Assessment Program, or iLEAP, in ELA and mathematics. The iLEAP has both a norm-referenced component and a criterion-referenced component. Louisiana is the only state in the United States that uses a norm-referenced examination as part of its SPS component to be compliant with NCLB (B. Ferguson, *New Orleans Schools Decline Following State's 'Double Standard' Takeover* [New Orleans, La.: Center for Action Research on New Orleans School Reform, 2010]).

The criterion for promotion to the next grade level is somewhat complicated in that students must score a "basic" or higher on one test and "approaching basic" or higher on the other in order to be promoted to the next grade. For example, a fourth- or eighth-grade student who scored "basic" on mathematics but "approaching basic" on ELA would be promoted to the next grade level. A student who scored "approaching basic" on both mathematics and ELA would be retained.

18. Included in the SPS are school attendance and dropout rates.

19. Cowen Institute, *Recovery School District of Louisiana.*

20. B. Ferguson, *New Orleans Schools Decline.*

21. UTNO, *No Experience Necessary.*

22. Ibid.

23. Interview notes, August 25, 2008.

24. Cowen Institute, *Recovery School District of Louisiana* (New Orleans, La.: Cowen Institute, Tulane University, 2010); UTNO, *No Experience Necessary.*

25. American Federation of Teachers, *"National Model" or Flawed Approach? The Post-Katrina New Orleans Public Schools* (Washington, D.C.: American Federation of Teachers, 2006), http://www.coweninstitute.com/our-work/applied-research/education-archive/education-transformation-archive/national-model-or-flawed-approach (accessed June 23, 2010); Eric A. Hanushek, John F. Kain, and Steven G. Rivkin, "The Revolving Door: Factors Affecting Teacher Turnover," in *Developments in School Finance: 2003,* ed. William J. Fowler Jr. (Washington, D.C.: U.S. Department of Education, National Center for Education Statistics, 2004): 7–15.

26. All names of participants are pseudonyms.

27. Eighty public schools are currently open in New Orleans. Seven of the eighty schools are run by the Orleans Parish School Board, thirty-three are run by the RSD, and the remainder are charters run by twenty-nine different charter operators (Cowen Institute for Public Education Initiatives, *The State of Public Education in New Orleans, 2008 Report* [New Orleans, La.: Author, 2008]).

28. Interview notes, March 30, 2009.

29. Sara Carr, "Equal Treatment in Short Supply for Special-Needs Students at New Orleans Public Schools," [New Orleans] *Times-Picayune,* [New Orleans] *Metro Education News,* February 1, 2010.

30. At the end of 1995, Gayarre had gone through the name-change process adopted by OPSB to ensure that the names of schools in the district reflected the

historic and cultural shifts from being racially segregated and predominantly white to being predominantly black. Charles E. Gayarre was a wealthy slave owner who led a crusade to legally restrict Creoles as being a classification for whites only.

31. Patricia Hill Collins, *Black Feminist Thought: Knowledge, Consciousness, and Politics of Empowerment* (New York: Routledge, 2000): 173; *Theorizing Black Feminisms: The Visionary Pragmatism of Black Women*, ed. Stanlie James and Abena A. P. Busia (London: Routledge, 1993), 44.

32. National Hurricaine Center, "Preliminary Report, Hurricane Andrew, 16–28 August, 1992," http://www.nhc.noaa.gov/1992andrew.html (accessed on March 1, 2009).

33. American Federation of Teachers, 2006.

34. B. Quigley, "HUD to New Orleans' Poor: 'Go F(ind) Yourself (Housing)!'" *Counterpunch*, 2006, http://www.counterpunch.org/quigley06192006.html (accessed June 27, 2010).

35. M. J. Kegel, "Despite Our Euphoria, New Orleans Is Struggling, *Des Moines Register*, http://www.unitygno.org (accessed June 27, 2010).

36. NOFA is chartered by the Leona Group, a charter school operator with more than seventy schools in Michigan (twenty-one), Ohio (twelve), Indiana (one), Arizona (twenty-two), Florida (fourteen), and its newest location in New Orleans, where it operates two schools.

37. Prior to Katrina, most public school students in New Orleans attended schools in their neighborhoods. Moreover, the district subsidized vouchers for students to use the public transportation system, the Regional Transit Authority (RTA), to travel to school. Currently, most charter schools pay for elementary age children to be transported by school buses and provide high school students with tokens. The cost for busing has increased from $18 million before Katrina to $24 million for the 2008–2009 school year even though the number of public school students has decreased by half from 64,000 in 2004–2005 to 34,000 in 2008–2009, http://www.nola.com/news/index.ssf/2009/03/school_busing_costs_in_orleans.html (accessed March 6, 2009).

38. *The New Orleans Parents' Guide to Public Schools* (*Parents' Guide*) was created in 2007 by former New Orleans *Times-Picayune* reporter Aesha Rashid. Ms. Rashid formed the New Orleans Parent Organizing Network to "support parents in organizing for excellent public schools" (i).

39. This appears to be a common timeframe for most students. http://www.nola.com/news/index.ssf/2009/03/school_busing_costs_in_orleans.htm (accessed March 6, 2009).

40. McDonogh 42 is a prekindergarten through grade 8 charter school that falls under the RSD but is run by the Treme Charter Association (TCA). It is TCA's only charter school. Both the principal and the board president are former principals in the New Orleans Public School district. Both were committed to hiring

veteran teachers who had a commitment to teaching all children and hence, the school is an open enrollment school.

41. School Facilities Master Plan for Public Schools in Orleans Parish, http://sfmpop.org/plans/School_Facilities_Master_Plan_for_Orleans_Parish.pdf (accessed March 2, 2009).

42. Interview notes, January 27, 2009.

43. Ibid.

44. Michael Apple, "Making Schools 'Right' Again: Whose Choice Is the Education Market?" in *Pedagogy, Policy, and the Privatized City: Stories of Dispossession and Defiance from New Orleans,* ed. Kristen Buras, Jim Randels, Kalamu ya Salaam (New York: Teachers College Press, 2010).

45. Apple, "Making Schools 'Right' Again."

46. American Federation of Teachers, *"National Model" or Flawed Approach? The Post-Katrina New Orleans Public Schools* (Washington, D.C.: American Federation of Teachers, 2006),

47. Interview notes, March 30, 2009.

48. Center for Community Change, *Dismantling a Community* (Washington, D.C.: Center for Community Change, 2006); http://www.communitychange.org/library/dismantling-a-community (accessed June 23, 2010); Theresa Perry, "The Plight of the Education Systems—Post Hurricane Katrina: An Interview with Dr. Brenda Mitchell and Dr. Linda Stelly," *High School Journal* 90, no. 1 (2006): 16–22; L. Quaid, "Obama Education Plan Speech: Stricter Standards, Charter Schools, Merit Pay," *Huffington Post,* 2009, http://www.huffingtonpost.com/2009/03/10/obama-education-plan-spee_n_173405.html (accessed June 23, 2010); and UTNO, *No Experience Necessary.*

49. Harper Smith left the RSD at the end of the 2008–2009 school year and took a post at another larger urban school district.

50. Interview notes, March 27, 2009.

51. UTNO, *No Experience Necessary.*

52. K. W. Crenshaw, "Race, Reform, and Retrenchment in Anti-discrimination Law," *Harvard Law Review,* 101, no. 7 (1988): 1331–87.

53. Field notes, March 15, 2009.

54. More than any other school of its type, it is 51 percent white on both of its campuses.

55. *New Orleans Parents' Guide to Public Schools (Parents' Guide),* 2007, 42, 68.

CHAPTER 6

Black and White, Unite and Fight?

Identity Politics and New Orleans's Post-Katrina Public Housing Movement

John Arena

Those who oppose neoliberalization must do more than merely point to its contradictions. . . . We must also find and make known the resistance that is already taking place. . . . We must understand and learn from their experiences, and we must contribute to their success.

—Mark Purcell, *Recapturing Democracy*

IN HIS PROVOCATIVE ESSAY, *"Why Is There No Black Political Movement?"* political scientist Adolph Reed defines a political movement as a "force that has shown a capability, over time, of mobilizing popular support for programs that expressly seek to alter the patterns of public policy or economic relations." Based on this definition, Reed, writing in the late 1990s, concludes that, at least at the national level, "There simply is no such entity in black American life at this point."[1] In this article I use Reed's working definition of a *political movement* and maintain his focus on policy issues particularly relevant to African Americans but alter the question and level of analysis. Drawing from the experience of the public housing movement in post-Katrina New Orleans, I ask "Why is there is *some* black political movement?" That is, how and why—in the face of a storm whose aftermath one reporter predicted would facilitate "the biggest, most brutal urban-renewal project black America has ever seen"—did a movement emerge to challenge a key component of that frightening agenda: the drive by local and federal officials to demolish thousands of badly needed public housing apartments? At the same time, what were the key impediments that blocked the movement from achieving its central, immediate goal—stopping demolition?[2] In short, why was there some movement, one that was able to partly, but not completely, change the patterns of public policy?

Several levels of analysis are required to fully evaluate the post-Katrina public housing movement, including the ideological role played by academics that demonized public housing residents and activists, and the state repression the movement faced, including the arrest of more than thirty activists between December 2005 and March 2008. While these are all important aspects of the story, in this study I hone in on the critical, but understudied, "intramovement," or "intraclass," component of the public housing movement. That is, I highlight the actions, decisions, analyses, and ideologies of the social movement organizations and actors who aided and undermined the effectiveness of the post-Katrina public housing movement.

To address these concerns, I begin by highlighting the grassroots organization Community Concern Compassion (C3)/Hands Off Iberville (hereafter C3) and their efforts to defend public housing in pre-Katrina New Orleans. This initiative, at the same time, clashed with the neoliberal development agenda of the city's post–civil rights black political leadership to radically downsize the city's public housing stock over the past twenty years, a policy that paralleled national, neoliberal trends. Nonetheless, despite this unfavorable environment, I explain how C3 was able to defeat an important component of the neoliberal agenda before Hurricane Katrina. This section concludes by making the case for the necessity of not only defending but expanding and improving public housing. In the second section, I address how Katrina created a favorable opportunity structure to advance the neoliberal transformation of the city and the policy measures and ideological legitimation used to advance a key component of that elite vision—the elimination of public housing. Attempts at transformation from above generated challenge from below, and I highlight this resistance, identifying the various organizations and personalities that emerged and the challenges they mounted and assess the mixed results of the public housing movement as of early 2009. The final section evaluates the period from September 2005 to November 2007, highlighting four critical strengths of the public housing movement and the actors, decisions, and ideologies, rooted in identity politics, that challenged and undermined these movement foundations. I conclude by identifying the broader theoretical and strategic insights the post-Katrina public housing case provides for a renewal of antiracist struggles in the United States.

The primary data source for this study was garnered from four years (2004 through 2008) as a central participant and observer of New Orleans's public housing movement. I attended, helped organize, and took notes of scores of meetings, public hearings, demonstrations, and forums, and I participated in many of the key discussions over strategy and tactics of one key organization in the movement—C3/Hands off Iberville—as well as in the broader collection of movement organizations and actors. I also drew on documents distributed by activists, emails, newspaper articles, and government documents. My approach to this study—theoretically, methodologically, and politically—is part of forging a "critical public sociology," in which sociologists "immerse themselves and their analysis in a social practice that embraces struggles and movements."[3] Thus, consistent with this approach to public sociology, the insights of this work are aimed not, as with liberal sociology, at "policymakers." Rather, the findings are designed to contribute to an intramovement dialogue designed to reflect on, and improve, the political practice of the New Orleans public housing movement, as well as the larger labor movement—understood as "the sum total of organizations and activities within the working class that promotes advancement, self-organization and power"—of which it is a part.[4] Thus, this study theorizes the public housing movement as a constituent part of the class struggle. A core assumption or postulate of this theorization is that while class may be anchored and sustained in production, it is not something that only happens there. Classes extend beyond their bases in the social relations of production or, as David Camfield puts it, "people do not stop belonging to classes when they leave their workplaces. Class relations [and struggle] pervade all aspects of social life."[5] This study, by highlighting a community-based public housing struggle and how race, gender, and space mediated and structured the manner in which this movement unfolded, helps us to specify the particularities of this terrain of class struggle. In turn, the findings garnered from this study can provide insights into the potential and obstacles for forging alliances between community and workplace struggles, bonds that are central to building a "social movement" or "social justice" unionism.[6]

Public Housing Struggles in Pre- and Post-Katrina New Orleans

In the year immediately preceding the storm, the main grassroots group organizing to defend New Orleans public housing was C3/Hands Off Iberville. C3 is a grass roots, all-volunteer, social movement organization funded, for the most part, by its members and supporters, rather than foundations, and was *not* registered with the Internal Revenue Service as a 501c(3), tax-exempt organization. While C3 emerged in 2001 as an anti-war group to oppose U.S. intervention in Afghanistan and then Iraq, the group always made a connection between what members termed the "war abroad" and the war of poverty, repression, and racism "at home." In 2004 C3 initiated a campaign against a key aspect of the "racist war at home": the destruction of public housing, and in particular the planned privatization of the Iberville public housing development, located adjacent to the famed French Quarter. Membership in C3 was not defined by a formal dues structure but rather by attendance at the weekly meetings and participation in protests and other actions organized by the group. On this basis, the membership varied over the years, but always involved a wide variety of black and white participants. Some of the core members included white activists such as myself, Mike Howells, and Elizabeth Cook, and African Americans, such as long time civil rights activist Andy Washington, and Iberville public housing residents, including Delena Moss (before the storm), Cody Marshall, and Cary Reynolds.

C3 activists, in their efforts to defend public housing, came up against the local, black-led and dominated city government's hegemonic neoliberal ideology and practice, or "mode of city governance."[7] In contrast to "twentieth century American liberalism [that] emphasized social compensation for the excesses of the market and private property," the key nostrum of neoliberal ideology, which informed the local black political elite's rule, is that the local state must work to lift and eliminate, at all costs, impediments to capitalist profit-making and freedom.[8] Neoliberalism is, essentially, a *class project*, in which the state intervenes to "dismantle its assistance for labor and the poor and increases its assistance for capital."[9]

The New Orleans power elite at the state and corporate levels identified public housing, partly due to its location in highly valued parcels of the central city, as a key impediment to its class project of developing and expanding the main engine, and source of profit, for the local corporate elite—tourism. Therefore, despite the fact that many low-income African American families relied on public housing for shelter—20 percent in the early 1980s, many of whom were the regime's most loyal supporters—the local black political leadership, and their white corporate backers, starting in the 1990s and continuing into the 2000s, began an aggressive effort in what Peck and Tickwell call the "roll back," or what Brenner and Theodore term the "destruction" phase—a particularly appropriate word choice in this case—of neoliberalism.[10] Between 1995 and 2005, the local political leadership, in collaboration with the federal Department of Housing and Urban Development (HUD) and their "HOPE VI" neoliberal revitalization program, demolished half of the city's public housing stock, dropping from approximately 14,000 to only 7,000, during this period. The New Orleans experience paralleled national trends, with the federal government, in cooperation with local housing authorities, demolishing approximately 100,000 public housing units during the same ten-year period.[11] The racially inequitable impact of public housing displacement across the country also placed New Orleans squarely in the mainstream, with African American and other minority, low-income families being disproportionally impacted. As a 2004 Urban Institute study concluded, "HOPE VI revitalization efforts [have] almost exclusively affected minority residents and communities."[12]

Emblematic of the local ruling elite's 1995–2005 frenzy of public housing destruction was the elimination of the 1,500 apartments of the St. Thomas community in 2001. Under the second, "roll-out" or "constructive" phase of neoliberalism, the development—now renamed "River Gardens"—was reinvented as a "mixed-income," privately run, for-profit enterprise with less than 200 public housing apartments and no right of return for the former tenants. A key political component of this neoliberal success story was the local elite's ability to harness a cadre of formerly radical community activists, and the St. Thomas resident council, to sign off on privatization as part of an exercise in racial "empowerment," as well as "political realism."[13]

In 2004, following the successful destruction of the St. Thomas community, real estate interests that had led the redevelopment at St. Thomas began to openly discuss similar plans for the Iberville public housing development.[14] In response to this threat, C3 became C3/*Hands Off Iberville* and, beginning in early 2005, initiated an organizing effort against the initiative. Through a movement that united residents and community activists, black and white, and primarily employing direct action, grassroots tactics—demonstrations, press conferences, denunciations at the Housing Authority of New Orleans (HANO), and city council hearings—the movement successfully defeated privatization plans in June 2005. Four sets of demands and strategies defined the C3/Hands Off Iberville–led effort: (1) uncompromising defense of public housing and services, including defense of remaining units, and reversal of neoliberal privatization of public housing; (2) class analysis—C3 advocated black and white working class unity, based on recognition of common material interests. Public housing privatization, while most directly relevant to poor black workers, was framed as part of a larger neoliberal assault targeting the entire working class; (3) identified direct action—protest and disruptions—is the key, strategic source of power for the public housing movement, rather than insider negotiations; (4) the last element was democracy—the weekly meeting, where attendees developed C3's agenda, was the highest decision-making body.[15]

The campaign to defend Iberville, by adhering to these core principals, helped to expose and exploit the various contradictions of neoliberal ideology and political practice as played out within the context of a majority black city. The central, glaring contradiction was between the neoliberal claim, promoted by the black political leadership, that privatization would improve housing opportunities and empower the poor and the reality of worsening housing opportunities for poor, black working class families—the black urban regime's political base. The public housing campaign made transparent these and other contradictions, questioned neoliberal "common sense," and thus helped construct the city's uneven, neoliberal landscape, with the continued presence of the Iberville, a "Keynesian artifact," coexisting along with neoliberal roll-out showcases, such as the privatized River Gardens.[16]

Why Defend Public Housing?

Some might ask, "Why defend a 'failed experiment' such as public housing"? The simple answer is that the for-profit housing industry, composed of real estate, construction, and banking industries, does a poor job of providing safe, sanitary, and affordable housing in both New Orleans and across the country for the great majority of working class people. The inadequacies of the private market have only become more apparent since Hurricane Katrina, the collapse of the speculative housing bubble, and the onset of economic depression in 2008. Before addressing how an adequately funded, well-built, and well-located expansion of public housing could address unmet housing needs, let us examine the abysmal record of the private market in pre-Katrina New Orleans.

Working class families in pre-Katrina faced a dearth of affordable housing, defined as housing costs (including utilities) that are no more than 30 percent of family income. For example, in 2002, a family in New Orleans earning 30 percent of the area median income—with 30 percent of the city's 188,000 households in 2000 making approximately this amount or less—could afford a monthly rent (including utilities) of $330, while the average rent for a two-bedroom apartment was $659, and for a one-bedroom, $529. At the same time, HANO's public housing and Section 8 voucher and "project-based" programs covered approximately 17,000 households, while the number of extremely poor households, those making at or just above 30 percent of the area median income, was over 57,000 according to the 2000 census.[17] Thus, unsurprisingly, before the storm, HANO had a combined waiting list for public housing and Section 8—lists the agency had closed for several years—of more than 25,000 applicants. On top of affordability issues, black renters faced rampant discrimination in the private housing market, with a 1996 study by the Greater New Orleans Fair Housing Action Center finding that "77 percent of the time African Americans were discriminated against when trying to find an apartment."[18]

Post-Katrina, access to affordable housing has become even more difficult, with a 2009 study showing that 60 percent of renters and 35 percent of homeowners pay more than 30 percent of their income for housing in New Orleans, with the median rent skyrocketing 44 percent between 2004 and 2007. In 2007, more than 70 percent of the families making less than $35,000 per year lived in "unaffordable housing"—that is, they were paying more than 30 percent of their income for housing.[19] In addition, working class African Americans have faced a series of thinly veiled racist ordinances that have created additional obstacles to finding housing. These barriers include bans, imposed by local authorities, on the construction of multifamily housing in surrounding, majority-white parishes, as well as in the predominantly black New Orleans East section of the city, and a "blood relative" ordinance in neighboring St. Bernard parish that banned homeowners from renting their properties to nonrelatives in a parish that was 93 percent white before the storm.[20] The *national* foreclosure crisis, the greatest since the economic depression of the 1930s, further underscores the failure of the private housing market and the need for a massive expansion of public housing. While bankers see a 1 percent foreclosure rate as alarming, in places like Detroit, currently 10 percent of homeowners are in foreclosure, while other non–Rust Belt states, from Florida in the East, to Arizona, Nevada, and California in the West, face similar scenarios. Millions more, in lieu of any government intervention, are expected to lose their homes in the next several years due to "ballooning" subprime loan payments, which disproportionally affects blacks and Latinos, and, increasingly, due to workers across the racial spectrum losing their jobs and thus being unable to make mortgage payments even on prime rate loans.[21]

In response to this abysmal situation, C3 and other social movement organizations are calling for a massive public works plan to rebuild the public sector, especially housing. Past experience shows it can be done. The Civil Works Administration (CWA), in just four months in the fall of 1933, built or repaired 33,850 public buildings, carried out 3,220 flood projects, built from scratch 1,000 airports and 3,700 playgrounds, and employed 4.2 million workers at its peak. The CWA was able to accomplish so much in so little time because it was based on *direct government employment*. No private contractors were used, but rather the government employed workers directly at union wages.[22] Employing this model to construct well-built and well-located public housing could address various problems in New Orleans and the Gulf region, including the lack of safe, affordable, well-located housing; the slowness of the recovery, which has blocked the return, disproportionately, of working class African Americans; the lack of well-paying jobs; and rampant racial discrimination in housing. A well-funded, democratically run public works initiative, relying on direct government employment rather than private for-profit contractors and exotic, unreliable financing mechanisms, could be the basis for meeting unmet housing and other social needs.

"Natural" Disasters and Neoliberal Opportunities

Hurricane Katrina, which struck the city on August 29, 2005, provided local and national power elites an opportunity to dramatically expand, and intensify, the human-made, destructive phase of neoliberalism.[23] This link between the storm and the opportunity it provided for furthering "neo-liberal roll back" was most graphically expressed by Louisiana Congress-man Richard Baker, who infamously exclaimed in the week after Katrina, "We finally cleaned up public housing. We couldn't do it, but God did." Indeed, authorities, maybe without the same frankness as the congress-man, did quickly move on this "opportunity," with the local housing authority (HANO) and HUD immediately declaring public housing "devastated" and refusing to reopen most of the developments, even while city authorities allowed property owners to return to their homes.[24]

Despite claims of devastation, the brick-and-plaster public housing buildings—many not flooded at all, being located on high ground—came through the storm in much better shape than most of the private housing. Activists in C3 attempted to expose this contradiction by highlighting—publicly, through writings, testifying at city council, and protests—the limited damage that public housing faced and the need for the developments to reopen. These efforts, including a December 2005 demonstration by the broader housing coalition known as the New Orleans Housing Emergency Action Team (NO-HEAT) demanding the reopening of Iberville, com-bined with direct-action reoccupations of Iberville by residents, led HANO to officially reopen the development by December 2005.[25] The pre- and post-Katrina efforts to defend Iberville made it politically impossible for housing officials to attempt to hand it over to developers. Even George Bush's HUD secretary, Alphonso Jackson, had to disassociate himself from any effort to privatize and demolish Iberville, telling a housing advocate in the spring of 2006, "I know people want to do it [Iberville] as a land grab, and it's not going to happen on my watch."[26]

C3, in its efforts to defend public housing in the weeks and months after Katrina, also began making contact with displaced residents through Internet postings, meeting residents at the developments while they attempted to check on and gather their belongings, and drawing on resi-dents' own extensive networks. For example, a St. Bernard public hous-ing resident made contact by telephone with C3 activist Elizabeth Cook after reading an Internet posting. This resident provided a network of St. Bernard residents who were in touch with each other in Houston, Texas, where the Federal Emergency Management Agency (FEMA) had evacuated many poor residents after the storm. Following weeks of telephone contact and networking, this writer took a Greyhound bus to

Houston in February 2006, and then rented a van to bring back displaced St. Bernard public housing residents to New Orleans. At a February 14, 2006, rally and press conference held at the development, residents and C3 activists demanded the reopening of St. Bernard and charged the local and national U.S. state with carrying out "class and racial cleansing" for their refusal to allow the almost all-black, low-income public housing residents to return to their homes. This policy, we underscored, violated a host of international human rights accords protecting internally displaced peoples.[27]

Between November 2005 and November 2007—the period on which I focus—C3 maintained regular weekly Thursday meetings and organized and/or participated in dozens of protests and actions in its efforts to reopen public housing. These varied interventions included reoccupation attempts of closed public housing apartments and complexes; marches, including to the home of the mayor and a city council person; and speakouts at the city council and HANO hearings. These efforts at times included new allies and organizations, such as Survivors Village, a group of St. Bernard residents, led by long-time black community activist and former head of the HANO board Endesha Juakali. C3 and Juakali organized a caravan of displaced St. Bernard residents, then living in Houston, to reoccupy their development on April 4, 2006—the anniversary of Dr. Martin Luther King's assassination. The reoccupation attempt produced a well-publicized clash with police that helped undermine neoliberal "common sense," promoted by the local media and public officials, that public housing residents did not want to return to their "dysfunctional" communities.[28]

Other activist organizations, including the Peoples Hurricane Relief Fund (PHRF), the Peoples Organizing Committee (POC, a Spring 2006 break-off from the PHRF), some activists associated with Common Ground Relief, the Revolutionary Communist Party (RCP), and MAYDAY Nola activist Jamie "Bork" Loughner, joined C3 and leading public housing tenant activists Sam Jackson, Sharon Jasper, Kawana Jasper, Cody Marshall, and Stephanie Mingo in the contentious public housing insurgency. In addition, lawyers Bill Quigley and Tracie Washington and a Washington, D.C.–based public interest law firm, the Advancement Project, filed a lawsuit to stop demolition in June 2006 (*Anderson et al vs. Jackson*). The suit was in response to the June 2006 announcement by HUD Secretary Alphonso Jackson to demolish four developments—Lafitte,

Cooper (Calliope), St. Bernard, and C. J. Peete (Magnolia)—encompassing some 5,000 apartments, and recreate them as "mixed income" developments, along the lines of River Gardens.[29] The Loyola University law clinic, as well as Common Ground legal services, also provided legal support for those arrested during protests.

This movement from below did generate concrete concessions from above. In early 2007, Congressional Representative Maxine Waters introduced bill H.R. 1227, which called for reopening New Orleans public housing and ensured one-for-one replacement—a significant break from past neoliberal practices—of all public housing units under any redevelopment. The bill, after its passage, moved to the Senate, becoming S.B. 1668, where it now languishes, as of this writing, in the Banking Committee. Nonetheless, while the public housing movement did stop demolition of Iberville and continues to demand one-for-one replacement, the authorities, after intense opposition, including occupations of buildings and the arrest of scores of protestors (such as during a well-publicized December 20, 2007, clash at the city council), HUD and HANO demolished most, but not all, apartments across the four targeted developments by Spring 2008.[30]

Despite not being able, in the short run, to completely alter the local and national power elite's neoliberal public housing plans, the post-Katrina New Orleans movement did present important challenges at the level of ideology and practice. In their efforts to eliminate public housing in post-Katrina New Orleans, neoliberal "reformers" used a mixture of traditional neoliberal antistatist ideas, combined with "humane," antipoverty, antiracist, and racial empowerment packaging. African American city councilman Oliver Thomas presents a prime example of this hybrid ideology at a February 2006 city council meeting, where he justifies denying the right of return to public housing residents:

> We don't need soap opera watchers right now. . . . We're going to
> target the people who are going to work . . . at some point there
> has to be a whole new level of motivation, and people have got
> to stop blaming the government for something they ought to
> do. . . . There's just been a lot of pampering, and at some point you
> have to say, "No, no, no, no, no." . . . If our legs don't hurt, you can
> walk somewhere. *I'm saying these things to motivate my people.*[31]
> [emphasis added]

Thomas went on to cite Malcolm X's argument that the welfare state was a form of modern slavery to further burnish his racial authenticity credentials and therefore more easily package his advocacy of blocking the return of poor black people as a form of racial empowerment. Others, such as white city councilwoman Stacy Head, a rabid opponent of public housing, restricted themselves to standard, academically-vetted "deconcentrating poverty" and "empowerment" arguments that sociologists, in particular, have developed to justify destroying public housing. Head expounded on her views in the context of opposing Congresswoman Waters' bill:

> Congresswoman Maxine Waters will hold hearings in New Orleans to decide whether to require HUD to reopen public housing . . . and ban all demolitions. I am opposed. . . . I am a strong believer in *mixed-income housing and deconcentrating poverty*. . . . I firmly believe that the decisions made with regard to public housing will greatly impact New Orleans recovery—from the immediate issues of health care delivery, education, and crime—to the long-term issues of revitalizing communities and empowering people to escape from poverty.[32] [emphasis added]

At city council hearings, press conferences, and through writings, the public housing movement consistently challenged the "progressive," anti-racist—as well as the openly racist and anti-poor attacks—on public housing. One key ideological weapon the public housing movement used to challenge the hegemony of neoliberal ideas was that of a human rights discourse. Activists used the language of human rights to press for the "right of return" for "internally displaced people," arguing the failure to reopen public housing violated that right, enshrined in various international human rights conventions. C3 and others employed the human rights rhetoric this way, but in a more confrontational form as well, highlighting the contradiction of the progressive "deconcentrating poverty" rhetoric and its real impact as "ethnic cleansing." The use of this terminology was strategic. In the tradition of the civil rights movement, C3 highlighted the contradiction between international rhetoric and ugly domestic realities; between human rights legitimated intervention and the U.S. imperial state carrying out flagrant, racially biased, human rights violations at home. Within the academy, a key incubator of progressive neoliberal ideas, movement allies, through writings and academic conferences, challenged the "deconcentrating poverty" thesis, regularly invoked by developers and state officials, to justify public housing demolition.[33] At the policy level the movement, by forcing intervention by the national state, undermined the neoliberal strategy of "hollowing out" the national, that is, "decreasing [the national state's] role as an institutional buffer between localities and the machinations of the global economy," which facilitates dismantlement of public services.[34]

Terrains of Conflict within the Public Housing Movement

The gains the movement made, in spite of significant challenges, arose through commitment to some of the key principles that guided C3's work: *uncompromising defense of public housing, interracial class unity, direct action, and popular democracy.* These core movement principles, centered on noninstitutionalized, rather than insider negotiations, helped make what appeared to be a powerless group, defending a particularly maligned and demonized public program, into the most dynamic of the post-Katrina grass roots movements. Nonetheless, despite this success, there were a number of intra-movement challenges that undermined adherence to these movement foundations. In this section I analyze the public housing movement by identifying the *actors, choices, actions, and ideologies* that pulled activists away from these core principles and sources of power.

Interracial Unity

Although blacks and whites worked together, there were several attacks and criticisms, primarily from left and nonprofit activists, rather than public housing residents, questioning or criticizing the interracial character of the public housing movement. For example, a black female organizer with the criminal justice reform group Critical Resistance told white C3 activists that they should not be involved in the public housing struggle since it did not affect them.

> *The white folks at C3 need to back off. Dealing with racism isn't your life's experience,* I would never presume to speak on behalf of white people, could one of you show me and other people of color the same respect. . . . This habit on speaking on behalf of those 'less

fortunate' is becoming more than just comically irritating but offensive and damaging to actual change . . . for me this [is] about very practical issues, *organize from where you personally and actually are.*[35] [emphasis added]

Also weighing-in against interracial organizing was a trainer for the Peoples Institute, a nonprofit group that organizes antiracist workshops. At the March 25, 2006 C3 meeting focused on an organizing a caravan of displaced public housing residents back to the city, this African American male organizer burst into the gathering to warn "the people of color" that white activists were leading them on a dangerous and adventuristic course. Implicit in both critiques of C3's interracial, class politics theory of organizing was support for an alternative rooted in identity politics. As Sharon Smith, a keen observer of past and contemporary social justice struggles, argues, this theory of organizing and power is based on the premise that *"only those who actually experience a particular form of oppression are capable of fighting against it. Everyone else is considered to be part of the problem and cannot become part of the solution by joining the fight against oppression."*[36] Exponents of identity politics, by insisting on "differences as the central truth of political life undercuts establishing a broad base as a goal of organizing," and thus undermines accessing a key source of working class power—numbers.[37]

The critique leveled against C3 by these two above cited activists was, for the most part, adhered to by the PHRF and POC Black Nationalist, organizational currents in the movement. Black Power or Black Nationalist politics, which is a version of identity politics, "treat racial affinity and political interests as synonyms. . . . (It) assumes some coherent transhistorical black interests in advance. These arguments tend to flatten class contradictions within the black community."[38] Indeed, "the key premise of identity politics," as elaborated by activist-writer John Anner, captures the central assumptions of nationalism: "all members of the group have more in common than the members have with anyone outside the group, that they are oppressed in the same way, *and therefore that they all belong on the same road to justice".*[39] [emphasis added]

Although the POC and PHRF did participate in the public housing movement, they were relative late-comers, and often inconsistent supporters. For example, the precursor of the PHRF, Community Labor United (CLU), never participated in the pre-Katrina public housing struggle, despite repeated requests. PHRF abstentionism is not surprising considering the contradiction between the racial and class dynamics of public housing and its adherence to identity politics. Facing a combined attack from white developers, the black controlled city hall, the latter's allied-black contractors, and significant opposition from middle class blacks and whites, public housing is an issue that exposes, rather than perpetuates, the myth of a unified "black community."

In the aftermath of Katrina, and the formation of the PHRF, public housing continued to be ignored by this leading grass roots group. For example, PHRF rebuffed a request by activist Mike Howells that someone specifically address the issue of public housing at their December 10, 2005 right of return rally.[40] The PHRF favored taking issues that could easily be framed as affecting the whole black community.[41] Consistent with this approach, the major actions that PHRF organized over its two years existence—including a mass march and international human rights tribunal for the first and second anniversary commemorations—tended to be framed as flagrant racial attacks affecting the whole black community. In fact, at PHRF's International Tribunal—organized to try "the U.S. Government and its officials for crimes against humanity" as part of the August 2007 second Katrina anniversary commemoration—there was not one panel dedicated, unbelievably, to public housing even though international observers identified its closing as one of the most egregious violations of international law. Through the Tribunal the PHRF did, to their credit, play a crucial role in exposing the widespread murder of black Katrina survivors by New Orleans and other police forces, as well as those committed by white vigilantes, especially in the city's unflooded Algiers section, during the storm's immediate aftermath. These crimes were later given wider attention through the reporting of independent journalist A..C. Thompson—exposure that forced the local newspaper of record, the *Times-Picayune*, to finally investigate the issue as well.[42] Nonetheless, Tribunal organizers did not have one panel addressing the equally outrageous crime of public housing demolition. Only after protests by public housing resident and activists was a hastily organized and unpublicized panel assembled. Although PHRF did eventually become involved in the public housing movement, it was never a central part of their work until late 2007, when demolitions began.

The POC, the result of an April 2006 split within the PHRF, was led by Curtis Muhammad, a retired trade union organizer, and his son, Ishmael, an attorney who relocated to New Orleans after Katrina.[43]

The POC and the Muhammads, unlike the PHRF, did make public housing a central part of their organizing. Yet, like others enthralled to identity politics, the POC also opposed white C3 activists playing a central role in the movement. Ishmael Muhammad elaborated on his organizing philosophy in November 2005 at a protest march to commemorate suburban Jefferson Parish police and sheriffs preventing mainly black Katrina survivors from evacuating across the Mississippi River Bridge in the days after the hurricane.

> One of the things that's important to put at the top of any list is that the self-determination of those most victimized in this situation must be respected. That they have to be in charge of how this city is rebuilt. They have to be in charge of how the money is spent, they have to be in charge of what happens here in repairing their lives. . . . *And any of those who are speaking on their behalf without being in touch with them, without organizing with them, without reaching out to them, cannot speak and should not be allowed to speak.*[44] [emphasis added]

These "rules of movement engagement," enunciated by Muhammad, seem reasonable. Nonetheless, in practice, Muhammad deemed white C3 activists as illegitimate leaders, even though this organization had extensive contacts and historical relationship with public housing residents—his own litmus tests for leadership and legitimacy. In practice, for Muhammad, leadership legitimacy is rooted in racial authenticity, rather than in substantive issues regarding a group's program, actions, or even opinion of public housing residents. The latter assumption was particularly demeaning to public housing and other black working class C3 members since it assumes they had no influence over the organization's direction. To undermine interracial unity and what they viewed as C3's illegitimate work, the POC began meeting at the same time as C3, denigrated the interracial C3 as a "white organization" that manipulates blacks, Ishmael Muhammad physically assaulted two white C3 activists, and had a white POC "ally" shout down a white C3 activist speaking at the 2007 Martin Luther King Day rally at the St. Bernard development.[45]

While attacking any legitimate role of whites in the public housing movement other than as "allies"—which dovetailed with Mayor Nagin's own attack on whites defending public housing[46]—Muhammad and his father, Curtis Muhammad, did recognize class differences within the black community, and the need for the black poor to be in positions of power. Curtis Muhammad, in an interview, emphasized that

> It is not enough . . . for organizations of color to lead the rebuild-
> ing efforts, but for those organizations to be made up of people
> most directly affected by the disaster. Many of our black leadership,
> non-profits and all, are from the middle class. Our coalition said
> upfront, we are listening to the voices of the poor.[47]

While recognizing class differences, Muhammad still sees the black poor—in this case black public housing residents—speaking as one, if only the arrogant advocates would listen. The problem with this approach, part of what the Muhammads' call their "bottom-up" organiz-ing philosophy, is that even among public housing residents there is not one voice. The reification of public housing residents negates political diversity and conflicting voices. Indeed, some residents, particularly tenant council leaders, supported demolition and "redevelopment." Thus, while recognizing class differences, the Muhammads', and their "bottom-up" organizing philosophy, continue, in practice, to create an idealized racial collective that negates real differences. This organizing model, con-sistent with nationalism, "assum[es] the voice of a putatively coherent black community" which then must be conveyed to policymakers. In this case, the POC ordained itself as the mediators that could help translate, for the broader public and policymakers, the true, authentic, "bottom up" message and demands of black public housing residents.[48]

In a manner similar to the Muhammad's, black minister Reverend Marshall Truehill Jr. attacked C3's leadership in the public housing move-ment based on a racial legitimacy deficit, rather than the substantive posi-tions held, and actions taken, by the group. In the spring and summer of 2007 C3 was spearheading protests against U.S. Senator Mary Landrieu for her failure to seriously push for passage of public housing legislation already approved by the House.[49] To undercut these protests, and strengthen his own position as an intermediary between cooperative tenant council lead-ers and elected officials, Truehill argued that the protests were "disrespect-ful" of the "true resident leaders" holding negotiations with the Senator's aide.[50] C3's protests—which included a march to the home of Landrieu's brother, then-Lieutenant Governor Mitch Landrieu—implied that the "true tenant leaders"—those recognized by HANO and Landrieu—"could not speak for themselves." Instead, Truehill argued, C3 should play a "supportive," "followship" role and not question whether black resident council leaders—who had a long track record of betraying residents' need and had played little or no role in the post-Katrina protests to reopen public housing developments—really "represent[ed] the interests of residents." Truehill ended his broadside lecturing that "residents"—as he collapsed the interests of vetted tenant leaders with those of rank and file tenants—"do not need the great White father and mother"—referring to myself and another white female member of C3—"to patronize them with their paternalistic attitudes toward their struggles." Truehill basically employed the racial authenticity trope to undermine C3's class-based, interracial form organizing equals, protect neoliberal state official from grass roots pressure, and, importantly, provide a shroud of racial legitimacy around the insider, collaborationist policy followed by tenant council leaders.

Direct Action and Consistent Opposition to Neoliberalism

Protest, noninstitutionalized forms of resistance, was the modal tactic employed by the movement to change government policy. At the same time, the use of institutionalized forms of redress—such as the courts—and the allure of the nonprofit accommodation to neoliberalism, under the guise of "self-determination," presented threats to the core principles of the movement.

A prime example of the dangers posed by insider strategies was the federal lawsuit *(Anderson et al. vs. Jackson)* human rights Attorneys Bill Quigley and Tracie Washington, along with the public interest law firm, the Advancement Project, filed in June 2006 to force the Department of Housing and Urban Development to reopen the developments. The public housing movement had early on asked lawyers to initiate a lawsuit. Yet, what prompted them to finally take the case was, according to leading activist Mike Howells, the "resistance in the streets," particularly St. Bernard public housing residents and supporters breaking through a phalanx of police to reenter their homes on April 4, 2006—the anniversary of Dr. King's assassination.[51]

Legal support, although requested by public housing activists, also presented a threat to the movement as well, which even some lawyers, such as Bill Quigley, recognized. First, and most importantly, the turn to the courts undermined support for direct action, a key source of movement strength. Second, the lawsuit increased the power of "movement" lawyers and their nonprofit organizations, to negotiate deals with the state independent of the desires and involvement of the broader movement. Indeed, as the terrain of struggle moved to the courts, the power and self-activity of residents and activists was relegated to the margins, while that of nongovernmental organizations (NGOs), who some have called the "trojan horses of global neoliberalism," strengthened. The NGOs, who have clearly gone into ascendancy with neoliberalism, "tend to be elitist, unaccountable . . . frequently conceal their agendas, and prefer direct negotiation with or influence over state and class power," rather than engage in confrontation.[52] The New Orleans experience finds support for that characterization.

To address this contradiction—of the lawsuit being a source of both power and weakness for the movement—C3 activists continually emphasized that "judges are nothing but politicians in robes" and that "our strength in the courts is only as strong as our struggle in the streets." Furthermore, C3 and others challenged the elitist and exclusionary practices of some top lawyers who did not share information with non–public housing activists—claiming they only represented their "clients" who were plaintiffs in the lawsuit—and engaged in unaccountable negotiations with authorities.[53] Nonetheless, despite these damage control efforts, the suit did lead some residents to step back from protest and worked to dampen the movement's militancy. For example, C3 member Mike Howells argued the failure to reoccupy the St. Bernard development at the June 3 and July 4, 2006, protests—as originally planned and announced, even to the press— was due, in addition to opposition by self-appointed Survivors Village leader Endesha Juakali, to the belief that "an occupation might jeopardize the court case . . . some residents and activists believed that the problem could now be resolved in the courts."[54]

Another factor that undermined commitment to direct action, and consistent opposition to privatization, was a proposal between the Housing Investment Trust (HIT), the investment arm of the AFL-CIO labor federation, and St. Bernard public housing residents. Endesha Juakali, the African American founder of Survivors Village, was the key to bringing together leading resident activists and the AFL in late 2006 and early 2007. Juakali, formerly known as Michael Williams, was raised in the St. Bernard development. In his youth and early adult life in the 1970s and early 1980s, he was a leading anti–police brutality activist and headed up various antipoverty programs serving the St. Bernard community. Mayor Sidney Barthelemy appointed the Tulane University law graduate, in 1988, as chair of the HANO board, with one key mission: remove Jesse Smallwood, the executive director. Smallwood had garnered the wrath of the mayor—and the support of public housing residents—because of her opposition to a mass demolition and privatization scheme for public housing being floated at the time by Barthelemy and developers in the form of the "Rochon Plan." After HUD forced Juakali to step down from the HANO board in 1991, he faced further problems as head of a city-created public corporation. City auditors charged him with gross misuse of funds, with monies designated for rehabbing housing and small business assistance being rerouted for salaries and perks. In 2003, after a series of suspensions of his law license, the Louisiana Supreme Court disbarred him for repeatedly collecting fees without performing services and other improper behavior committed against mainly low-income residents from the St. Bernard community.[55]

Despite his record, the charismatic Juakali exercised some influence with residents, and other elements of the public housing movement, and he used this to redirect people away from protest and into negotiations. By 2007 the residents, AFL banker Tom O'Malley, and Juakali had formed a nonprofit corporation, the St. Bernard Housing & Recovery Development Corporation, to develop their own privatization plan. Instead of demanding continued state ownership and defending all the public housing apartments, resident leaders, their advisors, and the AFL bankers proposed a new "mixed-income" development that would include only 425 public housing units, down from the original 1,462. The "new St. Bernard" would be owned as a partnership of the resident's nonprofit corporation and the AFL investment trust.[56]

The proposal, although never accepted by HUD, had three negative impacts on the public housing movement. First, the nonprofit proposal represented a break from a key movement principle—agreed to in earlier mass meetings—to defend all the units as public housing. Instead resident leaders and their advisors, under the guise of "self-determination," agreed to step back from their unconditional defense of public housing and accept a downsizing and privatization plan. Due to principles of identity politics, neither Juakali—nor his white AFL-CIO banker allies—faced any criticism, apart from C3, for their support for privatization. The second negative feature of the nonprofit scheme is that it fed into preexisting divisions among public housing residents. "Neighborhood conscious-ness," or "attachment to place," was very strong among New Orleans public housing residents and was a source of strength of the public housing move-ment. Yet, while on one level residents' attachment to their community strengthened solidarity, at another level this consciousness created ob-stacles to uniting all the project residents in opposition to privatization. The formation of the St. Bernard nonprofit, and floating a redevelopment deal just for this development, accentuated these preexisting divisions and created barriers for unified struggle. Finally, the formation of the nonprofit and the redevelopment deal took St. Bernard and other residents further away from the terrain of direct action—*the* arena for public housing resi-dents exercising power. Indeed, as negotiations proceeded with the AFL, Juakali became increasingly critical of protest, encouraging residents not to participate in various actions, such as the campaign C3 launched against U.S. Senator Mary Landrieu for not aggressively pushing pro–public hous-ing legislation.[57]

The grant proposal made by PHRF Executive Director Kali Akuno to the Venezuelan government, designed to create a community bank and land trust in the Lower Ninth Ward, is another example of move-ment groups and activists promoting "people's capitalism" solutions that accommodated neoliberalism and undermined direct action.[58] The request was not about how the Bolivarian Republic could assist local groups to pressure and confront the state in the midst of its neoliberal restructuring agenda but rather how to build a nonprofit alternative. Yet, for Akuno, a leading member of the Black Nationalist Malcolm X Grassroots Movement, the call for a land bank could be defended as a radical one, as a "transitional demand" for the larger objective of a black homeland in the U.S. South, a central plank of the organization.[59]

Another example of the amenability of seemingly radical organizations and their ideology to neoliberalism is that of Common Ground Relief, one of the best-known organizations that emerged post-Katrina. Founded immediately after the storm by former Black Panther Malik Rahim and two white, anarchist-inspired activists from Austin, Texas, Brandon Darby and Scott Crow, Common Ground has brought thousands of peo-ple to New Orleans, mostly young and white, to support reconstruction efforts. Yet, despite the radical roots of the Common Ground founders and their slogan of "solidarity, not charity," used to distinguish themselves from the myriad of nonprofit charity groups that have sprung up in the city, the outfit's focus has *not* been to oppose the destruction of public housing and other public services. Rather, Common Ground, in a manner not inconsistent with its anarchist and nationalist roots, focused on creating a nonprofit alternative to the public sector—a defining feature of neoliberalism.[60] Indeed, Rahim articulated his preference for nonprofits, as an alternative to state-delivered services, at a June 2008 national conference of cooperatives held in New Orleans. In response to a query by this writer on whether the focus by Common Ground and other groups to build up nonprofit services undermined the fight to defend public housing and other public service, Rahim responded: "I'm not a believer in public housing. It's always been a failure. It's easy to convert public housing into cooperative housing. We can do this."[61] Common Ground and Rahim's actions back up this philosophy: One of Common Ground's major initiatives, in addition to organizing a nonprofit health clinic, was acquiring (later lost) and managing a low-rent apartment complex. Thus, while some young people associated with Common Ground did become involved in public housing protests, the central role of the organization was to take people *away* from protest confronting the state and *toward* the private, nonprofit alternative. While, from above, this approach had clear material benefits for nonprofit leaders, from below it also resonated with the antistatist, anti–working class version of anarchism that holds sway among many of the radical youth attracted to Common Ground.[62] Thus, Common Ground's neoanarchism and Akuno and PHRF's nationalism are some of the radical packaging that neoliberalism can employ.

Direct Democracy

An important obstacle to employing direct action was the authoritarian and undemocratic actions taken by the African American founder of Survivors Village, Endesha Juakali. C3 forged a relationship with Juakali in March 2006, when they worked with him to bring displaced St. Bernard public housing residents from Houston back to New Orleans for an April 4 demonstration. Nonetheless, despite the alliance, C3 activists knew, as documented earlier, the proprivatization role he played at HANO and his unethical behavior as a lawyer. Thus, C3 made a pragmatic decision to work with Juakali, while recognizing his weaknesses, and opposed him when he took positions that contradicted the agreed-on aims of the movement. In contrast, many white leftists in the movement anointed Juakali as the authentic leader beyond reproach. For example, Common Ground Relief, while focusing on building a nonprofit alternative structure, did assign a liaison, Soleil Rodrigue, to work with the public housing movement and to involve their volunteers in various protest actions. Yet, Rodrigue operated in a support role to, as one observer noted, take "cues from local organizers working closely with public housing residents."[63] In practice there were real class, race, and gender biases in who the white left, such as Rodrigue, defined as a legitimate leader. Despite his support for the AFL privatization plan, and his efforts to put a damper on protests, much of the white left in the public housing movement uncritically anointed Juakali, as the "pulse of the community . . . , as bearer of the left's authentic race line" with respect to public housing.[64] Juakali was able to maintain this mantle as the authentic black leader of the public housing movement while "articulating views [and advocating strategies] that scarcely resemble views we normally think of as leftist."[65] The critique that Adolph Reed makes of much of the white left's response to black leaders is particularly relevant to the New Orleans experience and Juakali's rise to prominence:

> The key problem is that whites on the left don't want to confront complexity, tension, and ambivalence in black politics. In general, they do not see political differences among black people. They do not see that blacks are linked to social, political and economic institutions in a variety of ways, and that those different links, and the networks that flow from them, shape interests and ideological perception no less . . . than among whites.[66]

Thus, with this legitimacy, Juakali could more easily make decisions without any accountability to the rest of the movement. For example, at early Survivors Village meetings, held in front of his FEMA trailer next to the St. Bernard development, activists decided to occupy the development, first on June 3, 2006, and then again on July 4, 2006. Juakali himself made public pronouncements about this as well. Observers, such as historian and antiracist educator Lance Hill, argued that the willingness of the displaced to defy the law and retake their homes would mark an historic turning point in efforts to challenge the local elites drive to displace the poor.[67] Nonetheless, undemocratic decision making undermined the movement's ability to realize these historical possibilities. On both dates, Juakali unilaterally decided—including at the 200-person-strong July 4 march around the development, which included residents and support-ers from across New Orleans and the country—that the march would not culminate with an occupation.[68] Although people were disgruntled, pro-testors did not challenge this decision by the self-appointed voice of the community. This unilateral, unchallengeable diktat was not an outlier. For example, on Saturday, December 23, 2006, following a successful march the week before to Mayor Nagin's house to protest his support for demo-lition, Juakali, along with a black, male PHRF leader, called off a second march to the mayor's house, even after scores of people had assembled. Juakali's claim that "there were not enough people" went unchallenged for the most part as well. Challenges to this decision would have been accused of "disrespect" for the black indigenous organizer, particularly if it had come from white activists. The white-left's practice of anointing— or at least not contesting self-coronations—authentic black leaders hand-cuffed the ability of activists to beat back gross violations of democracy.

Another example of this contradictory behavior by the white left, at the national level, is their relationship with Common Ground Relief leader Malik Rahim. In the aftermath of Katrina, the former Black Pan-ther was regularly invited to speak at national antiwar events, and other national leftist gatherings, as a voice of the post-Katrina social justice movements. Nonetheless, as mentioned, he has been scarcely involved in the post-Katrina public housing movement, nor has he mobilized his followers to defend other public services, such as health care and education, whose destruction have been central components of the post-Katrina "disaster capitalist" agenda. Indeed, just as with public housing, Rahim and Common Ground's health care initiative cen-tered on creating a nonprofit clinic—their signature program—rather than mobilizing its volunteers to reopen New Orleans's shuttered, and little-damaged, Charity Hospital. Conversely, Rahim had no problem per-sonally rallying and leading his troops to embrace private, philanthropic, nonprofit initiatives led by celebrities. The Common Ground founder and his followers organized a welcoming committee to "meet and greet" right wing, former Democratic President William Clinton and Holly-wood celebrity Brad Pitt when they both descended upon the city's still battered Lower Ninth Ward on March 17, 2008. These political and cul-tural components of the global power elite, who also run into each other at places like Davos, Switzerland, for the World Economic Forum, were there to launch their joint Make It Right–Clinton Global Initiative paltry 150-unit nonprofit, green-housing initiative.[69] The radical welcoming committee did not put a damper on the festivities by reminding the attendees—or the honorees—of the former president's destruction of over 7,000 of New Orleans's *public* housing apartments in the 1990s.

Amy Goodman, the radical journalist and host of the most widely heard leftist radio show, *Democracy Now*, further burnishes Rahim's leftist credentials by regularly turning to him for critical perspectives of ongoing developments in New Orleans. The prominence bestowed upon Rahim and Common Ground by Goodman would lead one to assume that they are at the cutting edge of left, radical resistance in New Orleans. In fact, the organization, through its promotion of non-profit services, is actually abetting the rulings class's privatization agenda. Again, we have the white left defining the "true," African American grassroots voices, without any serious interrogation of the political stances and work that people like Rahim are undertaking, a practice that further undermines the honest, democratic debate needed to develop an effective challenge to the racist neoliberal agenda. The contradiction between image and substance is also embodied in *Floodlines*, journalist Jordan Flaherty's chronicle and analysis of post-Katrina social movements. In his admirable attempt to "amplif[y] the [marginalized] voices of Black New Orleanians" and show "the world . . . it's not too late to make a difference," he too often substitutes cheerleading for the hardnosed critical, honest analysis of popular movements that we so desperately need. Activists and organizations that do not fit his image of racial authenticity are either reviled, dismissed, or ignored.[70]

Identity Politics: Symptoms, Sources, and Solutions

The immediate focus of this study was to identify the intramovement impediments facing New Orleans post-Katrina public housing movement. That is, what were the key obstacles preventing this movement from realizing its major public policy aim—the defeat of state and corporate attempts to destroy thousands of viable public housing apartments and displace poor, African American communities? Yet, while this movement addressed a public policy issue that most clearly impacted and concerned the city's low-income black families, the issue also had great political and economic importance for black and other working class communities in New Orleans, and across the country.

The drive to destroy and privatize New Orleans' public housing was one key component of an overall neoliberal capitalist restructuring effort to further dismantle and shred the United States's remaining public services and civil liberties.[71]

While the stakes in the public housing movement, and the overall struggle for the city, were and are high, the political choices made by the movement, informed by particular ideologies, undermined achieving stated objectives. That is, ideological obstacles undermined the movement's ability to exploit what Therborne calls its "class capacities," its "capacity . . . to act and to achieve its objectives in relation to other classes."[72] The key, pernicious ideology identified in this in-depth case study was the theory and political practice associated with identity politics. This model of organizing, in its various manifestations, played a central role undermining and sapping the strength of New Orleans's post-Katrina public housing movement. Repeatedly, the ideas and actions associated with identity politics blunted the movement's ability to exercise key sources of power rooted in direct action, legitimated undemocratic decision making, provided a cover for conciliation to privatization, and created obstacles to interracial unity through struggle.

Thus, as William Robinson emphasizes, ideology—in this case, the identity politics' variety—and its intellectual purveyors and practitioners operated as a political force, that is, a "*material force*," in the way they "orient[ed] and set limits on human action by establishing codes of conduct which organize entire populations."[73] More broadly, the central role that identity politics played in the public housing movement among "progressive" forces underscores its place as a key component, indeed expression of, the official, elite-sanctioned, "antiracism" of the neoliberal era. "Neoliberal multiculturalism"—the vetted, neoliberal version of antiracism that has superseded Keynesian era "racial liberalism," and old-style white supremacy—"sutures official anti-racism to state policy in a manner that prevents the calling into question of global capitalism."[74] The chief characteristic of this neoliberal-era "antiracism" is a fetish placed on superficial "multicultural" appearances, while ignoring deepening substantive material inequalities.

This dichotomy between appearances and substance was also a defining feature of identity politics' exponents in the public housing movement. Political interventions informed by identity politics focused more on maintaining outward antiracist appearances, rather

than effectively fighting the substantive racism of neoliberal public
housing reform. My study found that the most consistent and enthusiastic practitioners of identity politics were found in the nonprofits,
which underscores that this ideology is not simply a free-floating one.
Rather, identity politics is rooted in a particular organizational and
socioeconomic matrix. James Petras, a keen observer of nonprofits,
provides some insights into the class roots of identity politics and the
objective interests its proponents serve.

> There is no national coherent social movement in the US.
> Instead we have a collection of fragmented "Identity groups"
> each embedded in narrow sets of (Identity) interests, and totally
> incapable of building a national movement. . . . *The proliferation*
> *of these sectarian "non-governmental" "identity groups" is based in*
> *their structures, financing, and leadership.* Many depend on private
> foundations and public agencies for their financing, which
> precludes them taking political positions. At best they operate
> as "lobbies" simply pressuring elite politicians of both parties.
> Their leaders depend on maintaining a separate existence
> in order to justify salaries and secure future advances in
> government agencies.[75] [emphasis added]

It is clear that class-based organizing is necessary for mounting an
effective challenge to the bipartisan-supported public housing demolition and other components of the neoliberal agenda. At the same time,
this study has found abundant evidence that the nonprofits and their
operatives—funded as they are by major foundations—are major purveyors of identity politics and its associated practices that frustrate efforts
to forge class-based, antiracist struggles. Indeed, those groups that placed
race at the center of their politics were, conversely, the least effective at
challenging the deeply racist neoliberal agenda, particularly around public
housing. Clearly, the New Orleans case—the current epicenter for disaster capitalism in the United States—underscores the need of movements
to effectively neutralize the pervasive nonprofit "progressive sector" and
their identity politics' ideology. Being able to marginalize these actors and
their debilitating ideology is a prerequisite for reigniting a substantive,
antiracist movement in this country that can confront the racist, capitalist
neoliberal agenda.

Notes

1. Adolph Reed, *Class Notes* (New York: The New Press, 2000), 3.

2. Cited in Mike Davis, "Gentrifying Disaster," *Mother Jones*, October 25, 2005,www.motherjones.com/commentary/columns (accessed July 10, 2009).

3. W. Katz-Fishman and J. Scott, "Comments on Burawoy: A View From the Bottom-up," *Critical Sociology* 31, no. 3 (2005): 371–4.

4. Bill Fletcher Jr. and Fernando Gapasin, "Politics of Labor and Race in the USA," *Socialist Register* 39 (2002): 259.

5. David Camfield, "Re-Orienting Class Analysis: Working Classes as Historical Formations," *Science and Society* 68, no. 4 (2004): 421.

6. Fletcher and Gapasin, "Politics of Labor and Race in the USA"; and Gay Seidman, *Manufacturing Militance: Workers' Movements in Brazil and South Africa, 1970-1985* (Berkeley: University of California Press, 1994).

7. Jason Hackworth, *The Neoliberal City: Governance, Ideology, and Development in American Urbanism* (Ithaca, N.Y.: Cornell University, 2007), 2.

8. Neil Smith, "New Globalism, New Urbanism: Gentrification as Global Urban Strategy," *Antipode* 34, no. 3 (2002): 429.

9. Mark Purcell, *Recapturing Democracy* (New York: Routledge, 2008), 15; and C. Jones and T. Novak, *Poverty, Welfare, and the Disciplinary State* (London: Routledge, 1999), 133.

10. Jamie Peck and Adam Tickwell, "Neoliberalizing Space," *Antipode* 34, no. 3 (2002): 380–404; Neal Brenner and Nik Theodore, "Cities and the Geographies of 'Actually Existing Neoliberalism,'" *Antipode* 34, no. 3 (2002): 349–79.

11. By 2009, the numbers had increased to 140,000 units demolished. See letter from Rep. Barney Frank and Rep. Maxine Waters to HUD Secretary Shaun Donovan, June 15, 2009, in possession of the author.

12. Susan Popkin, Bruce Katz, Maty Cunningham, Karen Brown, Jeremy Gustafson, and Margery Turner, *A Decade of HOPE VI: Research Findings and Policy Challenges*, (Washington, D.C.: The Urban Institute and The Brookings Institution, 2004), 8.

13. Hackworth, *The Neoliberal City*, 11; and John Arena, "Winds of Change before Katrina: New Orleans' Public Housing Struggles within a Race, Class, and Gender Dialectic," PhD diss., Tulane University, 2007.

14. Bruce Eggler, "Sweeping Overhaul Outlined for Canal," *Times-Picayune*, March 1, 2004, A1.

15. C3. "Movement Principles," May 2008, in possession of the author.

16. Hackworth, *The Neoliberal City*, 12; and Purcell, *Recapturing Democracy*, 14.

17. Jessica Pardee and Kevin Gotham, "HOPE VI, Section 8, and the Contradictions of Low-Income Housing Policy," *Journal of Poverty* 9, no. 2 (2005): 9, 18.

18. Cited in Nayita Wilson, "Housing Discrimination Is Significant in New Orleans," *Louisiana Weekly*, March 7, 2005, 1.

19. Katy Reckdahl, "Housing Costs Strap Residents," *Times-Picayune*, June 28, 2009, B1; and National Economic & Social Rights Initiative, "Human Rights E-Newsletter," Summer 2009.

20. For documentation on these racially discriminatory measures, see the archives of the Greater New Orleans Fair Housing Action Center, available at www.gnofairhousing.org/archives.html. On black renters being driven from their homes by arson in St. Bernard parish, see Lizzy Ratner, "New Orleans Redraws Its Colorline," *The Nation*, August 27, 2008.

21. Les Christie, "1.5 Million Homes in Foreclosure in '09," *CNN Money*, July 16, 2009, www.money.cnn.com/2009/07/16/real_estate (accessed July 24, 2009).

22. Mike Howells and Eric Lerner, *Public Works to Rebuild New Orleans* (New Orleans: Workers Democracy Network, 2007). For the modest program called for by the Gulf Coast Civic Works Project, go to www.solvingpoverty.com.

23. Naomi Klein, *The Shock Doctrine. The Rise of Disaster Capitalism* (New York: Metropolitan Books, 2007); and Kevin Gotham and Miriam Greenberg, "From 9/11 to 8/29: Post-Disaster Recovery and Rebuilding in New York and New Orleans," *Social Forces* 87, no. 2 (2008): 1042.

24. Cited in Charles Babington, "Some GOP Legislators Hit Jarring Notes in Addressing Katrina," *Washington Post*, September 10, 2005, A4. For press echoing of HUD/HANO claims, see Gwen Filosa and Gordon Russell, "Faltering Safety Net," *Times-Picayune*, October 9, 2005, B1.

25. M. Black, "Basin Street Blues: Iberville Human Rights March," *Indymedia*, December 5, 2005; www.nyc.indymedia.org/en/2005/12/61297.html (accessed July 1, 2009).

26. Author's interview with James Perry, July 10, 2009, New Orleans.

27. Graham Burke, "Residents Rally to Re-Open St. Bernard Housing Development," February 14, 2005, 26; neworleans.indymedia.org/news/2006/02/7033.php (accessed May 2009).

28. Fluxrostrum, "New Orleans St. Bernard Public Housing," *Youtube*, April 2006, www.youtube.com/watch?v=4JYMh13viMU&NR=1 (accessed July 27, 2009).

29. Gwen Filosa, "Four N.O. Developments Will Be Demolished," *Times-Picayune*, June 15, 2006, A1.

30. "New Orleans City Council Shuts Down Public Housing Debate," *Youtube*, December 20, 2007, www.youtube.com/watch?v=cMBWAXfGsc4 (accessed July 27, 2009).

31. James Varney, "Thomas Stands by Rules for Re-entry," *Times-Picayune*, February 25, 2006, A1; and "HANO Wants Only Working Tenants; Council Members Applaud Screening," *Times-Picayune*, February 21, 2006, A1.

32. Stacy Head, "Email, Re: Congressional Hearing on Thursday," February 21, 2007, in possession of the author.

33. Adolph Reed and Stephen Steinberg, "Liberal Bad Faith in the Wake of Hurricane Katrina," *ZNET*, May 4, 2006 www.zmag.org/content/showarticle.cfm?ItemID=10205 (accessed May 16, 2009).

34. Hackworth, *The Neoliberal City*, 12.

35. Mayaba Liebenthal, "Email, Response on Race and Class Debate," March 17, 2006, in possession of the author. Two minor spelling corrections insert by author.

36. Sharon Smith, "The Politics of Identity," *International Socialist Review* 57 (2008).

37. Reed, *Class Notes*, xxii.

38. Cedric Johnson, *Revolutionaries to Race Leaders: Black Power and the Making of African American Politics* (Minneapolis: University of Minnesota Press, 2007), xxviii. For a further critique of the conservative role and legacy of Black Nationalism, particularly its obscuring of class divisions and interests, see Dean Robinson, "Black Power Nationalism as Ethnic Pluralism," in *Renewing Black Intellectual History*, ed. Adolph Reed Jr. and Kenneth W. Warren (Boulder, Colo.: Paradigm Publishers, 2010), 208–9.

39. John Anner, *Beyond Identity Politics* (Boston: South End Press, 1996), 9.

40. Author's interview with Mike Howells, May 10, 2008, New Orleans.

41. Unsurprisingly, well-known black film director Spike Lee *(When the Levees Broke)* and television host Tavis Smiley (PBS's *Right to Return* series) have taken a similar approach in their analysis of post-Katrina New Orleans. Their works downplay class divisions by largely ignoring post-Katrina neoliberal privatization, particularly public housing, and the central role the black political establishment played imposing this agenda. Likewise, well-known national black activists Al Sharpton and Jesse Jackson also failed to show any support for defending New Orleans public housing, despite repeated requests (see Brenda Stokely, "Email, re: Sharpton," December 6, 2007, in possession of the author).

42. Common Ground Relief founder Malik Rahim provided key testimony at the Tribunal on white vigilante violence in Algiers. For A. C. Thompson's coverage, see "Katrina's Hidden Race War," *The Nation*, January 5, 2009.

43. For Curtis Muhammad's perspective on the split, allegedly based on differences with his "bottom-up" organizing philosophy, see "How We Got Where We Are," May 1, 2006; www.peoplesorganizing.org/how_wegot.html; on his differences with the U.S. left, see, "A Farewell Letter on the Second Anniversary of Katrina," *ZNET*, March 2, 2007, www.zmag.org/znet/viewArticle/14592 (accessed July 27, 2009).

44. Ishmael Muhammad, "March to Gretna Speech," November 9, 2005, neworleans.indymedia.org/news/2005/11/6255.php (accessed May 10, 2009).

45. C3, "C3/Hands Off Iberville Statement Against Physical and Verbal Attacks of Ishmael Muhammad," March 2007, in possession of the author; for a defense of the assault, see Peoples Organizing Committee, "The People's Organizing Committee Asserts the Importance of Local Black Leadership 'by the Tenants Themselves' in the Movement to Reoccupy Public Housing," January 16, 2006, www.peoplesorganizing.org/archives.html#jun07 (accessed May 8, 2009).

46. For a critique of Nagin's attempt to delegitimate white public housing activists, see Mike Howells, "Why Ray Nagin Doesn't Want White People to Stand Up for Public Housing," January 8, 2007, neworleans.indymedia.org/news/2007/01/9837_comments.php (accessed May 8, 2009).

47. Interview of Curtis Muhammad by Walidah Imarisha, January 9, 2006, www.neworleans.indymedia.org/news/2006/01/6754_comment.php#6779.

48. See Reed, *Class Notes*, 71–76, for further elaboration of this critique.

49. For criticism of Landrieu from Maxine Waters, a member of her own party, for failing to seriously push the legislation, see "Congressional Leader Faults La. Officials on Recovery; Landrieu Accused of Faltering on Housing," *Times-Picayune*, June 4, 2007, B1.

50. All quotes on this episode are taken from "Email: Response to Jay Arena's Call to Tell the Landrieu's: Do the Right Thing," June 2, 2007, in possession of the author.

51. Interview with Howells; and Fluxrostrum, "New Orleans St. Bernard Public Housing."

52. David Harvey, *Spaces of Global Capitalism* (Verso: New York, 2006), 52.

53. Elizabeth Cook, "Email: Letter to Advancement Project," July 9, 2007, in possession of the author.

54. Interview with Howells; and Gwen Filosa, "Tenants Vow to Retake Housing Complex," *Times-Picayune*, June 1, 2006, A1.

55. For role at HANO and Armstrong Redevelopment Corp, see Joan Treadway, "HANO Fires Smallwood Despite Protests," *Times-Picayune*, June 15, 1988, A1; author's interview with Jesse Smallwood, January 21, 2004; Christopher Cooper, "Public Aid Firm's Spending Questioned," *Times-Picayune*, February 13, 1994; for documentation on suspension of his law license, and then disbarment, see *Louisiana State Bar Ass'n v. Juakali*, 854 So. 2d 307, ladb.org/NXT/gateway.dll/?f=templates$fn=default. htm$vid=ladb:ladbview (accessed July 26, 2009).

56. Housing Investment Trust, "Proposal for the St. Bernard Redevelopment Site," May 1, 2007, in possession of the author.

57. Interview with Howells.

58. Peoples Hurricane Relief Fund, "New Orleans Community Land Trust and Cooperative Credit Union," April 2007, in possession of the author.

59. Malcolm X Grassroots Movement, "Why We Say Free the Land," 2008, mxgm.org/web/programs-initiatives/why-we-say-free-the-land.html (accessed March 26, 2009).

60. Purcell, *Recapturing Democracy*, 16–17; Harvey, *Spaces of Global Capitalism*, 50–55.

61. For more on Common Ground's aim to create a nonprofit alternative to state-delivered services, listen to the interview with the organization's new operational director, Thom Pepper, "Interview by KNYO Radio," November 29, 2007, http://knyo.libsyn.com/index.php?post_id=282870 (accessed March 26, 2009).

Of course, Common Ground founder Brandon Darby later revealed himself as an FBI informant, and there are numerous accounts of his disruptive role. Nonetheless, his FBI role was not, fundamentally, what pushed Common Ground in the nonprofit direction. For more on the FBI and Darby, see David Winkler-Schmit, "Brandon Darby-FBI Informant and Common Ground Co-founder," *Gambit*, January 26, 2009.

62. For a critique of identity politics anarchism, and in support of a version that places the working class at the center of social transformation, see Wayne Price, "What Is Class Struggle Anarchism?" February 7, 2007, nhindymedia.org/newswire/display/5429/index.php (accessed July 26, 2009).

63. M. J. Essex, "Anarchism, Violence, and Brandon Darby's Politics of Moral Certitude," June 26, 2009, neworleans.indymedia.org/news/2009/06/14041.php (accessed July 26, 2009).

64. Reed, *Class Notes*, 72.

65. Ibid., 72.

66. Ibid., 73.

67. Lance Hill, "Thoughts on June 3rd as the Turning Point for New Orleans Displaced Poor," June 1, 2006, in possession of the author.

68. Interview with Howells; and Filosa, "Four N.O. Developments Will Be Demolished."

69. Debbie Pfeiffer, "Students Join Ex-President, for Green Change," *San Bernardino County Sun*, March 18, 2008. For anti-immigrant views, see Gwen Filosa, "Employ Tenants, HANO Is Urged; Work to Begin Soon on City's Complexes," *Times-Picayune*, May 17, 2007, B1.

70. Unsurprisingly, Amy Goodman wrote the forward for the book. Jordan Flaherty, *Floodlines* (Chicago: Haymarket Books, 2010), 2.

71. Klein, *The Shock Doctrine*; and J. Arena, "The War at Home," *ZNET*, November 12, 2005, www.zmag.org/znet/viewArticle/5033 (accessed July 26, 2009).

72. Göran Therborne, "Why Some Classes Are More Successful than Others," *New Left Review* 138 (1983): 40.

73. William Robinson, "Latin America in an Age of Inequality: Confronting the New Utopia," in *Egalitarian Politics in the Age of Globalization*, ed. Craig Murphy (New York: Palgrave, 2002), 30.

74. Jodi Melamed, "The Spirit of Neoliberalism: From Racial Liberalism to Neoliberal Multiculturalism," *Social Text* 24, no. 4 (2006): 16.

75. J. Petras, "US Middle East Wars: Social Opposition and Political Impotence," July 9, 2007, petras.lahaine.org/articulo.php?p=1704 (accessed March 24, 2009).

· III ·

Planning

CHAPTER 7

Charming Accommodations

Progressive Urbanism Meets Privatization in Brad Pitt's Make It Right Foundation

Cedric Johnson

And if the levees had just been built right the first time, with respect for the people who lived amongst them . . . if they'd just practiced a little preventative medicine and spent a little more, well then we wouldn't be faced with the tens of billions it is costing to fix it today. But that didn't happen. And we have to fix it. And not make the same mistakes again.

—Brad Pitt, Preface to *Architecture in Times of Need* (2009)

I N THE WANING MONTHS OF 2007, New Orleans fell in love with Brad Pitt, the Hollywood actor with runway-model looks and the conscience and chutzpah of Sean Penn without the self-righteous attitude. Uniting residents, activists, and some of the most renowned architects in the world, Pitt launched the Make It Right (MIR) Foundation, a private sector effort to reconstruct 150 homes in one of the hardest-hit and neglected New Orleans's neighborhoods, the Lower Ninth Ward. MIR would oversee the design, financing, and construction of state-of-the-art, ecologically sustainable homes. This project quickly garnered international recognition and extensive media coverage, including featured stories in design magazines like *Azure* and *Architectural Digest*. Pitt frequently appeared on television programs like *Larry King Live* to focus public attention on the beleaguered Lower Ninth Ward and a season of HGTV's *Holmes on Homes* show was dedicated to MIR's work.[1] The familiar sight of Pitt cycling along St. Claude Avenue clad in faded jeans, sport coat, and driver's cap lifted the spirits of some Ninth Ward residents and others in a city that had been brought to its knees. In a polity where citizens seem increasingly willing to choose their politicians based on the allure of celebrity rather than actual leadership skills and unique political vision, Pitt seemed to have it all. Infatuation with the city's adopted favorite son ran so high that some residents launched a symbolic "Brad Pitt for Mayor" campaign. Such a mayoral campaign was improbable given residency requirements for mayoral candidates and Pitt's stated disinterest in the job. This "campaign," however, served as rough measure of public approval of Pitt's approach to rebuilding.

MIR evolved within the postdisaster context of highly publicized, racist violence and concerted efforts to bar the return of the city's black precariat. The project took concrete form amid local reactions to the Bring New Orleans Back (BNOB) commission's initial rollout of a plan that would shrink the pre-Katrina footprint of the city and encourage more dense development along the natural levee. Activists and residents within New Orleans and beyond contested these plans. MIR emerged as a powerful voice of neighborhood preservation and racial justice alongside other efforts to defend the city's most flood-ravaged areas, such as that of actor Wendell Pierce in his native Pontchartrain Park and Father Vien Nguyen of Our Lady Queen of Vietnam in New Orleans East. Ideologically, however, MIR was propelled by a moderate rendition of "right of return" arguments made by progressive and radical left activists who sought redistributive public policy to facilitate the resettlement of displaced residents. The Lower Ninth Ward emerged as a compelling touchstone of the "right of return" claim because of the area's majority black demography and unusually high rates of homeownership. Unlike the more volatile issue of public housing provision, the Lower Ninth Ward offered the opportunity to craft a resettlement project that appealed to mainstream notions of the deserving poor. Within the context of MIR's house-by-house rebuilding strategy, the right of return was construed as the right of homeowners to rebuild and resettle without regard for smart planning and a comprehensive flood-management strategy. The MIR project evolved as a challenge to racial inequality and displacement, but the project is hobbled by an approach to rebuilding that is rooted in bourgeois notions of homeownership and private real-estate development.

The architectural approach of MIR might be characterized as *urban homesteading*, essentially the advancement of housing forms that introduce the aesthetics and modalities of suburban housing into inner city settings. Here the norms and expectations regarding nuclear family cohabitation, self-reliance, and neighborhood life are constituted by bourgeois, individualistic assumptions rather than by collectivist values. Single-family detached housing is treated as a normative form within a neoliberal urban context whose physical landscape has beenreshaped by the massification of building practices and enormous state subsidization of single-family dwellings over apartment construction since the Cold War era. The concerted efforts of New Democrats and New Urbanists under HOPE VI to demolish high-rise apartment buildings for low-income citizens and replace them with vinyl-sided, balloon frame homes and faux townhouses has altered the urban fabric and set in motion a new set of practices concerning how urban space is imagined and constructed in the United States.[2]

The MIR project and its individual houses are charming manifestations of this new landscape of neoliberal urbanism. Brad Pitt and the supporters of MIR should be commended for their attempts to promote sustainable building practices in South Louisiana and defend the interests of residents who have been perennially left behind in the designs of city fathers. With rain water–recycling systems, photovoltaic panels, and other green technological features, each MIR house models eco-sustainability and energy independence. At the same time, such features are especially valuable in a depopulated, convalescent city where public services are not guaranteed. Ten-foot concrete pillars and roof-top escape hatches are not merely nifty amenities. Rather, these features are technological accommodations to a regional and national political context where flood protection is not what it used to be and the continued provision of effective levees, flood walls, and pumping systems remains a huge question mark in public deliberations and fiscal ledgers.

Rather than engage in open political struggles for a socially just reconstruction of the city, the MIR project has focused on a house-by-house rebuilding strategy and is guided by communitarian mythology that pervades the world of liberal, do-good architecture and posits that vibrant neighborhood life can be engineered primarily through good design. Like the substitution of micro-technology for comprehensive flood control strategies, this approach to neighborhood development privileges design solutions over social processes and democratic politics. MIR does not embrace a more systemic view of resettlement and planning, but rather, this project complements the broader scheme of privatization and uneven development that has enveloped the city. This chapter concludes by briefly sketching an alternative path to reconstruction that might have merged progressively redistributive public policy to foster greater economic security and vibrant urban life for residents and land use planning suited to the region's unique geomorphology and flood hazards.

Gentrification Dreams Versus the "Right of Return"

The social chaos that ensued after the flooding was characterized by the blatant demonization of the city's black poor and accelerated efforts to remake the city in the image and interests of the local ruling elite. After officials finally ended the misery of thousands of stranded residents and initiated their evacuation, some local elites openly celebrated the departure of the city's poorest residents.[3] Republican Senator Richard Baker was overheard telling lobbyists, "We finally cleaned up public housing in New Orleans. We couldn't do it, but God did." Finis Shellnut, a local New Orleans real estate magnate, was especially enthusiastic about the disaster's social consequences, "The storm destroyed a great deal and there's plenty of space to build houses and sell them for a lot of money. . . . Most importantly, the hurricane drove poor people and criminals out of the city and we hope they don't come back."[4] Equally jubilant was James Reiss, a descendant of an old-line family, who contracted an Israeli security firm to protect his Audubon Place mansion as rumors of looting and mayhem gripped the city. While much of the city still lay underwater, Reiss and other local elites summoned New Orleans Mayor C. Ray Nagin to Dallas to plot the city's future. Although his comments were more tactful than Shellnut's, Reiss shared the same vision of a radically different New Orleans. Speaking with the sense of noblesse oblige and universality that has often cloaked imperial designs, Reiss asserted, "Those who want to see this city rebuilt want to see it done in a completely different way: demographically, geographically and politically. . . . I'm not just speaking for myself here. The way we've been living is not going to happen again, or we're out."[5] Although their use of the phrase is certainly hyperbolic when compared to global-historical instances of genocide and forced exodus, some activists began referring to these attempts to rid the city of its black population as nothing less than "ethnic cleansing." In the weeks and months after the disaster, these unvarnished expressions of antiblack and antipoor sentiment and plans for gentrification were given an air of respectability as various social scientists and planning technocrats entered the public conversation, touting the virtues of deconcentrating poverty and drafting plans for reconstruction that merely retraced the standing outlines of uneven development that divided the city.[6]

Progressive and radical left activists in the city and beyond articulated the "right of return" in response to these gentrification schemes. Although the phrase was gleaned from Cold War international human rights discourses, the most progressive expressions of this claim were made by those activists who fought the demolition of habitable public housing stock across the city and efforts to curtail affordable housing policies in the adjacent parishes.[7] Organizations like Community Concern Compassion (C3)/Hands Off Iberville, the People's Hurricane Relief Fund, and the New Orleans Coalition for Legal Aid and Disaster Relief were foremost in these efforts to counter the war against the poor in post-Katrina New Orleans. Amid the flurry of blueprints for rebuilding, celebrity telethons, and federal pledges of billions in aid that followed in the weeks after Katrina devastated the Gulf Coast, activist and Loyola University law professor Bill Quigley identified systematic attempts to rid the city of its working poor population by tearing apart the remaining threads of the social safety net. He described the evolution of a two-tiered system of relief and recovery that favored property owners over renters even though the latter constituted the majority of New Orleans's pre-Katrina population. Although much of the city's public housing stock survived the disaster with little flooding and relatively no structural damage, the Housing Authority of New Orleans (HANO) moved forward with the demolition of the Lafitte and St. Bernard housing complexes despite reports that concluded that renovation would cost significantly less than razing and redevelopment.[8] The war against affordable housing was not restricted to New Orleans proper and radiated into the suburban parishes. In neighboring Jefferson Parish, residents halted the construction of a 200-unit, assisted living complex by passing a resolution that prohibited all low-income tax-credit, multifamily housing. And in St. Bernard Parish, residents supported a blood relative ordinance on rental agreements that effectively barred blacks and the area's expanding Latino migrant labor population from securing apartments in the almost exclusively white suburb. Quigley argued that school privatization, the lack of investment in public health care especially in regard to mental health services, and the uneven restoration of water and utilities all constituted a systematic attempt to remake the city's racial and class composition.

Focusing on the unjust distribution of wealth and power, the "right of return" argument crafted by Quigley and other activists is consistent with the New Left slogan of the "right to the city." This concept was first offered during the late 1960s in the writings of French social theorist Henri Lefebvre, and in recent years the idea has been taken up again by intellectuals and activists amid the immense urban social misery and precarity produced by neoliberal restructuring. Although this notion has liberal and mainstream renditions as well, its more radical iterations refocus attention on redistributive politics as a possible rallying point for diverse urban social movements. As David Harvey notes, the right to the city is not merely the individual liberty to access urban resources. Rather, the right to the city is "a right to change ourselves by changing the city," and it is by definition "a common rather than an individual right since this transformation inevitably depends upon the exercise of a collective power to reshape the processes of urbanization."[9] This "freedom to make and remake our cities and ourselves is" according to Harvey "one of the most precious yet most neglected of our human rights." This concept shifts focus from recognition and inclusion within the established capitalist growth coalitions that govern most contemporary cities towards the possibility of an egalitarian urbanity where the interests and passions of living labor determine the course of public life, the shape of the built environment, and how the wealth created through urban productive relations is distributed. In asserting that housing should be a fundamental right of the city's inhabitants, the struggles against public housing demolitions, discussed at greater length in John Arena's contribution to this volume, constituted a direct challenge to capitalist visions of the city. Unfortunately, the "right of return" arguments offered by progressive activists were eclipsed by those of more conservative forces who promoted an approach to resettlement and reconstruction that was grounded in property rights. The MIR Foundation's mission of rebuilding the Lower Ninth Ward community where it formerly stood was undoubtedly shaped by the "right of return" discourse as well as heated public debates over the Urban Land Institute (ULI)'s footprint recommendations issued in the immediate months after Katrina made landfall.

The Footprint Debate and the Death of Planning

The BNOB Commission tapped the Urban Land Institute to draft a strategy report for rebuilding the city. This internationally recognized think tank was created by the National Association of Real Estate Boards in 1939 amid the urban renewal efforts of the New Deal era as a vehicle for advancing propertied interests and thwarting the construction of public housing stock in U.S. central cities.[10] The commission was racially diverse, but its membership was drawn heavily from the city's managerial and ruling classes.[11] One of the most divisive figures on the commission was wealthy real estate developer Joseph Canizaro. A top Republican campaign contributor in a majority Democratic city, Canizaro had developed the reputation as a formidable civic leader who was willing to speak against the grain of prevailing opinion. He was a major force in Nagin's local machinery, a confidant of GOP strategist Karl Rove, and the former president of the ULI. His presence on the BNOB commission and close ties to the ULI heightened many residents' concerns that sinister motives would taint the planning process. Canizaro's public comments on how the city should be rebuilt did little to ease this discomfort. As most observers were beginning to predict that post-Katrina New Orleans would be a smaller, whiter, more affluent city, Canizaro attempted to rationalize this demographic change as a matter of simple market economics rather than an outcome of intentional public policy: "As a practical matter, these poor folks don't have the resources to get out of our city. So we won't get all those folks back. That's just a fact."[12] Simmering suspicions that the new New Orleans would be a radically gentrified city reached a boiling point when the ULI publicized its recommendations for rebuilding the city.

The ULI report held that the "failure to create an immediate and forward-thinking plan can result in scattered, uncoordinated, dysfunctional redevelopment; an ineffective infrastructure policy; and a greatly impaired urban fabric."[13] The final report is characterized by a cautious tone that repeatedly embraced the platitudes of inclusion: "Diversity, equity and cooperation are of critical importance. The recovery must not be held back by the racial issues that have slowed progress in the past." "Every citizen," the report holds, "has the right to return to a *safe* city" [emphasis in original]. The report recommends that all federal contractors pay a living wage, health benefits, and vacation days. With respect to public housing, the panel called on HANO to "repair and reopen all public housing units in appropriate areas" and to expand the use of Section 8 vouchers. The ULI panel also recommended the passage of an inclusionary housing ordinance that would require 10 to 15 percent of all new housing stock—for sale and rental units—to be affordable to families earning no more than 80 percent of the city's median income. Beneath these socially liberal gestures, however, the ULI report's economic and social policy recommendations favored the city's propertied strata and recommended only modest redistribution of resources and minimal disruption to the structures that reproduced inequality in the city.

The ULI report proffers its own rendition of the "right of return," which gestures toward the universal claims advanced by liberal and progressive activists in and beyond New Orleans, but makes more detailed stipulations favoring homeowners and developers. The ULI panel stopped short of endorsing full enforcement of Davis-Bacon Act's prevailing wage requirements, citing the potentially adverse impacts on small contracting businesses. The report also expressed commitment to diversity within the entrepreneurial class, concluding that the "number of successful opportunities for African American businesses to share in New Orleans's economic rebound will be a bellwether to the nation of the city's commitment to rebuilding a diverse city."[14]

The most controversial section of the ULI report recommended that New Orleans be rebuilt on a smaller geographic footprint. The intellectual rationale of this recommendation was consonant with emerging remedies to industrial decline and population loss across the global North. In cities as far flung and demographically varied as Dessau, Germany, and Youngstown, Ohio, local elites have either proposed "right-sizing" plans or already initiated the conversion of boarded-up, vacant housing and brown fields into park space.[15] The expressed rationale is that green space amenities provide additive value for both urban dwellers and real estate development and might allow for a more efficient delivery of urban services in cities with dwindling populations, tax bases, and resources. In a few words, the panel asserted that New Orleans should be built on a smaller footprint determined by real estate values and future flood hazards: "The city should be rebuilt in a strategic manner. Areas that sustained minimal damage should be encouraged to begin rebuilding immediately, while those with more extensive damage will need to evaluate the feasibility of reinvestment first and then proceed expeditiously in a manner that will ensure the health and safety of the residents of each neighborhood."[16]

The ULI panel report operates from the assumption that flood hazards either cannot or will not be rectified by comprehensive, publicly financed engineering projects. More importantly, the report outlines an approach to flood protection that suspends consideration of the man-made factors that created the 2005 disaster, namely, the flood hazards created by the Mississippi River Gulf Outlet and the Industrial Canal's proximity to residential neighborhoods; the negative ecological impacts of both the Army Corp's reengineering of the Mississippi River and corporate oil and natural gas drilling on coastal wetlands; and, finally, the consequences of fiscal conservatism and infrastructure divestment on flood risks and public safety. The ULI report outlined a program of storm water management that was guided by an implicit critique of the strategic approach administered by the Army Corps since Hurricane Betsy. Instead of flood control, the ULI report encourages the introduction of "new concepts and technologies for storm water management, such as bioretention areas, vegetated swales, storm water wetlands, green roofs, permeable pavement, and conservation areas."[17] Their plan reflected the new terms of public divestiture and encouraged local and state officials to reduce construction and maintenance costs for storm water infrastructure. The panel asserted that the city's future flood management plans "must accept and embrace the city's surrounding hydrology, establishing every opportunity for canals, rivers, lakes, ponds and wetlands to become urban amenities from the scale of the neighborhood to the entire city."

The report divides the city into three zones with each determined by the extent of damage and prospects for long-term recovery. Investment Zone A was composed of the lowest-lying and most flood-damaged areas of the city, namely, those portions of the city north of the French Quarter and bordering Lake Pontchartrain and the Industrial Canal. The panel essentially concluded that these areas would require too much capital investment to be fully repaired and, therefore, they should not be resettled en masse.[18] Instead of full-scale reconstruction, the ULI panel suggested that these neighborhoods be converted into parkland and integrated into a more effective, storm water management system. Investment Zone B was composed of those areas of the city with more varied impact. The ULI panel recommended a composite strategy of neighborhood revitalization and the creation of "open-space systems" that "connect and span from one neighborhood to another, to enhance the walkable nature of New Orleans."[19] Investment Zone C was given the top priority in the proposed rebuilding schema of the ULI panel. This zone encompasses the areas closest to the natural levee and the city's original settlement. "These areas," the panel held, "also constitute much of the city's tourism base and can help its preliminary economic recovery as well as provide housing."

In his 2006 book *Breach of Faith*, *Times-Picayune* journalist Jed Horne argues that city officials in New Orleans should have approached reconstruction with the same posture as civic leaders in Kobe, Japan, after the massive 1995 Hanshin earthquake. Although the Hanshin disaster was deadlier—6,401 people were killed, over 300,000 were left homeless, and 2.6 million lost electrical power—Kobe makes for an interesting comparison with New Orleans. Both are port cities that possessed extensive historical housing stock at the time of their respective disasters. Although more ethnically homogeneous than New Orleans, Kobe possessed a small Korean immigrant population that endured considerable scapegoating and harassment in the aftermath of the disaster. Horne is enamored by the leadership displayed by Mayor Kazutoshi Sasayama in the aftermath of the quake. Sasayama, a trained urban planner, assembled his team and ventured out into the city to assess the damage and develop a plan for reconstruction. Rather than risk future calamity or blighted tracts in Kobe's urban fabric, Sasayama developed a plan that relocated some residents to safer areas away from fault lines. His plan created neighborhood greenspaces with water features that doubled as a public amenity and fire deterrent and also replaced antiquated, frail wooden structures with concrete and steel ones. Sasayama pursued this reconstruction agenda in the face of resistance from residents and activists who often referred to city planners as *kajibadorobo*, or "thieves at the scene of a fire."[20]

Horne's brief comparison with Kobe suggests that New Orleanians might have undertaken a more technocratic path to reconstruction guided by sound design principles and free of politics. Horne's instincts regarding the need for sound planning are correct, but his comparative analysis evades the central problem of meaningful democracy in New Orleans and other North American cities on matters of real estate and economic development. The lack of substantive participation was the root problem of the BNOB commission's work and the wellspring of opposition to the ULI's footprint recommendation. Many residents felt that they were being politically bulldozed by the commission that, despite its token diversity, was essentially an organ of the city's ruling class. It was not enough to enlist residents' opinions during public hearings for the purpose of securing legitimacy for elite designs. The concerns about displacement might have been reconciled through more democracy. Town hall meetings and design charrettes are inadequate means of pursuing a citizen-led, democratic rebuild. More extensive use of new information technologies might have lent a more substantive democratic dimension to post-Katrina rebuilding and created opportunities for more extensive participation among New Orleanians temporarily residing in other cities. The post-Katrina planning process unfolded in a context where an isolated, small group of elites proceeded without any serious intention of including the concerns and interests of thousands of displaced residents in an extensive and sustained manner.

The idea that post-Katrina New Orleans should be rebuilt on higher ground is sensible. The initial settlement of the Lower Ninth Ward, New Orleans East, and much of St. Bernard Parish was driven by short-term, selfish economic interests rather than sound planning or long-term concern for human welfare. Such accelerated expansion away from the original French settlement during the twentieth century was driven by the same confluence of automobile dependency, highway construction, industrial restructuring, real estate speculation, and racial fears that fueled the radial growth of cities nationwide. Disasters create the opportunity to start anew and to build better than before. The Great Chicago Fire of 1871 fundamentally transformed that American city.[21] Architects and planners descended upon the city and gave birth to radical innovations in commercial building and housing construction. In many ways, New Orleans has become a similar laboratory for architects and planners, but its fate may in the end approximate that of postdisaster San Francisco more closely than Chicago. The 1906 San Francisco earthquake and fire saw similar abandonment of planning in favor of political expediency and profit as city officials waived new building codes to speed up the reconstruction process. The Katrina disaster afforded city leaders an opportunity to rebuild smarter with an eye toward sustainability and flood control. The promise of a safer, well-planned New Orleans was derailed by political expediency.

In his January 2006 speech commemorating the Martin Luther King Jr. holiday, Nagin reassured black constituents that New Orleans would remain a "chocolate city," and he proved again that he could garner black electoral support through skillful use of emotive rhetoric that evoked the city's unjust economic-spatial legacies while at the same time advancing policies that were antagonistic to the interests of the city's black working classes. Perhaps tasting his own blood in the political waters, Nagin backed away from the ULI's footprint recommendations and did not call for a moratorium on building in any part of the city, saying, "I have confidence that our citizens can decide intelligently for themselves where they want to build, once presented with the facts."[22] Other black politicians like Cynthia Willard-Lewis, who represented New Orleans East on the City Council, and Oliver Thomas, a native of the Lower Ninth Ward and at-large councilman in the aftermath of the disaster, followed suit and balked at the ULI/BNOB commission recommendations. In essence, Nagin and the council approved a plan that would devolve responsibility for planning back to the neighborhoods. This move serviced two ends—it restored a glimmer of hope to those neighborhoods that would have been marked for demolition if the ULI recommendations became public policy and yet, simultaneously, this maneuver ensured that those very neighborhoods with the greatest damage and most economically and politically marginal residents would face a steep uphill climb toward reconstructing their lives and communities. Affluent neighborhoods, like the black enclave of Eastover and majority-white Lakeview, which possessed neighborhood associations, political connections, and individual and collective resources would be able to rebuild quickly and retain city services, while the less affluent residents who lacked access to capital and social networks would be doomed to stagnant recovery, municipal neglect, and broken hearts.[23]

In all likelihood, the strict implementation of the smaller footprint plan would not have enriched Canizaro and his cohort in the manner speculated in "land grab" charges made by opponents, but rather powerful real estate holders would have benefitted from a land pinch as more concentrated development sprouted closer to the natural levee and drove up the value of already precious tracts of real estate. This scenario was not inevitable, however. Historical-spatial practices are not frozen in time, and despite power asymmetry, political struggle can alter the course of public policy and create a more humanistic vision of the city. Public authorization of rent controls, housing subsidies, and other measures might have offset the negative effects of concentrated real estate development and ensured a place for working people in the new New Orleans. Nonetheless, the rejection of the ULI plan surrendered the debate over the remaking of the city to political insiders and set in motion a rebuilding process defined by market forces rather than sensible planning practices and generous and sustained public input.

For politicians, the "right of return" slogan provided a means for expressing symbolic support for an inclusive vision of New Orleans without making the kinds of concrete political commitments that would enable the return of citizens to a viable, sustainable urban environment with effective services, low crime, cherished neighborhood life, and vibrant economy. In fact, many local elites appropriated the right-of-return mantra even as they moved aggressively to demolish public housing in the city. This wholesale retreat from public planning has been embraced by a diverse ensemble of local activists, nonprofit organizations, celebrity benefactors, politicians, New Urbanist architects, and planners. The politics of deregulation accommodated and enhanced various agendas of community empowerment and grassroots rebuilding. Five years after the disaster, the reports of mainstream think tanks such as the Brookings Institution and major news media routinely praise the resiliency of New Orleans and Gulf Coastal residents and tout the grassroots civic spirit that has flourished in Mid-City, Pontchartrain Park, and the Lower Ninth Ward as the key to the region's rebirth. The work of New Urbanist guru Andrés Duany and of Brad Pitt's MIR project are both illustrative of this tendency to fasten a socially liberal rhetoric of community empowerment to private sector development.

Duany argues in favor of laissez-faire building practice as a means of preserving the city's famous *laissez le bon temps roulez* culture. The Cuban expatriate architect and co-founder of the Congress for New Urbanism confides that New Orleans has served as "as a surrogate for [his] inaccessible Santiago de Cuba."[24] In response to those right-wing critics who admonished New Orleans's legendary cultural hedonism (e.g., Pat Robertson) and political mismanagement (e.g., FEMA Director Mike Brown) as root causes for the disaster and reasons to constrain full federal commitment to rebuilding, Duany argues that these commentators have not fully understood the historical, geographic character of the city or the source of its unique way of life. When viewed through the lens of the Caribbean, Duany argues, "New Orleans is not among the most haphazard, poorest, or misgoverned American cities, but rather the most organized, wealthiest, cleanest and competently governed of the Caribbean cities." He adds, "If New Orleans were to be governed as efficiently as, say Minneapolis, it would be a different place—and not one that I could care for. Let me work with the government the way that it is." Duany praises the low cost of living in the city and fears that in the place of "houses that were hand built by people's parents and grandparents, or by small builders paid in cash or by barter," returning residents will face higher construction costs and mortgages. The resulting homeowner debt and lifetime of work needed to settle accounts will, he argues, kill the casual, freewheeling culture of the city. "Everyone will have a mortgage," he writes, "which will need to be sustained by hard work—and this will undermine the culture of New Orleans." Duany is neither an anthropologist nor an historian, and his claim that hard work will undermine New Orleans's unique culture is ahistorical, counterintuitive, and dangerous. The city's legendary musical idioms from ragtime and jazz to latter-day sissy bounce, its manifold culinary contributions, and raucous carnival celebrations, brass band funerals, social aid and pleasure clubs, and Mardi Gras Indian tribes were largely crafted by the city's polycultural working classes—slaves, dockworkers, cooks, waiters, domestics, prostitutes, buskers, day laborers, immigrant street vendors, etc.—whose lives were characterized by crushing material poverty and exploitation. Hard work has always defined the lives of the majority of the city's inhabitants.

Duany argues that the best way to keep building cost down is to deregulate the construction industry and to remove all barriers to what he calls "grassroots 'bottom up' rebuilding." He favors the creation of an experimental "opt-out zone" unrestricted by typical American building codes and specifications. "There must be free house designs that can be built in small stages, and that do not require an architect, complicated permits or inspections." The real target of Duany's animus is what he terms the "nanny state." According to him, state building codes and standards are "so expensive and complicated that only the nanny-state can provide affordable housing." Such arguments neglect the historical role that deregulation played in the widespread death and destruction that ensued as the city's levees breached. Lax enforcement of building codes allowed contractors to create unnecessary hazards by constructing homes "slab on grade" on parcels that were below sea level and often in freshly drained swamps. Moreover, Duany dedicates little attention to the negative effects these cost-cutting measures might have on wage floors, safety, and working conditions for construction workers in the short run and on the longer-term safety of residents. Where Pitt expresses more disappointment and cynicism in response to government failures, Duany offers outright contempt for the concept of state planning.

Both arrive in similar places, however, in supporting a market-oriented approach to rebuilding.

Brad Pitt's MIR Foundation contests the notion that certain city neighborhoods are beyond repair and deserve to be abandoned, but this project does not challenge the broader distributive politics set in motion by Nagin and the BNOB commission. By developing a concrete path for displaced residents to return, Pitt's project has won accolades from mainstream media and activists alike. The MIR project's progressive elements — defense of black homeowners and incorporation of green building technologies, however, conceal tacit commitments to a socially unsustainable urbanism that is driven by the same market logics animating the larger neoliberal growth-recovery coalition. Like the New Urbanism, Pitt's MIR project is guided by nostalgia for community that neglects other important values like metropolitan planning and economic justice.

The Road to Privatization Is Paved with Good Intentions: Making It Right

In the weeks after Hurricane Katrina made landfall, the Lower Ninth Ward quickly emerged as a poignant symbol of the city's inequalities in the national and global, public consciousness of the 2005 disaster. By now, the broad outlines of the Lower Ninth Ward's origins and woes are well known and this locale's history reflects the broader political-economy of residential segregation that has defined American life over the past half-century.[25] The Ninth Ward voting district is bisected from north to south by the Industrial Canal, with the Lower Ninth Ward extending from the canal eastward to the St. Bernard Parish Line. The area was described as "lower" due to its downriver orientation relative to the original French settlement and the more-affluent uptown section of the city. Whereas as the French Quarter, the Central Business District, and Uptown all stood on the natural levee, much of the Ninth Ward was built on less-desirable, flood-prone land.

Because of its geographic isolation and decades of municipal neglect, the Lower Ninth Ward developed a vibrant neighborhood culture of mutual aid and self-sufficiency. Until relatively recently, the Ninth Ward contained considerable racial and class diversity, but like many American urban neighborhoods, the area was transformed by the post–World War II exodus of white residents to neighboring St. Bernard Parish. Between

Figure 7.1. A heavily damaged house near Jourdan Road, in the Lower Ninth Ward, October 2006. Photograph by the author.

1940 and 1970, the Lower Ninth Ward's "nonwhite" population rose from 31 percent to 73 percent. By 2000, African Americans comprised 90 percent of the Lower Ninth Ward's population and poverty rose from 28 percent in 1970 to 36.2 percent in 2000.[26] Although residents retained a sense of community pride and adoration for the neighborhood amid population decline and increasing violence, the popular image of the area was one of urban danger and utter blight, with some locals referring derisively to the Lower Ninth Ward as the "murder capital of the murder capital."[27]

Groping for the words to adequately describe the sheer destruction of the Lower Ninth Ward after Katrina, many commentators and residents quickly adopted the military language first used to describe the focal point of a bombing and later popularized after the September 11 terrorist attacks. The Lower Ninth Ward became "ground zero" in the Hurricane Katrina disaster. Rumors that the catastrophic flooding of the Lower Ninth Ward was the result of a bombing conspiracy also circulated widely in the months and years after Katrina and added to the sense of mounting public outrage. Some residents swore that they heard an explosion and speculated

that the Industrial Canal was detonated and the Lower Ninth Ward neighborhood sacrificed to relieve pressure on the more valuable real-estate
upriver. Such grapevine theories often intermingled with and embellished
accounts of the 1927 flood and faded recollections of 1965's Hurricane
Betsy. Even former mayor Marc Morial paused to assert that a federal
investigation should have been undertaken given the extent of testimo-
nies and allegations about a possible explosion.[28] In all likelihood, the loud
noise many residents heard was the sound of an Ingram Company barge,
ING 4727, that crashed through the floodwalls of the Industrial Canal near
North Claiborne Avenue. Like most conspiracies, however, the Lower
Ninth Ward residents' suspicions were rooted in a longer history of social
exclusion and an empirically grounded sense that there were forces in the
city who viewed the neighborhood and its residents as expendable.

A year after the Katrina disaster, while other parts of the city slowly
crept back to life, the Lower Ninth Ward was literally a cemetery. More
than 4,000 homes were destroyed. The force of gushing water from the
Industrial Canal swept away many of the homes, leaving behind only foundations and concrete steps in many yards that created the impression of
tombstones and crypts amid the overgrown grass and eerie silence. The few
scattered houses that survived the storm appeared slumped and defeated
like soldiers on a late battlefield. It was one of the last neighborhoods to
have power and water services resumed. The scale of devastation made the
Lower Ninth Ward a popular stop on the disaster bus tours that cropped up
in Katrina's wake and a literal tabula rasa for architectural revisioning.

The Lower Ninth Ward provided the perfect cause célèbre for
Hollywood philanthropists, dissident journalists, veteran activists, millennial volunteers, and do-gooders of all classes, faiths, and political creeds,
because the area was the poorest, most neglected, physically "bombed
out" neighborhood and yet, most of its residents possessed one of the
hallmarks of American bourgeois virtue—homeownership. According to
the 2000 census, there were 14,008 residents in the Lower Ninth Ward.
With approximately 60 percent of its households owner-occupied, the
Lower Ninth Ward outpaced homeownership in Orleans Parish generally
(53 percent) despite high levels of poverty and vacancy.[29] In an effort to
compel the Bush administration toward a more concrete expression of its
rhetoric of compassion, Peter Wagner and Susan Edwards of the progressive left magazine *Dollars & Sense* even described the Lower Ninth as a
"shining example" of Bush's "ownership society." As such, the Lower Ninth

Figure 7.2. Standing atop the ruins of a Lower Ninth Ward house, Jocelyn A. Sideco (third from the left) of Contemplatives in Action recounts the forensics of the Katrina disaster for a group of college students, March 2009. Photograph by the author.

Ward provided a more effective symbol for organizing moderate right-of-return claims than the public housing projects scattered about the city.

Pitt and MIR executive director Tom Darden assembled a diverse coalition to serve as MIR's principal players. GRAFT, an award-winning design firm, oversaw the development of the projects overarching design principles. Celebrated architect and "cradle-to-cradle" design proponent, William McDonough offered expertise in ecological sustainability. Preliminary feasibility studies were undertaken by Cherokee Gives Back Foundation, the philanthropic wing of Cherokee, a private equity firm specializing in brownfield redevelopment. In addition to its support of the MIR Foundation, Cherokee has also underwritten the projects by organizations such as Bhopal Hope and former President Bill Clinton's Global Initiative. The Lower Ninth Ward Stakeholder Coalition offered constant feedback on financial, design, and planning components. Since most of the MIR homes carry a $150,000 sale price, Ajamu Kitwana, director of Homeowner Services for MIR, was responsible for coordinating "gap financing" to bridge the residents' individual resources with the home purchase price. In addition to this central team, MIR has collaborated with numerous respected architects including local firms like Billes Architecture, Concordia, and John C. Williams Architects; national firms such as Kieran Timberlake of Philadelphia and Pugh + Scarpa of Santa Monica; and international firms such as Netherlands-based MVRDV and Shigeru Ban Architects, whose principal is renowned for his paper-tube emergency shelters. To his credit, Pitt did not cave in to the fashionable claims about deconcentrating poverty, which imply that working and poor people have no social relations, traditions, or values worthy of preservation and instead need more extensive cultural assimilation and tutelage from middle-class mentors. Unlike Oprah Winfrey, Canadian automotive magnate Frank Stronach, and others who built housing subdivisions for evacuees in suburban or rural sites, Pitt made a commitment to rebuild a working class urban community.

Pitt offered a progressive analysis of the disaster that focused on social and political factors rather than pure meteorology. In his foreword to *Architecture in Times of Need,* a catalogue of MIR homes, Pitt opens with a blistering critique of the disaster's underlying political dynamics, noting that "Katrina has been called the greatest natural disaster in U.S. history, but that description is incorrect. . . . Let's be clear, Katrina was man-made."[30] Pitt argues that in times of crisis, society's first priority should be to help the most vulnerable and he concludes that New Orleans is a microcosm of the world's problems, namely, "the marginalization of a people, the malpractice of providing low-quality housing for low-income people, even the victimization of oil greed. (If New Orleans had been receiving their fair share of profits from offshore drilling, they would have been able to autonomously secure their levees properly.)" Although he is keenly aware of the social and political factors that drove the disaster, Pitt does not challenge this state of affairs. Rather than serving as a starting point for collective action, which might contest how societal resources are distributed, these facts of political life give way to cynicism, symbolic protests, and the pursuit of "roll-up your sleeves" self-help.

Pitt's first act of symbolic protest was to erect 429 pink tents in November 2007. The tents resembled different components of a house (roof, walls, etc.) and were strewn across the deserted streets of the Lower Ninth Ward. These ghost structures were composed of steel tubular frames and clad with Earthtex fabric, a 100 percent recyclable material, and at night they were illuminated using solar power, bringing 24-hour attention to what was once a neighborhood. Pitt later asserted that he

Figure 7.3. The Make It Right Foundation's Pink Project Installation with the Industrial Canal's Lift Bridge and the Central Business District in the background. Photograph by Ricky Ridecós.

chose pink because "it screamed the loudest."[31] The Pink Project installation also evoked, perhaps unintentionally, other familiar, enduring symbols and narratives of the American Dream and, more succinctly, notions of success and economic security inextricably linked to homeownership. An immediate reference is to John Cougar Mellencamp's 1984 hit record "Pink Houses," an ode to small town self-reliance. Visually, the Pink Project also alludes to the small red houses of the Monopoly board game. Like the classic board game, which simulates the dynamics of an unregulated real estate market, the MIR Foundation sought private sector residential development within the essentially unrestricted rebuilding context of postdisaster New Orleans.

Houses That Float: Technology Surrogates Planning

William McDonough's "cradle-to-cradle" philosophy of industrial and building design forms a crucial intellectual component of the MIR vision.[32]

McDonough offers "cradle-to-cradle" as an alternative to the "cradle-to-grave" culture common to the developed world where linear production processes, planned obsolescence, and irrational use of natural resources have created unfathomable waste and ecological destruction. Recycling is only a marginally better alternative to normative industrial practices and is more accurately described as "downcycling" by McDonough, since this practice merely delays the inevitable trip to the landfill for products that were designed to be disposable. Instead, McDonough envisions the design of products and the built environment in a manner that emulates the regenerative and complementary properties of the natural world. Under his "cradle-to-cradle" philosophy, buildings should be designed to operate like trees that produce more energy than they consume. In a similar vein, commonly used products like books and magazines might be fabricated with synthetic materials rather than paper. Such technical nutrients can be continuously and indefinitely reintroduced into the production cycle. Guided by "cradle-to-cradle" design theory, the MIR homes have raised the bar for ecologically sustainable building practices in the region by insisting on extensive use of mold-resistant materials, South-facing roofs with active solar installations, home elevations that exceed FEMA requirements, inclusion of space within each home for composting and recycling, installation of graywater and rainwater recycling systems, and other cutting-edge green technologies.

Not only will such technologies reduce waste and the carbon footprint of the occupants, but these energy-related installations have important economic benefits as well. In MIR homes, surplus power collected through solar panels is fed back into the electrical grid helping to reduce overall energy costs. The durability of these systems and cost associated with future maintenance and replacement notwithstanding, this aspect of the MIR homes is commendable as an individualistic solution to matters of economic hardship. The homes designed by David Adjaye of Adjaye Associates and Thom Mayne of the Santa Monica–based firm Morphosis are elegant examples of how sustainable ecology and flood-deterrent elements are integrated into the MIR project. A number of the MIR houses address flood risks through elevation, but both of these architects have devised innovative solutions to building below sea level while maintaining a more typical interface between home and pedestrian life.

Born in Tanzania to Ghanaian parents and now based in London, Adjaye was selected to design the National Museum of African American

History and Culture in Washington, DC. Adjaye's innovative design for
the MIR Foundation was replicated in two Lower Ninth Ward homes, the
first on Deslonde Street and a second nearby on Tennessee Street. Named
"Asempa" or good news in the Twi language of his native Ghana, Adaye's
twin MIR homes are rather unassuming and simplistic at first glance.
Although their cubelike appearance is a visual departure from the city's
vernacular architecture, the floor plans of Adjaye's homes pay homage to
the spatial economy of the Shotgun House. With a building footprint of
24 × 44 feet and a little more than 1000 square feet of living space, the
design features a stilted, canopy roof that creates a shaded-outdoor living
space spanning the entire footprint of the house. Instead of a traditional
pitched roof, Adjaye's house incorporates a concave design that facilitates
solar and water collection. Hurricane proof windows and a foundation
of concrete grade beams and piles offer protection from seasonal storms.
In addition to panoramic views of the city, the rooftop deck provides a
means of egress in the event of catastrophic flooding. Rather than a more
conventional porch, Adjaye's homes offer another means for facilitating
interaction with the life of the sidewalk. The house features wide cast-in
concrete stairs that can double as stadium-styled seating for gatherings
with neighbors.[33]

The FLOAT house designed by Thom Mayne of the Santa Monica–
based firm Morphosis may represent one of the most effective attempts
to combine modernist lines, green components, and elements of the
local vernacular aesthetic and color palette.[34] The most celebrated feature
of the house is its ability to float as high as 12 feet in rising flood waters.
Inspired by the flexibility of a car chassis, the foundation was fabricated
from polystyrene foam encased in fiberglass-reinforced concrete. The
roofline and floor plan of the FLOAT house evoke the two most ubiquitous low-income housing forms in South Louisiana—the shotgun house
and the mobile home. The living room and kitchen constitute a large
entertaining space at the main entrance and the remaining bedrooms and
bathrooms follow in succession down a single hallway. Like other MIR
houses, the FLOAT house incorporates solar power and rainwater recycling systems. Like Adjaye's MIR home, the Morphosis' floating house
maintains connectivity with the sidewalk via a low-slung deck that is
skinned in ironwork reminiscent of French Quarter balconies.

Some have touted the development of floating houses and prototypical
amphibious communities in the Netherlands as a model for development

Figure 7.4. Asempa House designed by David Adjaye. Photograph courtesy of Adjaye Associates.

throughout New Orleans and other coastal regions of the United States.[35] Geoff Manaugh and Nicola Twilley argue that under the Army Corps of Engineers flood control approach, New Orleans's landscape "has never been under anything but martial law." In contrast to grandiose proposals to build massive sea gates or replenish depleted wetlands by pumping Mississippi River sediment through pipelines, Manaugh and Twilley favor a strategy of "managed retreat" and floating architecture for addressing the city's hydrological challenges. Manaugh and Twilley's arguments are largely focused on the history of Mississippi River flood control and as such are off the mark in ascertaining the more contemporary hazards facing the city—namely, flooding from Lake Pontchartrain. Their work also neglects indigenous approaches to building in the watery context of South Louisiana. For generations, elevated houses have stood out on the South Louisiana horizon near the various bayous and tributaries of the Atchafalaya Basin and along the Gulf Coast. As well, before industrial practices threatened coastal wetlands, local artisans relied on bald cypress trees as a vital building material because of its durability and water-resistant properties. More important than these historical omissions, Manaugh and Twilley suspend any serious discussion of politics and planning in a fashion common to contemporary progressive design circles. Their Netherlands comparison is problematic because unlike post–New Deal America, the experimental housing complexes in Rotterdam exist within a broader social democratic context where tremendous public investment fosters a greater degree of equality and also ensures more universal protection from the temperamental North Sea. In contrast, personal homeowner flood protections incorporated in the MIR designs are accommodations to state divestment. In this context, living "off the grid" is not so much an expression of one's commitment to twenty-first century environmentalism but rather a subtle concession to the neoliberal landscape of uneven development and increasing social precarity. Within the Lower Ninth Ward, these building innovations ensure survival in the absence of a cutting-edge and fully funded regional flood control system.

The Communitarian Myth

The MIR proponents set out to accomplish more than the mere provision of shelter to the displaced residents of the Lower Ninth Ward. They

Figure 7.5. FLOAT House at 1638 Tennessee Street designed by Thom Mayne / Morphosis Architects. Photograph by Iwan Baan.

want nothing less than to reconstruct a devastated urban community, and some supporters see this undertaking as potentially providing a model for neighborhood revitalization that can be replicated elsewhere. The principal architects of GRAFT note that by focusing on the Lower Ninth Ward, MIR "sought to identify a center of attention and action, a pressure point within the urban fabric of New Orleans, which will trigger the redevelopment of larger areas within the city and potentially identify techniques for providing shelter to those in need around the globe."[36] MIR's vision for the Lower Ninth Ward is animated by a nostalgia for the neighborhood that is fueled by three contingent factors: (1) the actual, dramatic loss of lives, livelihoods, institutions, and dense social networks in the 2005 Katrina disaster; (2) the prevalence of communitarian mythology within progressive architectural circles; and, finally, (3) the local tourist industry's incessant effort to capitalize on nostalgia as a means of branding the city and securing its niche as an exotic, almost foreign destination for American vacationers.

In elaborating the design philosophy of MIR, GRAFT architects assert that "Cultural considerations for rebuilding this community are every bit as crucial as finding proper resolution for the functional, safety and sustainability needs. As a culture rich in history, music as well as community interaction, the uniqueness of the Lower Ninth Ward can be reinvigorated, cherished, understood, and physically expressed as such."[37] This valorization of culture is yet another example of how progressive arguments for post-Katrina reconstruction have melded with the overarching tourist industry logic where cultural authenticity forms a crucial linchpin connecting the notions of place identity cherished by residents and the place branding of the city to attract visitors.[38] The centrality of tourism in post-Katrina narratives of recovery and reconstruction has alloyed the specific material interests of corporate elites in revitalizing tourism with those right-of-return advocates who argue that the city's renowned musical and culinary folkways will not survive without its black residents. The comments by GRAFT's architects regarding diversity reflects this seamless merging of agendas when they assert: "We must acknowledge the immense value of retaining cultural capital and preserving the world's ethnosphere as well as the biosphere."[39] The nostalgia for urban authenticity that drove the New Orleans tourist industry before Katrina has been compounded by the destruction and displacement experienced by Lower Ninth Ward residents.

GRAFT and other supporters of MIR share a similar fixation on recovering community through conscientious design that has been made popular by New Urbanists over the past two decades. Despite GRAFT's commitment to a more holistic understanding of neighborhood development, their approach fetishizes design and imbues the work of design professionals with an exaggerated power. They contend: "The psychological resonance the building has with its occupant, the sense of well-being it provides, and the ability to create a platform from which residents can meaningfully and creatively interact with the world around themselves is fundamentally the heart of design."[40] This passage overstates the causal relationship between good design practice and social well-being. Design certainly matters, but the composition and impact of the built environment are intimately mitigated by other economic, social, and political variables. One need only to walk through the traditional streetscapes of Detroit's eastside or Rochester's "Fatal Crescent" to realize that design alone cannot ensure vibrant urban life. Well-designed neighborhoods with tree-lined sidewalks, coherent zoning, and pleasant elements like front porches and pocket parks can play host to social misery and alienation just as easily as the much-maligned tower block. The health and vitality of neighborhoods and communities are determined more by the economic security of its inhabitants than by the built environment per se. New Urbanists' subsequent appropriation and degradation of Jane Jacobs's classic writings have spawned an architectural movement predicated on communitarian mythology.

In her writings and grassroots activism, Jacobs contested the elephantine urban renewal projects undertaken by Robert Moses that promised to decimate the dense, lively urban fabrics of Manhattan. Her most influential book, *The Death and Life of Great American Cities,* offered an enduring critique of the destructive power of high modernist urbanism and its neglect of human scale and social contexts. Her Cold War liberal economic perspective and emphasis on microsocial aspects of urban life have also enabled her work to maintain traction within academe and planning circles as more radical left perspectives of political-economy and urban development have fallen from grace.[41] Jacobs's affection for her Greenwich Village street and the peculiar development challenges facing Manhattan neighborhoods at mid century have unfortunately been taken up too often by her self-styled heirs as a normative model of local neighborhood planning and urban life. This is unfortunate because Jacobs is less concerned with the kind of repressive notions of community so common to contemporary American public debate. Rather, she is more adamant about encouraging the kind of diversity, complexity, and spontaneity that make large cities interesting and socially valuable places. When extracted uncritically from the temporal and spatial context that animated Jacobs's concerns, this interpretive focus on the quality of everyday life in the neighborhood and concomitant cynicism about large-scale state planning is uniquely suited to neoliberal times because it neglects how the character and quality of local and personal life is molded by broader dynamics of political-economy.[42]

In analyzing this romance of community that defines so much New Urbanist work, Peter Marcuse argues that "it purports to hearken back to a form of 'community' that in fact very rarely existed in the past. . . . It is false historically . . . it is the image of community, more than community that is recaptured."[43] Nostalgic notions of community have hampered creative thinking about how New Orleans might be rebuilt along more inclusive, egalitarian lines. Rather than fixed, static entities, neighborhoods and communities should be understood as dynamic, fluid social forms. Neighborhoods and communities are constantly transformed by the natural rhythms of birth and death; immigration and exodus; the marking of the life process via social and religious rites of passage; the "creative destruction" of capitalist development that converts drugstores into bingo halls, "mom and pop" grocers into convenience stores, and dormant factories into luxury condos; and also the various forms of self-activity and social struggles undertaken by city residents that challenge entrenched power and inherited traditions to carve out new modes of urban living.

MIR succumbs to the temptations of nostalgia and substitutes the aesthetic vestiges of community life for a broader approach to urban planning that might yield *socially* sustainable, vibrant neighborhoods. The MIR approach to rebuilding is characterized by an almost excessive fascination with "stoop sitting" and front porch sociality. If the MIR Project continues to repopulate parts of the Ninth Ward to its previous density, these design choices may enable vibrant community to arise once again along Lizardi, Deslonde, and Tennessee Streets. The front porch, however, does not foster lively streets by itself, but rather the forms of social interaction coveted by MIR architects are typically supported by other social structures and institutions. Without nearby newsstands, schools, bars, butchershops, salons, workshops, bookstores, clothing boutiques, social clubs, offices, mosques, churches, and other social institutions that might

encourage pedestrianism and spontaneous moments of contact and in-
terchange, the MIR porches lose their social utility. As Jacobs and others such as Samuel R. Delany have argued, these moments of cross-class
contact create and sustain a vibrant urbanism and also yield rich modes of
citizen engagement so vital to democratic public life. By and large, these
design features reappear in the post-Katrina landscape cut free of the living context that produced and sustained them over decades. Whereas
the decaying camelbacks and Creole townhouses of pre-Katrina New
Orleans carried an air of authenticity as well as gritty functionality, the
emerging neo–New Orleans cityscape is a mix of novelty and mimicry
that lacks the dense network of social relations and diversity that produced the city's unique urbanity.

The "Jack O'Lantern" effect dreaded by supporters of the ULI footprint recommendation has come to pass with many city streetscapes
defined by a rough patchwork of vacant lots, abandoned homes, pioneer
homesteads, slow renovations, and new construction. Although few
could dispute the immediate benefits of the MIR homes to their owners, the pace of MIR construction has been slow. As the city and the
nation marked the fifth anniversary of the Katrina disaster, MIR neared
the completion of only 40 of the 150 homes that have been pledged.[44]
The Lower Ninth Ward has one of the lowest rates of resettlement in the
city, and as of August 2010, the area was still without a green grocer, high
school, or post office. Inasmuch as it neglects sensible strategies like
urban infill and cross-use zoning, the MIR project promises to create a
sparsely populated neighborhood cut off physically from the resources
and services of the city.

Apartment buildings and townhouses that might provide affordable
housing to diverse social classes are largely absent from the rebuilding
projects that have been initiated by MIR and other charitable organizations in the city. Although a second round of MIR homes included du-
plexes and granny flats, most of the homes that have been constructed
adhere to the single-family, detached-home format. This housing form
achieved centrality within post–World War II America through massive
public investment via Federal Housing Administration lending, federal
interstate highway construction, and state and local outlays on public safety, maintenance, and infrastructure improvements (i.e., water treatment
and delivery systems, sewerage, snow removal, curb installation, traffic
signage, bridges, and railway crossings).[45] With little apparent concern for

Figure 7.6. The "Jack O'Lantern" effect near GRAFT's nouveau shotgun house (Tennessee Street side) in March 2009. Overgrown vacant lots, empty slabs, rehabbed homesteads, and new construction form an uneven patchwork instead of a dense, vibrant urban community. Photograph by the author.

the discrete historical and political motives that secured its hegemony, the GRAFT architects celebrate this Cold War model of middle-class suburban homeownership as a central component of the MIR strategy: "Landownership is a fundamental core belief that forms part of the American dream; it is the belief in this dream, the belief in their family and extended family of community that fuels what could best be described as a grassroots movement, MIR."[46] The rebuilding schemes undertaken MIR and other organizations, like URBANBuild, Catholic Charities, and Phoenix of New Orleans, are united in their neglect of renters.

MIR has been a trailblazer in eco-conscious design, but the decision to resettle a sparsely populated section of the city may ultimately foster inefficient use of the city's power grid and municipal resources. A more sustainable strategy for rebuilding might have encouraged more vertical development and urban infill. Parts of the Upper Ninth Ward and the Lower Ninth Ward's Holy Cross neighborhood, which sustained less damage and retained more population, were more viable starting points for dense urban reconstruction.

Instead of the high-tech homesteads we see rising slowly on the deserted lots of the Lower Ninth Ward, MIR might have supported mid-rise apartment buildings that combined mixed-income units and first floor retail and services. Although apartment buildings are conspicuously absent from the Lower Ninth Ward rebuild, Pitt recently announced a partnership with Newark Mayor Corey Booker to construct an MIR apartment building for lower-income residents. Oddly enough, some of the architects tapped by MIR to construct individual family homes in New Orleans have designed noteworthy multioccupant dwellings and public spaces elsewhere. William McDonough's Greenbridge apartment complex in Chapel Hill, North Carolina, and David Adjaye's Whitechapel Idea Store in London are two projects that embody design principles that could create a more inclusive, vibrant, and sustainable post-Katrina New Orleans.

McDonough's Greenbridge complex contains over 25,000 square feet of retail space and 100 condominium units. Like the MIR homes, Greenbridge incorporates various eco-sustainable features including a rooftop garden, solar thermal and solar voltaic collectors, low-flow toilets, waterless urinals, Energy Star appliances, and extensive use of renewable materials throughout the building. The ten-story dwelling received gold certification from the Leadership in Energy and Environmental Design (LEED) standard. The inclusion of comparably scaled, mixed-income and mixed-use developments in post-Katrina New Orleans might have facilitated a more rapid repopulation of the city and a pattern of residential rebuilding especially suited to the needs of students, seniors, modest-income workers, disabled residents, empty nesters, and others who are either financially or physically unable to pursue home ownership as an option. Instead of the nonprofit vehicle and private financing that excludes the needs of renters from the reconstruction of neighborhoods, MIR might have pursued cooperative ownership of apartment buildings as a way of fostering greater economic independence for residents and engendering a sense of rootedness and commitment to emerging post-Katrina neighborhoods. Vertical, multioccupancy dwellings built closer to the natural levee might have reduced future flood risks as well. More important, this rebuilding strategy might have allowed for greater diversity and vibrant social life that could never replace that of the old New Orleans but might surpass it in innovation, creativity, and overall quality of life.

The careful integration of commercial, residential, and public space embodied in Adjaye's Whitechapel Idea Store offers an instructive example of what good urbanism looks like. Built in Tower Hamlets, one of London's poorest neighborhoods, the Idea Store is a latter-day reinvention of the public library that interacts with the Third World aesthetics and cultural sensibilities of the neighborhood's large ethnic immigrant populations. The Idea Store is a hub of activity where residents go to borrow books, access internet resources, and also take courses in literacy, job-interview skills, Pilates, and Capoeira. The building's blue and green glass panels reflect the surrounding street vendors' stalls and facilitate a seamless blending of traditionally scaled commercial activity and the free circulation of ideas associated with the Information Age. With the exception of a small, green playground, the commissioning of public spaces has not figured prominently in MIR's plans for the Lower Ninth Ward. This is an oversight that threatens the longer-term social stability and desirability of the neighborhood. Instead of a sprawling patchwork of homes amidst ruins and vacant lots that defines the Lower Ninth Ward, Pitt, MIR, and other well-intentioned supporters of New Orleans might have aspired to create a denser streetscape of apartment buildings, viable public spaces, shops, workplaces, and more traditional homes that would have placed residents in walkable proximity to services. Such a vision, however, would have required a more egalitarian distribution of resources and a deeper commitment to public planning, which are both endangered qualities in post-Katrina New Orleans.

Conclusion

To his credit, Pitt made a commitment to a community that had been neglected and marginalized long before the 2005 disaster. Moreover, unlike many of his celebrity peers, he chose to address questions of inequality on American soil, a task that carries certain risks and challenges that international philanthropy do not. As well, Pitt used his fame and publicity to lambast authorities for their lack of leadership during and after the disaster. After noting the extent of official irresponsibility and alluding to the uneven spatial development of the city, however, Pitt stopped short of making a clarion call for public action, pivoting instead toward the do-good posture that characterizes most "activism" among U.S. celebrities. Melding personal hobby and public relations strategy, such celebrity causes encompass everything from adopting children from developing nations, to drilling freshwater wells in the Sudan, and sponsoring summer camp programs for "at-risk" youth. Rarely do these pet projects and tax write-offs target the fundamental political-economic motors of our contemporary social and ecological crises. The MIR project grafted left progressive impulses concerning racial justice to an otherwise market-oriented rebuilding approach that eschewed public planning. In the end, MIR substituted technology for political struggle and the aesthetics of community for the development of a fine-grained, socially sustainable urbanism.

The public debate over the footprint recommendations left the impression that there were only two alternatives to rebuilding the city. The ULI's position (and that embraced by Nagin until it became a political liability) would have shrunk the city and restricted rebuilding to the natural levee and more elevated adjacent areas. Low-lying neighborhoods would have been turned into parkland and incorporated into a broader flood-management system. The second alternative that materialized in the town hall debates over the ULI survey was to allow rebuilding throughout the city out of respect for the communities that had thrived in these areas for decades. Liberal and progressive left activists rallied around this approach as an antidote to what they perceived as a land grab by developers and an aggressive attempt to rid the city of its black poor and working class neighborhoods. At times, the contours of this debate precluded other options. A third and much more difficult alternative might have combined the ethical assertion of the "right of return" with sensible planning strategies that could address flood hazards and create vibrant neighborhood life.

Democratic, inclusive rebuilding and sensible planning are not necessarily incompatible. These two goals—the repopulation of the city by all residents who desire to return and the reconstruction of the city in ways that will secure its longevity have been counterposed within an elite-driven, racially charged plan for remaking the city. The struggles over public housing in the city of New Orleans and more broadly the struggle to secure the material basis for the resettlement of the city's working class represented a more progressive alternative to both MIR's emphasis on assisting property owners and the overarching antiplanning environment that resulted from the footprint debates. Left organizations, despite valiant efforts, have been unable to advance a progressive blueprint for rebuilding the city. The weaknesses of progressive left forces in New Orleans are those of the left in the United States more generally. Although an exhaustive discussion of these challenges would constitute subject matter for another dedicated thesis, the frailty of left progressive forces on the ground in post-Katrina New Orleans stemmed from the decimation of traditional bases of support and mobilization in the aftermath of disaster—namely, the wholesale exodus of entire blue collar neighborhoods, massive layoffs of the city's public employees and unionized teachers, and the corresponding over-reliance on publicity and carpetbagger volunteerism to fill the chasm left in the wake of these dramatic changes. With the exception of radical left activists who contested the demolition of public housing, much of post-Katrina activism, including that of the much touted Common Ground Relief, has converged with that of more mainstream NGOs and focused on job training, individual home construction, etc., rather than on mounting a forceful challenge to the central rebuilding designs hatched by the Crescent City's business elite.

Notes

I would like to thank John Arena and Adolph Reed Jr. for offering generous written feedback on an early draft. Their correctives spared me unnecessary embarrassment and provided just the right dosage of critical energy and support I needed to complete this chapter. As well, sincerest thanks to Roderick M. Sias, Sekile Nzinga-Johnson, and Marcus Watts for offering helpful feedback and insights on this chapter's core arguments.

1. Rachel Pulfer, "Making It (Kinda) Right in New Orleans," *Azure,* September 2009, 92–98; Elizabeth Pagliacolo, "Sometimes, It Takes an Actor to Raise a Village," *Azure,* December 2007, http://www.azuremagazine.com/newsviews/blog_content. php?id=732 (accessed February 22, 2008); Andrew Blum, "Saint Brad," *Metropolis,* March 2008, http://metropolismag.com/story/20080319/saint-brad (accessed July 22, 2010); Robin Pogrebin, "Brad Pitt Commissions Designs for New Orleans," *New York Times,* December 3, 2007, http://www.bradpittpress.com/artint_07_nytimes.php (accessed July 20, 2010); and Gerald Clarke, "Brad Pitt Makes It Right in New Orleans," *Architectural Digest* (January 2009): 60–69, 150.

2. Lizabeth Cohen, *A Consumer's Republic: The Politics of Mass Consumption in Post War America* (New York: Vintage Books, 2003); Marco D'Eramo, *The Pig and the Skyscraper: Chicago, A History of Our Future* (New York: Verso, 2002); Sudhir Alladi Venkatesh, *American Project: The Rise and Fall of a Modern Ghetto* (Cambridge, Mass.: Harvard University Press, 2000); Larry Bennett, "Transforming Public Housing" in *The New Chicago: A Social and Cultural Analysis,* ed.

John P. Koval, Larry Bennett, Michael I. J. Bennett, Fassil Demissie, Roberta Gardner and Kiljoong Kim, 269–76 (Philadelphia: Temple University Press, 2006); Henry G. Cisneros and Lora Engdahl, eds., *From Despair to Hope: HOPE VI and the New Promise of Public Housing in America's Cities* (Washington, D.C.: The Brookings Institution, 2009); and Larry Bennett and Adolph Reed Jr., "The New Face of Urban Renewal: The Near North Redevelopment Initiative and the Cabrini-Green Neighborhood," in *Without Justice for All: The New Liberalism and Our Retreat from Racial Equality,* ed. Adolph Reed Jr., 175–214 (Boulder, Colo.: Westview, 1999).

3. Christopher Cooper, "Old-Line Families Plot the Future," *Wall Street Journal,* September 8, 2005, A1.

4. Matthias Gebauer, "Will the Big Easy Become White, Rich, and Republican?" *Der Spiegel,* September 20, 2005, http://www.spiegel.de/international/a-375496. html (accessed October, 15, 2005).

5. Cooper, "Old-Line Families."

6. New Vision Institute, "Moving to Opportunity in the Wake of Hurricane Katrina," September 15, 2005, http://www.newvisioninstitute.org/Moving OppotunityScholarsPetition.pdf (accessed January 8, 2008); David Brooks, "Katrina's Silver Lining," *New York Times,* September 5, 2005, http://www. nytimes.com/2005/09/08/opinion/08brooks.html (accessed September 12, 2005); Jonathan Cohn, "The Golden Ticket: A Ninth Ward Family's Way Out," *The New Republic,* August 14 and 21, 2006, 13–17; Xavier de Souza Briggs, Susan J. Popkin, and John Goering, *Moving to Opportunity: The Story of an American Experiment to Fight Ghetto Poverty* (Oxford and New York: Oxford University Press, 2010); David Imbroscio, "'United and Actuated by Some Common Impulse of Passion': Challenging the Dispersal Consensus in American Policy Research," *Journal of Urban Affairs* 30, no. 2 (2008): 111–30; Stephen Steinberg, "The Myth of Concentrated Poverty," in *The Integration Debate: Competing Futures for American Cities,* ed. Chester Hartman and Gregory D. Squires, 213–27 (New York: Routledge, 2010); and Adolph Reed and Stephen Steinberg, "Liberal Bad Faith in the Wake of Hurricane Katrina," *Black Commentator,* May 4, 2006, http://www.blackcommentator.com/182/182_cover_liberals_katrina_pf.html (accessed June 20, 2006).

7. See Amnesty International, "The Right to Return: Rebuilding the Gulf through the Framework of International Human Rights" (Washington, D.C.: Amnesty International, n.d.), http://www.amnestyusa.org/us/AIUSA_Rebuilding_ the_Gulf_fact_sheet.pdf (accessed July 22, 2010); Amnesty International, *UN-Natural Disaster: Human Rights in the Gulf Coast* (Washington, D.C.: Amnesty International, 2010), http://www.amnestyusa.org/dignity/pdf/Un-Natural_ Disaster_report.pdf (accessed July 20, 2010).

8. Quigley, "The Right of Return"; see also Bill Quigley, "Bulldozers for the Poor, Huge Tax Credits for Wealthy Developers," *Counterpunch,* December 3, 2007, http://www.counterpunch.org/quigley12032007.html (accessed July 28, 2010); Mike Davis, "The Predators of New Orleans," *Le Monde Diplomatique,* October 2005, http://mondediplo.com/2005/10/02katrina (accessed January 6, 2007); and Michelle Chen, "New Orleans: Vanishing City," *Women's International Perspective,* February 7, 2008, http://www.thewip.net/contributors2008/02/vanishing_city_postkatrina_red.html (accessed February 8, 2008).

9. David Harvey, "The Right to the City," *New Left Review* 53 (September-October 2008): 23; see also Peter Marcuse, "From Critical Urban Theory to the Right to the City," *City* 13 (June-September 2009): 185–97; Henri Lefebvre, "The Right to the City," in *Writings on Cities,* ed. Eleonore Kofman and Elizabeth Lebas, 147–59 (Oxford, UK: Blackwell Publishers, 1996); and Don Mitchell, *The Right to the City: Social Justice and the Fight for Public Space* (New York: Guilford, 2003).

10. For more on slum clearance and the origins of the Urban Land Institute, see Kevin Fox Gotham, "A City without Slums: Urban Renewal, Public Housing, and Downtown Revitalization in Kansas City, Missouri," *American Journal of Economics and Sociology* 60, no. 1 (January 2001): 285–316; and Marc A. Weiss, "The Origins and Legacy of Urban Renewal," in *Urban and Regional Planning in an Age of Austerity,* ed. Pierre Clavel, John Forester, and William W. Goldsmith, 53–79, (New York: Pergamon, 1980).

11. Mike Davis, "Who Is Killing New Orleans?" *Nation,* April 10, 2006, 11–20; Jed Horne, *Breach of Faith: Hurricane Katrina and the Near Death of a Great American City* (New York: Random House, 2006), 315–26.

12. Quoted in Davis, "Who Is Killing New Orleans?" 14; and Gary Rivlin, "A Mogul Who Would Rebuild New Orleans," *New York Times,* September 29, 2005, http://www.nytimes.com/2005/09/29/business/29mogul.html?pagewanted=print (accessed May 22, 2007).

13. Urban Land Institute, *New Orleans, Louisiana: A Strategy for Rebuilding* (Washington, D.C.: Urban Land Institute, 2006), 11.

14. Urban Land Institute, *New Orleans,* 47.

15. Phillip Oswalt for Kultursiftung des Bundes, ed. *Shrinking Cities, Volume 2: Interventions* (Ostfildern, Germany: Hatje Cantz Publishers, 2006).

16. Urban Land Institute, *New Orleans,* 14.

17. Ibid., 44.

18. Ibid., 45.

19. Ibid., 46.

20. Horne, *Breach of Faith,* 282.

21. d'Eramo, *The Pig and the Skyscraper*; Carl Smith, *Urban Disorder and the Shape of Belief: The Great Chicago Fire, the Haymarket Bomb, and the Model Town of*

Pullman (Chicago: University of Chicago Press, 1995); William Cronon, *Nature's Metropolis: Chicago and the Great West* (New York: W.W. Norton, 1991).

22. Quoted in Horne, *Breach of Faith*, 326.

23. Gary Rivlin, "In Rebuilding as in Disaster, Wealth and Class Help Define New Orleans," *New York Times*, April 25, 2006, http://query.nytimes.com/gst/fullpage.html?res59E0DE4DB123FF936A15757C0A9609C8B63 (accessed May 22, 2007).

24. Andrés Duany, "Restoring the Real New Orleans," *Metropolis*, February 14, 2007, http://www.metropolismag.com/story/20070214/restoring-the-real-new-orleans (accessed May 22, 2007).

25. For a more detailed discussion of the Lower Ninth Ward's geography and history of settlement, see Richard Campanella, *Geographies of New Orleans: Urban Fabrics Before the Storm* (Lafayette, La.: Center for Louisiana Studies 2006); Richard Campanella, *Bienville's Dilemma: A Historical Geography of New Orleans* (Lafayette, La.: Center for Louisiana Studies, 2008); Juliette Landphair, "The Forgotten People of New Orleans," *Journal of American History* 94, no. 3 (2007): 837–45; and Craig Colten, *An Unnatural Metropolis: Wresting New Orleans from Nature* (Baton Rouge: Louisiana State University Press, 2006).

26. Landphair, "The Forgotten People," 837–9.

27. Ibid, 837–9.

28. Morial offered these comments on Spike Lee's 2006 documentary *When the Levees Broke*. Morial's willingness to flirt with conspiracy theory is especially curious given that he bears some responsibility for the broader disaster, like all other public officials who presided over the levee system's steady deterioration and the hypersegregation and impoverishment of the city's black precariat.

29. Wagner and Edwards, "New Orleans by the Numbers," 1.

30. Brad Pitt, "Foreword," in *Architecture in Times of Need: Make It Right Rebuilding New Orleans' Lower Ninth Ward*, ed. Kristin Feireiss, 7 (New York: Prestel, 2009).

31. Brad Pitt, "Idea, Concept, and Construction of Pink," in *Architecture in Times of Need: Make It Right Rebuilding New Orleans' Lower Ninth Ward*, ed. Kristin Feireiss, 372–85 (New York: Prestel, 2009).

32. William McDonough and Michael Braungart, *Cradle to Cradle: Remaking the Way We Make Things* (New York: North Point, 2002).

33. A much longer thesis might be dedicated to the visual staging of black life in the conceptual drawings of MIR houses and other projects in post-Katrina New Orleans. Such renderings are riddled with myths and prescriptions of African American life. Carrying their own commercial motives and conservative ideological freight, some of these renderings seem as if characters from one of Tyler Perry's gospel stage plays had been digitally cut and pasted into a Julius Shulman portfolio. From the child walking hand in hand with the caring patriarch, the well-placed Obama portrait, the ubiquitous barbecue, and the

spontaneous jazz performance on the front porch, these mock-ups draw on black middle class notions of respectability and right wing arguments about the primacy of heterosexual marriage and the nuclear family form and incur occasional debts to Hollywood and the local tourist industry. See *Architecture in Times of Need,* ed. Kristin Feireiss.

34. Doug MacCash, "Brad Pitt's Architect Thom Mayne Designs Floating House in New Orleans," *Times-Picayune,* October 7, 2009, http://www. nola. com/arts/index.ssf/2009/10/world_famous_architect_thom_ma.html (accessed November 9, 2009); and Wayne Curtis, "Houses of the Future," *The Atlantic,* November 2009, http://www.theatlantic.com/magazine/ archive/2009/11/houses-of-the-future/7708/ (accessed November 9, 2009).

35. Geoff Manaugh and Nicola Twilley, "On Flexible Urbanism," in *What Is A City? Rethinking the Urban after Katrina,* ed. Phil Steinberg and Rob Shields, 63–77 (Athens: The University of Georgia Press, 2008); Matt Bradley, "Dutch Design Lets Homes Float on the Floodwaters," *Christian Science Monitor,* October 26, 2005, http://www.csmonitor.com/2005/1026/p13s02-lihc.html (accessed March 2, 2009).

36. GRAFT, "Design in Times of Need," in *Architecture in Times of Need: Make It Right Rebuilding New Orleans' Lower Ninth Ward,* ed. Kristin Feireiss, 117 (New York: Prestel, 2009).

37. Ibid., 118.

38. See Kevin Fox Gotham, *Authentic New Orleans: Tourism, Culture and Race in the Big Easy* (New York: New York University Press, 2007).

39. Ibid., 118.

40. GRAFT, "Design in Times of Need," 118.

41. For a discussion of Jacobs's anti-communism, see Alex Sparberg Alexiou, *Jane Jacobs, Urban Visionary* (Piscataway, N.J.: Rutgers University Press, 2006), 31–34.

42. Jane Jacobs, *The Death and Life of Great American Cities* (New York: Random House, 1961); Anthony Flint, *Wrestling with Moses: How Jane Jacobs Took on New York's Master Builder and Transformed the American City* (New York: Random House, 2009); Roberta Brandes Gratz, *The Battle for Gotham: New York in the Shadow of Robert Moses and Jane Jacobs* (New York: Nation Books, 2010); see also Samuel R. Delany, *Times Square Red, Times Square Blue* (New York: New York University Press, 1999); James C. Scott, *Seeing Like a State: How Certain Schemes to Improve the Human Condition Have Failed* (New Haven, Conn.: Yale University Press, 1998), 132–46; and Richard Sennett, *The Uses of Social Disorder: Personal Identity and City Life* (New York: Alfred P. Knopf, 1970).

43. Peter Marcuse, "The New Urbanism: The Dangers So Far," *DISP* 140 (2000): 4–6; Peter Katz, ed., *The New Urbanism: Toward an Architecture of Community* (New York: McGraw-Hill, 1994); Andrés Duany, Elizabeth Plater-Zyberk, and Jeff Speck, *Suburban Nation: The Rise of Sprawl and the*

Decline of the American Dream (New York: North Point Press, 2000); see also David Harvey's concise, perceptive critique of the New Urbanism's communitarian mythology, David Harvey, "The New Urbanism and the Communitarian Trap," *Harvard Design Magazine*, no. 1 (Winter/Spring 1997): 1–3.

44. Emily Badger, "Getting It Right," *Good* (Summer 2010): 94–100.

45. Kenneth T. Jackson, *Crabgrass Frontier: The Surburbanization of the United States* (New York: Oxford University Press, 1985); Robert Fishman, *Bourgeois Utopias: The Rise and Fall of Suburbia* (New York: Basic Books, 1987); James Howard Kuntsler, *Geography of Nowhere: The Rise and Decline of America's Man-Made Landscape* (New York: Touchstone, 1993); Andrés Duany et al., *Suburban Nation*; Douglas Rae, *City: Urbanism and Its End* (New Haven, Conn.: Yale University Press, 2003); Dolores Hayden, *Building Suburbia: Green Fields and Urban Growth, 1820-2000* (New York: Vintage, 2004); and Dolores Hayden, *Redesigning the American Dream: Gender, Housing, and Family Life* (New York: W.W. Norton, 2002).

46. GRAFT, "Design in Times of Need," 119.

CHAPTER 8

Laboratorization and the "Green" Rebuilding of New Orleans's Lower Ninth Ward

Barbara L. Allen

I N THE DAYS AND MONTHS following the flooding from Hurricane Katrina in New Orleans in August 2005, no neighborhood received more coverage than the destruction of the Lower Ninth Ward. After the storm, the floodwall separating the neighborhood from a navigable industrial canal ruptured, releasing a torrent of water, literally washing away an entire section of the city, and taking many lives in its wake. Whereas houses closest to the floodwalls were literally erased, uprooted from their foundation, and carried away, other parts of the Lower Ninth Ward (L9) were left damaged but intact to varying degrees. Dramatic press coverage, YouTube videos, and blogs were only the beginning of the public engagement storm that was to follow Katrina and be centered, in part, in the L9. In the wake of the very visible government failure, at all levels, to help citizens in the days and months (and years) following the disaster, a phenomenal number of nongovernmental organizations, Katrina-oriented philanthropy groups, and civic and church volunteers filled the assistance void left by the government and for-profit sector.

Almost overnight, New Orleans became a full-scale neoliberal experiment in recovery and rebuilding. Everything from debris removal contractors and temporary housing to public education and the health service was part of this agenda, shifting via government contract what were formerly public provisions to private enterprises.[1] The void left in the formerly public services sphere combined with the dramatic needs of the residents formed a perfect storm allowing these grand neoliberal experiments to occur, largely, but not entirely, without protest from the distressed public. Not that other urban areas have not been touched by funding and policy changes effectively shifting formerly public goods and services to the private arena, but what made New Orleans unique in this regard was the scale, speed, and ease of the transformation. My research examines a significant technological transformation in one flood-damaged neighborhood. This transformation was in large part due to the neoliberal trends, made evident in built form, in the city after Katrina.

To examine this green transformation phenomenon, I use strategies from the interdisciplinary field of "science and technology in society," sometimes called "science and technology studies" (STS), as it provides some useful tools for understanding social, technological, and infrastructural changes. For my analysis in this chapter, I use several STS analytical frameworks; the primary one is a version of "laboratory studies" as developed by French STS theorist Bruno Latour. His version of laboratory studies is an applied methodological approach to track emerging technoscience innovation and transfer on-the-ground. It is demonstrative of the application of another broader theoretical and methodological approach that was developed in part by Latour—actor-network theory (ANT), as expanded on later in this chapter.[2]

A Neighborhood in Danger of Erasure

The Lower Ninth Ward (L9), magnified by the media, epitomized both the immense destruction of the storm and the racial inequalities embedded therein. While many help groups flooded into all parts of the city, there seemed a particularly intense focus on the L9. The density of outside groups and volunteers was easily visible to the naked eye: groups of college students in matching t-shirts busy at work in abandoned homes, church groups in marked buses lining the streets, and young, predominantly white volunteers typically outnumbering locals in neighborhood meetings. The initial focus of outside groups in the city was primarily gutting and cleaning homes and providing temporary assistance. The second wave of volunteers would be involved with permanent rebuilding, and those groups required a different focus. Since the obvious tasks, such as gutting and cleaning, were done, the new set of tasks in rebuilding required making some assumptions about what was to be rebuilt and the best way to go about doing it.

It is probably no surprise that the first city-wide rebuilding plan completed for then-Mayor Ray Nagin's "Bring New Orleans Back Commission" was done by the Urban Land Institute (ULI). The ULI's website describes it as a nonprofit organization "connecting the global real estate community" and "representing the entire spectrum of land use and real estate development disciplines, working in private enterprise and public service."[3] The notorious plan, dubbed "the green dot plan" by residents, was driven by a "flood-risk-damage rationale." Neighborhoods with minimal to moderate damage should be repaired immediately with services and infrastructure restored. The more heavily flooded neighborhoods would be turned into urban green spaces or otherwise redeveloped as part of an integrated environmental floodwater control system. The final map, released in January 2006, showed six green dots, almost entirely in majority African American neighborhoods and including the L9.[4] But the opportunistic environment enabled by the neoliberal approach to rebuilding not only attracted business-allied nongovernmental organizations but also created openings for other community, faith, and environmental groups as well. The "green dot plan," an anathema to many New Orleanians, across race and class lines, was hugely successful in bringing communities together even as most of their residents were living elsewhere. Suddenly, these neighborhoods were desperately looking for any help they could get, in rebuilding while at the same time fighting for their survival.

When most people think of the L9, they think of the neighborhood that was demolished with the collapse of the levee walls, followed by images of people on rooftops waving flags for help. This area immediately captured the public imagination and widespread indignation with broadcast images ensuring national and international attention. One the L9's most star-studded rebuilding efforts is Brad Pitt's "Make It Right" Foundation, which mobilized about two years after the storm, bringing together top architects from around the world to build 150 leading-edge sustainable houses to replace those that were demolished.[5] Pitt's project has been pivotal in saving and rebuilding the L9 of the media—that part of the L9 that was totally destroyed and flooded for many weeks. But this part of the Lower Ninth Ward is not the focus of my research. My interest is in a one-square-mile subdistrict of the L9 that fronts the Mississippi River on the higher ground of the natural levee—one historic neighborhood called Holy Cross (HC).

The HC neighborhood is adjacent to the devastated "green dot" section of the L9. It dates back to the early nineteenth century when it was a collection of sugar plantations. By the close of the Civil War, it had become a residential and light farming community of poor African Americans and newly arrived European immigrants. Many of the houses in HC were constructed using traditional Louisiana wood frame building styles in the late nineteenth and early twentieth centuries. In 1986, the neighborhood was made a National Register Historic District, the same year its neighborhood association was founded. By the time of the storm, the demographics of HC was 87 percent African American. As of the 2010 U.S. census, 41 percent of the houses in HC were still vacant compared to only 15 percent before the storm.[6]

HC is not below sea level. When the canal walls broke, the reason that this neighborhood was flooded was due to the massive hydrostatic pressure of the water rushing in, pushing a wall of water up onto the high ground, as it had no other place to go. The water took less than a week to drain from these houses as it receded to areas that were at or below sea level in other parts of the L9. Unfortunately, because the main bridge into this cutoff part of the city was also the main bridge into the devastated part of the L9, all residents were not allowed entry into their flooded houses

Figure 8.1. A typical street with housing in the Holy Cross neighborhood, mostly from the late nineteenth and early twentieth centuries. Photograph by the author.

until many months after the storm. Additionally, it was one of the last areas to have utilities and other services restored, leading many residents to believe that they were being implicitly told not to rebuild. That meant that carpets and wet materials sat in the houses and molded and otherwise ruined parts of the structure that could have been saved from extensive damage had residents been allowed in immediately after the water receded. So although the housing stock was older, more durable, and more resistant to water damage than their neighbors across the highway, the fact that they were not allowed entry to clean up until several months later meant that their damage fate was more extensive than it would have been otherwise.[7] Because of the type of housing that it was, while some interior walls had to be gutted, from the outside the houses looked as if there was little damage. In fact, in many cases the basic structure and roof of the house were undamaged. To former residents, their homes looked repairable, quite different from the dystopia across the highway in the other part of L9.

In the year following the storm, it was "green" nongovernmental organizations that focused their efforts on HC/L9, and it is now an evolving showplace for sustainable building products and practices. Given that the government's Road Home Program did not offer rebuilding help in a timely manner and initially considered most of the houses in this area of the city to be more than 50 percent destroyed, thus not eligible for rebuilding funds, these groups, their volunteers, material donations, and funding formed one of the main resource streams into the community.[8] Thus, the "green groups" were welcomed by many neighborhood residents, although it must be noted that their choices were few. Indeed, according to its website, HC hopes to become the nation's first sustainable, carbon-neutral urban neighborhood. So how did a poor minority neighborhood, following disaster, emerge at the cutting edge of the neighborhood sustainability and green building movement?

The Laboratory Studies Lens

To understand the dynamics of this exceptional post-Katrina transition from devastated neighborhood to a beacon of sustainability and green architecture, I am using some of the tools of STS, a field that examines the social and cultural dimensions of the construction of knowledge, artifacts, and practices. Laboratory studies, one of the theoretical and methodological tools of STS, has a set of interesting analytical approaches that are useful in understanding the dynamics of change and green technology transfer in the rebuilding of New Orleans.

The early laboratory studies of the 1970s and 1980s was an attempt to unpack the "constructed-ness" of facts from within their place of origin, namely, the scientific laboratory. [9] Using microsocial methodologies, such as ethnography and other observational methods, these scholars revealed the influence of local conditions and contingencies in the knowledge production process, disrupting the normative narrative of scientific and technical knowledge as being universal. These early laboratory studies scholars reinforced feminist claims, such as those of Donna Haraway, that there is no God's-eye view of knowledge from nowhere but that all knowledge is firmly situated in its context of making—in this case, the laboratory.[10] However, it is important to note that the primary contribution of these early studies was to uncover the construction of facts by focusing on what scientists actually do in laboratory settings.

Other scholars such as Bruno Latour and Steve Woolgar furthered laboratory studies, showing how the social world influenced the construction of varying degrees of factualness from speculations to taken-for-granted knowledge.[11] In their parsing of the term "fact," they continued to open the "black box" of knowledge-making in a more accessible manner. By the 1990s there was less interest in observational laboratory studies, but other types of lab studies and new interests of lab studies scholars added a rich dimension and diversity to this early endeavor. Latour, following his early ethnographic work, devised a new theoretical and methodological approach to studying the construction of facts and artifacts, that of ANT.

In essence, Latour and others had advanced their discoveries in microsocial laboratory studies toward a totalizing theory of "the social," that of knowledge-in-action or translations from one actor to another. They specifically eschew previous social theory approaches that look at ready-made analytical categories such as race, class, and gender as well as other economic and social structures. Instead, they are concerned with how new knowledge and practices emerge on-the-ground through alliances and synergies of interactions. It is no surprise that ANT and laboratorization methods and theories have been popular with business, marketing, and technology transfer scholars as they provide an explanation for how to "sell" new technologies to the public.[12] Latour describes the political program that his project engenders as giving one the ability to see the emergence of new politics as opposed to framing these emergences in the social scientists' own prepackaged structures.[13]

In his famous "Give Me a Laboratory and I Will Raise the World" article on the work of Louis Pasteur in the development and diffusion of the anthrax vaccine to the farmers, citizens, and government, Latour proposes a specific approach to laboratory studies "focusing not on the laboratory itself but on the construction of the laboratory and its position in the societal milieu."[14] In essence, the process of laboratorization destabilizes the local and the global, the micro and the macro, in fact challenging the notion that any real difference in actors or scale actually exists. In the same way that interests cannot be imputed to people or groups, according to Latour, social explanations cannot be overlaid onto knowledge-making in action as interests come via translations—the scientists or technologists (i.e., actors) translate what people want or make people want what they have to offer.[15]

In Latour's first phase of analysis, Pasteur transfers himself to the farm, a place untouched by the type of science he hopes to introduce (problem-itization)—social and physical worlds that would not come in to contact with each other in normal circumstances. To capture the interests of the farmers (interessment), Pasteur moves the lab to the farm, despite the lack of initial interest on the part of the farmers. Then the scientists commence to translate issues of concern for the farmers, learning from the local condition, to their own interests and laboratory language but having yet to interest the farmers. To enlist the farmers, a second phase is necessary (enrollment)—a move back to the lab with the "problem," emerging with a solution to the farmers' problem only if they pass through the lab. This miniaturization of the larger problem within the lab makes it such that Pasteur can do what others have not been able to do in the larger world outside the lab. The micro world of the lab allows something thought impossible to be possible. The third phase ensures that the lab does not simply remain there—the field trial is necessary, moving the lab's knowledge back into the world. Then via the success of the trial, others in similar situations know that they can solve their problems with the same scientific or technological discovery ordered from that lab or a similar lab. Thus, in the translational steps or phases, the social arena is transformed—the lab is now a representative for the community and for the larger "world" (mobilization).

Why Holy Cross Became a Green Laboratory

One way to frame what happened next was that New Orleans's Lower Ninth Ward (L9) neighborhood became an unlikely and unplanned green rebuilding laboratory following the disaster. To better understand the dynamics of the change of HC from disaster zone to the forefront of green building I want to explore the situation by using the moves or phases in Latour's version of Pasteur's story, informed by his later explications of ANT as theory/method. I will make visible the relationships and synergies within the HC green network that enabled its emergence, growth, and strength.

In this case, the green promoters, not unlike Pasteur, find a place untouched by the type of technology they hope to introduce. Many activists and entrepreneurs advocating sustainable communities and building practices find themselves up against immoveable traditions and infrastructures—the obduracy of the built environment and the technologies therein. Exactly how a variety of green nongovernmental organizations and other allied groups and agencies found HC and the Lower Ninth Ward is only speculation. It could be they saw an opening to begin transformation, one in which they would not have to deal with changing old infrastructures but instead a clean slate to be built anew. It could be that as the eyes of the nation were turned toward the L9, many of these groups saw an opportunity to help those who were left struggling—or they saw a chance to "perform" sustainable rebuilding in the bright lights of sustained media interest. It could also be that green activist groups were particularly philanthropic and wanted to help the least fortunate, most damaged neighborhood in New Orleans. Imputing motive is difficult, so it is best to simply look at actions and results in a pragmatic fashion, per ANT analysis.

In applying Latour's analytical technique to HC/L9, it is important to note that there is no one special green group or person on which I want to focus. Instead, I will mostly bracket together the green groups and begin the analysis by looking for movements, enrollments, and translations and their affiliated transcriptions. Because this is a huge project, I will admit that many activities will not be captured in my snapshot. However, I will attempt a representative picture of green neighborhood building-in-action for the purposes of analysis.

One of the problems facing the introduction of new sustainable technologies is that they can appear to be redundant. Adding new solar heating to your house when you already have a working system or replacing old windows with insulated ones can seem like a luxury reserved for the wealthy, especially since personal economic payback (i.e., the reduction in your electric bill) can take many years to equal the initial cost. Anique Hommels has shown that cities are composed of obdurate technologies whose dismantling is difficult, if not impossible, due to numerous reasons. She explains the tenacity of urban technologies (other than cost) in three ways. They are immoveable because of (1) "ways of thinking and interacting," (2) "the interconnectedness of social and technical elements," and (3) "the long-term persistence of traditions."[16] The green building movement has definitely come up against technological obduracy, making green transformation a slow process of accretion and replacement. A convincing, focused laboratory or case study neighborhood that could be made fully sustainable— absent the obduracy problem—was a welcome site indeed.

Greening in Action: The Laboratorization of Holy Cross

Within six months to a year after the storm, once the initial cleanup of the houses was under way, it was apparent to many residents that help from the government was not forthcoming. Additionally, any funds, including insurance reimbursement, that might be able to help them required lengthy wait times and often had multiple strings attached. While middle-class residents were able to rebuild using their charge cards or savings accounts to pay construction costs up front, those of lesser means could only wait and hope.

While green building groups and strategies emerged and continue to operate throughout the city, they are most highly concentrated in the Lower Ninth Ward and, in particular, the historic HC neighborhood. Talking with people in the neighborhood, a narrative emerges explaining the presence of all of these outside groups, a concentration of outsiders unrivaled in other parts of the city. According to locals, after the floodwaters subsided and volunteers rushed in to help gut and clean the houses. There was a particular focus on the Lower Ninth Ward as that was an area featured in the media where so many lost their lives and their homes in the canal wall break. After the cleanup, much of the upper part of the L9 was leveled or almost beyond repair; however, down the road across St. Claude Avenue was the lower part of the

L9, HC, a neighborhood on high ground that sustained only moderate damage and to the naked eye, looked practically inhabitable. In reality, the homes, which were structurally sound, had had most of their plumbing, heating, electrical, windows, and other systems damaged. Many of the homes were well built, constructed before World War I using materials and designs that were climate and location appropriate. This could be an ideal location for a green neighborhood test case.

Green groups, such as nongovernmental organizations, composed of environmentally conscious citizens, scientists, engineers, and business people had rarely had such an opening into a full-scale laboratory experiment. Relegated to slow change at an individualized pace or the grueling process of changing of regulations and codes, they saw in HC/L9 a chance to showcase what a green community could look like—the fact that it was a poor and minority community was a bonus in that it removed the upper middle class / white stereotype of sustainable communities.

So how did the green groups construct "interests" or, more precisely, how were citizens convinced that greening was a possible solution to their problem? How were they able to move their laboratory into HC such that it became a full-scale test site in the field? First, the earliest groups, such as Global Green and Historic Green, learned the language of the residents and then translated this into a technical language of their own.[17] The language of environmental justice (EJ), the linking of social and environmental harms, was one of the primary rhetorics of the neighborhood and the media covering the neighborhood. Global Green, an organization supported by Brad Pitt, who later created a spin-off project in the L9 with the Make It Right Foundation, also built a demonstration green house, with plans for a large development in HC that included more homes and apartment buildings. In terms of the activities of residents, many spent months cleaning their homes with the help of volunteers only to find they had reached a dead end in the rebuilding process without resources.

Building resources were what the green groups promised: labor, materials, and money. They were able to translate their activities into something both needed and recognizable to HC/L9 citizens—join with the green program to sustainably rebuild their homes and craft an environmentally just future. By January 2007, a year and a half after the storm and six months after the first major green groups arrived, the local neighborhood association began a new project called the Center for

Figure 8.2. Global Green's demonstration house in Holy Cross. More sustainable houses and apartments are planned nearby. Photograph by the author.

Sustainable Engagement and Development (CSED), which was funded by numerous nongovernmental organizations and university consortia. The project was the perfect umbrella to incorporate the new green activity in HC and become the entity to apply for and receive further funding. According to their website,

> CSED's mission is to encourage restorative rebuilding, sustain natural systems, support community leadership, and stimulate civic engagement through an informed, protected, engaged, repopulated Lower Ninth Ward. Through these initiatives, they hope to create a cohesive, prosperous, sustainable community that is *climate-neutral* by 2020 and *carbon-neutral* by 2030.[18] [emphasis added]

Thus, the new CSED project incorporated environmental justice language as well as the very technical language of sustainability. The HC Neighborhood Association was now fully enrolled in the green rebuilding project, with green rhetoric embedded in the mission statement of its most financially important project.

HC/L9 was now the official lab for sustainable rebuilding in the city, and dozens of other green groups quickly followed along with their allied volunteers. In the mix now, for example, was the Alliance for Affordable Energy with solar panels and radiant barriers to improve energy efficiency and lower energy bills. In 2008, the Home Builders Association of Greater New Orleans created a green builder certification program and it offers classes on installing many of the new technologies.[19] Building suppliers, such as Home Depot, began marketing many of the new materials, and Global Green provided a hands-on sample center where homeowners could come to see and feel the new materials and technologies before ordering them.

Because of the historic status of HC, the many preservation groups began positioning themselves as the "original" green building practitioners—Why not recycle your home that was built with climate appropriate design and materials in the first place? They featured con- ferences such as Historic Green, showing the linking of sustainability concepts and practices with that of preservation, thus making HC at the cutting edge of this new synergy. They brought craftsmen to teach traditional ways of working with historic materials and structures. The State Historic Preservation Office (SHPO), with a large grant from the federal government, began a regranting program to help rebuild historic homes. Significant amounts of funding were immediately given to the homeowners who applied. With the help of outside groups in writing the grants, the residents of HC received a lion's share of that money. Soon they had lists of reputable contractors as well as how-to manuals written for both professionals and the general public. Rebuilding Together, a part of the Preservation Resource Center in the city, also had a huge contingent of volunteers, probably one of the largest continuing single flows of such volunteers in the city.[20]

From the website they describe themselves:

> Historic Green is about the possibilities. About knowing a place. Respecting its rich heritage for future generations. And seeing the promise of sustainability to create healthier, safer, more livable communities. Historic Green represents a blending of the past, the present and the future. What was, meets what could be. New Orleans' Holy Cross Neighborhood and the Lower Ninth Ward offer one path

to what we're calling "sustainable preservation." Nowhere else could it happen on such a scale as here: an entire community brought to its knees in the aftermath of Hurricanes Katrina and Rita.[21]

There were also many citywide as well as neighborhood green rebuilding planning brochures, documents, and websites that became icons in the various groups' alliances and legitimizing campaigns. There were nongovernmental organizations, such as the Idea Village, focused on green business in the neighborhood. There were symbiotic relationships between the various green groups, whereby some groups would do plumbing and electrical work and other would follow with volunteers to paint and perform finish carpentry and yet others might install solar panels. The neighborhood was awash in green and was looking like a success in the eyes of those on the ground. In the analytical frame of Latour, the green groups had turned the field into the laboratory: they had persuaded the residents of the HC that their interests were the green groups' own.

But what is to stop interests from fading and the momentum to green from slowing, especially if the project remains isolated in the HC (and L9) neighborhood? Here Latour's third and final move is needed. The translation of HC must be staged to resonate on the macro scale. Thus, the media was enlisted by the green groups and played their part.

According to the Holy Cross Neighborhood Association website:

Thanks to Brad Pitt, Global Green and the *Today Show*, millions got their first look at what promises to be the most advanced, sustainable, affordable multi-family housing on the face of the earth. And closer to home, New Orleans' *Times-Picayune* summed it up the best in "Pitt Power." . . . The rest of the world seemed to be listening, too, as he and Global Green CEO Matt Petersen spoke of the Holy Cross Project becoming a national model for eco-friendly, low income housing. Stories ran in Canada's *Globe and Mail*, the *Seattle Times*, *Sydney Morning Herald* (Australia), *USA Today*, *ABC Online*, *FOX News*, *International Herald Tribune* (France), *People Magazine* and even *Pravda in Russia*.[22]

So the sustainable building groups find themselves in the middle of a neighborhood where they had never been before, possibly even the driving force behind that community's ability to rebuild and repatriate. Thus, the barrier between green building and the community of the HC has been breached. There is no inside and outside of the green technologies (or is there?). The actors have all been "displaced," to use Latour's terms—no one is untouched by this transformation. "The laboratory has gained strength to modify the state of affairs of all the other actors."[23]

According to Latour, laboratories are the sources where "fresh politics as yet unrecognized as such are emerging."[24] And if by politics he means sources that mold society, the sustainable building movement is certainly one of them. Technologies can transform society by transforming social relations in new ways. Thus, "laboratories are considered places where society and politics are renewed and transformed."[25]

Conclusion

So can this analytical method lead to a better understanding of the processes of urban redevelopment? Can this entrepreneurial-type lens explain the movement of actors, technologies, processes, and materials toward rebuilding after a disaster? What exactly can we know and what is not revealed in the "flat social domain" (i.e., without acknowledgment of relative power or politics) of ANT methodologies?[26]

While descriptions of the actors and networks in the green laboratorization of HC provide a complete catalogue of the situation at hand, it does not answer the question as to whether the community wanted to become a green lab at all. Did it agree to be a lab out of desperation or opportunity? This kind of description also neglects to ask whether the making of facts and artifacts will include, in a meaningful way, community voices or, better yet, will privilege those voices. The question: "Whose lab, whose technology?" never seems to arise from ANT/laboratory studies alone.

In their critique of Latour's approach, Whittle and Spicer argue that this "sociology of translation" or "production of detailed descriptions" comes with an inherently conservative political commitment.[27] Latour considers the political project of ANT to be the introduction of a "multiplicity of agencies" into an emergent version of the social and the political and has distanced himself from the idea of critique.[28] Others have argued that the political usefulness of ANT is not to verify or dispute social problems, such as structural inequalities, "but to trace their participation in assembling the social . . . [for example] how do some accounts of environmental justice, and not others, prevail and become instituted as 'matters of fact.'"[29]

I believe that a reason to use ANT as a methodological-analytical tool is that it is "good to think with": Latour's program of laboratorization, demonstrative of ANT, nicely fits the scheme of greening in HC. Made apparent are the movements of the actors and technologies as they coalesce and translate, breaching their respective discrete boundaries until a collaboratively enhanced movement is happening toward furthering green housing.

However, green housing, as one step toward carbon-neutrality by 2020, is only a part of what a sustainable community is about. Talking with community leaders, it is clear that their version if sustainability is a more enhanced "just sustainability," not simply sustainability as defined by preserving biodiversity and living in equilibrium with nature with an eye toward future generations. EJ advocates define "the environment" on much broader terms, including not only the natural world but also the social and economic conditions of its human inhabitants. Just sustainability is a hybrid of sustainability with environmental justice goals, which, broadly stated, are the need for distributed environmental goods and harms to all regardless of race or class.[30] This can be a point of tension between traditional sustainability movements and EJ movements, but the laboratorization/ANT analysis can help make apparent the strategies for moving forward, as well as show their points of tension and disconnect.[31]

As Julian Aygeman points out in his careful analysis of sustainability and EJ movements, the basic organizational structure of these two movements is very different. While EJ movements "can be understood as a local, grass-roots, or 'bottom-up' up community reaction to external threats to the health of the community," sustainability "emerged in large part from top-down international processes and committees, governmental structures, thinks tanks" and nongovernmental organizations.[32] The lab/ANT analysis process places these actors, along with the technologies and artifacts that they bring on a flat field, where interaction and translation is measured equally by what they actually do and say. On the one hand, this could be viewed as naïve, ignoring issues of power and social structure, but as Latour would say, "That's just the point."[33]

So the language of EJ emerged, as a major neighborhood focus, after Katrina, with the HC neighborhood association incorporating both sustainability and EJ language at the same time.[34] Thus, the EJ focus of the HC neighborhood association did not exactly build from the ground and later partner with just sustainability groups, the way that Aygeman suggests is most effective and equitable. Both of these groups and their discourses emerged almost simultaneously and immediately in communication and exchange with one another. These groups came together—the green groups because this was an ideal testing laboratory and the neighborhood because here was a huge alliance of people and resources to help them get back into their homes.

That the green groups and neighborhood groups had different environmental priorities was less important than the fact that they shared the same concerns, albeit with different emphases. In fact, many green groups present themselves, at least in their website language, as "just green building" organizations, to use Aygyman's framing of the "just sustainability paradigm." But the laboratorization lens, with its ANT approach, uncovers something else.

As Latour explains, "either we follow social theorists . . . or we follow the actors' own ways," allowing the actions to explain concepts and processes rather than having the analysts do all the talking, proffering their own prepackaged social and political concepts and aggregates.[35] Furthermore, by focusing on group formations, one can see traces of new emergences: "It is being performed and will then generate new and interesting data."[36] The actors are mapping the social theory rather than the other way round. Latour advocates limiting our studies to the agencies that result in acting—in other words, results in "doing something, that is, making some difference in a state of affairs."[37] Agency results in some sort of transformation (via action), and without that, there is no agency.

So now return to the HC green rebuilding assemblage of "actor-networks" and look at the action, the transformation. Or maybe, quicker to the point, where there is no transformation. While evidence of green structures, materials, and technologies is evident throughout the neighborhood, the evidence of the economic side of EJ is not present. While the three sides of "just sustainability" appear in print (environmental, social, economic), only the first one is predominant in actions. What is the problem? Why have the actor-networks not mobilized and acted around, for example, the economic parts of the EJ paradigm?

In speaking with both green nongovernmental organizations and local citizen groups, it was clear that they saw the lack of economic development as a problem. While no one had an easy answer, most believed that the government and its policies should be the primary catalyst in strengthening the economics of this impoverished neighborhood. These nodes of connection and transformation are missing from the actor-networks of HC/L9. But this could be framed another way, using traditional social science as explanation—the neoliberal policies of our current regime fail in fostering the economic viability of poor neighborhoods. And this failure, whether termed "absence of actions" or "neoliberal policies and their results," could be the unmaking of this green laboratory neighborhood—what could have become the first carbon neutral community in the urban United States.

The rebuilding on New Orleans is ongoing and will be for many years to come. The research on "best practices" and green rebuilding has only just begun. It is clear that a variety of analytical tools will be needed to cover the range of questions that needs to be asked of rebuilding strategies following disasters. It is, however, important that researchers understand both the promises and limitations of theories and methods chosen, carefully considering if their approach is the best one for answering the questions they pose. ANT models well the processes and products of neoliberalism in rebuilding a flood-damaged community but neglects to reveal issues of power and lack of social equity mechanisms in its focus on "emergences."

There are some other questions that need to be answered to understand the green trajectory in community rebuilding and development: Will other urban technologies emerge enabling further green economic and social transformation? Will there also be changes in transportation, recycling, food production, and other consumption practices that might shift everyday life in positive directions? Can exogenous movements adopted by desperate people to solve their problems in times of need ever really become local? Can urban laboratories become a catalyst for substantial environmental change? The answer to these questions is important in thinking about our collective future.

Notes

The research for this paper was supported with funding from the U.S. National Science Foundation, grant No. SES-0821353. The grant, titled "Dynamics of Citizens and Organizations in Knowledge Making, Building Practices, and Repatriation of New Orleans' Historic Neighborhoods," funds a comparative examination of different neighborhoods in the city. I expect the research for this project to be completed in 2012. The findings and analysis are my own.

1. Besides other chapters in this volume, other edited volumes to address this phenomena to some extent are: *There Is No Such Thing as a Natural Disaster*, ed. Chester Hartman and Gregory D. Squires (New York: Routledge, 2006) and *Race, Place, and Environmental Justice after Hurricane Katrina*, ed. Robert D. Bullard and Beverly Wright (Boulder, Colo.: Westview Press, 2009).

2. For a complete advanced introduction to ANT, see Bruno Latour, *Reassembling the Social: An Introduction to Actor-Network-Theory* (New York: Oxford University Press, 2005).

3. See ULI's website at http://www.uli.org/LearnAboutULI.aspx.

4. While the original "green dot map" is missing from the *New Orleans Times-Picayune* graphics archive online, a copy can be viewed at http://www.regional-modernism.com/2008/05/green-dot.html.

5. For information on Brad Pitt's Make It Right Foundation and the L9 sustainable house designs and building program, go to: http://www.makeitrightnola.org/. Also see *Architecture in Times of Need*, ed. Kristin Feireiss (New York: Prestel, 2009).

6. By comparison, the devastated part of the L9 had only a 19 percent home repatriation rate as of June 2009, the lowest repatriation rate in the city. It should also be noted that in the L9, almost half of the land *not* in the floodplain (i.e., above sea level) was flooded compared to 15 percent citywide. To access current demographic data on the city go to the Greater New Orleans Community Data Center at: http://www.gnocdc.org/.

7. For more on immediate postdisaster knowledge and practice failures, see Barbara Allen, "Environmental Justice, Local Knowledge, and After Disaster Planning in New Orleans," *Technology in Society* 29 (2007): 153–9; Barbara Allen, "Environmental Justice and Expert Knowledge in the Wake of a Disaster," *Social Studies of Science* 37, no. 1 (2007): 103–110.

8. For more on ACORN's role helping citizens with reassessment see Lisa K. Bates and Rebekah A. Green, "Housing Recovery in the Ninth Ward," in *Race, Place, and Environmental Justice after Hurricane Katrina*, 229–45.

9. For more on the evolution of laboratory studies, see Karin Knorr Cetina, *The Manufacture of Knowledge: An Essay on the Constructivist and Contextual Nature of Science* (Oxford: Pergamon Press, 1981); Michael Lynch, *Art and Artifact in Laboratory Science: A Study of Shop Work and Shop Talk in a Research Laboratory* (London: Routledge & Kegan Paul, 1985); Park Doing, "Give Me a Laboratory and I Will Raise a Discipline: The Past, Present, and Future Politics of Laboratory Studies in STS," in *The Handbook of Science and Technology Studies*, 3rd edition, ed. E. Hackett et al. (Cambridge, Mass.: MIT Press, 2008), 279–95.

10. Donna J. Haraway, *Simians, Cyborgs, and Women: The Reinvention of Nature* (New York: Routledge, 1991), 189–91.

11. Bruno Latour and Steve Woolgar, *Laboratory Life: The Social Construction of Scientific Facts* (Princeton: Princeton University Press, 1979).

12. See Steve Woolgar et al., "Does STS Mean Business?" *Organization* 16, no. 1 (2009): 5–30.

13. Latour, *Reassembling the Social*, 258–62.

14. Bruno Latour, "Give Me a Laboratory and I Will Raise the World" (1983), in *The Science Studies Reader,* ed. Mario Biagioli (New York: Routledge, 1999), 258.

15. Ibid., 259.

16. Anique Hommels, "Studying Obduracy in the City: Toward a Productive Fusion between Technology Studies and Urban Studies," *Science, Technology, and Human Values* 30, no. 3 (Summer 2005): 342.

17. Global Green is the U.S. affiliate of Green Cross International created by President Mikhail S. Gorbachev to foster a global value shift toward a sustainable and secure future. Nationally, its particular focus is on green buildings and cities. One of its main projects in the United States is in Holy Cross. Historic Green is the loose umbrella configuration under which preservation and sustainable groups, concepts, and practices converge and influence one another. It was founded in New Orleans following Katrina and has a major focus in Holy Cross.

18. See http://www.historicgreen.org/csed.php.

19. From an interview with Hampton S. Barclay, government relations representative, Home Builders Association of Greater New Orleans, December 11, 2008. For a list of all green groups active in HC, go to the Help Holy Cross website at: http://www.helpholycross.org/

20. The Preservation Resource Center (PRC) in New Orleans, founded in 1974, is a nonprofit advocacy and information center for the preservation, restoration, and revitalization of the city's historic neighborhoods. It houses two other important outreach arms: Rebuilding Together, the largest sustained volunteer coordination effort (founded 1988), and Operation Comeback, a project that buys blighted properties and restores them for sale to the general public (founded 1987).

21. See http://www.historicgreen.org/historic_green.php.

22. See http://www.helpholycross.org/2007/08/index.html.

23. Latour, "Give Me a Laboratory and I Will Raise the World," 266.

24. Ibid., 268.

25. Ibid., 269.

26. Latour, *Reassembling the Social*, 171.

27. Andrea Whittle and Andre Spicer, "Is Actor Network Theory Critique?" *Organization Studies* 29, no. 4 (2008): 611–29.

28. Latour, *Reassembling the Social*, 260.

29. Ryan Holifield, "Actor-Network Theory as a Critical Approach to Environmental Justice: A Case against Synthesis with Urban Political Ecology" *Antipode* 41, no. 4 (2009): 625.

30. Julian Agyeman, *Sustainable Communities and the Challenge of Environmental Justice* (New York: NYU Press, 2005).

31. For a substantive analysis of the sustainability/EJ divide, see Andrew Dobson, "Social Justice and Environmental Sustainability: Ne'er the Twain Shall Meet?" in *Just Sustainabilities: Development in an Unequal World,* ed. Julian Agyeman et al. (Cambridge, Mass.: MIT Press, 2003): 83–95. Sandra Harding both criticizes the work of Latour and, at the same time, shows its usefulness in making apparent the contributions of "outsiders" in technoscientific systems in her *Sciences From Below: Feminisms, Postcolonialities, and Modernities* (Durham, N.C.: Duke University Press, 2008).

32. Agyeman, *Sustainable Communities and the Challenge of Environmental Justice,* 1–2.

33. Latour, *Reassembling the Social,* 221.

34. There had been some environmental activism prior to Katrina. In 2003, the Holy Cross Neighborhood Association, Louisiana Environmental Action Network, and Gulf Restoration Network filed a lawsuit against the U.S. Army Corps of Engineers No. 03-0370 (Eastern District of Louisiana, February 6, 2003) to stop the dredging of the industrial canal and the disposal of the hazardous sediment near their neighborhood. They won their lawsuit after appeal receiving a favorable judgment in 2006. For more information, see http://www.helpholycross.org.

35. Latour, *Reassembling the Social,* 29-30.

36. Ibid., 31.

37. Ibid., 52.

CHAPTER 9

Squandered Resources?

Grounded Realities of Recovery in Post-Tsunami Sri Lanka

Kanchana N. Ruwanpura

Encountering Disasters

I had just returned from my usual early morning hours at the gym and found an e-mail from a British friend inquiring whether I was safe from the threat of the impending hurricane. I lived in upstate New York. Of course, I was! Still I found the e-mail a little peculiar because between 6:00 and 7:00 a.m. on August 29, 2005, the television news had not particularly overplayed the imminent storm—and possessing no television of my own, the only place I had access to a television was while at the gym. The e-mail got me surfing the BBC website and listening to BBC Radio 4's Today Programme where across the Atlantic Ocean serious attention was paid to the possible onslaught of Katrina. I half thought that this news made sense because my ten-minute walk from the gym to my apartment was through fairly strong winds, even by upstate New York standards.

It was through the day that the calamity of Hurricane Katrina was unfolding, and it is the next morning, once again at the gym, that I had access to the horrific images of the destruction of New Orleans. As I exercised on the ergo machine, watching the images of a battered and destroyed New Orleans, I found it incredulous that America seemed to be torn apart at the seams with entire world watching! My amazement also stemmed because my time in Sri Lanka that summer included being involved in a post-tsunami research project. Therefore, I had witnessed within close proximity the traumatic experiences of people in two locations in southern and eastern Sri Lanka. Another "natural" disaster was occurring? Or, yet another disaster triggered by a social calculus shaped by neoliberal policies?[1] The events of the day as well as the days and weeks immediately following the event seem to suggest that the social order mattered as much as in the United States as it had in Sri Lanka.

In what ways was the recovery and reconstruction process in post-tsunami Sri Lanka, still proceeding, finding parallels in the United States? At a superficial level, this ought not to be the case. The United States was a dominant superpower, whereas Sri Lanka is a "developing" country. Although Sri Lanka's human development indices are laudable and compare well even with many developed countries, the GDP per capita (as problematic as such averages tend to be) between the two countries differ markedly. Moreover, decades of Sri Lanka's protracted and bloodied ethnic conflict should imply that similarities are unlikely to be found between the two countries. But is this necessarily the case? The aftermath of Hurricane Katrina showed how uneven resources and development tendencies leave some people more vulnerable than others. Inequalities in our existing social arrangements lead to weaker members of the community bearing a disproportionate burden of the destruction to livelihoods and property.[2] Similarly, ignoring the ethnic, class, and gender fault lines of the affected communities was difficult to overlook. A preponderance of these social groups among the distressed was captured by the mainstream media. When the deck is already loaded against marginal communities, they inevitably bear the concomitant repercussions on who gets what, when, and how much in the emergency relief and reconstruction process.[3] As I discuss in the parts to follow, post-tsunami Sri Lanka was no different. Spaces of inequality along ethno-nationalist divisions perpetuated patronage and existing disparities, thus entrenching the powerful and excluding the weak.[4] The uneven ways in which the neoliberal approach transpires postdisaster was unraveling in both contexts. Previous cuts to welfare spending affected the social, political, and economic security of communities in the United States and is considered a key factor that turned a disaster into a catastrophe.[5] The fervent faith in the market, however, continues, with the postdisaster situation framed by corporate interests taking precedence over community welfare in the recovery process.[6] The deployment of neoliberal policies in Sri Lanka is more subtle in the post-tsunami context. I show in the subsequent sections the reliance on philanthropic giving and nongovernmental organization relief work leads to skirting the micropolitics of everyday life. Despite the touted importance of these institutional actors, close reading highlights how their activities more often than not tended to reproduce social hierarchies and inequalities.

My focus in this chapter is on the resettlement and reconstruction of temporary and permanent shelters in Sri Lanka. I use fieldwork done in Batticaloa and Hikkaduwa, eastern and southern Sri Lanka, respectively, to bring to light and articulate concerns and anxieties that were expressed by community members. Material realities of the political economy became coupled with prevailing fault lines of war and inequality in the ways in which people conveyed how they made sense of the tsunami experience. I draw upon the conversations with about thirty people who either directly bore the impact of tsunami and/or were involved in putting into place the rebuilding efforts of communities. Much of this information was gleaned through in-depth interviews and participant observation, and voices that are represented in this research come from affected members of the Burgher, Muslim, Sinhala, and Tamil communities.[7] At all times ethical convention is maintained by using pseudonyms when citing their tales and voices.

The Sri Lankan Space

War, ethnic cleavages, and uneven development processes are all attributes of the Sri Lankan social fabric, pointing to the need to pay attention to the politics of inequality in tsunami-affected communities.[8] Eastern Sri Lanka, for example, is war-ravaged and steeped in a highly fraught and politically contentious environment. In Batticaloa, the political tensions between the LTTE (Liberation Tamil Tigers for Eelam) and LTTE-Karuna factions meant not simply skirmishes and outbreaks of violence that add to the political turmoil in the area but also different diktats on the buffer zones to be maintained in the post-tsunami period. People tend to be caught between policy directives by the state, the LTTE, and LTTE-Karuna factions adding to existing insecurities and fear of unstable futures.[9] Security-led immobility, sporadic clashes, and outbreaks of violence together with LTTE-imposed draconian tax burdens also worsened structures of poverty and bore negatively on the welfare of local people.[10]

Batticaloa then hosts embattled ethnic communities facing widespread poverty and ethnic deprivation. Yet, the area is not without its spaces of hope. Eastern Sri Lanka is well known for matrilineal inheritance patterns and communities among Muslims and Tamils. Property, land, and wealth are inherited and passed onto young women through their mother's side, with husbands joining women in their parental residence, which place women in a favorable position. In many ways, it is socio-legally distinct from the rest of the country.[11]

The rest of Sri Lanka is not immune from these contradictory conditions. The liberalization reforms that began in 1977 witnessed gradual but steady transformations to the previous social safety nets, denting income distribution patterns in palpable ways.[12] The distributional impacts together with conspicuous consumption patterns culminated in the JVP (Janatha Vimukthi Peramuna: People's Liberation Party)–led insurrection during the 1980s. Social tensions, ethnic segmentation, and economic inequities underpinned this violent period of Sri Lanka's postliberalization phase.[13] Fragmented development and patterns of social exclusion continue to be widespread in the country, shaping politics of inequality in the everyday as well as during extraordinary events.[14] At the same time, however, Sri Lanka has held on remarkably well to high human development indices (HDI) for a developing country, with laudable gender equality achievements.[15]

This curious anomaly aside, much of the country is plagued by social ills of inequality, uneven development, and a bloody ethnic war. This was the backdrop against which the tsunami took place, where people had to make sense of a "natural" disaster. Although the fieldwork sites— Hikkaduwa and Batticaloa—were concentrated in southern and eastern Sri Lanka, respectively, thick descriptions of grounded realities facilitate dislocating recurrent articulations of natural disasters.[16] Anxieties echoed by affected people as they experienced their newfound and sometimes ill-fitting temporary and permanent shelters then need to be appreciated against the tumultuous and jagged Sri Lankan social space.

Reconstruction and Recovery

The tsunami destroyed a total of 127,105 houses and 11,002 buildings in a matter of twenty minutes.[17] This destruction alone meant that the challenge of rebuilding was colossal. It would, however, be rash to assume that the challenge was limited to the physical act of putting up houses.

Because communities are embedded in social structures, the act of offering permanent and temporary shelters has to be understood within its political context. The stories shared by affected communities on how they made sense of their accommodation, whether permanent or temporary, show how socioeconomic and ethnic tensions bear out in their everyday experiences. In the subsections to follow, some of these key themes are highlighted, as the case studies appear to reveal.

Ethnic(-ized) Aid?

The ethnic location of people was paramount in whether they were able to access temporary shelters. Indeed, people's experience of their new living arrangements was ethnically marked because of their previous direct and indirect exposure to war-related impacts. The prevailing political turmoil and ethnic tensions were critical pointers and tracing these instances also reveals regional specifics.

The Tamil community in war-affected regions has undoubtedly been on the receiving end of the ongoing ethnic war. A cost of directly bearing the brunt of the war has been that they have experienced displacement during temporary, sudden, or unending evacuations at vital moments of intense warfare.[18] Living in areas prone to recurrent turbulence at the same time, however, has made these people adapt to violently changing situations. There is recognition that often they don't have any control over the violent backdrop within which they inhabit and thus have to make the best of their circumstances. Because of their prior experiences, living in transitional camps where shelters were made of corrugated iron (where the hot sun would quickly heat up the interior) was never brought up as an issue of consternation. It is not only the heat that appeared to make living in such accommodation hard. During one of my field visits, when the North-East monsoon was pouring down, the inadequacies of the drainage system was made apparent with overflowing drains causing mild flooding into some premises. Despite inconveniences caused by the sun and the rain, the level of optimism and confidence that they were generally satisfied with their current shelters and will be the recipients of permanent dwellings within a reasonable period was recurrently noted. Renuka, a forty-two-year-old woman, noted, "We will get our permanent house built in two years time," and this time frame was perceived as necessary for ensuring that good houses could be built with solid construction material.

Resilience built through years of living in war zones partly explains their satisfaction with the temporary living arrangements. But also their ease with the new residential setting had to do with how their lives were shaping in comparison to their pre-tsunami living and their ability to maintain a seemingly ordinary day amid political violence and an environmental catastrophe. They seemed to suggest that the structurally poor situation of housing was less important. Yet, the whole picture is much more than this. Poverty and deprivation were features of their lives in the pre-tsunami period. Even as many families lost their few possessions to the tsunami and without discounting the personal trauma they underwent, Jonathan Rigg et al. note how the tsunami in Thailand also "afforded an opportunity to move to a larger, permanent and prime corner plot."[19] The situation in Sri Lanka was no less different. On the one hand, it is their grinding poverty and low-quality, makeshift homes that were easily demolished through the tsunami waves, underlying the political economy conditions that made their vulnerability acute and turned a disaster into a catastrophe.[20] On the other hand, there were also instances in which the tsunami brought with it opportunities for better-quality housing. Soundarie, a forty-one-year-old Tamil woman, said, "This new house is better than the earlier one. This is built with brick and this is very strong. The roof too is hardy. There is a proper concrete foundation and the roofing has tiles." The unequivocal appreciation she narrates suggests the asymmetrical outcomes of the tsunami, as does Renuka's optimism regarding having better-quality housing within a two-year period.

In this regard, it was not only Tamil women who shared their enthusiasm and hope for gaining better-quality houses. Madhavi, a twenty-seven-year-old Sinhala woman from Hikkaduwa, contrasted her new premises with her old destroyed home by saying, "The house we have got from the foundation is quite solid. It is plastered and colour-washed nicely." The few Sinhala people who had come to own new and permanent houses largely conveyed a high degree of satisfaction. Indeed, the common perception was that the new houses appeared to be "nice." Therefore, coming into ownership of such property was something people either directly or indirectly hinted as being an aspiration. These dwellings, however, were two-bedroom houses built on the assumption of a nuclear family size of four, while there were some larger families moving into such properties.

The satisfaction expressed by Tamil women with their temporary and permanent shelters was echoed by Sinhala women with regard to their new permanent dwellings; the experience of the Muslim community, however, point to the gaps in this narrative. Jayadeva Uyangoda notes how Muslims were the community to have fared the poorest in the Eastern Province.[21] He contends that they were the weakest link in the "peace talks," which took place between the state and the LTTE since 2002. Because the two dominant communities, the Sinhalese and the Tamils, deliberately crafted the political terrain on the basis of ethno nationalist agendas, casting aside the visibility of Muslims—and indeed other minority communities in the country—was an important move. The visibility of Muslims was at best peripheral to the ethno-nationalism espoused and propounded by both Sinhalese and Tamils. This political omission of minority voice and space had ramification for affected Muslims.

Neither the government nor the numerous nongovernmental organization actors appeared to have looked into the welfare of Muslim families we came across. The material support they received was haphazard. They lived in plastic tents or shacks put together through their own initiative, which were covered with plastic donated during philanthropic initiatives in the emergency relief stage. The only sustained support that they received was through an organization, SURIYA, which was involved in rights-based work. SURIYA's mandate revolves around linking the community voice to the relevant government authorities and legal awareness campaigns—and their commitment to the community had been established from six years prior to the tsunami. This was not torn asunder by the tsunami. It supports previous research in the area that underscores how social movements grounded in the lived realities of communities acquire a commitment to work through difficult periods and different tensions that transient development workers may not necessarily show.[22] Moreover, as John Telford and John Cosgrave point out, the "urgency to spend money visibly, worked against making the best use of local and national capacities."[23] This is unsurprising as process-based work is "the most contingent and most difficult to engineer," which tends to be overlooked by the international aid community looking for quantifiable outcomes.[24] Against this backdrop, even a year after the tsunami, they had not received any official directives or support on obtaining stable housing. Initial pledges made by a Hong Kong–based church group had yet to reach fruition. Hafsa, a thirty-eight-year-old Muslim woman, attributed this to "the land problem (meaning lack of clarity regarding the buffer zone) means that we don't know anything about our permanent housing."

State- and LTTE-dictated buffer zones pointed to the ways in which the everyday life of the people was made chaotic and insecure,[25] where there appeared to be little regard and respect for people's need for proper housing. The everyday difficulties encountered by Muslims were apparent simply in the appalling quality of their living quarters. They reasoned that this lack of permanent dwelling was attributable to their previous housing falling within the 200-meter buffer zone. Yet because their exclusion stems from the humanitarian relief efforts, a more reasonable explanation is offered by Telford and Cosgrave, who note the multiple ways in which marginal and politically invisible social groups fall through the gaps of humanitarian assistance.[26] The upshot for marginal communities was that the post-tsunami period created "spaces of fear and mistrust around which party politics and nationalist tensions were organized."[27]

This politically troubling experience is not novel to Sri Lanka, with "the greatest nation" on earth (a.k.a. United States) manifesting ethnic and racial demarcations in dealing with recovery and reconstruction. Forthergill et al., in their review of the literature on the intersections between race and ethnicity of people's experiences of disasters, point to the problems encountered by minority groups in securing permanent housing where there is evidence of racism in the housing process as well.[28] While the review carried by the authors was for the pre-Katrina era, a recent media article reports similar racist contours shaping the housing, relocation, and regeneration policies. MacAskill quotes an African-American woman who thinks that race will determine the shape of the city: "I think they only want a segment of the community to come back. The majority of people are black and they have not planned on them coming back."[29]

Humanitarian losses then are not the criteria used for rebuilding communities and regenerating disaster-destroyed areas. A convergence of grounded political realities, including the voice and social location of ethnic communities, determined the level of political patronage that each social group received. This ultimately shaped their social and domestic welfare as well. Aid intervention, too, has an ethnic face and phase, and the absence of recognizing its limits is more likely than not to perpetuate pitfalls rather than to realize its potential.

Squandered Resources?

The tsunami generated an unprecedented outpouring of funding, breaking records for "the most generous and immediately funded international humanitarian response ever."[30] How did this generally munificent resource base go toward meeting the needs of affected communities? What other social groups mattered? Or, put differently, does not paying attention to class locations of affected people result in the squandering of resources?

Jamiez-aiyya, a sixty-seven-year-old man from Hikkaduwa, captures the essence of this quandary eloquently:

> Take a look around and note the number of houses that are unoccupied. The agency just came and built wood houses. They did not ask who owned and wanted houses. So people who had extended family or property in the interior moved to those places, but nominally hold onto a temporary shelter. . . . But do the agencies ever wonder about the wastage of resources that they contribute towards by not asking and assessing the needs of each local community? I do not mean to criticize the agency, but it is hard not to be concerned with the squander of resources.

The squandering of resources is not the only unease Jamiez-aiyya captures in his conversation with us. He is also disclosing the lack of consultation with affected communities that was raised by numerous affected people and families. In fact, he is suggesting, as did many others, that the funding meant to meet their humanitarian losses did not necessarily do so because the recipients were never consulted in the first place.

Barring those affected from the review process leads to resentment because it had an impact on their living conditions in multiple ways. The problem with temporary shelters that were put up was not only that there were unused and empty premises, which indicate a waste of resources. Their complaints also had to do with how the plastic coverings, low-quality timber, and/or corrugated iron that were used led to rain beating into houses, unbearable interior heat, and loud noises that were caused by windy weather. All these factors affected the health of people and made living difficult. The lack of regard and respect for vernacular living conditions evoked the omission of democratic voices and inclusive politics in the everyday planning processes. Thus, irrespective of conventional rhetoric championing nongovernmental organizations as spaces for strengthening civil society, the grounded experiences suggest that embedded structures are unlikely to be eradicated without a committed and sustained negotiation processes. Such fieldwork evidence supports Telford and Cosgrave's assessment of how risk analysis carried out in a hasty manner in the post-tsunami setting tended to miss "more complex aspects."[31]

Not withstanding the hardships and difficulties encountered by the people, a notable amount of affected people did make do with their temporary shelters. The Tamils and Muslims discussed in the cited instances are cases in point. So, too, did many Sinhalese and Burghers. There are, however, two distinctions between the four communities that are worthy of consideration. I start with the ways in which split housing arrangements were observed among some Burghers and Sinhalese. At one level, their housing preferences offered further credence to the "squander of resources." These family units did not make use of their nominal housing structures, other than to ensure that they were not left out of any benefits that were passed onto affected communities. The hardships they would encounter if they were to live in the transitional homes, the inconvenience of being located away from the children's school and their extended family networks, and having to share common washing and toilet facilities were some commonly cited reasons for opting for the split living arrangements. These are widespread problems encountered by almost all affected communities, yet they were circumvented by segments of Burghers and Sinhalese. At another level, these social practices zone in on the central import of class since their capacity to maintain split housing arrangements was because they had the necessary middle-class connections that made such arrangements possible. Helen, a thirty-four-year-old Burgher woman, said, "We live in town in my grandmother's house as it is easy for my children to go to school. We don't live in the house in the Thiraimadu camp. We go spend some time there on some evenings and on holidays." Quite frequently, they took for granted their right to established conveniences and were unwilling to forfeit their comforts, despite witnessing others similarly affected by the tsunami living in poverty conditions. Consequently, they staked their nominal rights to shelter in the transitional camps with no critical reflection on the ways in which their lack of use could be aggravating social tensions and hierarchies. Instructive here is the waste of resources they were contributing toward even as they complained about their exclusion from recovery processes. The empty houses that Jameiz-aiyya pointed out then highlight the central importance of class in the ability of some social groups to manipulate their privileges in ways that result in a misallocation of resources—and thus, by extension, to its waste.

Despite the class markers, ethnic differentiation between the Burghers and Sinhalese vis-à-vis Muslims and Tamils also points to the imperative of the warring background and the ways in which different ethnic communities bore the impact of the conflict. The daily curfews, *hartals*, and disruption to electricity and schooling were part and parcel of war-torn Batticaloa, which affected Burghers living there.[32] However, they actively assumed a stance of impartiality adopted as a means of avoiding state- or LTTE-sponsored violence. As a result, they did not bear the direct onslaught of the war nor did they experience displacement. Dislocation from homes was a new experience for the Sinhalese living in the South, too. The perverse novelty of their displacement was another rationale used to justify their strident concerns with the difficulties encountered with their temporary shelters. Inappropriate use of raw materials, the poor housing structures, the use and abuse of transitional shelters, and their lack of voice were all frequently cited as testifying to their suffering. This difference in a couple of marginal ethnic communities (Muslims and Tamils) bearing the direct impact of the war in comparison with the dominant community (Sinhalese) indirectly experiencing the war along with a minority community (Burghers) actively carving out a neutrality posture was also paramount for the distinctive ways in which affected people conveyed their discontent or partiality toward their temporary dwellings. Indeed, ignoring those exiled from the war multiple times was displaced from the mainstream psyche. This turn of events also had to do with the marginal status, whether based on class, gender or ethnicity, of these war-affected communities; hence, their trials and tribunals lingered in the background, away from a tsunami-triggered generosity fund.[33] The unprecedented resources available then were disbursed in ways that were less about assessed needs and more about advocating a media-generated recovery process with unambiguous neoliberal underpinnings.

Beautifying Beaches

A much-contested aspect to the recovery process was the potential relocation of affected families to the interior of the country. There was much consternation in the public imagery about a potential second wave of forced displacement because of the keenness with which the buffer zones were advocated by both the state and the LTTE. The lack of clarity in the pronouncement by both these actors did add to the insecurity and uncertainty of people, intensifying political controversy and ethno-nationalist sentiment.[34] An additional reading was the loss of livelihoods such dispossession would bring about for the fishing communities, and hence the relocation to interior areas.[35] There is much credibility to these standpoints, with fishing families in particular mentioning the fear of losing a secure source of livelihood. Imali and Hettige (wife and husband, respectively) supported this contention by saying, "Because we are fisher folk, we want to be close to the sea as it is convenient for the men to go to sea."

The fieldwork, however, also suggested that there were factors beyond this simple narration. The obstinate refusal to relocate into the interior was not necessarily a collective stance, since some families viewed the opportunity to possess better-quality housing and land as signifying upward social mobility. Such prospects, however, did have a catch attached. The need for fairness and equity was emphasized repeatedly. Mistrust of motivations then underpinned the opposition or reception to relocation, which was continuously emphasized. Imali and Hettige best encapsulate this distrust and ambiguity of motivations: "There is also talk that the state is hoping to clear the coastline so that they can beautify the beach areas, make it more attractive for the tourists and the tourism industry."

Imali and Hettige's parlay of uncertainties in southern Sri Lanka were directed at the state, but the LTTE was no less immune from this criticism. What were their motivations? Whose interest were they espousing? Are the Tamil-speaking people, whom the LTTE claim to represent, a homogeneous group undifferentiated by class, caste, and ethnicity? A religious figure keenly engaged with the recovery process in his parish area in Batticaloa insisted that we visit a nearby beach that was cleared up. These clearing-up efforts caused such a degree of disquiet with the local community that a protest march was organized to challenge whose interest the LTTE was espousing. *"THE LAGOON IS OUR LIFE AND THE SEA IS OUR HOME—KEEP YOUR HANDS OFF THEM"* was the watchword around which people championed their voices. They thus questioned the interest of capital which the LTTE also was promoting. The LTTE's own alignment with neoliberal forces as espoused in the

ISGA (Interim Self-Governing Authority) proposal was articulated as the need to be "in-tune with the international community" on economic questions.[36] LTTE's alliance with neoliberal policies makes their plans for beautifying beaches banal. Such instances of not meeting the needs of the tsunami-affected communities exemplify the LTTE's quest for representing the Tamil-speaking people as quite distinct from that of radical economic democracy.[37]

The perception that capitalist interest was superseding the needs and priorities of affected communities thus was parallel across regional locations. Vasuki Nesiah argues that rendering beaches pristine for the tourist's gaze was at play from the moment the "former German Chancellor Helmut Kohl was airlifted from the roof of his holiday resort in Southern Sri Lanka" by the local air force. She proceeds to acknowledge that while Kohl is not representative of all tourists, the "aerial exit from debris and disaster is symptomatic of the tourist industries' alienation from the local community." This estrangement of local communities from the public use of land for livelihood sustenance, such as fishing, is likely where infrastructure development caters to a global tourist industry rather than the needs of local communities.[38] Beautifying beaches and buffer zones may be the blatant symptoms deployed by the state and the LTTE, less evident and as crucial, however, are the efforts to rebuild model villages just outside of the 100- to 200-meter buffer zone along coastline. The initiatives for numerous villages reawakening schemes did not necessarily come from the state and/or the para-state (i.e., the LTTE). Private philanthropic and nongovernmental organizations were crucial to building local houses to meet "Australian" standards, and setting up Munich or Victoria villages and other such seemingly laudable initiatives.

What is the appropriateness in building to Australian standards? Are these suitable for the local topography? The implicit logic suggests that it is poor housing structures rather than the poverty of people that lead to the destruction of their houses to the tsunami waves. No word is given here of the connection between people's poverty and poor housing conditions. More significantly, to protect tourists from the jarring and unseemly sights of poverty and ramshackle dwellings, the tsunami offered a significant opportunity to not just beautify beaches but also rebuild coastal communities dotting the interior of the coastline with at least attractive houses. Whether inhabitants made a living wage is not necessarily in the mind of tourists seeking rest and relaxation, given that they have criss-crossed the globe to consume Sri Lanka's "exoticism."[39] The state, the LTTE, and numerous philanthropic and nongovernmental organization initiatives appear to be complicit in promoting a neoliberal agenda with space for a tourist industry that was given priority over tsunami-affected coastal communities.

Conclusion: Global Fault-Lines?

The preceding discussions trace some of the notable lapses in post-tsunami recovery process in Sri Lanka. Telford and Cosgrave argue that these failures demonstrate the wider context of adopting "isolated and short-term approaches" that is media-driven. Putting "affected communities in the driving seat" was not a strategy consistently pursued.[40] There is much veracity to this viewpoint. I have argued here that affected communities negotiate the recovery process in diverse ways, much of which is based on the local patterns of stratification. Micropolitics based on ethnicity, class, and gender positioning continues to matter. The multiple intersections of spaces of inequality and existing fault-lines of the war constantly surfaced in the numerous conversations with affected communities in both southern and eastern Sri Lanka. However, does this analysis penetrate the multiple layers to unravel the particular politico-economic milieu within which global processes bear upon disaster and postdisaster contexts?

A close reading of the grounded transformation reveals that the gigantic outpouring of aid and funding is not without its stipulations. Yet, these caveats were not created by the tsunami or the post-tsunami recovery efforts. In Sri Lanka, like in New Orleans, the exacerbation of socioeconomic inequalities was also linked to the modus operandi of neoliberalism already set in place. The opening of the market to the world economy begun as early as 1977 brought with it worsening income distributions and unbridled consumerism. The disenchantment caused through the everyday violence of neoliberal initiatives found expression in Sri Lanka through more extraordinary moments of violence that came in the form of JVP-led insurrection in southern Sri Lanka as well as a lingering and bloodied ethnic war.[41] The United States, in contrast, is perceived globally as epitomizing the possibilities of economic growth when national economies are tied by its umbilical cord to a market system. This narrative line obscures the everyday violence—whether through guns or gangs—which is also associated with the fallout of class and social inequities of unbridled capitalism. Consequently, in post-Katrina New Orleans, the fallouts of capitalism could be neglected by marrying reconstructions efforts even more closely to the strictures of neoliberal economic policies.

There is certain predictability then that the complexities and class hierarchies inherent in the social fabric of both countries are likely to have made the "natural" disasters particularly harsh on the more vulnerable sections of the community. Paying particular attention to local patterns of social stratification and micropolitics is then crucial for many reasons; most critical, however, is the way in which resources are squandered. In the Sri Lankan context, Jameiz-aiyya pointed to the everyday squandering of resources through the nonuse of the various houses built and nominally held by middle-class segments of the affected community. Similarly, Imali and Hettige and the priest voice their concerns regarding the potential exclusion of local communities from their livelihoods by making beaches a potentially exclusive zone for tourists. As Nesiah shows, the global economic rationale for preceding the interests of hoteliers and global tourists over local communities ignores the impact of a fluctuating tourist market on the local economy.[42] I would push this line of thinking further to argue that the social tensions created by giving primacy to global hotelier interests are also about potentially aggravating the everyday and extraordinary violence that afflicts different social settings globally. Resources, then, are not only ravaged by the whimsical needs of consumer-friendly tourists but also intensified by the bloodied trajectory of violence that in Sri Lanka's case besieged the island for over two decades. The global rationale for an efficient use of resources tends all too easily to then neglect the longer-term consequences for local economies and communities, thus begging the question of whether it is the interest of local communities or hoteliers that the Sri Lankan state and the LTTE were tempting with the exclusionary buffer zones?

The dependence on fickle-minded tourists is not the only parallel between the exotic beaches of Sri Lanka and jazz-based New Orleans. The fervent faith in the market in both countries also led to a retrenchment of public-sector support and a gradual assault on safety nets that made the ineptitude of state authorities in both locales glaring. The unwillingness to engage and accept the limited resource base with which the state has had to work is a worrying outcome in and of itself. Moreover, the continued reliance on private philanthropy, private sector initiatives, and the nongovernmental organization sector activities is not without its pitfalls. Even as the Sri Lankan state and occasionally even the LTTE are denounced for their top-down approach to postdisaster recovery, the limits to facilities offered by philanthropic and nongovernmental organization actors tended to be coded and could be educed only with some prodding. The humanitarian aid offered by these non state actors is marked by ethnic differences, with the experience of Muslims poignantly illustrating such "humanitarian" lapses or for building houses for "ideal-sized" nuclear families. Yet often criticisms of this sector tended to be cautiously expressed with constant optimism for change with on-going efforts extolled. The incongruous ways in which affected people deal with the state, quasi-state (LTTE), and the non state institutions point more fundamentally to a transfer of social and political capital from the state to the philanthropic private sector. The hegemonic positions that private philanthropic sectors have come to occupy, thus hint at a complex power nexus that finds expression via a globally integrated world.[43] By promoting philanthropic and nongovernmental organization initiatives, which are least of all accountable to the locale within which they operate, it becomes possible to displace any engagement with the resource-poor base with which state authorities operate. The latter engagement calls for a more fundamental conversation about the value of placing market values above the sense of place and space that communities nurture through their habituation of everyday values. This is a dialogue that is too often avoided as it lays bare the global fault-lines at play. A focus on the unprecedented humanitarian aid implicitly justifies the solidification of the shift towards the non state sector, and thereby conveniently masks the uneven global-local dynamics and processes. New Orleans has been no less immune from these shifts. It points to the need for care and critical evaluation of these processes at play—wherever they may be taking place.

Spotlighting the global fault-lines is not to deny importance of ethnic differentiation in Sri Lanka (or racial segregation in the United States) and all its attendant challenges. Time and again, the local patterns of stratification appear to matter as the narration of affected people's experiences seems to tell. However, the uneven and laissez-faire emphasis of the recovery process also has as its consequence the fortification of power asymmetries, which appear to side with "big" interest over the small—which is a position staked by the state and the LTTE. Economic disempowerment often is coupled with various discriminatory processes. As much as the latter requires our consistent consideration, so do the causes of economic disempowerment. Because the latter is intricately bound to global fault-lines and the global economy with neoliberal impulses, a focus on the misuse of resources uncovers the ways in which local communities are disrupted and destroyed. This occurs not necessarily and merely through a "natural" disaster, as the tsunami or Katrina may seem at first glance, but through processes of social, political, and economic disempowerment that has a prior history and unfortunately continues unabated.

Notes

This chapter draws upon my research with Neloufer de Mel on the project "Gendering the Tsunami: A Report of Women's Experiences." See Neloufer de Mel and Kanchana N. Ruwanpura, "Gendering the Tsunami: Women's Experiences from Sri Lanka"—Report Series 3, August 2006. Colombo, Sri Lanka: International Centre for Ethnic Studies 2006. Some themes of this paper were also animated during conversations with Anushaya Collure, who was my research assistant during fieldwork during 2005–2006. I was fortunate to have excellent follow-up research assistance from two dedicated and enthusiastic students during the summer of 2007 and 2009, both funded by the Summer Student Bursary, School of Geography, University of Southampton. Andrew Morgan helped gather updated information on the rebuilding process in Sri Lanka, and Lisa Boorman helped finalize the nitty-gritty details required at the very last stages. I also wish to acknowledge that this chapter is a revised version of a previous article: Kanchana N. Ruwanpura, "Putting Houses in Place: Rebuilding Communities in Post-Tsunami Sri Lanka," *Disasters* 33, no. 3 (July 2009): 436–56.

1. See S. Nanthikesan, "Post Tsunami Posturing," *Lines-Magazine*, 2005, http://www.lines-magazine.org/Art_Feb05/Editorial_Nanthi.htm (accessed August 23, 2007); Neil Smith, "There Is No Such Thing as a Natural Disaster," 2006, http://understandingkatrina.ssrc.org/Smith/ (accessed August 27, 2007); and Lisa Schipper and Mark Pelling, "Disaster Risk, Climate Change, and International Development: Scope for, and Challenges to, Integration," *Disasters* 30, no. 1 (March 2006): 19–38.

2. See Alice Fothergill et al., "Race, Ethnicity, and Disasters in the United States: A Review of the Literature," *Disasters* 23, no. 2 (June 1999): 156–73; Joni Seager, "Noticing Gender (or Not) in Disasters," *Geoforum* 37 (2006): 2–3; and Smith, "There Is No Such Thing as a Natural Disaster."

3. See Ahilan Kadirgamar, "The Fourth Person and the Politics of Aid," *Lines Magazine*, 2005, http://www.lines-magazine.org/Art_Feb05/ahilan.htm (accessed August 19, 2007); and Susan Cutter, "The Geography of Social Vulnerability: Race,

Class, and Catastrophe," 2006, http://understandingkatrina.ssrc.org/Cutter/ (accessed August 27, 2007).

4. See also Kadirgamar, "The Fourth Person and the Politics of Aid"; Cutter, "The Geography of Social Vulnerability"; and Smith, "There Is No Such Thing as a Natural Disaster."

5. Smith, "There Is No Such Thing as a Natural Disaster"; and Andrew Lakoff, "From Disaster to Catastrophe: The Limits of Preparedness," 2006; http://understandingkatrina.ssrc.org/Lakoff/ (accessed August 2, 2007). See also Schipper and Pelling, "Disaster Risk, Climate Change, and International Development," 19–38.

6. Smith, "There Is No Such Thing as a Natural Disaster."

7. A detailed account of fieldwork method and scope can be found in De Mel and Ruwanpura (2006); Ruwanpura, "Temporality of Disasters: The Politics of Women's Livelihoods 'After' the 2004 Tsunami in Sri Lanka," *Singapore Journal of Tropical Geography* 29, no. 3 (November 2008): 325–40, and Ruwanpura, 2009; the interested reader is referred to these works.

8. See James Sidaway and Peggy Teo, "Editorial: Lessons in Geography," *Singapore Journal of Tropical Geography* 26, no 1 (2005): 1–3; John Telford and John Cosgrove, "The International Humanitarian System and the 2004 Indian Ocean Earthquake and the Tsunamis," *Disasters* 31, no. 1 (March 2007): 1–28; Jennifer Hyndman, "The Securitization of Fear in Post-Tsunami Sri Lanka," *Annals of the Association of American Geographers* 97, no. 2, (2007): 361–72; and Neloufer De Mel, "Between the War and the Sea: Critical Events, Contiguities, and Feminist Work in Sri Lanka," *Interventions* 9, no. 2 (July 2007): 238–54.

9. Hyndman, "The Securitization of Fear in Post-Tsunami Sri Lanka," 361–72.

10. See Jonathan Goodhand et al., "Social Capital and the Political Economy of Violence: A Case Study of Sri Lanka," *Disasters* 24, no. 4, (December 2000): 390–406; Benedikt Korf, "War, Livelihoods, and Vulnerability in Sri Lanka," *Development and Change* 35, no. 2 (April 2004): 275–95; and M. Sarvananthan, *Economy of the Conflict Region in Sri Lanka: From Economic Embargo to Economic Repression*, Policy Study Series (Washington, D.C.: East-West Centre, 2007).

11. Dennis McGilvray, "Mukkuvar Vannimai: Tamil Caste and Matriclan Ideology in Batticaloa," in *Caste, Ideology, and Interaction*, ed. D. McGilvray (Cambridge: Cambridge University Press, 1982), 34–97; and Dennis McGilvray, "Households in Akkaraipattu: Dowry and Domestic Organization among Matrilineal Tamils and Moors of Sri Lanka," in *Society from the Inside Out: Anthropological Perspectives on the South Asian Household*, ed. J. N. Gray and D. J. Mearns (London: Sage Publications, 1989), 192–235.

12. David Dunham and Sisira Jayasuriya, "Equity, Growth, and Insurrection: Liberalization and the Welfare Debate in Contemporary Sri Lanka," *Oxford Development Studies* 28, no. 1 (February 2000): 97–110.

13. Dunham and Jayasuriya, "Equity, Growth, and Insurrection," 97–110; Goodhand et al., "Social Capital and the Political Economy of Violence," 390–406; and Jayadeva Uyangoda, "Ethnic Conflict, the State, and the Tsunami Disaster in Sri Lanka," *Inter-Asia Cultural Studies* 6, no. 3 (September 2005): 341–52.

14. Jayadeva Uyangoda, *Ethnic Conflict in Sri Lanka: Changing Dynamics*, Policy Studies Series 32 (Washington, D.C.: East-West Centre, 2007).

15. Jane Humphries, "Gender Inequality and Economic Development," in *Economics in a Changing World, Volume 3: Public Policy and Economic Organization*, ed. D. Bos (New York: St. Martins Press, 1993), 218–33; and UNDP, *Human Development Report, 2001* (Oxford: Oxford University Press, 2001).

16. Goodhand et al., "Social Capital and the Political Economy of Violence"; and Mark Pelling, "Natural Disasters?" in *Social Nature: Theory, Practice, and Politics*, ed. Noel Castree and Bruce Braun (Blackwell: Oxford, 2001), 170–88.

17. Department of Census and Statistics, *Final Report—Census on the Buildings and People Affected by the Tsunami Disaster—2004*, http://www.statistics.gov.lk/ Tsunami/ (accessed April 25, 2007).

18. Goodhand et al., "Social Capital and the Political Economy of Violence"; and Pradeep Jeganathan,"Philanthropy after the Tsunami," *Lines-Magazine*, February 2005, http://www.lines-magazine.org/Art_Feb05/Pradeep.htm (accessed August 22, 2007).

19. Jonathan Rigg, Lisa Law, May Tan-Mullins, and Carl Grundy-Warr, "The Indian Ocean Tsunami: Socio-Economic Impacts in Thailand," *The Geographical Journal* 171, no. 4 (2005): 374–79.

20. Uyangoda, "Ethnic Conflict, the State and the Tsunami Disaster in Sri Lanka," 341–52; Telford and Cosgrove, "The International Humanitarian System and the 2004 Indian Ocean Earthquake and the Tsunamis," 1–28; Hyndman, "The Securitization of Fear in Post-Tsunami Sri Lanka"; and de Mel, "Between the War and the Sea."

21. Uyangoda, "Ethnic Conflict, the State, and the Tsunami Disaster in Sri Lanka," 343.

22. Kanchana N. Ruwanpura, "Awareness and Action: The Ethno-Gender Dynamics of Sri Lankan NGOs," *Gender, Place, and Culture* 14, no. 3 (June 2007): 317–33. See also Fothergill et al., "Race, Ethnicity, and Disasters in the United States," 156–73, and Wade Rathke and Beulah Laboistrie, "The Role of Local Organizing: House-to-House with Boots on the Ground," in *There Is No Such Thing as a Natural Disaster*, ed. C. Hartman and G. D. Squires (London and New York: Routledge, 2007), 255–70, for similar experiences in the United States.

23. Telford and Cosgrove, "The International Humanitarian System and the 2004 Indian Ocean Earthquake and the Tsunamis," 21.

24. Goodhand et al., "Social Capital and the Political Economy of Violence," 404.

25. Uyangoda, "Ethnic Conflict, the State and the Tsunami Disaster in Sri Lanka," 341–52; and Hyndman, "The Securitization of Fear in Post-Tsunami Sri Lanka."

26. Telford and Cosgrove, "The International Humanitarian System and the 2004 Indian Ocean Earthquake and the Tsunamis," 18.

27. Hyndman, "The Securitization of Fear in Post-Tsunami Sri Lanka," 366.

28. Fothergill et al., "Race, Ethnicity, and Disasters in the United States," 167.

29. MacAskill, "Summertime—And after Katrina, Life Still Isn't Easy," *The Guardian*, August 29, 2007, http://www.guardian.co.uk/katrina/story/0,,2157829,00.html (accessed on August 29, 2007).

30. Telford and Cosgrove, "The International Humanitarian System and the 2004 Indian Ocean Earthquake and the Tsunamis," 2.

31. Ibid., 17–18.

32. de Mel and Ruwanpura, *Gendering the Tsunami: A Report of Women's Experiences*; and de Mel, "Between the War and the Sea."

33. See also Jeganathan, "Philanthropy after the Tsunami."

34. Hyndman, "The Securitization of Fear in Post-Tsunami Sri Lanka," 365.

35. Sunil Bastion, "Limits of Aid," *Polity* 2, no. 3 (2005): 21–23; Rajan Phillips, "After the Tsunami," *Polity* 2, no. 3 (2005): 8–9; and N. Shanmugaratnam, "Tsunami Victims' Perceptions of the Buffer Zones," *Polity* 2, no. 4 (2005): 13–15.

36. See Ahilan Kadirgamar, "ISGA and Economic Democracy," *Lines-Magazine*, November 2003; http://www.lines-magazine.org/Art_Nov03/Editorial_Ahilan. htm (accessed September 1, 2007). LTTE's appropriation of neoliberal forces and policies is shown to hold in recent years in the manner in which labor rights were ignored in a general cross-country strike initiated by health care workers. The health care workers, across multiethnic groupings, challenged neoliberal measures that would have affected the health care sector as well as the extreme anomalies in salaries and wages between physicians and health care workers. Kadirgamar ("ISGA and Economic Democracy,") points out how the LTTE not only did not back the workers on this strike but also openly backed the government for its pro-neoliberal stance. The ways in which the policies of the LTTE, which purportedly works for the "oppressed" people, dovetails with hegemonic economic policies propounded by the Sri Lankan state is a telling illustration of the lack of radical economic democracy initiatives being part of its political mantle.

37. Ibid.

38. Vasuki Nesiah, "The Political Economy of Tourism: Reconstructing New Vistas for the Tourist Gaze," *Lines-Magazine*, February 2005; http://www. lines-magazine.org/Art_Feb05/Editorial_Vasuki.htm (accessed August 22, 2007).

39. See also Vasuki Nesiah, "Fisherfolk Out, Tourists In," *Dollars & Sense* July/August 2005; http://www.dollarsandsense.org/archives/2005/0705nesiah.html (accessed September 2, 2007).

40. Telford and Cosgrove, "The International Humanitarian System and the 2004 Indian Ocean Earthquake and the Tsunamis," 22.

41. The late Newton Gunasinghe traced the impact of the open economy on ethnic relations in Sri Lanka, pointing to how the ethnic program against Colombo-based Tamils in 1983 had much to do with rapidly changing economic structures that worked against the Sinhala working classes. He points out how their economic dissonance found an easy expression against a minority community (Tamils), where there were a notable number of burgeoning industrial capitalist in the immediate post-1977 period. This displacement of economic grievances by the working classes was easily manipulated by some politicians in the ruling party toward Tamils rather than against the upper-classes—since the latter would be to acknowledge their own complicit role in creating a class war (Newton Gunasinghe, "The Open Economy and Its Impact on Ethnic Relations," in *Economy, Culture, and Civil War in Sri Lanka,* ed. Deborah Winslow and Michael Woost [Bloomington: Indiana University Press, 2001], 99–114 [initially published in 1985]).

42. Vasuki Nesiah, "Fisherfolk Out, Tourists In."

43. See also de Mel and Ruwanpura, *Gendering the Tsunami: A Report of Women's Experience.*

· IV ·

Inequality

CHAPTER 10

How Shall We Remember New Orleans?

Comparing News Coverage of Post-Katrina New Orleans and the 2008 Midwest Floods

Linda Robertson

M ANY OF AMERICA'S most influential television journalists vowed to take from their experience in New Orleans a commitment to covering issues related to race and poverty in America. The massive flooding during June and July 2008 in the Midwestern states of Illinois, Indiana, Iowa, Michigan, Minnesota, Missouri, and Wisconsin provided an opportunity to act on that commitment because the natural disaster revealed an underlying—and underreported—economic exigency, just as it had in New Orleans. But while right-wing talk radio hosts compared what happened in New Orleans to the flooding in the Midwest, as did television comedians, no comparison based on either race or socioeconomic conditions was offered by the major television cable and network news outlets—ABC, CBS, NBC, and CNN. (FOX network is excluded because it rarely sends correspondents to cover news stories.) The failure of mainstream news to report the nexus of natural disaster with economic hardship in the Midwest made it possible for right-wing talk radio and other similarly ideologically driven outlets to deploy the myth that the predominantly African American population trapped in New Orleans were victims of their own "mentality of dependence" fostered by a welfare society, while the predominantly white population of the Midwest signified the virtues instilled by rugged individualism and self-reliance as they filled their sandbags and braced for the worst.

How the coverage by the mainstream press opened the way for this invidious comparison will be presented in four sections: (1) an explanation of what is meant by "framing" in news analysis; (2) an analysis of the two journalistic narratives—semantic conventions and experiential reporting—used to construct the memory of the flooding in New Orleans[1]; (3) a discussion of how and in what ways the Midwest floods can be compared with what happened in New Orleans; and (4) an exploration of how commentators compared post-Katrina New Orleans with the Midwest floods. This analysis will conclude with an argument that the reasons why mainstream television news failed to compare New Orleans with the Midwest floods have serious implications for how Americans understand the country's social and economic condition.

Framing the News and Breaking the Frame

Simply defined, a news frame is the equivalent of a genre in literature or film; that is, it draws upon persistent or well-known patterns of what media critic Todd Gitlin calls "selection, emphasis, and exclusion."[2] Said another way, it provides recognized organizing principles for the presentation and interpretation of events. News framing entails not only—or even especially—the individual reporter but is a consequence of news production; that is, it reflects the practices of a news organization, including its owners but particularly the editors.[3] The typical frame for a natural disaster can be summarized as human ingenuity / expertise / civil authority confronts the danger of nature unleashed and restores order.

Television news coverage gave the nation two ways to remember what happened in New Orleans between August 29, 2005, when the levees gave way, and September 4, 2005, when the evacuation of the Superdome and Convention Center was completed. One journalistic narrative relied upon semantic conventions for covering disasters in urban areas. "Semantic convention" is used here to mean how stories are typically scripted within a generic frame and refers to both the visuals and the words used to explain them. The semantic conventions applicable to the flooding of a major city include covering (1) the rescue and recovery efforts of government agencies, (2) the protection of and losses to private property, and (3) law enforcement efforts to ensure order. The semantic conventions used in reporting what happened in New Orleans included the inappropriate use of "looting" to describe the efforts of those trapped in the city to provision themselves.[4] In addition, there was a spate of alarmist reports of murder, rape, gun violence, and what Matthew Power, a contributing editor to *Harper's*, called "shades of racial hysteria."[5] Later, journalists would acknowledge with considerable chagrin that these reports were based upon unsubstantiated rumors and were either untrue or grossly exaggerated. In other words, the first narrative relied upon either the thoughtless application of semantic conventions to what reporters witnessed or repeating rumors that seemed to support them.

In sharp contrast, the second journalistic narrative was experiential; that is, it was based upon not only what the journalists witnessed but also their emotional connection to it, particularly the desire for mercy toward suffering human beings. This break with semantic convention was prompted by the failure of government agencies to comply with the anticipated frame: officials failed to respond to the natural catastrophe while those trapped without aid died from the extreme conditions. The experiential narrative promised to teach Americans the need for civil society and public provisioning as necessary to ameliorate the predations of poverty, inequality, neglect, and corruption.

Semantic Conventions: New Orleans and the "Looters"

The coverage of "looters" in flooded New Orleans illustrates how news reports are produced from generic frames and semantic conventions. The allegation of racial bias in the coverage was brought to widespread public attention because of two pictures that circulated on the Internet within a day of the flooding. *Yahoo! News* uploads photographs from a variety of news agencies, usually with the original captions. Someone spied two photographs and their captions, placed them together, and uploaded the new image to Flickr—another Yahoo! service that allows users to upload and access photographs. The first picture has the caption: "Associated Press (AP) Tuesday, August 30, 11:31 AM ET: Young man walks through chest deep flood water after looting a grocery store in New Orleans on Tuesday, Aug. 30, 2005."[6] The second picture was taken the same day and distributed by Agence France-Press (AFP)[7]: "Two residents wade through chest-deep water after finding bread and soda from a local grocery store after Hurricane Katrina came through the area in New Orleans, Louisiana." This image of the two photographs was quickly transmitted by numerous bloggers, along with accusations of press bias: "White People 'Find,' Black People 'Loot'?" was the accusatory headline attached to it by many bloggers.[8]

The two pictures were taken by two different photographers for two different news agencies at two different locations in New Orleans in the morning and afternoon following the collapse of the levees. At that time, there were no services available for those who had been trapped in the flood: no provisions for food, water, or medical assistance except for the limited and inadequate provisions at the Superdome. The first photographer, Jack Martin, worked for the AP and was following the scripted guidelines for reporting what happens after a natural disaster. He saw the young man in the picture go into an empty store and come out again with goods from the store. Martin did not interview the young man. According to editorial guidelines, the appropriate label for what Martin saw is "looting." It was a semantic meaning, applied without reference to the actual circumstances faced by those caught in the floodwaters of Katrina.[9]

Chris Graythen took the picture of the two white people for Getty Images. Graythen, who lives in New Orleans, reacted passionately to the controversy over his caption in a posting to SportsShooter.com (he is a sports photographer for Getty Images):

> Jeasus [sic], I don't belive [sic] how much crap I'm getting from this. . . . I have not seen my wife in 5 days, and my parents and grand parents HAVE LOST THIER [sic] HOMES. As of right now, we have almost NOTHING. . . . I wrote the caption about the two people who "found" the items. I believed in my opinion, that they did simply find them, and not "looted" them in the definition of the word. The people were swimming in chest deep water, and there were other people in the water, both white and black. I looked for the best picture. There were a million items floating in the water. . . . These people were not ducking into a store and busting down windows to get electronics. They picked up bread and cokes that were floating in the water. . . . I spent 4 hours on a boat in my parent's neighborhood shooting [photographs], and rescuing people, both black and white, dog and cat. I am a journalist, and a human being—and I see all as such. . . . Please, please don't argue symantics [sic] over this one. This is EXTREMELY serious, and I can't even begin to convey to those not here what it is like. . . . Thank you all—Chris Graythen.[10]

The caption attached to Graythen's photograph may reflect differences in the editorial standards of AFP compared with the AP. The facts about the captions ultimately have had little or nothing to do with how they are remembered. The notorious pictures continue to be characterized as examples of racism by those who insist the pictures represent a latent cultural racism even if journalists deny it.[11] Even worse, Graythen's recognition that people taking food in order to survive does not constitute "looting" failed to influence the captioning of other pictures. There is a Kafkaesque absurdity to insisting upon applying the semantic meaning "looters" to people who have no food, water, or provisions for their babies (such as diapers) and who are compelled to take food from stores without refrigeration and are chest deep in water. The food in those stores would never be sold and would have to be written off by the owners.

The absurdity of sticking to the conventional use of the term "looting" under the circumstances cannot be overemphasized.[12] Tens of thousands of people awoke on August 29, 2005, to find themselves trapped in a flooded city with no way out. Approximately 80 percent of New Orleans—a city of just under half a million people—was flooded. There was no available water, food, electricity, communications, sewage treatment, or transportation; medical care was scarce because hospitals flooded or were forced to evacuate. Many police and firemen had already left New Orleans with their families. There was a nearly complete breakdown in civil authority at the local level, ineffective support at the state level, and a very slow response from the federal government. The majority of residents in New Orleans who had their own transportation evacuated the city before the flooding, but plans made by officials of the City of New Orleans to evacuate those without transportation by bus and train were never acted upon. The majority of those without their own transportation lived in the part of the city hardest-hit by the flooding. More than sixty thousand people were stranded in New Orleans, many in their homes. Just over half of these—thirty-three thousand—were rescued by the Coast Guard.

The only passable highway out of New Orleans was the Crescent City Connection, which linked to United States Highway 90. Initially, police permitted sixty thousand evacuees to cross over to what is called locally the Westbank, where they were shuttled by buses to safe locations. But in the days following the hurricane, local officials established a roadblock, preventing anyone from crossing over. The explanations ranged from the concern that relief supplies had been exhausted to the reaction following the looting and burning of a major shopping mall in Oakwood Center. The damage was blamed on evacuees from New Orleans. Police at the road-block threatened to shoot anyone who attempted to cross through.

One picture exemplifies the downright cruelty and indifference required to maintain this semantic meaning of "looters." Caught in the lens of a photojournalist is a policeman man-handling a man who has just come out of store. Both the policeman and the man are ankle deep in water. The policeman has torn the man's shirt almost off his body. Floating in the water are what look to be three ice cream bars, which was what the man had evidently "looted." The caption employed a cruel wit: "In New Orleans, police flush out looters on Canal Street on Tuesday as flood waters continue to rise." Who would you have to be to write such a snide comment? What does sniggering at such a caption make of those who read it?

On September 1, 2005, the State of Louisiana declared war on the survivors in New Orleans. Three hundred Arkansas National Guard arrived in New Orleans with orders from Louisiana Governor Kathleen Babineaux Blanco to "shoot to kill."

> These troops are fresh back from Iraq, well trained, experienced, battle-tested and under my orders to restore order in the streets. They have M-16s and they are locked and loaded. These troops know how to shoot and kill and they are more than willing to do so if necessary and I expect they will.[13]

The governor oversaw an influx of a small army composed of off-duty law enforcement officers and armed mercenaries (privately contracted) in addition to the National Guard. The extent to which the reporting of widespread looting contributed to this extreme decision will probably never be fully determined. Numerous alarmist reports by news outlets ignored the reality that a significant number of "looters" were trying to survive.[14]

On the other hand, pre-Katrina New Orleans had been the homicide capital of America and many neighborhoods were regular battlegrounds for extremely well-armed gangs.[15] Not surprisingly, the criminal element took advantage of the lack of civil authority after the flooding. Pre-Katrina New Orleans had also been plagued by a corrupt police force. In a number of instances, police officers were accused of looting electronics and other high-end goods after the levees broke.[16] In addition, there were tens of thousands of very desperate people trying to survive in New Orleans. Major news agencies—CNN and NBC, for instance—moved their headquarters out of New Orleans because of the reports of armed gangs shooting at the police. Reporters with cars feared carjacking by those desperate to get out of the city and believed it was unsafe to take water and food into the streets.[17] The problem with the coverage was the tendency to make the victims the cause of the danger without acknowledging that the failure of civic authority created the opportunities for both criminals and corrupt police to act with impunity. And, the extreme conditions caused by the breakdown in civil authority drove others to desperation.

The Experiential Narrative: One Bright and Shining Moment

In the crucial days from August 29, 2005, when the levees gave way, until September 1, 2005, when the evacuation of the Superdome and the Convention Center began, journalists rebelled against the disconnect between the official words used to describe the efforts being made to assist the victims of Katrina (the semantic version) and what the journalists could see was happening (experiential meaning). Between August 29, 2005, and September 1, 2005, the people of New Orleans lacked any officially organized response to their plight, with the exception of the rescue operations by the Coast Guard. On September 1, 2005, Anderson Cooper fought back tears as he called out Louisiana Senator Mary Landrieu for her cheerful appreciation of all the heartfelt concern expressed by other politicians and President Bush:

> I have to tell you, there are people here who are very upset and angry, and when they hear politicians thanking one another, it just, you know, it cuts them the wrong way right now, because there was a body on the streets of this town yesterday being eaten by rats because this woman has been laying in the street for 48 hours. . . . There are people that want answers, and people want someone to stand up and say: we should have done more.[18]

Cooper could not bring himself to go so far off script as to substitute "I" for the indirect "there are people," but that is clearly what he meant.

Rather than waiting for officials to provide them with the news, reporters discovered they had to tell officials what they did not know, but ought to have known, about the conditions on the ground in New Orleans. On September 1, 2005, NPR's Robert Siegel informed Homeland Security Chief Michael Chertoff that there were several thousand people trapped at the Convention Center without food or water. Chertoff responded that the press should not listen to rumors. Immediately following the interview, Siegel interviewed John Burnett, NPR reporter in New Orleans, who reported that four people had died of conditions at the center. He contradicted Chertoff's assurances that people were being told to go to "staging areas" to receive food and water by reporting that people had been told to go to the Convention Center because it was a staging area [it wasn't]. Later that day, Chertoff contacted NPR to say that supplies would be sent to the Convention Center.[19] On September 2, CNN's Soledad O'Brien challenged Federal Emergency Management Agency (FEMA) Director Michael Brown for not realizing people were trapped at the Convention Center. Since CNN had been covering the story, including National Guard reports that fifty thousand people were trapped there, O'Brien asked: "How is it possible that we're getting better intel [intelligence] than you're getting." Brown admitted he heard about the conditions in the Convention Center from listening to news reports. Finally frustrated beyond usual journalistic restraint, O'Brien challenged Brown: "Do you look at the pictures that are coming out of New Orleans? . . . And do you say, I'm proud of the job that FEMA is doing on the ground there in a tough situation? . . . Or do you look at these pictures and you say, this is a mess and we've dropped the ball; we didn't do what we should have done?"[20]

Of all the television journalists, it was Brian Williams who won the most accolades for his coverage: four Edward R. Murrow Awards, his fifth Emmy Award, the duPont-Columbia University Award, and the George Foster Peabody Award. He spent the night of the hurricane in the Superdome and stayed in New Orleans to cover the aftermath. In a thirty-minute retrospective documentary, Williams reflected on his response:

I kept putting myself in their [the survivors in New Orleans] place. It's part of who I am and I can't help it. I've been married for 20 years. I'm a father of two kids. And I'm enough of an idealist to believe that string of presidents I've grown up with telling me that we're all of equal value, that if you take my two kids and their two counterparts in a family of color in New Orleans, that those children have the same worth, the same value.

And, it's gonna take a long time to shake one of the lessons of this story, which was that I didn't see that there. I didn't see people of equal value. Starting with the treatment of the people in the Superdome.[21]

What the conditions in New Orleans meant to Brian Williams was simply that the value of human life was degraded. The premise that human life is intrinsically and equally valuable poses the fundamental challenge to neoliberal economic policies. His explanation merges semantic memory (the foundational values of American democracy) and experiential memory (he is a husband and father) along with the emotional connectives that are inherent in experiential meanings; that is, he could see himself and his family in the faces of those suffering around him:

> The point of Katrina is that because of a natural disaster, one, and because of the government response, or lack of it, two, human behavior degraded in New Orleans that day. . . . I remember seeing wild eyes that day. Desperation. The inability to feed yourself or your family. Really, the common sense which gets clicked off. And, we don't become recognizable to ourselves or our families anymore.[22]

For Williams and his team of reporters, September 1, 2005—the day reporters realized that FEMA officials did not know there were people trapped at the Convention Center—was the breaking point, the day when reporters became outraged and showed it.

> We beat the first responders to Hurricane Katrina. That made us witnesses. And that gave us license to come at these government officials who were in the other side of that screen, the split-screen America we lived through for a week there, who were saying, "You know what? Everything's fine."[23]

The split-screen technique projected rolling video of the horrors taking place in New Orleans on one side of the picture while showing an interview with a government leader responsible for providing assistance on the other side.

Many media critics lamented how short-lived was the departure from usual journalistic practice. Matthew Power, a contributing editor to *Harper's*, approved of the "call for justice" in the reporting during the time when New Orleans was abandoned to its fate. But "the brief reanimation of journalistic responsibility could not last: they would not stay off-script for long." Soon, "broadcast news returned to its default setting as the pornography of disaster." Merrill Morris, who teaches journalism and mass communication theory at George State University, also saw a hopeful opportunity that the realities New Orleans would force journalists to abandon their conventional narratives: "To report on the poor, the press chooses from a narrow range of proven narratives about drug addicts, welfare mothers, or heroes in the projects standing up to criminals." But rather than focus on the issues of race and class, which the tragedy revealed all too plainly, journalists turned to a familiar narrative: bureaucratic ineptitude. "The moment for the media to look at race and class, to change the old narratives, the familiar stories of heroes and villains . . . had passed."[24]

Critics and journalists alike have vowed to change the old narrative, to use what posthurricane New Orleans revealed to begin a serious examination of a national issue: race and class in America. David Kurpius, the associate dean at the Manship School of Mass Communication at Louisiana State University, is among those who lamented the "lopsided" focus on race. But he felt it was positive that the issue of poverty came to the forefront. "My fear is that journalists in particular and viewers and readers are only going to pay attention to it for this brief moment, and then the story fades away. And that is unethical."[25] The "it" is not only the disparity of incomes in New Orleans, but race and class inequalities in major American cities. As Brian Williams said: "If we come out of all this crisis and in the next couple of years don't have a national conversation on the following issues: race, class, petroleum, the environment, then we the news media will have failed by not keeping people's feet to the fire."

Comparing the Forces of Nature with Recovery Effort

The opportunity to apply this resolve presented itself with the record-breaking flooding in the Midwest. While the natural causes and consequences of the two disasters were very different, a comparison of the recovery efforts reveals how much more efficient local, state, and federal agencies were in the Midwest than they were in New Orleans—and to a great extent, because of the lessons learned from New Orleans. Most significantly, remarkable similarities emerge from a comparison of the preflood socioeconomic conditions. As with New Orleans, the crisis precipitated by a natural disaster reveals a yawning gap between the "haves" and "have nots" in America's heartland that is just as troubling as the poverty afflicting New Orleans. This aspect of the flooding in the Midwest was not covered by the national, mainstream press nor were comparisons made with New Orleans or the Gulf Coast in general. To see why this omission is important, the points of possible comparison need to be understood.

Comparing the Forces of Nature

According to the National Hurricane Center, Hurricane Katrina was one of the five deadliest hurricanes in the history of the United States, and it was by far the costliest. Although it caused extensive damage as far as one hundred miles from the storm's epicenter, the greatest concentrated loss of life and property damage occurred in New Orleans, because the levees protecting the city gave away under the force of the waves and the wind and the city is below sea level. Estimates range from 1,577 to 1,836 killed as a direct consequence of the storm in all areas of the Gulf Region. Over 1,464 deaths were from Louisiana; 828 bodies were recovered from the floodwaters of New Orleans.[26]

How do the conditions in New Orleans compare with the June floods in the Midwest? First and most obviously, the flooding in the Midwest did not come as the result of a massive hurricane; rather, there were widespread rainstorms equal to the worst nonhurricane precipitation since recordkeeping began in 1895 along an extensive watershed of numerous rivers. For the most part, it was possible to predict when rivers would crest and residents could evacuate to higher ground. No city of the size of New Orleans was flooded or left without services to the extent that New Orleans was — and, of course, no city along the affected rivers is below sea level, either. Because residents were alerted to the coming high waters, and because the areas were generally rural rather than urban, there were no large concentrations of evacuees in shelters. The total number of displaced people in all of the flooded areas — thirty-five thousand to forty thousand — is far less than even the numbers of people trapped in New Orleans and seems small in comparison with those displaced throughout the Gulf by Hurricane Katrina, ranging from several hundred thousand to a million people. Estimates of the loss of crops in the Midwest due to the flooding are substantial: $7 billion. The United States Department of Agriculture estimated crop losses due to Hurricane Katrina at $900 million.[27] These comparisons are not offered to diminish the loss and suffering in the Midwest states in June 2008. They are intended to point out the difficulty of comparing the flooding with the effects of Hurricane Katrina on New Orleans.

Comparing Recovery Efforts

Comparisons can, however, be made of the recovery efforts. Herculean efforts were made by those engaged in rescue operations in New Orleans and those who worked tirelessly to fill sandbags along the rivers of the Midwest. In both instances, people dedicated themselves to helping their communities, often against daunting odds. But there is a stark contrast in the responsiveness of local, state, and federal agencies. In New Orleans, over twenty thousand people crowded into the Superdome, where they encountered increasingly squalid conditions. Although designated as an emergency shelter, government officials had provided the Superdome with only minimal supplies. One portion of the building was set aside for individuals in need of medical care. The stadium section was set aside as a shelter-of-last-resort for able-bodied people, who were told to bring their own food and water. Lacking were any water purification equipment, cots, or sufficient bathrooms. And after Hurricane Katrina hit, the medical supplies proved inadequate. By August 30, the Superdome lacked both power and a water supply, so that sanitary conditions deteriorated to intolerable levels. At the same time, the Superdome began to flood. Both adults and children suffered from dehydration, lack of food, water, and medical supplies. Ten people died in the Superdome as a result of the neglect. Their bodies were left to decay in the heat because there was nothing else to do with them. It was not until September 1 that buses began to arrive to take those suffering in the Superdome to the Reliant Astrodome in Houston, Texas. The evacuation was completed on September 4.

Conditions were even worse at the Convention Center, which had never been intended for use as a shelter and lacked food, water, and electricity. Some officials sent evacuees to the Convention Center as the Superdome filled. Rescue workers dropped people they had rescued at the Convention Center on the understanding that buses were scheduled to pick them up and take them to another facility. No buses came. Eventually, those assembled outside the Convention Center broke into it, with the total population growing to twenty thousand. Four people died in the Convention Center, again with nowhere to put the bodies. The survivors were evacuated at the same time as the stranded people in the Superdome.

In the Midwest, there was no general breakdown in civil authority. In areas affected by the flooding, many families lost all of their food to the flood or because of power failures. In contrast to the conditions that prevailed in New Orleans, state and local governments as well as local charities and food banks provided emergency relief. FEMA was generally acknowledged to have learned a valuable lesson from the agency's slow and ineffective response to the crisis in New Orleans. FEMA was credited with responding quickly and effectively in the Midwest. In early June, FEMA provided 13 million sandbags to shore-up levees, and as the extent of the flooding became clear, delivered 3.6 million liters of water and 192,000 meals ready-to-eat (MREs), as well as supplying emergency generators and trucks to haul away debris. FEMA deployed 650 inspectors and quickly processed 45,000 applications for housing assistance, distributing $81 million in housing assistance funds. Local, state, and elected officials to Congress praised FEMA's responsiveness in comparison with the agency's performance in the aftermath of Hurricane Katrina. The governors of the hardest-hit states asked the Bush Administration to increase the amount of funding available to areas declared federal disaster zones.[28]

Socioeconomic Conditions in the Midwest

But, in some instances, the relief was needed more quickly than it was provided. On June 24 in Milwaukee, 2,500 people stood in line waiting to receive rumored food vouchers to replace food lost in recent floods and power outages. Lines to the Human Services Center began to form at 7:00 a.m. When the door opened at 8:00 a.m., it was torn from its hinges as the crowd surged forward. Charline Britt, age fifty-two, was crushed against a door and trampled on before she passed out. In fact, the agency was only taking applications for vouchers. Upon learning this, Yvonne Love became frustrated, "Now I have to try and get [to] a food pantry. . . . I have to feed my children." Love, who is unemployed, has three children, ages eight, ten, and fourteen. Milwaukee Common Council President Willie Hines said in a statement: "We expect long lines for free food in

Third World countries; we don't expect a line of 2,500 people waiting for food vouchers at the Marcia P. Coggs Center."[29]

Long lines also formed in other states where federal food stamps or food debit cards were provided to the tens of thousands who had lost food to the flooding or from loss of power. But the issue was not only the loss of food to flooding. The additional and salient issue was the poverty in the affected areas. The assistance was made available only to those who qualified—a family of four could have no more than a total monthly income of $2,295 after any storm-related expenses. Despite this income constraint, agencies in Omaha reported "lines stretching for several blocks in all directions" each day for several days. An estimated twenty thousand to thirty thousand Nebraskans from the three most affected counties were expected to apply.

The panic in the food lines in Milwaukee merited only two sentences in various mainstream television news reports. In an unrelated story during the time of the floods in the Midwest, the *New York Times* reported that, according to the U.S. Department of Agriculture (USDA), the cost for a minimally nutritious diet had risen 7.2 percent nationwide in the past year, which is the largest increase since 1989.[30] The television coverage of the floods concentrated on the consequences for the average consumer of the loss of food crops, not the impact on women and children dependent on food stamps.

The demand for emergency food reflected not only the effects of the flood but also the economic decline in the Midwest. The near-panic at the Milwaukee office indicates how the flooding exacerbated the problems of poverty, declining wages, and unemployment plaguing the population before the flood. On August 29, 2005, the U.S. Census Bureau released statistics showing that Wisconsin's poverty rates were rising faster than any other state—almost 2 percentage points in the past two years. Eleven percent of the population was defined as poor, which was the highest rate in the state for over a decade.[31] The Center on Wisconsin Strategy (COWS) at the University of Wisconsin at Madison released an economic report on September 1, 2005; it confirmed the Census Bureau's report. Real median household income fell more than $4,000 in six years. There has been a steady and serious decline in employer-provided health insurance. In the words of the report, "The social contract in Wisconsin is shredding." The report also found that "trends in the economy are felt particularly hard among black Wisconsinites, who have much higher rates of poverty and unemployment than whites, and are clustered in lower paying occupations and among employers with even lower rates of insurance coverage." The alarming reality is: "Wisconsin has done better the past few years than much of the depressed Midwest region," according to UW-professor Joel Rogers, who is the director of COWS.[32] In Nebraska, the unemployment rate according to the 2004 U.S. Census was 10 percent, compared with 12.7 percent nationally. In June 2004, food stamp use in Nebraskan households was at an all-time high, despite improving economic indicators. Milo Mumgaard, executive director of the Nebraska Appleseed Center for Law and the Public Interest, commented: "We don't see it as a lagging indicator. We see it as a revealing indicator, revealing that the economy is not reaching down and boosting the income of those at the bottom."[33] One of the wealthiest men in the world, Warren Buffet, lives in Omaha, Nebraska, which is the location of more Fortune 500 companies (five) than any other U.S. city. Yet, according to a report in the April 15, 2007, *Omaha World-Herald*, Omaha has the third-highest black poverty rate among the hundred largest metropolitan areas in America and the highest percentage of African American children living below the poverty line of any American city. Only one other city, Minneapolis, has a wider income gap between white and African American populations: "Omaha's black poverty figures are even more dismal than those in New Orleans, where the stark plight of poor blacks in the wake of Hurricane Katrina put a spotlight on troubling national issues of poverty and race."[34]

A number of factors contribute to these statistics. A significant percentage of the educated black middle class has left Omaha, while the number of Hispanics—who compete with low-income African Americans for the lower-paying jobs—has surged. Between 1990 and 2000, the Hispanic population grew by 139.9 percent (total Hispanic population 39,735; 5.5 percent of the total population of Omaha). During the same period, the non-Hispanic black population grew 24 percent (total non-Hispanic black population 63,134; 8.8 percent of the total population). In 1999, the poverty rates by race or ethnicity in Omaha were Asian 13.3 percent, black 27.6 percent, Hispanic 16.9 percent, and non-Hispanic white 5.7 percent.

Socioeconomic Conditions in Pre-Katrina New Orleans

There is ample evidence that pre-Katrina New Orleans was a city in decline because of a profound neglect of the public good. The city had the highest homicide rate in the United States, and the majority of those reflected black-on-black crime.[35] The two most vibrant economies in pre-Katrina New Orleans were the illegal drug trade (primarily crack cocaine) and the tourist economy, which provided relatively low-paying jobs in the service sector. Pre-Katrina New Orleans was the most dangerous city in America because of an unchecked, violent drug culture made possible by an ineffective and corrupt police force and an equally corrupt judicial system.[36]

New Orleans has lost more than one-fifth of its population since the 1960s; those who left between 1990 and 2000 were young and educated. One reason was oil-industry consolidation, which took jobs from New Orleans to Texas; but the long-term reason is that investors are turned off not only by the high homicide rate but by the widespread corruption in city government. According to James Bernazzani, head of the FBI office in New Orleans, "Outside companies don't invest because they are sick and tired of the kickbacks." In the summer of 2005, four cronies of the previous mayor—including his uncle—were indicted for public contract abuses. The FBI was also investigating alleged widespread abuses by the school board, while New Orleans schools were generally regarded as failed institutions of learning. [37]

There is no doubt that many people in New Orleans were poor prior to Hurricane Katrina. According to most recent census figures, 12 percent of the population in the United States was poor—20 percent of the total population of Louisiana and 28 percent in New Orleans. But changes in the rules for public assistance have reduced the funding available to all but those in the most extreme poverty. Stated another way, in the United States as a whole at the last census, 87 percent of those living in poverty in the United States received no cash assistance; the figure for Louisiana was 87 percent; and for New Orleans, 90 percent. Far from the stereotype that poor, urban blacks are highly dependent on government subsidies, the fact is that in 2002 only 3.6 percent of the families in New Orleans received cash welfare payments.[38] Many of those counted as poor are working people; the unemployment rate in 2004 was a relatively stable 5.2 percent.

How much different the understanding of America would have been if the news had connected the aftermath of Katrina, the tens of thousands of people who lined up for food vouchers in the Midwest, the socioeconomic decline in both New Orleans and the Midwest states, and the emerging crisis in making sure America's children are fed. But no news outlet offered that comparison.

Who Compared New Orleans and the Midwest Floods—and How?

The mainstream television news networks did not examine what the flooding revealed about the socioeconomic realities of the Midwest. Instead, they reported the floods using a generic frame and semantic conventions (i.e., "Violent Nature vs. Stout-Hearted Individuals" or, more usually, "Violent Nature vs. Private Property Defended by Stout-Hearted Individuals"). Here is one typical example. On June 20, 2008, CNN reported the efforts to shore up a levee at Winfield, Missouri, after one levee had failed. In what follows, it is very easy to imagine the visuals that accompanied this unctuous condescension:

> REYNOLDS WOLF, CNN METEOROLOGIST: I'll tell you, the spirit here still remains really good. See this? This is not the white flag of surrender. This is a sandbag, sandbags they've been filling up here all morning. In fact, we've had millions of these things that have been filled up and down the Mississippi. At this place we've got Lorenzo. Lorenzo's been working like crazy. He's over here with Taylor. Check out Taylor. Taylor is working awfully hard. They both have been working. Everyone has been here putting them together. It's been a community effort filling up these sandbags like this one you see right here. . . . No one's relaxing just yet. And we see Lorenzo. He hasn't stopped. He's been here since early in the morning. The man is a workaholic. So it is a great thing to see.[39]

The reliance on generic frame and semantic conventions opened the door to invidious comparisons with New Orleans, an opportunity seized upon by right-wing talk show hosts. They compared the semantic narratives of New Orleans and the Midwest floods in order to show how much better the Midwest responded to flooding. A particularly virulent comparison came from Rush Limbaugh on his daily radio program (June 17, 2008):

> I look at Iowa, I look at Illinois—I want to see the murders. I want to see the looting. I want to see all the stuff that happened in New Orleans. . . . I see devastation in Iowa and Illinois that dwarfs what happened in New Orleans. I see people working together. I see people trying to save their property. . . . I don't see a bunch of

people running around waving guns at helicopters, I don't see a bunch of people running shooting cops. I don't see a bunch of people raping people on the street. I don't see a bunch of people doing everything they can . . . whining and moaning, "Where's FEMA, where's Bush?" I see the heartland of America. When I look at Iowa and when I look at Illinois, I see the backbone of America.[40]

Rush Limbaugh has twenty million listeners nationally to his weekday radio program and in 2008 signed an eight-year contract for $400 million with Clear Channel Communications. More people tune into his program than to any other radio program in the country, and his listeners are loyal fans, which makes his program highly attractive to advertisers.

Two days later, Neal Boortz on his nationally syndicated radio show offered a similar if even more poisonous comparison:

Why is it that the people who are being affected by the floods in Iowa and the upper Midwest, why is it that they seem to be so much more capable of taking care of themselves and handling this disaster than were the people of Katrina in New Orleans? . . . I think the answer's pretty clear, is that up there in that part of the country, you find a great deal of self-sufficiency. Down there in New Orleans, it was basically a parasite class totally dependent on government for their existence.[41]

Neil Boortz is based in Atlanta, Georgia. His weekday program is syndicated throughout the country on 230 radio stations, with about five million listeners.

Limbaugh and Boortz were echoed by *Tonight Show* host Jay Leno, who dedicated the proceeds from his June 26 Las Vegas performances to the Cedar Rapids Community Foundation. Even as he was raising money for the victims of the floods in Iowa, Leno implied the same deleterious comparisons with New Orleans as did Limbaugh and Boortz: "I don't see anyone in Iowa asking for money. These people are not looking for favors. I don't see anybody whining. I see people working hard, with shovels and brooms trying to clean the places."[42]

The reliance on semantic conventions for disaster coverage allows for the promulgation of stereotypes that link "race" with "dependency" or "lawlessness," a set of stereotypes that favor the economic arguments for mercilessly blaming of the victims not only of natural disasters but of a level of government incompetence that amounted to criminality. The reality hidden by the neoliberal railings against a "culture of dependency" is that the largest percentage of those who died in New Orleans were the elderly—those over sixty—and over half of the casualties were not residents of the poorest neighborhoods. The floodwaters were indifferent to income.[43]

The right-wing message was that the whining, dependent denizens of New Orleans deserved to find themselves in one of the deeper rings of Dante's hell, but Midwesterners can count on finding themselves sitting close to the right hand of God in the heaven that awaits such independent, hard-working individuals. The unstated implication is that the flood victims in New Orleans were black (hence, lazy, dependent, lawless) while those in the Midwest were white (hard-working, independent, individualistic, law-abiding). The deeper implication, however, was the neoliberal mantra: a society lacking in basic social provisioning for the poor produces citizens of stronger virtue or character, with the corollary implication that the poor deserve to be poor because they lack the basic virtues necessary to succeed. These are two tenets essential to neoliberalism, and they are the foundational assumptions not only for right-wing talk radio but also for mainstream conservatism—such as that expressed by the self-satisfied Jay Leno. One of the most influential conservative magazines in the United States—*The National Review*—published an article by John McWhorter in which he offered his Olympian judgment on those trapped by the flood: "What Katrina revealed was the result of one especially unsuccessful attempt to address black poverty: 30 years of teaching poor black people not to work for a living."[44] Similar excuses for allowing people to die in New Orleans using the semantic conventions of "welfare dependency" were echoed in other right-wing partisan magazines and newspaper editorials.[45]

The *Daily Show*'s "fake news" compared the coverage of the flooding in the Midwest with the coverage of the flooding in New Orleans. The segment "Wet Hot American Bummer" (June 18, 2008) played off Kanye West's electrifying condemnation of the coverage of the looting in New Orleans. Rapper West appeared with comedian Mike Myers as part of a celebrity benefit for the Red Cross that aired September 2, 2005, on NBC.

West ignored the script that scrolled on the teleprompter. Instead, he began his personal statement: "I hate the way they portray us in the

media. You see a black family, it says, 'they're looting.' You see a white
family, it says, 'they're looking for food.'" Mike Myers, who was standing next to Kanye West, took his turn and read from the teleprompter
as if nothing out of the ordinary had happened. When it was time for
Kanye to speak again, he said: "George Bush doesn't care about black
people." At that point, the telethon producer, Rick Kaplan, turned
off West's microphone and cut to the befuddled comic Chris Tucker.
Obviously, Kaplan would brook no intrusion of experiential discourse
into a carefully orchestrated evening of semantic narratives for celebrity
charity appeals.[46]

Two *Daily Show* correspondents—Jason Jones and Wyatt Cenac—
stood in windbreakers in front of a flood scene labeled "Live: Quincy,
Illinois." Jones played the persona of both the hapless Mike Myers and the
typical correspondent mouthing platitudes about the victims—reporting
the "devastation," "tragic loss," and "psychological damage." Cenac played
the "Kanye West" qua correspondent role, blurting out: "George Bush
doesn't care about white people."

> JONES (confused and pointing at the teleprompter): That's not
> what you're supposed to say. . . . He's clearly going off script
> here.
> STEWART: Wyatt, we just said the president is heading out to Iowa
> tomorrow.
> CENAC: These people have been under thirty-feet of water for a
> week, and he's finally coming now. . .
> STEWART: The president is in Europe, Wyatt.
> CENAC: So what. What's your point? It took him forever to get to
> Katrina. So what? By being late to Iowa it shows he's equally
> indifferent to the suffering of all people?
> [Applause and cheers]
> JONES (reading from teleprompter): . . . It's been inspiring for
> this reporter to see neighbors helping neighbors, working the
> sandbags, manning the levees, all in a spirit of solidarity and
> humanity.
> CENAC: George Bush doesn't care about wet people.
> JONES: OK. That's enough. You know what, man, we're done here.
> I'm going to go stand on the dry side of the street.[47]

It ruins a joke to explain it. But the satire is so canny here that it begs dwelling upon. Cenac brings to the fore what is implicit in the comments of Limbaugh, Boortz, and other commentators who agree with them: the Midwest is "white." Logically, then, if Bush delays in coming to the Midwest as he did visiting New Orleans, he hates "white people," and if not them, then all "wet" people. This is at once a deliciously barbed thrust at Bush's genial initial indifference to any of the many disasters he faced in office—particularly the catastrophe in New Orleans—and a swipe at those self-satisfied conservatives who think that victims of a disaster ought to figure out how to get out of it on their own.

Intertextuality and News Coverage

The critical term "intertextuality" helps explain how generic framing created the opportunities for the invidious comparisons of the post-Katrina New Orleans with post-flood Midwest. The term refers to the simple reality of communication: what is said is shaped by generic convention, as is what is understood. A reader knows what to expect from a novel purchased today because he or she has read other novels, just as the writer who sits down to write a novel has the idea in mind of the attributes of a novel. What delights the reader is the extent to which the writer either uses those conventions or violates them—but without the generic attributes in mind, that delight in the writer's novelty simply could not occur. Said another way, one has to know what a "kiss" is before one is kissed, or serious misunderstandings can occur.

As a rough generalization, what the public knows about post-Katrina are their recollections of what was shown on television and written about in newspapers. Rush Limbaugh, Neal Boortz, and the other like-minded commentators have made New Orleans stand for all that the neoliberal agenda deplores. Their commentary draws upon the memories of the coverage of New Orleans held in the minds of their listeners or readers, and then construes those memories—or codes them—according to a prior set of references—that is, according to the ideological premises they uphold. No unmediated reality enters into this equation; none of the commentators are required to have actually been to New Orleans in the aftermath of the hurricane in order to assign meaning to what was shown on television.

Sadly, in the United States, being male, black, and poor and residing in a city are coded in some sectors of the population as "dangerous" if unchecked by the police. This is an example of a cultural stereotype that feeds intertextuality. The unfounded reports of New Orleans as in the clutches of murderers, snipers, rapists, and thieves fell on some ears receptive to invidious stereotypes. These failings have been both admitted and criticized by journalists and media critics, and they cannot be repeated too often if they are to be prevented in the future.[48]

But the harm has been done, and those afterimages and the words attached to them remain. They are used by those who promote social and economic division by retailing the memories of New Orleans as if they had not been debunked. Rush Limbaugh has every reason to know that he is promulgating lies in his characterization of what happened in New Orleans. Subsequent reports debunked accounts of anyone firing at a National Guard rescue helicopter ("waving rifles at helicopters," in Limbaugh's words) or of widespread murder or rape in the Superdome. By his repeated use of "bunch of people," Limbaugh reproduces the illusion that the population of New Orleans fell into complete and violent anarchy. He is to be condemned for spreading his racially laced poison in the absence of fact; but journalists have to bear some of the blame for providing commentators of his ilk fodder for their lies. Journalists did, indeed, rely on semantic meanings rather than careful, experiential reportage when faced with the overwhelming visions of human suffering that confronted them in New Orleans.

The major networks inadvertently provided the opportunity for invidious comparisons between the Midwesterners and New Orleans when their reporting of the floods reverted to the semantic convention. By doing so, they reinforced the slant on what happened in New Orleans promoted by right-wing talk show hosts as well as more mainstream conservatives. Right-wing talk shows pointed to the pictures of the sandbag-shoveling Midwesterners as exemplary of determined individualism in contrast to the so-called culture of dependency and crime revealed by the flooding in New Orleans. These commentators who applauded the Midwesterners for not asking for handouts ignored the massive influx of support from FEMA precisely because of the disaster in New Orleans, and they ignored as well the call by the governors of the affected states for emergency funding above and beyond what would usually be allocated.

Missing the Story

Brian Williams spoke for many journalists and academics when he said: "If we come out of all this crisis and in the next couple of years don't have a national conversation on the following issues: race, class, petroleum, the environment, then we the news media will have failed by not keeping people's feet to the fire." These are solemn words and doubtlessly seriously meant. But the *Daily Show* astutely satirized the return to generic frames and the semantic conventions in the coverage of the Midwest floods.

Hurricane Katrina represents the failure of the central tenets of neoliberal orthodoxy: that is, unfettered free-market capitalism cannot address problems of public safety and health; reducing government spending for natural disaster relief makes it impossible for government to step into those areas where the free-market fails—as in the case of the catastrophe that was Katrina. Moreover, the American public evidently learned a lesson from watching the catastrophe unfold on their television screens, and the lesson played at least a supporting role in routing the Republicans from power.[49] Moreover, one of the props for neoliberalism—to blame the poor and create divisions along lines of race and class—failed to keep the Republicans in power as the first African American was elected president by a wide demographic. Thus, the optimistic conclusion might be drawn that democracy works when the public is sufficiently informed about social and economic problems—as it was by the coverage of Hurricane Katrina.

The problem with this assessment is that it ignores the glaring, central factor in the coverage of Hurricane Katrina and the aftermath: it was crisis coverage. All that was visited upon New Orleans by the winds of the hurricane was predicted and the loss of property and the cost in human life and suffering could have been prevented. But the pressures of the twenty-four-hour news cycle on cable news channels, and the cutback in funding for network and newspaper reporters, means that there is less and less coverage of emerging issues as they evolve over time. Said another way, the tragedy that befell those who lived in New Orleans might have been prevented with a different kind of coverage, one that over the years educated the public to the larger policy issues that ought to have been addressed before Hurricane Katrina struck. And equally important, the implications of what happened to New Orleans for the nation as a whole— and particularly what the natural disaster revealed about the conditions of poverty—would have been perceived with a different kind of coverage, one that connected the dots linking the economy of New Orleans with the economy of the Midwest as part of the disaster coverage. Instead, the national economic collapse hit the nation several years after Katrina as if it, too, were a crisis that could not have been predicted or prevented.

Reporting standards have not kept pace with President Obama's call for a new mindset, one which envisions the nation as a whole, and not as distinct regions, as a set of playing chips colored blue or red or as a set of identity groups to be played off, one against the other. One recent post-Katrina story provides an instructive illustration. On March 10, 2009, CBS/AP carried a story about the efforts of Brian Bordainick, a Teach for America volunteer at George Washington Carver High School in the Ninth Ward of New Orleans. Bordainick, twenty-three, who is a remedial teacher and the athletic director, set out to raise $1.8 million to build a football stadium and Olympic-quality track to replace sports facilities destroyed by Hurricane Katrina. The story focused on his efforts, and the grant awarded in March by the National Football League, which put the school well on the way to meeting its goal.

The story was presented by CBS News correspondent Bill Whitaker, who covered the immediate post-Katrina effects on the Mississippi gulf. He later acknowledged that the assignment was essentially a "feel good" story about post-Katrina New Orleans. Returning to the area for the first time since 2005, he anticipated that much of New Orleans would be restored. He was shocked by what he found in the Ninth Ward. The 531 students who attend George Washington Carver are less than half the number of pre-Katrina enrollments (1,200). The mostly poor and African American students attend school in prefabricated buildings; many of them were homeless after Katrina, and a number have missed up to two years of schooling as a result of their displacement.[50]

The CBS News editors did not think that there would be a national audience for news about policies which serve to bar the poor from returning to their homes in New Orleans because that is a "regional" issue. But they did think that the story about essentially private sources funding an athletic facility would interest a national audience, and particularly the grant from the NFL.[51] The reasoning is not far to seek if the intertextuality of generic frames is taken into account. After all, the story tied in sports, volunteerism, and private enterprise with helping the young, black, male, and poor in New Orleans. The story had all the elements of neoliberalism with the implied message that the power of the market can address all needs. Who needs taxes or urban planning with this winning combination of volun-teerism and donations? The story carried the message of individual self-improvement despite overwhelming odds. Marshall Faulk, a former National Football League star and a graduate of George Washington Carver, extolled the power of sports to overcome the limitations of poverty: "My coach got me off the street and taught me to believe in myself. That's what football can do in a school where kids don't have a lot of other things." In this instance, the "a lot of other things" includes permanent classrooms.

Bill Whitaker was shocked by the devastation he saw all around him when he visited the Ninth Ward in March 2009. While the CBS story did not reveal the extent of the damage, this writer can attest to the devasta-tion of the Ninth Ward. From the air, it looked at that time as if a gap-ing giant's mouth had all but a few of his teeth knocked out. Block after block of leveled houses and empty lots are punctuated by a few houses, here and there, rendered uninhabitable by the floods. On the ground, the most immediate comparison is with a bombed-out district. While Whitaker's report referenced these issues, they were not developed; nor was the implication that the school had to rely on a young, white male volunteer from New York to teach and coach.

In *The Predator State: How Conservatives Abandoned the Free Market and Why Liberals Should Too*, James K. Galbraith challenges liberals to stop acting as if the conservative ideology still drives politics in the United States:

> Hurricane Katrina stripped away the illusion that the federal government retains the capacity to move quickly to serve the needs of ordinary citizens in a time of crisis and peril. Katrina illustrates exactly what to expect in the event of further natural disaster or cataclysmic attack. But where, again, is the liberal political organiza-tion that places this issue at the center of a program? Nor have we yet come to grips with the growing crisis in housing and housing finance: a crisis that . . . is generating foreclosure notices every month nearly equal to the numbers displaced by Katrina.[52]

Galbraith argues that those newly in power need to take these issues on in a way that does not simply tinker with the superficial symptoms but takes on the systemic weaknesses of neoliberal capitalism. Because liberals are still reacting to the perceived power of neoliberalism (which has been abandoned by all but the most virulent defenders on the right), they are paralyzed, trapped in a "stasis of the liberal mind," and as a result, "new economic issues emerging under the influence of pressing events are dangerously underexamined."[53]

The problem of politicians underexamining key issues of importance to the nation is exacerbated by the dominance of coverage that is driven by the appetite for "crisis" news rather than coverage of emerging stories or following up on important stories. It is also driven by the reality that a significant percentage of mainstream news frames are reactionary to the semantics of the right; for example, how Supreme Court nominee Sonia Sotomayor was understood was constructed out of a reaction to the allegations from the right that she is a "racist." This charge is based upon the intentional misconstruction of a sentence taken out of context in a speech she gave. It is easy for an editor to assign a news anchor to construct a reactionary frame from inflammatory rhetoric and call it "news": just invite one "right-wing" guest and one "left-wing" guest to state their views. This is much easier, cheaper, and potentially more entertaining than assigning a knowledgeable reporter to provide a considered assessment of Sotomayor's judicial record on the appeals court. The ease of putting together that kind of story is made all the more necessary because of the cuts in budgets for reporters, the reduction in the number of permanent network press bureaus in our major cities, and the editorial blinders that fail to identify issues that ought to define us as a nation—the notion that the failure to rebuild the infrastructure of New Orleans is a "regional" story, but the NFL making a charitable contribution to a football stadium at a New Orleans school is worthy of national attention.

While there may be those who understand the lesson of Katrina as discrediting neoliberalism because it tragically revealed its flaws, the reality is that the news coverage only briefly broke from its generic frames and semantic conventions to challenge the failures of a particular administration at a particular time and in a particular place. While that breakout moment undoubtedly saved many lives and contributed to the Republican fall from the power, the conventions of news coverage—particularly television news—have not undergone the paradigm shift that a deeper examination of our moment in history requires.

Notes

1. The particular use of the terms "semantic convention" and "experiential meaning" was suggested to me by my reading of Umberto Eco, *The Mysterious Flame of Queen Loana,* trans. Geoffrey Brock (Boston: Houghton Mifflin Harcourt, 2005).

2. Todd Gitlin, *The Whole World Is Watching* (Berkeley: University of California Press, 1980).

3. Claes H. de Vrees, "News Framing: Theory and Typology," *Information Design Journal + Document Design* 13, no. 1 (2005): 51–62.

4. Kathleen Tierney, Christine Bevic, and Erica Kuligowsky, "Metaphors Matter: Disaster Myths, Media Frames, and Their Consequences in Hurricane Katrina," *The Annals of the American Academy of Political and Social Science* 604 (March 2006): 57–58.

5. Matthew Power, "Immersion Journalism," *Harper's Magazine,* December 2005, 73.

6. The AP is a cooperative news service. Newspapers as well as television and radio news sources own AP and contribute news stories and photographs to it; each of the 1,700 contributors can use any of the reports or photographs. Other news outlets can purchase reports and images for a fee.

7. AFP is the oldest news service in the world. While its primary client is the French government, AFP provides photographs and news stories to news agencies throughout the world.

8. Xeni Jardin, "Black People Loot, White People Find?" *Boing Boing,* August 30, 2005, http://boingboing.net/2005/08/30/black_people_loot_wh.html; Aaron Kinney, "'Looting' or 'Finding'?" *Salon.com,* September 1, 2005, http://www.salon.com/news/feature/2005/09/01/photo_controversy; and T. Armstrong, "In New Orleans White People 'Find,' Black People 'Loot,'" *HungryBlues,* September 1, 2005, http://minorjive.typepad.com/hungryblues.

9. Tania Ralli, "Who's a Looter? In Storm's Aftermath, Pictures Kick Up a Different Kind of Tempest," *New York Times,* sec. C, September 5, 2005, late edition–final edition.

10. Chris Graythen, "Finding vs. Looting (word choice in AP caption)," *Sports Shooter.com,* August 31, 2005, http://www.sportsshooter.com/message_display.html?tid=17204.

11. Samuel R. Sommers, Even P. Apfelbaum, Kristin N. Dukes, Negin Toosi, and Elsie J. Wang, "Race and Media Coverage of Hurricane Katrina: Analysis, Implications, and Future Research Questions," *Analysis of Social Issues and Public Policy* 6, no. 1 (2006): 43; and Michael Eric Dyson, *Come Hell or High Water: Hurricane Katrina and the Color of Disaster* (New York: Civitas Books, 2005), 164–5.

12. Sommers et al., "Race and Media Coverage of Hurricane Katrina," 43; Tierney et al., "Metaphors Matter," 66; and Dyson, *Come Hell or High Water*, 166.

13. Australian Broadcast Company News, "Troops Told 'Shoot to Kill' in New Orleans," *ABC News Online*, September 9, 2005, http://www.abc.net.au/news/newsitems/200509/s1451906.htm.

14. Tierney et al., "Metaphors Matter," 66–69.

15. Dyson, *Come Hell or High Water*, 172; Nicole Gelinas, "Who's Killing New Orleans?" *City Journal*, Autumn 2005, http://www.city-journal.org/html/15_4_new_orleans.html; and Mark J. VanLandingham, "Murder Rates in New Orleans, La, 2004-2006," *American Journal of Public Health* 97, no. 9 (September 2007): 1614–7, proquest.umi.com.

16. Nicole Gelinas, "Witnesses: New Orleans Cops among Looters," *CNN.com*, September 30, 2005, http://articles.cnn.com/2005-09-29/us/nopd.looting_1_police-officers-eddie-compass-police-department?_s=PM:US.

17. Brian Williams, "Brian Williams: We Were Witnesses," *MSNBC*, August 28, 2006, http://www.msnbc.msn.com/id/14518359/ns/nightly_news-after_katrina/t/brian-williams-we-were-witnesses/.

18. Anderson Cooper, "Anderson Cooper Interview with Senator Landrieu," youtube.com, September 1, 2005.

19. Robert Siegel, "Looting, Snipers Mar New Orleans Evacuation," *National Public Radio*, September 1, 2005, http://www.npr.org/templates/story/story.php?storyId=4828774; and Robert Siegel, "U.S. Aid Effort Criticized in New Orleans," *National Public Radio*, September 1, 2005, http://www.npr.org/templates/story/story.php?storyId=4828771.

20. Soledad O'Brien, "Soledad O'Brien Interviews Michael Brown," youtube.com, September 1, 2005.

21. Williams, "We Were Witnesses."

22. Ibid.

23. Ibid.

24. Power, "Immersion Journalism," 73; and Merrill Morris, "A Moment of Clarity? The American Media and Hurricane Katrina," *Southern Quarterly* 43, no. 3 (Spring 2006): 41, 43.

25. Katie O'Keefe, "Ethical Firestorm," *The Quill* 93, no. 9 (December 2005): 22–26.

26. Mark Schleifstein, "Katrina Weaker than Thought; Category 3 Hit Land, Study Says," *Times-Picayne*, sec. national, December 2005, proquest.umi.com; National Oceanic and Atmospheric Administration (NOAA), "Dennis, Katrina, Rita, Stan, and Wilma 'Retired' from List of Storm Names," *NOAA News*, April 6, 2006, http://www.noaanews.noaa.gov/stories2006/s2607.htm; FEMA, "Mitigation Assessment Team Report: Hurricane Katrina in the Gulf Coast/Building Performance Observation, Recommendations and Technical

Guidance," *US Government*, July 2006; Senate Committee on Homeland Security and Governmental Affairs, *Hurricane Katrina: A Nation Still Unprepared. Special Report* (Washington, D.C.: US Government Printing Office, May 2006), 37, http://www.gpoaccess.gov/serialset/creports/katrinanation.html; and David Zucchino, Nicholas Riccardi, and Doug Smith, "Katrina Killed across Class Lines," *Los Angeles Times, Archives*, December 18, 2005, sec. A-1, http://articles.latimes.com.

27. Michael Abramowitz, "President Visits Inundated Eastern Iowa," *washingtonpost.com*, June 20, 2008, washingtonpost.com/wp-dyn/content/article/2008; American Farm Bureau, "AFBF: Weather Damaged Crop Costs Top $8 Billion, *American Farm Bureau: The Voice of Agriculture*, June 25, 2008, http://www.fb.org/index.php?fuseaction=newsroom.newsfocus&year=2008&file=nr0625.html; Delta Farm Press, "USDA: Katrina Crop Damage at $900 Million," September 20, 2005, http://deltafarmpress.com/usda-katrina-crop-damage-900-million; NCDC, "Climate of 2008: Midwestern U.S. Flood Summary," *NOAA Satellite and Information Service*, July 9, 2008, http://www.ncdc.noaa.gov/special-reports/2008-floods.html; and Senate Environment and Public Works Committee, "The Midwest Floods: What Happened and What Might Be Improved for Managing Risk and Responses in the Future," 2008, http://www.lexisnexis.com/.

28. "Governors Ask Bush for More Flooding Money," *McClatchy-Tribune Business News*, June 25, 2008, proquest.umi.com; and Associated Press, "Victims of Midwest Flooding Praise FEMA," *USA TODAY*, June 23, 2008, http://www.usatoday.com/weather/floods/2008-06-23-fema_N.htm.

29. Associated Press, "Food-Aid Rumors Spark Milwaukee Scuffle," *chicagotribune.com*, June 24, 2008, http://www.chicagotribune.com/news; and Associated Press, "Scuffles Break Out among Flood Victims Seeking Food Voucher," *USA TODAY*, June 23, 2008, http://www.usatoday.com/news/nation/2008-06-23-food-vouchers_N.htm.

30. Leslie Kaufman, "Food Stamps Buy Less; Families Are Hit Hard," *nytimes.com*, June 22, 2008, http://www.nytimes.com/2008/06/22/nyregion/22food.html.

31. Charity Elison, "Poverty Rates Rise Substantially in Wisconsin," *Wisconsin Council on Children and Families*, August 28, 2007, www.2020wi.org/pdf/povertyrates_082807pr.pdf.

32. Joel Rogers and Laura Dresser, *Wisconsin Economic Picture Darkens* (Madison: Center on Wisconsin Strategy, University of Wisconsin-Madison, 2005), www.cows.org/pdf/pr-soww-05.pdf.

33. Nancy Hicks, "Food Stamp Use Continues to Rise," *JournalStar.com*, June 9, 2004.

34. Henry J. Cordes, Cindy Gonzalez, and Erin Grace, "Poverty Amid Prosperity: Alarming Figures Reveal the Reality of a Metro Area in Which Economic Hardship Has a Stronger and Stronger Grip on the Black Community," *Omaha World-Herald*, April 15, 2007, sunrise edition, http://www.lexisnexis.com/.

35. Gelinas, "Who's Killing New Orleans?"

36. Ibid.; Ben C. Toledano, "New Orleans—An Autopsy," *Commentary*, July 10, 2008, http://www.commentarymagazine.com.

37. Gelinas, "Who's Killing New Orleans?"

38. Peter Wagner and Susan Edwards, "New Orleans by the Numbers," *Dollars and Sense*, 2006, http://www.dollarsandsense.org/archives/2006/0306wagneredwards. html; and Timothy Brezina, "What Went Wrong in New Orleans? An Examination of the Welfare Dependency Explanation," *Social Problems* 55, no. 1 (2008): 25–26.

39. Reynolds Wolf, "Dozens of Levees Fail or Soon May in Midwest," *CNN Newsroom*, June 20, 2008, http://www.lexisnexis.com/.

40. Rush Limbaugh, "Rush Limbaugh: People of Iowa Better than New Orleans," *The Young Turks*, June 18, 2008, youtube.com.

41. A.C.S., "Boortz Again Referred to Victims of Hurricane Katrina as 'Parasite[s],'" *Media Matters for America*, June 19, 2008, http://mediamatters.org/mmtv/200806190009.

42. Marshall Allen, "Review: Leno's Flood Benefit Show Keeps 'Em Laughing," *McClatchy-Tribune Business News*, June 26, 2008, proquest.umi.com.

43. Louisiana Department of Health and Hospitals, "Reports of Missing and Deceased," August 2, 2005, http://www.dhh.louisiana.gov/offices/page. asp?id=192&detail=5248; and David Zucchino, Nicholas Riccardi, and Doug Smith, "Katrina Killed across Class Lines."

44. John H. McWhorter, "Katrina's 'Secrets': They're Not What Liberals Think," *National Review*, September 25, 2006, 20–22.

45. Brezina, 23–28; Joel Kotkin, "Ideological Hurricane," *The American Enterprise* (January/February 2006): 24–29; and Robert Tracinski, "Hurricane Katrina Exposed the Man-made Disaster of the Welfare State," *Pittsburgh Tribune Review*, September 11, 2005.

46. Kanye West and Mike Myers, "YouTube—Bush Doesn't Care about Black People," youtube.com, April 16, 2006.

47. Jon Stewart, Jason Jones, and Wyatt Cenac, "Wet Hot American Bummer," *The Daily Show/Comedy Central*, June 18, 2008, http://www.thedailyshow.com.

48. Keith Woods is a former newspaper reporter and editor at the *Times-Picayune* in New Orleans. He is now dean of the faculty at the Poynter Institute, a school for journalists in Florida. Appearing on the *Lehrer NewsHour* on September 29, 2005, Woods commented that journalists had already given considerable reflection to the "coverage of the looting that focused so much on material things in many cases at a time when human life was still at risk . . . you had much more important things to be talking about than whether someone was stealing a television set or not." On the same program, conservative news and talk radio show host Hugh Hewitt condemned the alarmist excesses as exemplary of a particular kind of ill-informed elitism: "Why was the media so eager and

willing to circulate these stories? Is it because we were dealing with the urban under class, largely black, and largely a community with which the elite media does not often deal? And as a result they were willing to believe stories about this community that they might not have given any credence to in a different situation" (NewsHour, "Online NewsHour: Katrina Media Coverage," September 29, 2005, *NewsHour with Jim Lehrer,* http://www.pbs. org/newshour/bb/weather/july-deco5/media_9-29.html); Morris, "A Moment of Clarity?" 44; O'Keefe, "Ethical Firestorm"; MSNBC, "Auditing the Early Reporting from New Orleans," September 7, 2005, http://www.msnbc.msn. com; Robert Pierre and Ann Gerhart, "News of Pandemonium May Have Slowed Aid," *Washington Post,* sec. A.08, October 5, 2005; Susannah Rosenblatt and James Rainey, "Rita's Aftermath; Katrina Takes a Toll on Truth, News Accuracy; Rumors Supplanted Accurate Information and Media Magnified the Problem. Rapes, Violence, and Estimates of the Dead Were Wrong," *Los Angeles Times,* September 27, 2005, proquest.com; Brendesha Tynes, Carla Hunter, Helen A. Neville, and M. Nicole Coleman, "'Bush Doesn't Care about Black People': Race, Class, and Attributions of Responsibility in the Aftermath of Hurricane Katrina," *The Black Scholar* 36, no. 4 (Winter 2006): 32–42.

49. NBC/*Wall Street Journal,* "Poll Question: Bush, George W., Accomplishments," National Broadcasting Company, December 11, 2008.

50. CBS News, "New Orleans' Own Field of Dreams," March 10, 2009, http://www.cbsnews.com/stories/2009/03/10/national/main4856627.shtml

51. Bill Whitaker, presentation, Hobart and William Smith Colleges, February, 2009.

52. James K Galbraith, *The Predator State* (New York: Free Press, 2008), 13.

53. Ibid.

CHAPTER 11

The Forgotten Ones

Black Women in the Wake of Katrina

Avis Jones-Deweever

We down here have been forgotten.

—A sixty-six-year-old grandmother, Orleans Parish resident,
and Hurricane Katrina survivor

FOR MOST AMERICANS, the horrors of Katrina have devolved into nothing more than a sad, but distant memory. We have written our checks, said our prayers, and, if we were especially generous, volunteered a few days or weeks of our time toward rebuilding efforts. Yet, for many who call home the various cities, towns, and vast rural stretches all along the Gulf Coast that felt firsthand the wrath of Katrina, the daily struggle to reclaim some semblance of the life they once knew remains. In many ways, that struggle is a lonely, tumultuous challenge, wrought with shifting rules of the game and a cycle of frustration that begets progress in one respect, with simultaneous retrenchment in several others.

Nearly all of those within the crosshairs of this historic storm have their own tales of challenge and heartache. But like what is commonplace around the world, in times of natural disaster, those groups who are most marginalized before tragedy strikes bear the brunt of ill-effects during the disaster and long afterward. As a result, the on-the-ground impacts of natural disasters are anything but "natural." Instead, they are shaped by social constructs that value some and devalue others as they relate to race, class, and gender in broader society. Katrina was, and is, quite ordinary in that respect. Although it threatened all, those most vulnerable to its effects were the ones with the fewest resources—both formal and informal—to draw upon when it mattered most.

But with the pain of Katrina, at least for a brief moment in time, came a great awakening to the implications of race and class disadvantage in America and what that really means in times of crisis. The shocking images of primarily black faces stranded, tired, and hungry in those days initially following the storm along with controversial banter regarding President Bush's alleged lack of affinity for black people made the issue of race one that was undeniably clear.[1] Issues of gender, however, were largely ignored. But a closer look at those same images would show largely women and primarily black women, doing the best they could to ease the hunger and thirst of babies and toddlers left in their care in the sweltering heat and the inhumane conditions associated with postdisaster survival. It was largely elderly women, both black and white, who were stranded in nursing homes, waiting for help that for far too many, came much too late. And it was largely, but of course, not exclusively, women who stayed behind in flooding hospitals to care for patients unable to care for themselves. Yet, their service and suffering were all but invisible, as are their continuing struggles to this day.

Today, women are doing the healing work associated with life after Katrina. They are comforting children still traumatized by the memory of this life-changing event. They are taking care of elders who are still mourning the loss of a lifetime of memories washed away with the storm. They are themselves, disproportionately the aged, who now in the twilight of their lives are forced to begin again. They also make up most of those who head families essentially barred from returning home, due to the impending destruction of the majority of public housing units within the city of New Orleans. And on the ground, they make up a sizeable mass of those community leaders left with the charge of bringing people together and demanding action more directly focused on those needs still left to be met for those tomorrows still to come.

This chapter tells their stories, and in so doing, it provides an analysis of women's increased vulnerability during times of natural disaster while determining to what extent the experiences of those women impacted by Katrina align with the experiences of women around the world impacted by disasters in their homelands. It also provides an overarching race/class/gendered analysis of women's post-Katrina experiences with a special emphasis on what they are doing now to rebuild their lives, reconstruct their homes, restore their families, and reclaim their communities. As such, the report puts to paper the perspectives of women gathered through a series of semistructured one-on-one and small-group interviews with thirty-eight women in New Orleans and Slidell, Louisiana, as well as in Biloxi and Gulfport, Mississippi. The women included in this study ranged in age from nineteen to sixty-six and are of diverse racial/ethnic backgrounds, including black, white, Creole, and Latina. Each woman contributed to their communities as a volunteer, activist, community organizer, or professional engaged in public service careers. Many, but not all, were involved with organizations that focused specifically on issues of concern to women. But each sought to, in some way, not only meet the immediate needs clear in the communities examined here but also to work toward making those communities better over the long haul by acknowledging and seeking to address long-standing pre-Katrina persistent structures of advantage and disadvantage that ultimately led to the tragic circumstances viewed around the world in the storm's immediate aftermath.

Background: Women and Natural Disasters

Natural disasters can wreak havoc on the human condition. Their impacts are felt economically, environmentally, psychologically, and physically. They have the power to wipe out entire communities, leaving only death and devastation in their wake. Yet, as powerful and unforgiving as natural disasters can be, their impacts are not universally felt across the human experience. Disasters occur within societies, and societal norms and structures typically serve to advantage some, while disadvantaging others. The resulting set of advantages and disadvantages ensure that some are more likely than others to have access to potentially lifesaving resources in times of crisis and are more apt to make due and more swiftly recover in the postdisaster period. When disasters occur, individuals experience vast differences in their ability to mitigate its negative effects typically based on their predisaster societal positioning.

It has been widely established that women are especially disadvantaged in times of natural disaster.[2] Women, though are not alone in their increased vulnerability to disastrous events. Also disproportionately impacted are the poor, the elderly, subordinated racial and ethnic groups, children, and the disabled.[3] But when gender intersects with other areas of disadvantage, it is women who are especially negatively impacted.

Around the world, women's social subjugation places them at severe risk, even under what is considered to be "normal" circumstances. They are much more likely than men to live on both the social and economic fringes of society. They are less likely than men to be literate or have access to information, transportation, social networks, or spheres of influence. They are also less likely to have paid employment outside the home, and when they do, they tend to earn low wages and have no benefits or union representation. Women are also particularly vulnerable to sudden unemployment and therefore lack economic stability. As a result, they are less likely to have access to income, credit, savings, and assets and, often, have limited capacity to control those resources that are (at least theoretically) available to them within their own homes. Because of these and other disadvantages, women make up the vast majority of the world's poor and account for fully 70 percent of those who live in abject poverty—subsisting on less than $1 per day.[4]

Decreased access to income and other critical nonmonetary resources such as access to information and social networks are significant barriers to women's ability to effectively respond to impending disasters and to swiftly recover after disaster strikes. Complicating matters, too, are women's traditional caregiving responsibilities. Caring for children, the elderly, and others reduces one's mobility during a crisis. And when time is of the essence, this can mean the difference between life and death.

When women lack the information to be adequately forewarned of an impending disaster or lack the resources to get out of harm's way even when a disaster is fully anticipated or find themselves attempting to make a hasty retreat with children in their arms or elders by their side, it is little wonder that they tend to be least likely to escape with their lives. It has been estimated that roughly three times as many women died as men in the deadly tsunami of 2004 that claimed the lives of well over 200,000 people,[5] and about 1.5 times as many women died as a result of the massive 1995 earthquake in Kobe, Japan.[6] Other research suggests that women are on average about fourteen times more likely than men to die during natural disasters.[7]

But for those who survive, life after disaster proves more difficult for women as well. In the immediate chaos that often ensues after disastrous situations, women's safety and security are particularly at risk. Rape, gang rape, and physical violence are common occurrences both domestically and abroad.[8] In the wake of California's 1999 Loma Prieta earthquake, sexual assault rose by about 300 percent,[9] while requests for restraining orders were said to have increased by 50 percent.[10] In some cases, women have been forced to exchange sex for food, shelter, or protection as a means of survival. We know also that women's vulnerability to sexual assault grows when living in refugee camps or non–gender-segregated shelter situations. Women and children of both sexes experience increased vulnerability to falling victim to the sex trade during this time as well.[11]

Once the immediate crisis is abated, survivors are left to pick up the pieces and start their lives over. With this comes a whole new series of challenges. The need to procure housing, food, water, and, eventually, a new source of income compounds an already stressful situation. As the days drag into weeks, months, and, in some cases, years, the slow pace of regaining "normalcy" heightens the stress associated with daily living. It is this overwhelming level of stress that is thought to contribute to the increased occurrences of domestic violence in the recovery period. Due to housing scarcity, women are often unable to escape abusive situations. In other instances, those who may have left known abusers before a disaster find that they must return afterward for lack of other housing options. This is particularly true since postdisaster aid typically is distributed on a head-of-household basis and, thus, nearly universally accessed by men.[12]

Women also have special physical and psychological concerns in the wake of disaster. Lacking sanitary conditions, their reproductive health is threatened. Also, pregnant women or those who may have given birth just before, during, or soon after the disaster run the very real risk of having their special needs go unaddressed.[13] Further, women's traditional domestic responsibilities become an even greater challenge in the postdisaster period. Preparing food and caring for children and others becomes an even more laborious process in strange surroundings and with limited resources. The increased workload is said to add to women's stress and may also serve as a threat to their health if the well-being of others is consistently prioritized. These and other stressors likely explain why women are said to, in many cases, be more likely than men to express symptoms of post-traumatic stress syndrome following a disaster.[14]

The disproportionate likelihood of prior economic insecurity makes it that much more difficult for women to pull their lives back together afterward. For some, the death of a partner may necessitate a search for paid employment. In other instances, postdisaster "male flight," which occurs when men leave their families to fend for themselves after securing relief aid for their own personal use, creates the immediate need for women to pursue paid employment.[15] In other situations, understanding the importance of increased income, women may seek employment to add to their partner's contributions, but finding employment is often especially challenging for women. The targeting of relief investments to postdisaster reconstruction ultimately leaves women shut out of jobs that are traditionally reserved for men. Although rebuilding is an obvious necessity in the postdisaster period, so too are the daily economic needs of women. And while employment for many is hard to find, an even rarer commodity is child care.[16]

Together, these disadvantages and others place women at increased peril before, during, and after disastrous events. In sum, their areas of vulnerability can be said to take place primarily across four streams: (1) decreased economic capacity both before and after disasters; (2) heightened exposure to violence and sexual assault in the immediate aftermath and during the protracted postdisaster recovery phase; (3) decreased mobility and increased resource needs due to caregiving responsibilities; and (4) policy practices that privilege male-headed household structures and the economic reintegration of men in postdisaster recovery efforts. Each of these levels of disadvantage reduces women's capacity to adequately prepare for impending disaster and then to swiftly rebound once disaster strikes. As a result, women face unique challenges in the face of natural disasters and only through adequate, gender-specific predisaster and postdisaster planning and action can their specific needs be properly addressed.

Remembering Katrina

Unless one has witnessed it with their own eyes, it is hard to even imagine the vast nature of destruction that Katrina wrought. There is no panoramic lens wide enough, no plasma screen television large enough, and, frankly, no language vivid enough to adequately relay the storm's level of devastation. In its wake, Katrina left miles and miles of obliterated structures, vast areas of broken and barren trees, and only sparse remains where vibrant communities once stood. In combination with Hurricane Rita, the storm did much more than flood one American city; it literally leveled an area the size of Great Britain,[17] left over 1,500 people dead,[18] and caused the displacement of some 1.2 million. Economically, the area was ravaged as well, resulting in estimated infrastructural damage of up to $130 billion. By just about any measure imaginable, this storm was of historic proportions, and one that will require many years of rebuilding in order to come within striking distance of anything resembling a full recovery.

Now, over two years post-Katrina, focus has deservedly shifted to issues of recovery and rebuilding. And while these issues are, of course, essential to the process of moving on, many of the women that we spoke to had an overwhelming need to share their survival stories—not as a way of eliciting pity, but perhaps as a survival mechanism itself. Relaying these stories to open and willing ears seemed to, in some way, help release at least of portion of the anxiety and stress that for so long, had been internalized. Most seemed relieved that others *wanted* to know what they had been through, how they had survived, and what they were doing now to "keep on keeping on." Nearly every woman bemoaned the fact that their voices had not been heard, and as a result, their stories have been left untold. We honor those voices here by relaying a sampling of their experiences, in their own words, as a way to promote a broader understanding of the true horror of Katrina and as a way of remembering and giving tribute to those whose lives remain forever changed.

Below, a woman who ultimately spent five days under an overpass relays her survival story and her courageous struggle to remain with her son.

> They tried deliberately to separate our children from us. I was one that fought for my child. They had the children on [one] truck . . . and we were placed on the trucks behind them. However, I did not want to be separated from my son so I said, "Why can't we be placed on the same truck?" They stated that we all were going to the same place. Well, I put up a fight about it until I was convinced by the other ladies that, you know, we can see the truck in front of us, so we can watch our children. So I agree. . . . They dumped the children first [in front of a bridge]. So I thought they were going to make a left turn, so I'm waiting. They did not make the left turn. The kids are under the bridge. They went to the very next stop so I'm thinking they're going to make that one, however, after they didn't make that one, I asked the National Guard, asked him, what kind of rifle he had? He told me. Of course, I don't remember, but I told him he may as well take that rifle and start putting bullet holes in my head cause I'm getting off this truck and getting my baby. . . . So I jumped off that truck and [was] cut up so bad. And then they turned the truck around to bring me to my child. And they had the audacity to say to me that um, oh, you are a brave mother and excuse my expression— I said, "No bastard, I am a mother. God did not want me separated

from him during the storm, man is not going to separate me from
him now." . . . And I'm screaming at them [the other mothers] saying
get your child, get your child! They were afraid to move because
they were told not to move, to stay there. So that's why I know they
deliberately separated us from our children. But I refused to let it go
on. I was willing to die for my child.

So we were dumped under the bridge for five days. It was scary.
It was dark. We had no food. Water was being dropped out of
helicopters like—like we were slaves. . . . Of course you know we
were like pretty nasty, dirty, funky. It was like a lot of red ants and
urine, waste, and we [other adults who were left there, but not the
parents of the children who were left there] had to make cardboard
beds for the children to sleep on and we sat around in a circle
[at night] to watch the children because it was so dark. And it was
a whole lot of activity going on up over the bridge, up on top of the
bridge. Right up over us there's the prisoners, so they had them at
gunpoint, with these large spotlights that was on all of us, so we feel
like we were being held at gunpoint also because every time we look
around, there was either National Guard, police officers, and everybody we seen with these guns and these big lights. They were
slamming people around and thousands and thousands of people
they drop off each night. That put us farther and farther back into
the woods. . . . The little things that we were able to salvage, they
took it away from us. They just threw it and just tossed it in the
street. They had raping going on. One of the National Guard actually shot a guy in the head. It was devastating, it was scary. . . . The
people were just fighting and crying and grown men crying and it
was a lot of praying. We did a lot of praying. It was a sight, it was
sight that I would not want to see or go through again. . . . Because
I mean, anytime you can hear grown men screaming and hollering
and crying out loudly, and children and babies. . . . Can you imagine
what it was like? . . . It was like the end of the world. It was like life
was over, but it was only for those that given up and I just kept
praying and knew there was a bright light on the other side.

After waiting for days for some means of escape, a bus finally arrived to
pick up those left stranded on the highway. But the struggle did not end

here for this mother and son. After being dropped off in a small town on the outskirts of Texas, the two bounced around for a period of time from shelter to shelter, some legitimate, and some, apparently not. One shelter, run by a pastor and his wife, required $800 for their stay. Unable to come up with the money, they were turned away. Ultimately, they crossed paths with a young lady who was willing to take both her and her son into her home. The apartment was small, but clean. Just starting out, the young lady who had opened her home to them only had an air mattress for furniture, but they made do. With $2,000 in FEMA assistance, she helped to set up the apartment with the basics—pots and pans, utensils, beds and bed linen, a small TV, and food. What she didn't know though, was that this young lady was behind in her rent. And before too long, they were evicted. Most of what she had purchased for that home now gone, she made the decision that she had had enough and decided to return. *"I made that move back to New Orleans. I said, I'm going home."*

Next, another woman relays her friend's story—a friend who lost a child in the storm's deadly aftermath.

> I had a friend of mine who had two kids, a son and a daughter. Son's 15, daughter's 12. They decided to leave when the water started going up, trying to get to the Superdome or Convention Center or whatever. It's two kids walking through the water and the little girl got stuck, so the brother went to go help her and he got his sister loose, but he got sucked into a manhole. They still haven't found his body. Fifteen years old . . . I mean he saved his sister, but it cost him his life. Everybody's got a story, some worse than others. I don't want no pity party, we don't want people to feel sorry for [us], we don't want a handout. . . . I work for what I want. I don't want nobody to give me anything, but assist me.

Across the Gulf region, women relayed precisely the sentiments expressed above. Although they had an abundance of tragic tales of loss and sacrifice, they didn't want to be pitied; they didn't want to be patronized in any way— they just wanted to be heard. They wanted to feel like their lives mattered. And for them, that feeling of being valued could only occur when their needs— and by extension—their very humanity was adequately acknowledged and addressed.

Life after the Storms

In conversations with women in and around New Orleans, three primary issues remained at the forefront of their concerns: housing, health care, and economic well-being. Each of these issues had multiple, and often interlocking reverberations on their lives. Although all whom we contacted expressed a deep commitment to their communities and an overwhelming desire to face those challenges that remain, the slow pace of recovery and the resulting prolonged lack of normalcy have played out in their lives in ways that have compromised their wellness, their sense of security, and, for some, even that small, but persistent kernel of hope that had for so long sustained them, even in the face of unparalleled disaster.

Perhaps no issue is as disruptive in the lives of women and their families as the loss of a place to call home. Obviously, a disaster of this magnitude levels entire communities and, as a result, wreaks havoc on the availability of housing stock. Due to the combined impact of Hurricanes Katrina and Rita, over 1.8 million housing units were damaged throughout the Gulf region, with over 300,000 homes totally destroyed.[19] Louisiana bore the brunt of destructive power of the storms, suffering fully four times the housing damage as neighboring Mississippi.[20] Yet, parts of Mississippi were ravaged as well, as communities all along the Gulf Coast were quite literally leveled due to their unfortunate positioning directly in the center of Katrina's path.

As one might expect, with a severely limited availability of housing units, the cost of those which were inhabitable increased precipitously. In New Orleans, for example, rental rates skyrocketed. The latest estimates indicate that fair market rental units have gone up some 46 percent from their pre-Katrina value.[21] As a result, an apartment that would have rented for $661 per month the year before the storm now demands a rental rate of $990 for inhabitance. In all, the city of New Orleans saw some 142,000 housing units severely damaged or destroyed as a result of the storm, and roughly 80 percent of the units that were most severely damaged were affordable- to low-income housing. Among the limited number of affordable units that withstood the storm, those set aside for the most disadvantaged—the city's public housing units—face impending demolition. On December 20, 2007, the New Orleans City Council, through a unanimous vote, gave the final go-ahead to the U.S. Department of Housing and Urban Development's (HUD) plan to demolish 4,500 public housing units to be replaced by mixed-income housing, which, it is anticipated, will set aside only 744 units for low-income residents.[22] These homes are slated to be demolished not because they were rendered uninhabitable by the storm; in fact, many proved to be among the sturdiest in the entire city. These homes have seemingly fallen victim to politics and the apparent desire to create a "new" New Orleans devoid of the city's most vulnerable population—it's deeply impoverished. All indicators suggest that this strategy is working, particularly to the detriment of poor single mothers, over 83 percent of whom have been unable to return home and begin the business of reclaiming their lives.[23]

As one can imagine, this mix of man-made disastrous decision-making along with the storm's lingering ravages makes finding housing extremely challenging in New Orleans and beyond, and finding *affordable* housing, a near impossibility. The resulting housing crunch has severe implications on the safety and well-being of women. Because of the limited availability and exorbitant cost of housing, many women and their children must now share tight living quarters with extended family, friends, or acquaintances. And since most sexual assaults do not occur at the hands of a stranger, this situation has, unfortunately, led to occurrences of sexual assault specifically tied to the Katrina experience.

Sexual assault counselors describe the problem below:

> Since Katrina, sexual assault has gone sky high. Because you have more [women] staying with relatives . . . it's the sexual assault that you're hearing a whole lot more of. I mean the sad thing about assault is when you think about sexual assault you think about strangers [but] more sexual assaults happen with the people that you know, that's related to you, people you trust. So on top of, you know, dealing with the hurricane situation . . . these women have a whole lot of things that they have to deal with that's making it . . . twice as hard.
>
> Now what we're seeing is kids who have been abused as part of their Katrina experience. They are living with seventeen different cousins and sharing bedrooms and uncle so-and-so is in the trailer . . . it's very upsetting to me that sexual abuse is becoming a part of the Katrina experience for children. Moms are having to take their children back to homes where moms were abused because they have no place else to go. They're having to live with perpetrators

that they know were perpetrators because where else are they going to go? Or, they're living with perpetrators that they don't know are perpetrators and they're finding out. It breaks my heart that this is what we're dealing with. The more that the government fails to provide housing, the longer this goes on and the more children are at risk; not just at risk, but this really happened to them, and we're starting to see it.

Another service provider adds:

> Our clients need for the abuse to stop . . . they need to get their children to safety and themselves to safety. Without having a pool of rental properties, people are stuck where they are. They can't just say, "I've had enough of this abuse" or "You can't have access to my kids" or whatever, "I'm leaving. I'm going to a shelter for a while and then I'll get my own place." People are coming into shelter but there's not a place for them to rent, to move on to. Housing would alleviate that pressure and let people leave and get out of the abusive situation.

In addition to the increased risk of sexual abuse, the lack of affordable housing has also put women at increased risk of domestic violence. Many have found themselves in the unenviable position of having to choose between shelter and safety. The shortage has in some instances caused women to return to known abusers. In other cases, the prolonged exposure to stress inherent in the post-Katrina experience has led to new occurrences of abuse in relationships that had once been free of violence. The lack of alternatives in terms of housing and shelter space has made it particularly difficult for women to escape dangerous situations.

It's important to keep in mind that when Katrina washed away homes, it also washed away domestic violence shelters. Only one shelter in the entire city of New Orleans survived the storm, and that one facility is full with a lengthy waiting list. But even that one remaining place of refuge could not operate at full capacity months following the storm since a staffer, unable to afford the exorbitant housing costs in the city, had made the shelter her temporary home; not because she needed to escape an abusive situation but instead because she couldn't afford to live anywhere else. Yet, compared to her clients, she is one of the lucky ones. As shelter staff describes, many women have found that limited housing options have only further constricted their ability to live life far away from a batterer's reach.

> Some women are opting to stay with their abusers simply because there's not enough housing to go around and our shelters are currently full, so the options to leave right now are really not there because we have limited space, there's limited housing here in the area, everything's booked up, taken up, you know, and affordable housing is just impossible to find right now. And if the female isn't in imminent danger than she's considered, you know, homeless and we have to find referrals for that particular shelter and there's been an influx of that, too, where women who are calling aren't necessarily in danger, but are in need of shelter.
>
> Well, this disaster caused a lot of women who [had been] separated from their batterers to go back to their batterers because they lost their homes. They've got the children. They have no place else to go. So they went back to batterers. Okay now they're with their batterer in a much smaller place, what is it? Six by thirty? [referring to the dimensions of the typical FEMA trailer]

In short, the longer the severe shortage in affordable housing continues, the longer the most economically vulnerable women and children will be forced to live in danger, and the more women and children will be needlessly exposed to the daily risk of molestation, sexual assault, and physical abuse, only because they have nowhere else to go.

In addition to the tragedy associated with the loss of a feeling of safety and security in one's own home, women are also dealing with the additional strain of starting over while mourning the loss of the familiar and, ultimately, the loss of community, in its most holistic sense. Such a loss is hard on everyone, but for the elderly, the pain is especially severe.

> You realize a lot of people lost everything. My grandmother is eighty-six. She's been in the house that she's in for about forty years. My grandfather built this house for her. My grandfather and my grandmother were married sixty-six years when he passed . . . he passed [one year before Katrina]. So sixty-six years of her life

with him, forty years in the house she's in . . . her house withstood every hurricane that ever passed through here. Every hurricane, she went untouched. And for the first time, and she's eighty-six years old, she lost everything she owned. . . . Every day my grandmother is like, "I want to go back home." How do you make somebody eight-six years old realize, there ain't no more home right now? Ain't nothing to go back to. Keep in mind that she lost her husband [before Katrina]. She's been in the same house forever. Normalcy to her, is being back in *that* house, nowhere else.

Today, this woman is one of the lucky ones. A family member who is a carpenter helped put the structure that is her house back together. She now lives once again in a space that she can call her own. But with so many of her sentimental belongings gone, along with most of her neighbors, the loss of the very sense of community that makes a house a home has now created an existence that is far different from the life she once knew. And it's that sense of community that some miss the most. Several women relayed despair over this loss, one they deemed much more tragic than the destruction of material goods.

I didn't do too much crying about the house, it was more the community aspect of it. A house can be replaced. My neighbors coming back, that's a long shot and that's what the problem is. That's harder to do.

I was born in that community and I was raised in the community. . . . I couldn't go two blocks without having a family member there, I knew all of my neighbors . . . everybody had been there for thirty years or more . . . people don't want to give up on the Lower Ninth Ward, particularly the North Side. When my parents moved there in the 1940s there was only one neighbor on the block and, then, my great grandmother moved and made the second and my grandparents made the third. So, they watched their community grow. They watched it grow and develop and people clinged to it, not because you're traditional or you don't know any better or [you] haven't been exposed [to anything else] or [you're] marginalized or whatever, but because we love it. It's ours and we love it.

And I think that's the dilemma a lot of people are in now. They
might have the means, the insurance, the motivation to rebuild
their individual homes . . . but is there a community that will be
here? Are there going to be two houses that are on this block? So
how do I live with that? So I think there is a bit of a waiting game,
trying to figure what they, meaning the government, is planning.

Home for these women, and for most of us, is far more than just a
specific physical structure. Home, in its broader sense, is a neighborhood,
a community, a social network of family and friends that together results
in a sense of belonging that is not easily replicated in unfamiliar places.
Perhaps one of the biggest tragedies of Katrina is that for so many, home, in
this broader sense, will never be the same again. Even if one makes it back
to their old house, on their own street, in their own neighborhood, that
victory is hollow when it's done in relative isolation.

In addition to the loss of housing and communities, women consistently lamented the lack of health care availability. Before Katrina,
Louisiana had in place the only state-supported charity hospital system
in the nation.[24] Charity Hospital, as it was commonly referred, provided
emergency and long-term treatment to the state's most vulnerable
population—impoverished citizens who lacked health insurance. Since
the storm, Charity has remained unopened, making it particularly
difficult for the most vulnerable to received swift and quality care.

> Charity Hospital . . . worked. It served the people. You had a
> Diabetic Clinic, you had Hypertension Clinic, literally, these were
> the name of these clinics—not the "Lisa Richardson's Clinic for
> Whatever," no, Hypertension Clinic. It was a teaching hospital, LSU
> and Tulane, you might not ever see the same doctor when you go
> because it's residents, it's a teaching hospital. They fed into even the
> education level of the people who lived in the city. We have a high
> illiteracy rate, high dropout rate, and that's why the clinics were
> labeled what they were: "Diabetic Clinic," "Sugar Clinic." . . . I've
> seen elderly people who had "Sugar Clinic" on their paperwork.
> That's so they can relate to it. . . . Charity Hospital had to have had at
> least 200 clinics. Two-hundred clinics serving not just New Orleans,
> but outside, in rural areas of Louisiana people came into the city
> because it was a state hospital, and anything you needed, could be
> done at Charity Hospital. . . . I don't think that's ever coming back.

The loss of Charity has resulted in the need for people to seek treatment, in some cases, miles away, only to wait for hours in overcrowded emergency departments just to spend a few fleeting minutes with overwhelmed medical staff. Further complicating matters is the area's increasing uninsured population. When the storm obliterated structures, it also took away jobs. And when jobs were washed away, for many, so too was health insurance coverage.

> I was a teacher for twenty-five and a half years and was arbitrarily fired because they fired all Orleans Parish School Board employees right after Katrina. My performance spoke for itself. You didn't see me not going to work. You know, I had so much leave, I could give it to people when they got sick. They [the school system] told me that I was not old enough to retire, but I could retire [with reduced benefits] since I had enough years. Then they told me that if I wanted to get insurance, I would have to pay six hundred fifty dollars a month. With reduced benefits, six hundred fifty dollars per month? That's more than a third of what I'd be getting. I said, "I can't afford that." So now I'm an unemployed school teacher with no health benefits, living in a house where I'm paying more rent than I was paying for my house note, and I'm just now getting assistance from FEMA. That's where I am.

Even among those who were able to regain employment upon return, the acquisition of a regular paycheck did not always mean the reclamation of health insurance coverage.

> I guess some people wouldn't consider me the "working poor," I do consulting work, I have a job, I make money, I travel . . . not the working poor, but if you ask me, right now my struggle is that I had [health] insurance pre-Katrina, I don't have insurance post-Katrina. One of my consulting jobs, the exchange was that they would just give me health care, and I would do what I do for them. . . . I had been having trouble with thyroids [and] I had a partial hysterectomy scheduled twice. . . . I went in for the blood work, did all the prep work, and the woman came in, "I know that you're scheduled for surgery in two days, but you have no insurance." The insurance company said that they weren't paid during Katrina . . . your agency didn't pay.

An added wrinkle to this matter is the significant increase in the number of Latinos in the area who have severe difficulty finding Spanish-speaking health care providers and who, some evidence suggests, avoid seeking treatment all together due to fears concerning challenges to their legal status. This situation has special implications for pregnant Latinas who, due to issues of language barriers and concerns regarding deportation, often forego prenatal care altogether and instead seek only emergency department care when it comes time for delivery. Hospitals, then, are required to provide care to all of those, regardless of immigration status, who arrive in labor at an emergency department. Once there, Medicaid provides coverage for delivery and up to a forty-eight-hour hospital stay depending upon the method of delivery.[25]

But according to one immigrant rights worker, the dearth of English translators and the fear of general anti-immigrant sentiment effectively shut many women out of the prenatal care that they need to best ensure safe and healthy development during their pregnancy.

> I mean we have documented situations where immigrant worker women are being denied prenatal care, you know? I mean like because of language access issues, because of questions of their immigration status. I mean we're talking about the most basic care. Right?

The need for expanded health care services through the region is not limited to the need for treatment of the body. The overwhelming prevalence of stress has also spawned a need for increased services for the treatment of the mind as well. Many have become mentally fatigued with the lack of normalcy in their lives and the increased pressures associated with daily living. Women find themselves in particularly stressful situations. They are the caregivers, the comforters, and the supporters. And it's not unusual for women to fulfill these roles with such loving devotion that they prioritize the needs of others over their own. The overwhelming pressure of this responsibility has led many to sink into protracted bouts of depression. Several women included in this study either were on antidepressant medication themselves or knew someone who was. All recognized the need for more mental health care services in the area, such as a need for the increased availability of free and culturally competent counseling as a way of helping people cope with the constant stress associated with living in a protracted state of recovery and rebuilding.

Stress is the biggest problem we're having, and I'm trying to get everybody to understand . . . a lot of us are coping, but a lot of us aren't. Even at my office, and I work in a government office, we've had people who've had nervous breakdowns because of all the stress. They have no home to go to, they are working ten and twelve hour shifts, and when they get home and they try to do a little work and nothing is working out—it's too dark, it costs them a fortune for lumber—it weighs down on you after a while.

Adults, though, aren't the only ones who are struggling. Dealing with life after Katrina ultimately takes a strain on young and old alike.

We were seeing lots and lots of stress on families, lots of stress on kids . . . twenty people living in a space that should have housed two or three so the stress level and the coping abilities of people [are] really at their max.

I see the young people are depressed and don't even know they're depressed, and they're acting out sexually. Many of them are now in Central City because that is the area that's up and running and extremely densely populated. One of the things that we've really been advocating for is to get some serious, nontraditional mental health services in this city. We need mental health facilities; we need programs that do mental health in concert with other things. We need places to refer people. [For example,] we can't do HIV/AIDS prevention with youth now unless we start talking to them about what do they need. What have you gone through since Katrina? How is this affecting your behavior? How is this all factoring into your self-concept and your ideas about the future? And then we can begin to talk about how your emotional state and your mental state can make you take high-risk action that are going to put your life in danger . . . [and] when I say nontraditional—we don't need a therapist one-on-one, we need small groups. We need . . . small group facilitated conversations. And they work. To me, they work well for our [the black] community. They work for us.

The drastically reduced capacity of the health care system post-Katrina has ultimately cost lives. One study published in the *Journal of the American Medical Association,* on disaster medicine and public health preparedness found that the New Orleans post-Katrina death rate has risen by nearly 50 percent.[26] Other research has shown that in the first several months after Katrina, suicide rates shot up nearly 300 percent.[27] Over time, as the city tries to rebound, a severe shortage of health care workers in both the mental and physical health fields ultimately means that many are going without desperately needed health care services. As a result, the people are dying. As one woman told us, "They're dying like flies."

Certainly adding to the health care and housing vulnerabilities women face are the tight economic circumstances many find themselves navigating largely in isolation. Their once broad familial networks, which were, of course, critical to their daily survival, have now been obliterated with families scattered across the nation— some literally as far away as Alaska—as a result of the chaotic evacuation that followed the storm. Those who have made it back home now must face daily challenges largely on their own. Even though the women of the Gulf Coast were among the poorest in the nation before Katrina hit, they were able to make it due to the tight bonds of family and friends that helped each other get by, even in the worst of times. In New Orleans especially, it wasn't unusual for grandma to live in the house next door, auntie to live across the street, sister to live two doors down, and so forth. With family all around you, there was always a house to go to if you are were running low on food, or if you needed someone to watch your children while you went to work, or if you just needed someone to talk to. With these critically important networks gone, those who have come back have done so in relative isolation, and now find life much more difficult than it ever was before.

> You grow up in a neighborhood, where you know your neighbors and you know their kids, and you know the grandkids . . . one family to another family, and everybody is close and help each other out but times right now is, everybody is struggling. You know, I can't help you because I can barely help myself.

In this and other ways, women appear to be doing significantly worse post-Katrina. In New Orleans, for example, women's representation in the workforce has decreased, as has their wages, while the opposite is true, on both accounts, for men. Although much of the post-Katrina employment landscape is now beginning to show signs of rebirth some two years after the storm, those industries where women are heavily concentrated have suffered the greatest levels of job loss. For example, the accommodations and food service industry is down some 21,000 jobs, as are the health care and social assistance fields (also down 21,000 jobs) and the education services industry, which has 16,000 slots that remain unfilled.[28] Clearly, the relative absence of women in the workforce has reverberations across the entire community. Without adequate numbers of health care workers, social service workers, educators, and workers within the bread-and-butter areas of a tourist economy, it becomes clear to see that when women are shut out of the jobs landscape, everyone loses.

The lack of workers, though, in some cases, has led to post-Katrina wage increases. But even though some jobs now pay more, it's typically not enough to offset the sharp jump in the overall cost of living in the area. High costs are not limited to the outrageous increase in the price of housing but also include jumps in the cost of utilities, food, health insurance, homeowners' insurance, even costs associated with building supplies that are, of course, a necessity for those seeking to rebuild their homes so that they may once again have some semblance of the familiar in their daily existence.

These increased costs pose a severe threat to the overall economic well-being of women and their families. Some women, though, have spoken of seeking to mitigate these costs through attempting to gain employment in the construction industry, as these jobs typically pay more than the types of jobs women traditionally fill. But in practice, the very real specter of hiring discrimination makes the chances of implementing that option quite remote. As one community volunteer relayed:

A lot of people came into the city after the storm because they heard that there was a lot of work. Men were able to benefit from that because there was lots of construction work to do. At the same time, women were hearing there was lots of work, but it's been harder for women to get jobs in construction because a lot of time people won't hire women for construction—even for house gutting. I know many many women who have called inquiring about a job and when they find out they are women, they say that they don't need them anymore, or they say that they will call them back, and they never do.

For other women, particularly immigrant women, finding hiring success in the construction industry wasn't problematic, but once on the job, many experienced blatant exploitation, were given substandard wages, or, in some instances, not paid at all.

> [Latinas] are doing construction work. You see women are on roofs . . . because they need both incomes to make it. So they are leaving the kids with family members and then sending the money back. This is a situation where it's not just immigrant workers, it's migrant workers from around the country. Migrant workers were recruited off of reservations, from factories and urban centers from around the U.S. . . . they were told that they could come here, that they could make a lot of money, they could find housing and then they could leave. What's happening is that they haven't found housing, their jobs have been underpaid or not paid at all, or they haven't been given the jobs that they were guaranteed so they've ended up going into debt. It's really intense to watch the situation with the city because there's this dual attitude. We need the labor, we need the work, but if you're black, get back, you can't even get access to the jobs. If you're brown, stick around, we may or may not pay you, we're going to keep you in a very low [wage] working situation.

New Orleans's once double binary labor market, split between black and white, and men and women, has changed significantly post-Katrina; it now includes a healthy dose of brown. Yet, many of these latest arrivals are clinging on economically, at extremely low rates of pay, while others seemingly can't even get in the game. The result has been the emergence of a very different New Orleans, a "new" New Orleans that in many ways has settled into a quite different city than what was the case before Katrina. The observers below, though, give their insight into this new New Orleans.

> People who have come back are coming back to houses or apartments that they can afford to rent. That's a certain socioeconomic level that's coming back. You have to be able to make it on your own to come back because there's just not enough to prop people up. You have to have a job to come back. If you're not in that group

of people, you can't live here. So much of New Orleans was not that group of people.

It's amazing to see, not just the demographic shift, but the sense of propriety like, "this is *our* space." We're going to push out this population—actually circumstances have removed this population, and we're going to do everything we can on a policy level to keep those people from returning . . . to public housing, to public schools, to public hospitals, we just aren't going to have those things anymore. We're going to take those things off the landscape of services that are provided to the inhabitants of this city. Hopefully, if we do that, they won't come back, or if they come back, they won't be able to sustain. It's so clear because it's across the board. It's not that we just don't have health services, we don't have public schools, we don't have daycare.

Perhaps for women, though, this issue of child care remains one of the most enduring barriers to coming back to New Orleans. To date, fully two-thirds of the child care facilities in the city of New Orleans remain closed.[29] Certainly, without this basic need fulfilled, mothers will be unable to obtain and maintain employment in their effort to begin anew.

But it doesn't have to be that way. Along the Mississippi Gulf Coast, some have met the challenge of rebuilding child care networks with some level of success. The Mississippi Low Income Child Care Initiative has been particularly active in raising rebuilding funds to meet the state's child care needs. To date, they've amassed over $600,000 to go toward rebuilding in the state. In the summer of 2007, Moore Community House, a historic child care facility for low-income families, will be reopening in Biloxi, Mississippi. This new "House" has the capacity to serve seventy children, nearly tripling its pre-Katrina capacity of twenty four.

As an example of what can be done when public and private interests work together, in Mississippi, industry has helped in no small part, to meet child care needs. Seeking to hasten the return of its workers, the Chevron Corporation funded the rebuilding of all licensed child care facilities within Jackson County, Mississippi. Certainly this example shows a deep awareness of the link between child care availability and employee availability and should serve as a model for what could be done elsewhere to help meet this overwhelming need.

Policy Recommendations

Many of the women whose perspectives are weaved throughout this report felt as if their voices had gone unheard both in the initial chaos of the first few days after the disaster and throughout the long recovery period. The following set of policy recommendations addresses many of their concerns and point toward what a gender-informed disaster relief strategy would entail. Such strategies serve to not only address those women still reeling from the ravages of Katrina but also as a way of thinking proactively about how we might better address the needs of women before, during, and after disasters yet to come.

- *Make the provision of affordable housing a top priority.* The safety of women and girls remains in jeopardy with each day that severe housing shortages go unaddressed. The Louisiana Hurricane Housing Task Force has estimated that the city of New Orleans alone needs roughly thirty thousand affordable housing units immediately to even begin to address the current demand. Land grabs and postdisaster upscale condo development fail to address this need. Focusing instead on the provision of affordable housing not only is the right thing to do for the safety of women and girls but also makes sense for business owners who now find themselves scrambling to attract and retain employees who find it difficult to keep up with skyrocketing housing costs.
- *Incorporate women in the rebuilding economy through nontraditional training and enforcement of antidiscrimination laws.* Women by and large have been shut out of the most lucrative aspects of the rebuilding economy and have suffered as a result. In the immediate aftermath of the storm, carpenters in the region were demanding and getting $50 per hour or more for their labor. Although wage rates have subsequently returned to normal, even these "normalized" rates still far outpace those of traditional female employment in the area. Providing women training in the skilled trades would help increase their chances of earning a rate of pay that would allow them and their families some level of economic well-being. And buttressing that training with aggressive enforcement of antidiscrimination laws in hiring and pay would help to alleviate some of the difficulties women report facing in trying to gain access to the trades.

- *Increase the availability and quality of child care and schools.* As the population of the region continues to expand, so too does the need for child care and educational institutions. For women and families to return the region, these two services are nothing short of a necessity. The opportunities for critical public and private partnerships are there, particularly with regard to the redevelopment of child care facilities. Yet more needs to be done to turn these opportunities into realities.

- *Address both physical and mental health care needs, especially among the most needy.* Health care post-Katrina, for many, has become yet another disaster. The aggressive recruitment of health care providers, including bilingual providers, is a critical necessity, as are investments in the full reconstruction of health care facilities throughout the region. Facilities that will properly care for those without health insurance and those who speak only Spanish are especially crucial. Reopening Charity Hospital and additional health care clinics must be a high priority to reach out to these particular populations. As New Orleans and the Gulf Coast continue to inch closer to their pre-Katrina population density, the area's health care demands will only increase. Meeting that need is critical to the reconstruction of safe and vibrant communities. The broad availability of counseling and other mental health services is critically important as stress levels remain greatly elevated throughout the population. Women face special demands as caregivers, comforters, organizers, and planners and often do so under the pressure of extremely limited material resources. Also, special attention should be given to those women and girls whose Katrina experience has included domestic violence or sexual assault to help them work through the lingering emotional scars such violations leave behind.

- *Include a broad representation of women on decision-making bodies addressing disaster recovery and any future bodies formed for the purpose of predisaster planning.* Women in this study expressed time and again the belief that their voices too often went unheard and their needs too often unaddressed. It is easy to overlook that which is not represented. To make sure that the particular needs and concerns of women are included as recovery efforts go forward, a significant representation of women must be included on decision-making bodies. And just as important, it is critical that predisaster planning improve and that planning must, from the beginning, be inclusive of women and address their particular needs and vulnerabilities.

The women of New Orleans and the Gulf Coast, much like women under similar circumstances around the world, have been distinctly challenged by Hurricane Katrina. Their economic vulnerability and caregiving responsibilities limited their mobility before the storm, and afterward they continue to face distinct challenges to their safety, well-being, and economic stability. Yet despite these challenges, the women represented here have become critical partners in the rebuilding of "community" in every sense of the word. They have been on the ground, from the very beginning, doing everything from trudging through the post-Katrina sludge, lending their sweat to the rescue and clean-up efforts, to organizing family, friends, and neighbors to push through seemingly impossible odds, to make sure their communities were saved and not erased from existence. They have done their part. They now deserve, at the very least, to have their voices heard and their needs addressed and to be assured that future disasters will not replicate many of the horrors that they have in fact endured. Through their voices, we hope to learn, take those lessons to heart, and then properly plan for those disasters yet to be.

Conclusion

The women of New Orleans have, in many respects, been abandoned. Not only in the immediate aftermath of the storm, but still today—years later— by the dearth of adequate policy response to their lingering, yet severe needs. Women deserve a chance to rebuild their homes, their lives, and their peace of mind. That chance will only be available to them when they can live in a place free of the constant threat of physical or sexual abuse, when they can obtain fair and equal access to employment opportunities that provide the level of wages that are necessary to live a life free of abject poverty, and when they can have their mental and physical health care needs addressed in a timely and appropriate manner. Only through the provision of these opportunities will the women of New Orleans have the chance to rise from the tragedy that was and is Katrina in a way that maintains their dignity, while honoring their continued struggle toward a better tomorrow.

Notes

1. Michael E. Dyson, *Come Hell or High Water: Hurricane Katrina and the Color of Disaster* (New York: Basic Books, 2006).

2. L. Chew and K.N. Ramdas, *Caught in the Storm: Impact of Natural Disasters on Women* (San Francisco: Global Fund for Women, 2005); Elaine Enarson and Betty Hearn Morrow, *The Gendered Terrain of Disaster: Through Women's Eyes* (Westport, Conn.: Praeger Publishers, 1998); Elaine Enarson, "Women and Girls Last? Averting the Second Post-Katrina Disaster," 2006, http://understandingkatrina.ssrc.org/Enarson; Oxfam International, "The Tsunami's Impact on Women," Oxfam Briefing Note, 2005, http://www.oxfam.org/en/files/bn050326_tsunami_women/download; Soroptimist International of the Americas, Inc, "Reaching Out to Women When Disaster Strikes," 2007, http://www.soroptimist.rg/whitepapers/wp_disaster.html; Tamara Tutnjevic, "Gender in Crisis Response: A Guide to the Gender-Poverty-Employment Link," 2003, http://www-ilo-mirror.cornell.edu/public/english/employment/recon/crisis/download/gender3.Pd; and World Health Organization, Department of Gender and Women's Health, "Gender and Health in Disasters," 2002, http://www.who.int/gender/other_health/en/genderdisasters.pdf.

3. Enarson and Morrow, *The Gendered Terrain of Disaster*.

4. Pan American Health Organization, "Gender and Natural Disasters," 2001, http://www.paho.org/english/dpm/gpp/gh/genderdisasters.pdf.

5. Chew and Ramdas, *Caught in the Storm*.

6. Joni Seager, Editorial comment: "Noticing Gender (or Not) in Disasters," *Chicago Tribune,* September 2005, http://www.gdnonline.org/resources/seager-geoforum-katrina.doc.

7. Soroptimist International of the Americas, Inc, "Reaching Out to Women when Disaster Strikes."

8. Enarson and Morrow, *The Gendered Terrain of Disaster*; Theresa Braine, "Was 2005 the Year of Natural Disasters?" *Bulletin of the World Health Organization* 84, no. 1 (January 2006): 4–6; and World Health Organization, Department of Gender and Women's Health, "Gender and Health in Disasters."

9. Women's Edge Coalition, "Fact Sheet: Women, Natural Disaster, and Reconstruction," 2005, http://www.womenthrive.org/index.php?option=com_kb&page=articles&articleid=5.

10. World Health Organization, Department of Gender and Women's Health, "Gender and Health in Disasters."

11. Ibid.

12. Chew and Ramdas, *Caught in the Storm*; Enarson, "Women and Girls Last?"; and Tutnjevic, "Gender in Crisis Response."

13. Chew and Ramdas, *Caught in the Storm*.

14. Enarson, "Women and Girls Last?"

15. Reported by the World Health Organization, this phenomenon has been observed in Miami, rural Bangladesh, the Caribbean, and Brazil.

16. See Tutnjevic, "Gender in Crisis Response."

17. Karen Rowley, *GulfGov Reports: One Year Later: First Look at the Recovery, Role, and Capacity of States and Localities Damaged by the 2005 Katrina and Rita Hurricanes* (New York: The Nelson A. Rockefeller Institute of Government, and Baton Rouge: Public Affairs Research Council of Louisiana, 2006).

18. John Brown Childs, ed., *Hurricane Katrina: Response and Responsibilities* (Nampa, Idaho: New Pacific Press, 2007).

19. Oxfam International, "The Tsunami's Impact on Women."

20. Louisiana Recovery Authority, "LRA Report: Recovery Funding Inequities," September 2007, http://lra.louisiana.gov/reports.html.

21. Greater New Orleans Community Data Center, "Metro New Orleans Fair Market Rent History," 2007, http://www.gnocdc.org/reports/fair_market_rents.html.

22. Gwen Filosa, "Mayor Applauds Council's Vote," *Times-Picayune*, December 20, 2007, http://www.nola.com/news/index.ssf/2007/12/mayor_applauds_councils_vote.html; and Bill Quigley, "HUD Sends New Orleans Bulldozers and $400,000 Apartments for the Holidays," The Smirking Chimp, 2007, http://www.smirkingchimp.com/thread/11370.

23. Erica Williams, Olga Sorokina, Avis Jones-DeWeever, and Heidi Hartmann, "The Women of New Orleans and the Gulf Coast: Multiple Disadvantages and Key Assets for Recovery" (Washington, D.C.: Institute for Women's Policy Research, 2006).

24. John Salvaggio, *New Orleans's Charity Hospital: A Story of Physicians, Politics, and Poverty* (Baton Rouge: Louisiana State University, 1992).

25. Eduardo Porter, "Katrina Begets a Baby Boom by Immigrants," *New York Times*, December 11, 2006.

26. Ed Stoddard, "Post-Katrina New Orleans Death Rate Shoots Up," Reuters, June 21, 2007.

27. Peter Eisler, "New Orleans Feels Pain of Mental Health Crisis," *USA Today*, January 16, 2007.

28. Louisiana Recovery Authority, "LRA Report."

29. Greater New Orleans Community Data Center, "Open Child Care Facilities in Orleans Parish as of February 29, 2008," 2007, http://www.gnocdc.org/maps/orleans_child_care.pdf.

CHAPTER 12

Hazardous Constructions

Mexican Immigrant Masculinity and the Rebuilding of New Orleans

Nicole Trujillo-Pagán

FOR A COUPLE OF WEEKS, media images of New Orleans flooded television sets and computer screens as they documented the devastation of Hurricanes Katrina and Rita. Less visible amid these images were the Latinos who had lived and worked in the area prior to the hurricanes. Those who returned to the city were joined by other Latinos who took on work and participated in efforts to rebuild the city. Having largely ignored the experiences of Latino evacuees, the media instead cast all Latino workers as "imported labor." Local and national radio stations, newspapers, and politicians questioned Latinos' right to work and characterized Latinos in the city as "illegal aliens."

The media participated in a relationship between construction businesses and government agencies that extracts profit at the expense of workers' rights. This chapter argues the media produced a perspective on Latinos that highlighted a controversial position in the city as migrant workers and undermined a view of Latinos as residents.

Although Latinos' limited visibility had negative consequences on their access to relief, it helped cleanup and recovery contractors secure profits. Contractors often exacerbated undocumented Latino workers' vulnerability and maximized the profitability of post-Katrina contracts. For example, contractors denied the presence of undocumented workers among their work crews when media reporters questioned their labor practices. Contractors also hired undocumented Latinos but refused to pay their workers once they determined that these workers lacked appropriate documentation. By strategically cooperating with U.S. immigration laws and limiting Latino workers' visibility, contractors minimized their cost of compliance with workplace regulations.

The relationship between contractors and policy decisions surrounding Hurricane Katrina are reflective of the shifting roles of local government and the development of the neoliberal state. The construction industry is generally considered "the most turbulent and unstable major sector of the economy" and requires government regulation of construction workers' wages to ensure a skilled labor force.[1] In response to Hurricanes Katrina and Rita, however, U.S. President Bush suspended worker documentation requirements and the Davis-Bacon Act, which guarantees a minimum wage for construction workers on federal contracts. In this way, the federal government promoted a "race to the bottom" in terms of basic worker protections. In addition, the federal government cooperated with contractors' interest in maximizing profits through a vulnerable workforce. In this deregulated environment, U.S. government agencies ignored the nature of workplace discrimination and did not enforce health and safety regulations. Agencies like the Occupational Safety and Health Administration (OSHA) reduced their operations in New Orleans to an advisory capacity.

Despite the significance of concrete actions in the form of employer discrimination and policy decision, the ways Latinos were represented by the media, employers, and government agencies undermined Latino workers' already precarious work experiences. For instance, government agencies used Latino workers' limited visibility to claim they did not know of any workplace abuses. In this way, OSHA not only eschewed responsibility for workplace health and safety regulation enforcement but also helped shift responsibility for worksite safety onto already vulnerable Latino workers.

In the past, where scholars of occupational health and safety have gone beyond Latino workers' limited visibility, they emphasize the role that Latino workers' deficiencies have on workplace illness, injuries, and fatalities. In other words, scholars argue that Latino workers are deficient. For instance, in the case of the 9/11 World Trade Center disaster, Barbara McCabe et al.[2] found that Latino workers "did not understand hazards or how to protect themselves." Scholars studying occupational risk share a direct-intervention approach with many other occupational health and safety specialists. Both scholars and industry specialists emphasize providing Latino workers with linguistically and culturally appropriate training and personal protective equipment (PPE) and reproduce an emphasis on the worker rather than the employer.

The following chapter provides preliminary evidence from Latino workers who argue that it is neither their lack of skill nor their linguistic or cultural deficiencies that account for a dramatic rise in workplace illness, injury, and fatalities among them. Instead, in my interviews with Latino workers in New Orleans, they inverted the deficiency argument. Many undocumented Latino workers believed contractors assumed they were "hard workers," which accounts for workplace discrimination. Specifically, Latino workers believed they were given more dangerous and risky work assignments because employers knew Latino workers would do the work. Latino workers felt their location in the labor market was premised on their ability to assume risks on the job. In this way, workplace discrimination is bolstered by the ways Latino workers were represented by the media, employers, and public policy, which this chapter considers a reflection of Latinos' "limited visibility."

Methods

This study is based on open-ended interviews within New Orleans and its surrounding areas of Metairie and Kenner. Interviews were conducted in a church, in restaurants, food stores, behind vacant businesses, on the street, and in parking lots where Latino workers congregated. The interview format asked Latino workers about their jobs, experience, use of PPE, and major work-related concerns. The final sample of Latino workers interviewed in this format was forty, with interviews varying in length from ten minutes to two hours.

Beyond interviews with workers, the study included other methods for identifying Latino workers' experiences of cleanup and recovery work. Ethnographic observations of work and worksites in New Orleans Parish and its surrounding areas (Jefferson Parish and St. Bernard Parish) were conducted during the period from October 5 through 15, 2005. Interviews were also conducted with community leaders, health and worker advocates, and state and federal agency representatives and staff. Content analysis was conducted on Spanish-language information available online from federal, state, and local agencies and local, state, and national media sources, which included OSHA, National Institute for Occupational Safety and Health (NIOSH), the Centers for Disease Control and Prevention (CDC), and the Environmental Protection Agency (EPA). Finally, several follow-up interviews with a subset of Latino workers were conducted via telephone.

Context

In the weeks following Hurricane Katrina and amid the extensive media coverage of the disaster, few media reports addressed Latinos in New Orleans. The few media reports in September 2005 that did address the Latino community suggested that Latinos hadn't understood many English-language public announcements about the pending hurricane or had failed to evacuate their homes because they were afraid of immigration officials and had died as a result.[3] These limited reports exposed the lack of a Spanish-language infrastructure in New Orleans and highlight one way policy decisions (using immigration officials for emergency response) promoted Latinos' increased vulnerability amid a natural disaster.

One reason why the Latino community failed to gain significant media attention was because the 2000 U.S. Census documented only a small population of Latinos in New Orleans. As a result, scholars have largely neglected this population and both reporters and relief agencies were at a loss for accessing the community. For example, an NIOSH staff person explained that NIOSH was concerned about Latino workers but his team "hadn't seen any Latinos in the area." In our conversation, he explained that the city was largely cordoned off and many relief workers required identifying clothing, which most likely undermined their efforts among undocumented Latino workers. In the weeks and months following the disaster, relief workers engaged in public work, including operating emergency response stations. This work limited their exposure to many who arrived in the city and worked in private businesses, such as hotels. As a result, government relief workers continued to struggle in identifying the community for outreach purposes.

My exploratory research found that a large population of Latinos lived in New Orleans, which was only partly a result of post-Katrina migration from beyond the impacted areas. Latino residents claimed that they represented over 30 percent of Kenner's resident population before the hurricanes and that Latinos commuted from Kenner to New Orleans for work. They pointed to housing complexes that had significant undocumented Latino populations and to social service, religious, and cultural organizations that had been serving the city's Latino community over the past five years. They also claimed that both the Latino population and organizations serving Latinos had recently increased but that this growth included a large percentage of undocumented migrants. Recent and emerging scholarship on Latinos in the U.S. South also finds that recent demographic growth and legal status are central factors affecting the Latino community's well-being.[4] As a result, the dramatic growth of the undocumented Latino population within the U.S. South poses unique challenges to "small Latino places," both rural and urban, that do not have a history of dealing with Latino immigrants, lack a Spanish-language infrastructure, and understand racial dynamics along a black–white binary.[5]

Recent scholarship on Latinos in the U.S. South demonstrates that the migration of young, male, foreign-born Latinos is "playing out in that region with a greater intensity and across a larger variety of communities—rural, small towns, suburbs, and big cities—than in any other part of the country."[6] Scholars recognize the important lessons the U.S. South offers the country for predicting future demographic trends, including the role that local economies have on stimulating new migration of not only Latinos but also whites and blacks. The rapid growth of the Latino population is also tied to current labor trends, and some scholars hold that Latinos will increase their representation in the workforce to 36 percent over the next ten years.[7]

Latinos' occupational risk involves a variety of local and national institutions, including immigration and labor policy, medical care, and education. Studies of Latinos' occupational risk in the U.S. South offer scholars opportunities to understand how these institutions interact and new challenges resulting from Latinos' rapid demographic growth in the United States. For instance, as the Latino population has grown, occupational injuries among Latinos have also increased. According to Maria Brunette, Latinos currently have "higher fatal and non-fatal occupational injuries than any other ethnic group in the United States," and their fatality rate "is about 20 percent higher than the rates for white and black workers."[8] This trend is particularly marked among foreign-born Latinos, who demonstrated a fatal work injury rate 44 percent higher than the national rate in 2004.[9] This trend may also be magnified within the U.S. South. For instance, a case study of Latino health and mortality in Georgia demonstrates that the leading cause of death among Latinos is unintentional injury, which contrasts national trends in Latino mortality.[10]

Occupational data also demonstrate that demographic growth alone is an inadequate explanation for work-related injuries and fatalities. For instance, J.C. Robinson's 1989 study found a statistically significant difference between Latinos and non-Hispanic whites in work-related injury and illness in California. More recent national data confirm a trend of shifting occupation risk, finding that national rates of occupational injury and illness dropped 35 percent between 1992 and 2001 but increased 67 percent for Latino workers. Occupational risk is influenced by higher-risk industries. In segmented labor markets, Latinos were more likely to work at construction jobs than at any other except for a similar seasonal industry—agriculture.[11]

In the U.S. South, the construction industry has employed Latinos at rates much higher than their migration into the region. The construction industry's growing interest in recruiting Latino workers is evidenced in their increased attention toward the population. For instance, industry publications suggest the widespread use of English-Spanish dictionaries of construction terminology. In local business journals within the U.S. South, construction industry leaders estimate their Latino workers at any-where from 30 to 50 percent of their workforce.[12] These business leaders also popularize and reinforce racialized assessments of Latino work-ers. For instance, the headline "Construction Industry Owes Hispanic Employees for Boom" ran in the *Memphis Business Journal*, which quotes a construction company's president: "They [Latinos] were one of the best things that ever happened to the construction industry.... Days don't mean anything to them. They'll work 12 hours. And they can do many things."[13] The same paper ran an article three years later whose author insisted that Latinos had proved "themselves capable, dependable, hard working and loyal to employers."[14] Similarly, in Charlotte, the president and CEO of another construction company asserted "Latino workers are productive, rarely miss work and are willing to put in long hours."[15] These examples demonstrate how construction companies and contractors recast their own economic interests and sense of opportunity as a set of cultural values unique to a specific racial or ethnic group.

Contractors' racialized assessments of the Latino workers fit within a broader context of racial discrimination in workplaces. Latinos' "hard-working" abilities are frequently contrasted with similar racialized con-structions of blacks' laziness. Scholars have critiqued the "model minor-ity," arguing the social construction of a particular racial/ethnic group as hard workers presumes all individuals within the group are "silent, effi-cient, uncontentious labor."[16]

The idealized constructions surrounding "Latinos'" capacity for work are an interpretation of productivity that contractors use to control work-ers' productivity. The construction industry not only plays an important role in the U.S. South's high economic growth rates but also leads all industries in fatal accidents. In this way, the construction industry demonstrates how greater profits are secured by shifting the burden of occupational risk onto Latinos. For example, the construction industry reduced nonfatal occupational injuries by 40 percent at the national level but is now the largest source of nonfatal occupational injuries for Latinos.[17] Similarly, Scott Richardson et al. find that the construction industry reduced fatalities by 3 percent at a national level but increased fatalities among Latinos by 24 percent.[18]

The dominant explanation for foreign-born Latinos' disproportional occupational risk reverts to worker-centered perspectives that emphasize improving upon workers' lower educational attainment, fewer job skills, and lack of English proficiency.[19] For instance, Maria Brunette argues that providing adequate health and safety training is "one of the most critical factors in reducing and preventing injuries."[20] In a disaster scenario, Barbara McCabe et al. found that Latinos working in cleanup after the 9/11 World Trade Center disaster were "given ordinary cleaning tools," were not trained or told of hazards, were not given PPE, and "did not understand hazards or how to protect themselves."[21] Despite the recommendation's apparent requirement for employer involvement, however, the studies emphasize workers to make claims about workers' difference and the provision of culturally and linguistically appropriate information. For instance, Maria Brunette argues that Latino construction workers have a "unique 'cultural' mindset towards the perceptions of different levels of hazards."[22] Other scholars assumed this "unique cultural mindset" involves gendered constructions of risk.[23] Similarly, McCabe et al. dedicated over a third of their paper to the role of language in written and oral communication for Latinos.

Scholarly emphasis on culturally and linguistically sensitive training cannot adequately address the problem of segmented labor markets or discrimination among foreign-born workers. For instance, Loh and Richardson's work suggests that foreign-born workers have different experiences in the workplace—Mexicans represented 27 percent of foreign-born workers but 42 percent of foreign-born worker fatalities in 2000.[24] Similarly, Justin Pritchard's award-winning coverage of Mexican labor in 2004 found they were "nearly twice as likely as the rest of the immigrant population to die at work."

Scholars' approaches to Latinos' disproportionate occupational risk eschews the problem of segmented labor markets and employers' roles in shifting occupational risks onto vulnerable Latino workers. In contrast to scholars' emphasis on workers, Latinos working on cleanup and recovery in a post-Katrina New Orleans explained their occupational risk in ways that promoted structural understandings of their vulnerability. First, Latinos felt that their relative lack of education, job skills, and English proficiency had a minor influence on their work. Instead, they felt their employer discriminated against Latinos in work assignments, which increased their likelihood of injury and death. Second, the Latino workers I interviewed in New Orleans included Mexican-, Honduran-, and Cuban-born workers. They distinguished themselves based on legal status, which increased Mexican workers' vulnerability. More specifically, Mexicans distinguished themselves among other foreign-born Latino workers when they referred to their potential for legalizing their status, which included their ability to gain temporary-protected status (TPS). Finally, unlike scholars who assert Latino construction workers possess a "unique 'cultural' mindset," Latino workers saw their culture as one that allowed them to strategically redefine their right to work and empower their sense of social value amid significant occupational risk.

Latino workers' emphasis on employers resonated with many concerns about the nature of contracting work in post-Katrina New Orleans. A host of scholars, activists, and media commentators protested the contracting of industry giants, like Halliburton, Bechtel, and Flour, for a variety of reasons that included the loss of local control over recovery, the preferential nature of no-bid contracts, and the expansion of "disaster capitalism."[25] These giants subcontract a lot of their work, which threatens employers' accountability and occupational health and safety. For instance, an occupational risk specialist in post-Katrina New Orleans explained that many health and safety standards could not be systematically enforced by the masses of cleanup and recovery subcontractors that had flooded the area. Similarly, on a larger scale, Joe Reina, the leader of OSHA's Hispanic Taskforce, explained that "ninety-five to 99 percent of the time, there's going to be noncompliance with a standard that could have prevented the fatality."[26]

The problems Latinos experience were largely invisible to the occupational health and safety specialists who arrived in the area. As the nature of work in New Orleans moves toward recovery and new construction, the risk of occupational accidents like falls, which has consistently been the major source of occupational fatalities for Latinos, also increase. In the data that follow, I argue that the major factors influencing this pattern of disproportionate occupational risk are that federal agencies ignore Latino workers and facilitate employers shifting the burden for occupational risk onto Latino workers.

A Critique of Skills-Centered Approaches

My interviews with Latino workers distinguished two types of workers. Former residents included a large percentage of Central American migrants who had been living in New Orleans and its surrounding areas for anywhere from eight to twenty-five years. These residents frequently had legal U.S. citizenship, permanent residency, or TPS. More recent undocumented Honduran immigrants believed their legal status would soon be regularized by the federal government and that they would receive an amnesty because they were affected by the disaster. Hondurans were also more likely to arrive in New Orleans through personal contacts rather than through a recruiter.

At least some of these residents included recent Mexican migrants who migrated after the year 2000 and believed the Mexican population in New Orleans had grown only recently. These relative newcomers were more likely to reside outside of New Orleans and in the immediate surrounding areas of Chalmette and Kenner. Mexican residents were much more likely to see their interests aligned with the recent influx of Mexican workers migrating to New Orleans after Hurricanes Katrina and Rita. Mexican residents and post-Katrina migrants shared a sensitivity regarding their legal vulnerability. For instance, Juan, a post-Katrina migrant recruited from Houston, distinguished himself from "Central Americans" because they had TPS.[27] Juan also reflected on the politicized nature of this vulnerability, which undermined many workers' trust in government-led initiatives. Juan said Mexicans were "trapped because [President] Bush was angry with [Mexican President] Fox for not supporting the [U.S.] invasion of Iraq and was 'taking it out on us' (*desquitándose con nosotros*)." Although my interviews did not ask about U.S.–Mexico relations, other Mexicans volunteered similar criticisms of U.S. immigration policy and its relationship to the war in Iraq. As a result of these beliefs, Mexican residents and post-Katrina migrants knew of the ongoing negotiations over the guest worker program but did not believe their legal status would soon be regularized.

Latino residents' response to the influx of new Latino workers differed dramatically from the public reaction demonstrated in local politics and the national media. On the one hand, Mexican residents did not distinguish themselves from those who are currently migrating into the area. One Mexican respondent who has lived in New Orleans for over four years explained that her family has gone to work in cleanup and recovery and "now they're all sick." On the other hand, non-Mexican Latino residents were neutral about the recent migration into the area. For instance, one group of Honduran workers that resided in the New Orleans area claimed they didn't care about the race of workers or whether they had resided in the area before Hurricane Katrina. They argued that it didn't matter if workers were white, black, or Latino as long as workers had some construction experience and could bring New Orleans back quickly.

Latino residents' emphasis on work experience reflected their own sense of place within the New Orleans labor force. They had worked primarily in construction and cleaning occupations prior to Hurricane Katrina and saw no reason why this should change. The few Latina workers I was able to interview told me they held jobs in cleaning, which typically involved domestic work or a combination of domestic work and after-hours cleaning in business offices. The Latino men I asked told me they had pre-Katrina jobs in the construction or fishing industry.[28] All Latino men I asked detailed at least some experience in painting, drywall installation, roofing, and shipbuilding. As a result, Latinos thought they had experience and did not see themselves as "low-skilled labor."

Worksites as Toxic Basements

Driving through New Orleans in early October was like driving through a ghost town. In some areas, I would find individuals or couples wandering from their homes to their cars, stopping frequently on the curb to contemplate what could be salvaged from their former lives. After a few trips of carrying out handfuls of items, they would inevitably stand outside, stopping to stare blankly at their former homes, and then drive away.

Residents' solemn routine contrasted that of bustling teams of workers. In other areas, these teams similarly moved back and forth from homes to the curbside, following one another endlessly and silently, each one carrying furniture, heavy carpeting, or sheetrock. Unlike residents' shocked resignation, however, workers seemed locked in an arduous struggle with each home or building to restore an order it had once offered. The silence of their work was repeatedly pierced by the trucks that came to take away what was now garbage. Workers sweat under the sun without face masks that would obstruct their breathing. They might stop at the doorway, peering inside, perhaps wondering where to step in fear that the loose flooring or any other part of the house might become a new casualty of the disaster.

I walked up and down New Orleans' streets repeatedly observing the same patterns. I straddled a world of difference between the zombie-like residents and the sweating workers as I observed the damage and the work and as I gingerly stepped over garbage, broken glass, and the endless power lines snaked across the ground. I entered several homes and found a chaotic world of multicolored mold, waterlines, and the signs of lives that the flood had reduced to wet garbage. In many homes I entered, rooms seemed small and the lack of windows made me feel suffocated. My headaches increased in intensity, and I could only briefly tour each building. After a couple of hours, I felt tired and weak.

As I drove around, I saw Latinos working outside. They were not only removing debris but also setting up makeshift structures and blue plastic tarps that would shield construction work from public view. At times, I saw Latinos who worked alone and carried heavy, wet carpeting out to the curbside. I stopped and spoke with a small team of Latinos who had stopped to rest. Inside the house they worked on, they had piled broken sheetrock on the floor of a home they worked in, leaving little room for mobility. I stepped through the rubble toward the center of the house and struggled to maintain my balance. They used ladders but did not use helmets. Although one wore gloves and a dust mask, they all wore simple shoes or sneakers. They repeat a common workday: ten to twelve hours. Four times Latino workers told me they worked fifteen hours per day. Most worked Saturdays, but only a few also called Sunday a workday.

I changed neighborhoods and headed for nearby Metairie, where businesses had been already opened and where I could see groups of people. The streets were busy with trucks transporting workers. As I watched one after another pickup truck wiz by, as if in a caravan, I couldn't distinguish I-10 from any other Texan or Mexican highway. From the open-air back, Latinos watched cars pass. I exited and followed one of the trucks and found myself in an area that, despite the activity in Metairie, initially seemed abandoned. I kept driving and found Latinos tucked away from public view. They were resting in the shade, behind buildings, or gathered outside of vans with their work crews. Others continued working. I drove into a hotel parking lot and found three vans surrounded by approximately twenty Latinos. I parked and headed toward the vans, but was approached by a well-dressed Latino. From his clean clothing and perfect Texan English, I assumed he was a foreman. He asked if he could help me and I asked him what happened to the hotel. He told me there were no vacancies in the hotel and waited until I walked back to my car and left.

My observations, combined with interviews in parking lots and restaurants, eventually distinguished two main types of work.[29] Workers I met in a restaurant explained that they not only worked on a large project in a hotel but also lived there. They had a specific job in a single locale. During the day, these workers were hidden within the building and to me by contractors who came and went throughout the day. They were less likely to lounge behind buildings or parking lots. As they described work putting up new sheetrock, I worried they would be systematically exposed to a more limited, but equally dangerous, set of occupational risks. Without adequate access to these worksites, however, I assumed this isolated population worked in what might have been a "toxic basement."

The workers I could access on the street or in parking lots explained they lived in company trailers, hotels, or makeshift housing within buildings they worked on. They were informally contracted for undefined periods of time or "until the work ends." In the morning, they received their work assignments, formed teams, and were transported to different locales and affected areas to work for the day. Their worksites changed frequently, which increased their exposure to a variety of occupational risks according to locale and neighborhood. The majority of workers I spoke with came from this group of workers.

After leaving the field, interviews with occupational health and safety workers and worker advocates found alarming evidence of occupational risk. For instance, an industrial hygienist at NIOSH observed Latino workers pushing glass out of an office building's "eleventh- or twelfth-story window" with no demarcation on the street below. Although this industrial hygienist contacted OSHA, he never heard back from OSHA about whether they had followed up with the contractor. When the industrial hygienist returned to the site five hours later, he found a Latino worker sweeping the sidewalk and assumed that the contractor had not followed what he could only offer as a "recommendation" because NIOSH did not have the power to enforce workplace safety regulations.

Regardless of the nature of work arrangements, the study found a generalized lack of services specific to a Spanish-speaking population throughout New Orleans and its surrounding areas. Both male and female workers consistently expressed confusion about what they "had heard" regarding toxins and were uncertain of what risks these toxins posed. They were uncertain about whether the materials they handled might potentially be hazardous. Among the workers I interviewed, no one used a hardhat. None wore any type of uniform that could decrease the likelihood they would transport any contaminants from their work-site to their home. Latino workers were generally unaware of why respirators or Tyvek suits could be useful as PPE. They consistently reported that they were not using PPE, although approximately 8 percent of the sample used gloves, 20 percent of the sample reported using dust masks, and 75 percent of the sample demonstrated or reported consistent use of construction boots. Latino workers were also generally unclear of important distinctions between types of PPE. For instance, one group of four workers said they believed their coworkers pulling down sheetrock used respirators. Upon further questioning, their definition of a "respirator" consisted of simple dust masks.

When I explained the utility of PPE, some workers explained that they did not have access to this equipment. Often, they did not know whether their employer had any PPE for workers or whether it was available to them. The generalized lack of training on occupational risks meant that workers were more concerned about how using PPE would affect their work performance. For instance, in the one case where a recently arrived worker believed PPE was available to him at his worksite, he did not know its purpose or how to use it. He believed using PPE was cumbersome.

Latinos were also concerned about how employers would respond to their request for training or use of PPE. A few Latinos were concerned about their employer perceiving them as weak, unwilling to work, or as someone who *hace problemas*, i.e., makes problems, or is a "troublemaker." Although respondents claimed they didn't need PPE, most believed they had been hired because "Latinos have a reputation for hard work." They were generally concerned that using PPE would negatively impact what they perceived to be already tenuous employment. More specifically, Latino workers were concerned that using PPE would reflect negatively on their ability to handle difficult tasks. As a result, they were unlikely to risk their jobs by asking their employer for training or PPE.

Brunette argues Latino workers have a "unique cultural mindset towards the perceptions of different levels of hazards," but Mexican workers used structural interpretations to understand the risks they faced at work.[30] For instance, one worker succinctly summarized his negative responses to my battery of questions regarding PPE by referring to his work "a la Mexicana," i.e., in the Mexican way. When Mexicans use this term outside of its culinary reference to color in a dish, "a *la mexicana*" refers to the raw, unadulterated nature of an experience. This worker's expression overlapped a general claim among Latino workers that redefined culture. Latino workers understood that their work involved hazards and risks not because of their own lack of education or information but because they were subjected to discrimination in their work assignments. As Jose, an undocumented Honduran worker who had migrated from Ohio, explained:

> They [employers] give us [Latinos] work because they know that Latinos work more. We work harder and faster and take risks. I used to work in demolition in New York. I worked from 8 am to 2 am and made $200 a day. Other workers don't care about finishing the job in a day. We are the ones who break our backs here (*da el lomo aqui*) and leave our suffering families behind (*familias sufrienda allá*).

Latino respondents believed that accepting the ambiguous risks they encountered in their work were necessarily a part of, or an aspect of, their ability to secure and perform work. They assumed their ability to withstand a tough working situation was part of why they were hired and what they were paid for. In follow-up discussions with respondents, it was evident that these risks had already become real concerns. By November, Jose was sick and suffering from what he believed was a cold. He explained that he did not have time to see a doctor and did not perceive his illness as serious. In minimizing his illness, however, he also explained that he was concerned about reporting his illness to his employer, seeking medical care, and losing his pay or his job. This case demonstrated that Latino workers minimized the effects of conditions over which they feel they have little control.

The finding that Latino workers minimize the effects of conditions over which they feel they have little control has two important implications. First, this finding implies that any efforts to improve workers' safety and health must take seriously the need mediate discrimination against Latinos that promote their vulnerability. Second, this finding implies that Latino workers' ability to control the terms of their work is hindered because they will neglect or ignore the negative consequences of a work arrangement they feel they cannot control. This finding also fits within a broader context of Latino workers' vulnerability in government-contracted business. As one respondent explained, when a company might be a U.S.-government contractor or when a contractor is protected by federal agents, undocumented workers fear reprisal and are less likely to report workplace hazards and risks. As a result, Latino workers' repeatedly reconciled themselves to controlling their individual responses to a threatening context. For instance, a widely shared response among Latino workers was that there was "one thing they knew" about what conditions they were working and living in, which was that simply that expecting an outcome would increase the likelihood it would happen.

Workplace Vulnerability

One experience gave me the impression that contacting workers at their worksite would have increased their vulnerability. On an evening that I was handing out some Spanish-language information from NIOSH in the French Quarter, I attempted to give a flyer to a Latino working inside a hotel. He was working with another Latino male who calmly stood nearby, clearly supervising his work in repairing the hotel's floor. I spoke in Spanish in a friendly tone and slid the papers through a gap in the locked doors. Immediately, the man who appeared to be a supervisor rushed to the papers and barked "What is that?" in English. As I explained, he glanced at the paper briefly and quickly cast it aside. I was left with the suspicion that the man who supervised the worker sought not to protect him [the worker] from threats or even work disruptions but from the possibility that the worker would interact with others in ways he [the supervisor] could not control.

In New Orleans, the construction industry has experienced significant changes over the past twenty-five years that facilitate its control over workers. The "free enterprise system" means that fewer contractors employ union labor, unions have lost significant influence and membership, and aging workers have been difficult to replace.[31] In light of the economic challenges facing the city before Hurricanes Katrina and Rita, the "exponential link between the overall business cycle and the construction business cycle" meant that New Orleans was positioned to depend heavily on "imported workers" without union representation.[32] As a result, laborers migrating to New Orleans for cleanup and recovery confronted a variety of occupational risks amidst other local changes that undermined both construction contractors' liability and workers' ability to pursue workers' compensation. Although OSHA is supposed to enforce job safety rules, it had already been criticized before Hurricanes Katrina and Rita hit the city for lacking a "standing with the construction industry."[33] These local factors promoted Latino workers' vulnerability in cleanup and recovery work. For example, Latino workers' labor arrangements made them insecure about any activities they perceived as threatening their jobs, such as exposing dangerous conditions at their worksites. Latino workers' insecurity appeared validated by other reports that suggest Latinos are considered disposable workers:

> Contractors are hiring immigrant workers right here in Houston and taking them to New Orleans to do cleanup. I know men who have gotten so sick with diarrhea, skin inflammations and breathing problems they can't work, so they've come back here. The contractors just hire more."[34]

The source of problems involving Latino workers' health and safety arose from workers' relationships to individual subcontractors. Often, the only contractor Latino workers knew was the same person who had recruited them and who they only knew on a first-name basis. Labor recruiters' methods for contracting workers included deception that negatively impact Latino workers' health. For instance, a Mexican worker that had been recruited in Houston claimed that his misplaced trust in a labor recruiter resulted in a worksite where he was "sequestered." He had only received one meal and one 0.5-liter bottle of water per day for outdoors work. Ironically, this worker was less concerned about the adverse consequences this could have on his health than he was about the fact that, although he worked over ten days at the site, he had not received any payment. His lack of money meant that he was extremely cautious about food expenses, which further threatened his health.

The threat to Latino workers' health and safety is compounded by the nature of contracting cleanup and recovery work in New Orleans. Specifically, despite media portrayals of competition among contractors for labor, this study found that workers were often quite concerned about being paid and securing work. The majority of workers interviewed were on verbal and informal contracts. Some workers expected to be paid every two weeks, but this group included those who were not paid by contractors. A significant number of respondents either had direct experience or knowledge of not being paid by employers after working one or two weeks. Some accepted partial payments in favor of long-term employment "until the work ended." Workers who were paid partial or who were paid sporadically were worried about how they could secure the remainder of their earnings. Workers who had already been paid fully were satisfied with biweekly and despite advertisements of jobs with greater pay, were not actively seeking better-paying jobs.

As a result of tenuous work relationships, all but one respondent lacked any form of insurance, including employer-based health insurance. Undocumented Latino workers are less likely to be listed on a subcontractor's workers compensation policy and know of their rights for protection under this policy, which make them less expensive and more desirable to contractors. In often uncertain subcontractor arrangements, many Latino workers may also fall beyond the scope of worker compensation statutes because they either do not know who their employer is or may be defined as independent contractors by the Louisiana Department of Labor.[35] When I asked government officials in the area about how contract clauses relating to occupational health and safety could be enforced among subcontractors, they lamented the high degree to which work was subcontracted (e.g., subcontractors for subcontractors) and the lack of occupational health and safety specialists in the area. One public health worker explained that there simply was no ability to enforce subcontract clauses on occupational safety that could protect workers. Finally, as a result of tenuous and abusive work relationships where Latinos are simultaneously exploited by contractors, foremen, and hawkish labor recruiters, Latino workers cannot avail themselves of initiatives that have been successful in other contexts, such as the "blue hardhat program" that identifies English-speaking personnel at a construction site.

The Case of St. Bernard Parish

The areas of Chalmette and Meraux in St. Bernard Parish are a unique case for understanding Latino workers' limited visibility to occupational risk workers. These areas were severely affected by Hurricane Katrina and only gradually opened to resident access in mid-October. Meraux is also considered a major toxic hotspot, covered in what has been referred to as a "toxic gumbo" of sludge caused by the Murphy Oil Refinery crude oil spill, which the U.S. Coast Guard stated represents among the worst Katrina-related environmental problems.[36] Although these toxins are unevenly distributed through the area, they cause both immediate- and long-term health problems. Early estimates are that cleanup alone will cost approximately $250 million, which will stimulate efforts to cut labor expenses.

In October, the streets of Meraux seemed empty of workers except for U.S. military soldiers, an occasional van filled with humanitarian relief workers, and handfuls of high-tech workers in white DuPont Tyvek suits. Latinos were not immediately visible among these groups, but the disaster medical assistance teams (DMATs) in the area confirmed the presence of Latinos in the area.[37] Although I visited the two DMAT sites on separate occasions and spoke with several DMAT workers, they were not willing to comment on what proportion of their patients Latinos represented. They refused to discuss any issues specific or common to Latinos and repeatedly insisted that they do not discriminate or ask people about their racial or ethnic background. They use intake forms to report their activities to the CDC, but the forms did not capture information relating to race, ethnicity, or nationality DMAT personnel limited collecting identifying patient information to a first name. At least one DMAT worker was concerned that their forms also failed to capture data relating to chronic conditions, such as asthma. In this way, DMAT workers colluded with the CDC and ignored data that could allow researchers to detect any distinguishing patterns among workers based on race, ethnicity, or nationality.

The DMAT treats only immediate, minor emergencies, but workers there explained that the medical problems they encountered had escalated. By the time I visited the sites in early October, DMAT workers explained that more people, including workers, were injured as they entered homes and were bitten by snakes that had settled in bathtubs, stepped on nails, fell from ladders, or scraped themselves with overturned furniture inside homes. They explained that they could not handle significant injuries and emergencies and, if these should occur, people would be evacuated to hospitals "in the area." The nearest hospital, the Chalmette Medical Center, remained closed in January.

I visited both DMAT sites twice, asking questions of several DMAT workers, and found they were either uncertain of any Spanish-speaking staff or uncertain as to where their one Spanish-speaking staff member could be found. Nonetheless, several DMAT workers confirmed that Latinos who could not speak English arrived for medical care, but the DMAT lacked Spanish-speaking personnel. I posed similar questions to different staff people in order to verify this information before locating this DMAT's single Spanish-speaking staff member. Although he had not been consistently present at both sites, he confirmed that some Latino workers required immediate medical care. Where Latinos required medical care, he explained that they most commonly presented with upper-respiratory problems.

The frequency of medical complaints involving upper-respiratory problems was confirmed as far as Gonzalez, about an hour away from New Orleans, where a physician who attended many Latino evacuees had found that attended similarly experienced upper-respiratory problems. These findings are also consistent with other research that finds high occupational risk for work-related asthma and/or wheezing among cleaners and construction workers, which may be primarily caused by mold exposure.[38]

The Spanish-speaking DMAT worker elucidated a critical intervention beyond issues surrounding the availability of Spanish-language staff and the adequate provision of adequate medical care when he observed that the number of Latinos coming to the DMAT sites for diphtheria-tetanus (DT) vaccinations had recently increased. "Now," he said, "contractors are bringing groups of workers in pick-up trucks and they all get vaccinated together." By early October, as subcontractors were educated about DT vaccines, he had seen more subcontractors bringing Latino workers to the DMAT site on their employees' first day. Although a then recent development, the case of St. Bernard Parish demonstrated that outreach to employers had been a successful intervention in Latino workers' health.

Interagency Cooperation and Institutional Mismanagement of Occupational Risk

As in the 9/11 World Trade Center disaster, significant interagency cooperation was immediately evident in New Orleans. Although this comparison is limited by the relative size of impacted areas and the nature of the disasters, several "lessons" arising from interagency cooperation in New York City were not applied in New Orleans, which negatively impacted Latino workers' ability to mediate the way they were affected by cleanup and recovery work. Specifically, in the case of 9/11, the Operating Engineers National Hazmat Program (OENHP) compensated for a lack of adequate cleaning tools, training, and PPE by building upon the social networks and trust that organizations like the New York Committee for Occupational Safety and Health (NYCOSH) had already established with the Latino community, which facilitated outreach to Latino workers and distribution of Spanish-language information on hazards and protection.[39] In contrast, federal agencies in New Orleans faced a relatively weak Spanish-language infrastructure and no comparable committee for occupational safety and health. Although the Houston Initiative for Worker Safety has made some efforts to improve undocumented Latino workers' access to medical care, these efforts are restricted to an advocate that pressures contractors into paying the basic fee required for care for returning workers who have been "dumped" in Houston.[40]

The lack of an adequate local infrastructure to support Latino populations' growth demonstrates how other states without a recognized history or presence of Latinos in their populations could produce occupational risks for Latino workers. In the short term, the glaring lack of Spanish-speaking federal agents and relief workers in the area undermined efforts to limit the negative impacts of cleanup and recovery work on Latino workers. In the long term, a lack of local and federal ties to community leaders and organizations prevented effective coordination with community leaders and organizations that could have carried out this work.

The lack of federal agency outreach to Latinos increased these workers' vulnerability. OSHA, NIOSH, and the CDC did not develop any outreach efforts and these agencies lacked Spanish-speaking personnel to speak directly with Latino workers. Amid the ubiquitous presence of U.S. government officials in the New Orleans area, Latino workers could not distinguish among different types of federal agents—i.e., those agents who could harm them (U.S. Immigration and Customs Enforcement officials) and those who could help them (OSHA and NIOSH). NIOSH officials also compromised this distinction in early September as they wore clothing that identified them as federal officers and traveled the city accompanied by police officers. As a result, although collaboration among federal agencies *seems* efficient, conflicts of interest among federal officials ultimately mean that vulnerable, undocumented Latino workers are more likely to be "injured" by OSHA. In the worst case scenario, U.S. Immigration and Customs Enforcement officials recently arrested undocumented Latino workers who had arrived for a "mandatory" OSHA training in North Carolina.

Agencies that were visible in New Orleans, notably the CDC, NIOSH, and OSHA, did not target Latinos in their efforts and rendered Latino workers invisible in their efforts. CDC data did not capture patients' nationality or ethnicity, thereby forgoing the possibility that patterns or trends specific to Latinos could be identified. NIOSH efforts in the area did not target the Latino population until this investigator identified sources for distribution of CDC materials, which began one week before NIOSH ceased operations in the area on October 22, 2005. Finally, OSHA efforts to do outreach among Latino workers in the area were limited to already existing initiatives, including a Spanish-language option on its toll-free help line (1-800-321-OSHA).

Federal agencies' attempts to access the Spanish-speaking population through their literature was limited by several factors. First, efforts to distribute this information were limited, brief, and curtailed by alternate agency priorities. Second, providing Spanish-language information was a secondary priority and it was only made available late in September, after similar information was provided in English. Third, a content analysis of OSHA, NIOSH, CDC, and EPA online documents conducted in the first week of November reveals that the extent of health and safety information translated to the Spanish language was limited. For instance, of the sixty-two documents listed on NIOSH's webpage, only nine (15 percent) were translated into Spanish.[41] Although not all NIOSH documentation was immediately relevant to the nature of Latinos' work in the area, critical documents on chemical safety, musculoskeletal hazards, PPE and clothing, respirator cleaning and sanitation, work in confined spaces, tree removal (chain saws), and burning of hurricane debris was only available in English over two months after Hurricane Katrina and well beyond the immediate postimpact phase of the event. A document relating to the prevention of "Chain Saw Injuries During Tree Removal After a Hurricane" was available on the CDC's webpage, "Index of Printable Hurricane and Flood Materials," but the availability of this and other health-related documents from the CDC is limited by the extent to which Latinos are not aware of the agency's work, are not informed about the availability of these documents, or are illiterate.

Subcontractors ignored measures that could contain occupational risk and the immediate efforts to promote to improve occupational health and safety among highly vulnerable Latinos seemed to rest squarely on their own (workers') shoulders. As a result, I began assisting NIOSH efforts in the area by including information distribution at the end of interviews. More specifically, once in the field, I obtained recently published Spanish-language CDC information from an NIOSH-affiliated federal agency that I distributed to Latino workers. The limits of this approach were apparent when I compared CDC information[42] to NIOSH information[43] that I had obtained at the October 11 meeting of the Hispanic Chamber of Commerce in Kenner. In other words, the two-page flyer available to Latino small-business owners was of greater relevance to workers than the six circulars the NIOSH-affiliated federal agent provided me for distribution to workers, which were Spanish-language publications of greater relevance to Latino residents.

Federal agencies attempt to minimize their efforts to contain occupational risk among Latino workers by leaving health and safety training up to already vulnerable workers. By relying on a simple and cost-effective method of providing Spanish-language information on their website, federal agencies obfuscated the role of government contractors in promoting occupational risk. Unfortunately, Latino workers lived in units that lacked access to the Internet through which this information is provided and could not educate themselves via Internet resources. In short, the nature of work in New Orleans prevented Latino workers from compensating for federal agents' lack of outreach to them.

Conclusion

Undocumented Latino workers in a post-Katrina New Orleans demonstrated how social disasters can unfold over weeks and months after a "natural disaster." Their occupational risk was produced in part by their limited visibility. Latino workers were clearly recognized by contractors and sought after by labor recruiters but largely invisible to agencies responsible for regulating safe and healthy working environments. In these ways, Latino workers' experiences in New Orleans demonstrated how their invisibility was structurally created.

Media depictions developed Latinos' limited visibility by racializing job competition in New Orleans. For instance, the *Times-Picayune*,

New York Times, *LA Times*, and NPR reported that Latinos made anywhere from $15 an hour to hundreds of dollars a day.[44] In this way, the
media constructed cleanup and recovery work as desirable and financially
rewarding. Although contractors' profits were no doubt profitable, however, vulnerable Latinos' wages averaged $10 an hour. Latino workers also
faced significant occupational risk and the persistent threat of not being
paid for their work.

In New Orleans, contractors were responsible for work arrangements
that promoted occupational risk. These arrangements demonstrated that
Latino workers' disproportionate injuries were not solely, or perhaps even
in large part, a result of their lack of educational attainment, job skills, or
English proficiency. Neither was it a result of a "unique cultural mindset" in
their perception of hazards. Although many Latino workers may have been
unaware of the specific risk their jobs involved, they recognized that their
"right to work" was premised on being unable to control the risks their work
involved. Latino workers became an inexpensive and disposable workforce
for construction contractors because they were legally vulnerable.

Political and economic factors reproduced Latinos' racialization.
New Orleans's Mayor Nagin capitalized on Latino workers' limited political visibility when he expressed concern that the city would be "overrun
by Mexican and Latino contractors." Similarly, contractors racialized Latinos
as hard workers, which promoted the illusion of job competition with
black residents. In the case of Latinos, however, the dual location of being
a "model minority" and an "illegal alien" meant that both blacks' place and
Latinos' right to work within New Orleans were jeopardized. For instance,
the increasingly politicized rhetoric surrounding Latino migration in the
city did not serve to increase regulatory agency initiative but rather to
jeopardize Latino workers' security as police and Border Enforcement officers round up increasing numbers of Latinos.

New Orleans demonstrated that Latino workers' occupational risk
resulted not only from contractors' discriminatory work assignments but
also from federal agency neglect whose outreach efforts focused on workers rather than on employers. Educational outreach to the Latino population, in terms of elucidating occupational risks, was only partially successful because it shifted the burden for minimizing occupational risk onto
vulnerable workers. In contrast, the case of DT vaccination demonstrated that employer outreach had a broader impact in terms of promoting
Latino workers' health. Unfortunately, regulatory agencies, and their

tenuous relationship with construction contractors, meant they ignored both health and safety standards and the ways in which employers promoted occupational risks for Latino workers.

Scholars' projections that the southern region's relative lack of experience with immigration, its traditional understandings of race along a black-white binary, and its general lack of a Spanish-language infrastructure could negatively impact Latinos' wellbeing were borne out after Hurricane Katrina.[45] Although recent immigration may not be immediately invisible in New Orleans, it is similarly reflected in the economic, demographic, and physical expansion of many Southern cities and rural areas. Cities and towns could reach out to prospects for growth that are sustainable for the greatest number of residents, which include Latinos.

Notes

1. Peter Philips, "Dual Worlds: The Two Growth Paths in US Construction," in *Building Chaos: An International Comparison of Deregulation in the Construction Industry*, ed. Gerhard Bosch and Peter Philips (London: Routledge, 2003).

2. Barbara McCabe, Cliff Carpenter, and Danielle Blair, "The Worker Component at the World Trade Center Cleanup: Addressing Cultural and Language Differences in Emergency Operations," *Waste Management Symposium Conference*, February 23–27, 2003.

3. Nicole Trujillo-Pagán, "Katrina's Latinos: Vulnerability and Disasters in Relief and Recovery," in *Through the Eye of Katrina: Social Justice in the United States*, ed. Kristin Bates and Richelle S. Swan (Durham, N.C.: Carolina Academic Press, 2007).

4. Rakesh Kochar, Roberto Suro, and Sonya Tafoya, *The New Latino South: The Context and Consequences of Rapid Population Growth* (Washington D.C.: Pew Hispanic Center, 2005); Rogelio Saenz et al., "Latinos in the South: A Glimpse of Ongoing Trends and Research," *Southern Rural Sociology* 19, no. 1 (2003): 1–19.

5. Roberto Suro and Audrey Singer, "Changing Patterns of Latino Growth in Metropolitan America," in *Redefining Urban and Suburban America: Evidence from Census 2000*, ed. Bruce Katz and Robert Lang (Washington, D.C.: The Brookings Institution, 2000); Barbara Ellen Smith, *The New Latino South: An Introduction* (Memphis: University of Memphis, Center for Research on Women, 2001); and Deborah A. Duchon and Arthur D. Murphy, "Introduction: From Patrones and Caciques to Good Ole Boys," in *Latino Workers in the Contemporary South*, ed. Arthur D. Murphy, Colleen Blanchard, and Jennifer A. Hill (Athens: University of Georgia Press, 2001).

6. Kochar et al., *The New Latino South*, i.

7. Maria J. Brunette, "Construction Safety Research in the United States: Targeting the Hispanic Workforce," *Injury Prevention* 10, no. 4 (2004): 244–48.

8. Ibid., 245.

9. Scott Richardson, "Fatal Work Injuries among Foreign-Born Hispanic Workers," *Monthly Labor Review* (October 2005): 63–67.

10. Liany Arroyo and Natalie Hernandez, *Latinos in Georgia: A Closer Look*, Statistical Brief (Washington, D.C.: National Council of La Raza, October 31, 2005).

11. Peter Phillips, "Dual Worlds: The Two Growth Paths in U.S. Construction," in *Building Chaos: An International Comparison of Deregulation in the Construction Industry*, ed. Gerhard Bosch and Peter Philips (London: Routledge, 2003); Brunette, "Construction Safety"; Xiuwen Dong and James W. Platner, "Occupational Fatalities of Hispanic Construction Workers from 1992 to 2000," *American Journal of Industrial Medicine* 45, no. 1 (2004): 45–54; Katherine Loh and Scott Richardson, "Foreign-Born Workers: Trends in Fatal Occupational Injuries, 1996-2001," *Monthly Labor Review* 127, no. 6 (2004): 42–53; R. Fernando Vásquez and C. Keith Stalnaker, "Overcoming the Language Barrier Improves Safety," *Professional Safety*, (June 2004): 24–28; and Katherine M. Donato, Melissa Stainback, and Carl L. Baukston III, "The Economic Incorporation of Mexican Immigrants in Southern Louisiana: A Tale of Two Cities," in *New Destinations: Mexican Immigration in the United States*, ed. Victor Zuñiga and Ruben Hernández León (New York: Russell Sage Foundation, 2005).

12. See, for instance, Ed Hicks, "Construction Industry Owes Hispanic Employees for Boom," *Memphis Business Journal*, October 19, 2001, Edward Martin's June 2004 article in *Business North Carolina*, or Marta Hummel's January 1, 2006, article in *Builder Online*.

13. Hicks, "Construction Industry Owes Hispanic Employees for Boom."

14. Lynne W. Jeter, "Wanted: Dependable, Hard Workers for Challenging Jobs: Hispanics Filling Niche in Construction Industry Around the State, South," *Mississippi Business Journal* 26, no. 28 (2004), http://goliath.ecnext.com/coms2/gi_0199-276645/Wanted-dependable-hard-workers-for.html.

15. Edward Martin, "Los Obreros: Latino Labor Influences the Way Things Are Built-and What They're Built With, across the State," *Business North Carolina*, (June 1, 2004), http://findarticles.com/p/articles/mi_qa5314/is_200406/ai_n21350158.

16. Eric Mark Kramer, "Gaiatsu and Cultural Judo," in *The Emerging Monoculture: Assimiliation and the "Model Minority,"* ed. Eric Mark Kramer (Westport, Conn.: Praeger Publishers, 2003).

17. Vázquez and Stalnaker, "Overcoming the Language Barrier."

18. Richardson, "Fatal Work Injuries."

19. Mike Flory, "Solving the Language Barrier," *Occupational Health & Safety* 70, no. 1 (2001): 37–38.

20. Brunette, "Construction Safety Research."

21. McCabe et al., Cliff, "The Worker Component."

22. Brunette, "Construction Safety Research," 244.

23. Thomas DeLeire and Helen Levy, "Gender, Occupation Choice, and the Risk of Death at Work," *NBER Working Paper*, no. 8574 (2001), http://www.nber.org/papers/w8574.pdf.

24. Katherine Loh and Scott Richardson, "Foreign Born Workers: Trends in Fatal Occupational Injuries, 1996–2001," *Monthly Labor Review* (June 2004): 42–53.

25. Naomi Klein, *The Shock Doctrine: The Rise of Disaster Capitalism* (New York: Picador Books, 2007).

26. Justin Pritchard, "AP Investigation: Mexican Worker Deaths Rise Sharply Even as Overall US Job Safety Improves," *Associated Press*, March 14, 2004.

27. Although the respondent generalized TPS to all Central Americans, only Hondurans, Salvadorans, and Nicaraguans benefit from TPS protection.

28. These categories overlapped when Latino respondents claimed experience in shipbuilding. Katherine Donato similarly demonstrates that a recent wave of Mexican immigrants arrived in Louisiana to work in "shipbuilding and fabrication yards in coastal areas of the state" (Donato et al. [2001]: 105). My respondents included a Honduran immigrant who has worked with one shipbuilding company for fifteen years. He explained that there were few Latinos when he began working at the yard, although the majority of his coworkers are now Latino.

29. It is important to note that other concerned activists, such as the National Employment Law Project (NELP), report alternate work arrangements. For instance, NELP argues that independent contractor agreements are present in the area, which allows subcontractors to underpay workers by paying for a task rather than the hours this task absorbed. Although this tendency was not observed in my sample, activists are concerned that these arrangements further intensify the pace of work and promote occupational risks.

30. Brunette, "Construction Safety Research," 244.

31. Deon Roberts, "Union Labor Gives Way to Free Enterprise for Construction Work," *New Orleans City Business*, April 25, 2005.

32. Philips, "Dual Worlds," 162.

33. Roberts, "Union Labor."

34. Alvarez, cited in Brendan Coyne, "Groups Urge Congress to Protect Gulf Workers," *The New Standard*, October 21, 2005. Juan Alvarez is the director of the Latin American Organization for Immigrant Rights in Houston.

35. The NELP has recognized this problem and released a series of online documents relating to worker's rights, including fact sheets and documents relating to recruiter and subcontractor abuse of workers, misclassification of workers

as "independent contractors," the right to be paid, and health and safety. For instance, their "Post-Katrina Fact Sheet" alerts workers to their rights to safety on the job and to compensation benefits in the event of injury, regardless of immigration status. Unfortunately, these online documents are not readily accessible and have not been translated into Spanish.

36. Murphy's Oil Refinery had a breach that leaked 1.1 million gallons of crude oil into the area, although the amount of crude oil spillage is disputed. For instance, 1640 AM radio station in the area frequently cited the spill in terms of 4 million gallons. Murphy's October 24 press release limited the spill to 25,000 barrels of crude oil. On September 7, ABC News estimated it would cost $250 million for cleanup of the Murphy oil spill. This area also elucidates the nature of controversies surrounding EPA testing, upon which habitability and health risk assessments are made. A Louisiana environmental group, the "Bucket Brigade," had soil samples collected from September 16 through 29 and found benzo(a)pyrene in levels thirty-three times higher than the EPA recommendation for a residential area in Chalmette and arsenic levels on two sites in an area covered by Murphy's oil spill that were twenty-nine times greater than standards set by the Louisiana DEQ.

37. DMATs rotate on two-week government contracts. They operated at two public sites in Chalmette.

38. Ahmed A. Arif et al., "Occupational Exposures Associated with Work-Related Asthma and Work-Related Wheezing among US Workers," *American Journal of Industrial Medicine* 44, no. 4 (2003): 368–76; and Jeroen Douwes and Neil Pearce, "Invited Commentary: Is Indoor Mold Exposure a Risk Factor for Asthma?" *American Journal of Epidemiology* 158, no. 3 (2003): 203–6.

39. McCabe et al., "The Worker Component."

40. Personal communication, Diana Cortez, Houston COSH, February 15, 2005.

41. The number of translations may be higher but they are not easily accessible from the "NIOSH Safety and Health Topics: Hurricane Response: Storm and Flood Cleanup" page at http://www.cdc.gov/niosh/topics/flood/. For instance, this topic page does not list one document's Spanish-language translation of "NIOSH Interim Guidance on Personal Protective Equipment and Clothing for Flood Response Workers," although it is available in Spanish.

42. Spanish translations of CDC information included "Worker Safety After a Flood" and "Protect Your Health and Safety After a Hurricane."

43. Spanish translations of NIOSH information included "NIOSH Interim Guidance on Personal Protective Equipment and Clothing for Flood Response Workers."

44. Nicole Trujillo-Pagán, "From 'Gateway to the Americas' to the 'Chocolate City': The Racialization of Latinos in New Orleans," in *Racing the Storm: Racial Implications and Lessons Learned from Hurricane Katrina*, ed. Hillary Potter (Lanham: Lexington Books, 2007).

45. Smith, *New Latino South*.

Contributors

BARBARA L. ALLEN is the director of the graduate program in science, technology, and society at Virginia Tech's Washington, D.C., campus. She is the author of *Uneasy Alchemy: Citizens and Experts in Louisiana's Chemical Corridor Disputes* and coeditor of several books, including *Dynamics of Disaster: Lessons on Risk, Response, and Recovery*. Her articles on environmental justice and repatriation have appeared in *Journal of Architectural Education, Social Studies of Science, Technology in Society,* and *Projections: MIT Journal of Planning.*

JOHN ARENA is assistant professor of sociology at the College of Staten Island, City University of New York. He has written widely on social justice issues in post-Katrina New Orleans and is involved in various campaigns to defend public services and establish a national public works project open to both immigrant and native workers. He is working on a study of the role of nonprofits in the privatization of public housing.

ADRIENNE DIXSON is associate professor of critical race theory in the Department of Education Policy, Organization, and Leadership in the College of Education at the University of Illinois at Urbana-Champaign. Her scholarship focuses on educational equity in urban schooling contexts, looking specifically at the relationship between race and educational opportunity.

ERIC ISHIWATA is assistant professor of political science at the Center for the Applied Study of American Ethnicity at Colorado State University. Specializing in issues of race and immigration, his work has appeared in *Cultural Values* and *Japanstudien.*

CEDRIC JOHNSON is associate professor of African American studies and political science at the University of Illinois at Chicago. He is the author of *Revolutionaries to Race Leaders: Black Power and the Making of African American Politics* (Minnesota, 2007), which was named the 2008 W. E. B. DuBois Outstanding Book of the Year by the National Conference of Black Political Scientists. His writings have appeared in *New Political Science, Monthly Review,* and *In These Times.*

AVIS JONES-DEWEEVER is the executive director of the National Council of Negro Women, where she formerly served as the director of the Research, Public Policy, and Information Center for African American Women. She is author of numerous publications focused on policy issues of importance to women of color.

CHAD LAVIN is assistant professor of political science and social, political, ethical, and cultural thought (ASPECT) at Virginia Tech. He is the author of *The Politics of Responsibility* and has published essays in *Theory & Event, New Political Science,* and *American Studies.*

PAUL A. PASSAVANT is associate professor of political science at Hobart and William Smith Colleges. He is author of *No Escape: Freedom of Speech and the Paradox of Rights* and coeditor (with Jodi Dean) of *Empire's New Clothes: Reading Hardt and Negri.* His essays have appeared in *Political Theory, Theory & Event,* and *Constellations.*

LINDA ROBERTSON is founder and director of the Media and Society program at Hobart and William Smith Colleges. She is author of *The Dream of Civilized Warfare: World War I Flying Aces and the American Imagination* (Minnesota, 2005).

CHRIS RUSSILL is associate professor of communication at Carleton University, Ottawa, Canada. His work on the relationship of environmental, climate, and geophysical sciences to twenty-first-century media has been published in *Public Understanding of Science, Global Environmental Change, Environmental Communication, Media International Australia, BSTS,* and *Critical Environmental Security.*

KANCHANA N. RUWANPURA is senior lecturer in development geography at the School of Geography, University of Southhampton, England. A native of Sri Lanka, she completed her PhD at Newnham College, University of Cambridge, and has worked on a UNICEF-funded project, "Gendering the Tsunami."

NICOLE TRUJILLO-PAGÁN is assistant professor of sociology and Chicano-Boricua studies at Wayne State University. She has authored numerous publications on Latinos in post-Katrina New Orleans. Her current research focuses on Latino immigrant labor in the construction industry.

GEOFFREY WHITEHALL is associate professor of political science at Acadia University, Nova Scotia. His articles have appeared in *Theory & Event, International Studies Perspectives, Borderlands,* and *Millennium.* His research focuses on international political theory; contemporary political thought; and discourses of culture and technology.

Index

Able Security, 111

Abramowitz, Michael, 297n.27

accountability, xxxvii, 65; NGO, 130, 260; school, LEAP program and, 134

Ackerman, Robert, 57n.89

active state-building, neoliberal state as project of, 91

activism, post-Katrina: black, 65; among celebrities, 217–18; human rights language and, 163; organizations, 161; refugees debate and civil rights activism, 63–66; right of return and, 188, 190–92, 194, 199, 203–4, 211; weaknesses of left progressive forces on the ground, 218–19. *See also* Make It Right (MIR) Foundation; public housing movement

actor-network theory (ANT), 226, 230–31, 232, 238–41; critiques of, 238; flat social domain of, 238, 239; reason to use, 239

Adjaye, David, 207–8, 209, 216; Whitechapel Idea Store in London, 216, 217. *See also* Asempa House

Advancement Project, 161, 169

affirmative action policies, University of Michigan, 36–37; Bush's anti-affirmative action position, 36–37, 41

affordable housing. *See* housing

African Americans: "black community," myth of unified, 166, 168; Chicago heat wave (1995) and, 12, 13; discrimination against, in private housing market, 158; economic decline in Midwest and, 282, 283; entrepreneurial, ULI report's commitment to, 194; experience with school choice, 139–44; first, elected as president, 291; hyper-incarceration of, 107, 108; identity politics of, 45–46; in Lower Ninth Ward, 202; media depictions of race during Hurricane Katrina and, 21, 22, 30n.60; "mentality of dependence," myth of, 269; political leadership, neoliberal development agenda of, 153, 155–56, 157; post-Katrina police and vigilante violence toward, xxxiv–xxxv, xlviiin.47; problematization of black family, 44–45. *See also* black women in wake of Katrina

Agamben, Giorgio, 66, 82n.10, 120n.12–13; biopolitics theory, 90; on Katrina refugees, 67–68

Agence France-Press (AFP), 271–73, 295n.7

agency: crisis as fundamentally about, 15–16; Katrina disaster as